Copyright © 2020 by Austin Benham

All rights reserved worldwide. No part of this book may be reproduced or transmitted in any form or by any means, electronic or mechanical, including photocopying, recording or by any information storage and retrieval system, without written permission from the publisher, except for the inclusion of brief quotations in a review.

Warning-Disclaimer

The purpose of this book is to educate and entertain. The author or publisher does not guarantee that anyone following the techniques, suggestions, tips, ideas, or strategies will become successful. The author and publisher shall have neither liability or responsibility to anyone with respect to any loss or damage caused, or alleged to be caused, directly or indirectly by the information contained in this book.

CONTENTS

INTRODUCTION 7
- Why Masterbuilt? 7
- Types of Smoker 7
- How to use a Smoker 9
- Safety Tips 10

Vegan and Vegetarian Recipes 11
- Smoked Eggplant 11
- Smoked Watermelon 11
- Smoked Portobello Mushrooms With Herbs De Provence 11
- Herby Smoked Cauliflower 11
- Smoked Potato Salad 11
- Smoky Corn On The Cob 12
- Delicious Portobello Mushrooms 12
- Squash Casserole 12
- Smoked Potato Salad 12
- Smoked Squash Casserole 12
- Twice Pulled Potatoes 13
- Smoked Portobello Mushrooms With Herbs De Provence 13
- Smoked Green Beans With Lemon 13
- Smoked Brussels Sprouts 13
- Smoked Summer Vegetables 13
- Smoked Volcano Potatoes 14
- Smoked Volcanic Potatoes 14
- Smoked Lemony-garlic Artichokes 14
- Smoked Salsa 14
- Smoked Green Beans With Lemon 15
- Smoked Volcano Potatoes 15
- Groovy Smoked Asparagus 15
- Smoked Apples with Maple Syrup 15
- Smoked Baked Beans 16
- Smoked Bananas for Sundaes and Smoothies 16
- Smoked Brussels Sprouts 16
- Smoked Curried Almonds 16
- Smoked Watermelon Skewers 17
- Smoked Summer Vegetables 17
- Smoked Lemony-garlic Artichokes 17

Side Dishes, Snacks & Desserts Recipes 18
- Smoked Yellow Squash 18
- Kimchi Coleslaw 18
- Mixed Vegetables 18
- Deviled Eggs 18
- Smoked Sweet Onions 19
- Maple-glazed Nuts 19
- Smoked Peaches Drowning In Rum With Ice Cream 19
- Smoked Portobello Mushroom 19
- Roasted Pears 20
- Burnt End Baked Beans 20
- Pork Belly Burnt Ends 20
- Jalapeno Poppers 20
- Cheesy Potatoes 21
- Smoked Avocados With Strawberry-mango Salsa 21
- Smoked Pineapple With Honey 21
- Naan 21
- Beef Jerky 22
- Applesauce 22
- White Chocolate Bread Pudding 22
- Southern Smoked Potato Salad 22

Cornbread 23
- Hamburger Jerky 23
- Smoke Roasted Apple Crisp 23
- Smoked Cabbage 23
- Pizza Jalapeño Poppers 24
- Alligator Eggs 24
- Teriyaki Smoked Venison Jerky 24
- Smoked Caesar Salad 24
- Bacon & Endive Salad 25
- Smoked Banana Foster 25
- Four Cheese Smoked Mac 'n' Cheese ... 25
- Tangerine Smoked Flans 25
- Smoked Peaches 26
- Bananas Calypso 26
- Stuffed Cabbage 26
- Smokey Pimento Cheese Appetizer 26
- Smoky Okra 26
- Smoked Trout Potato Skins 27
- Smoky Beans Barbecue 27
- Pork Tenderloin Appetizers 27
- Hasselback Potatoes 27
- Smoked Chocolate Bread Pudding 28
- Pecan Tassies 28
- Bacon Wraps 28

Beef, Pork & Lamb Recipes 29
- Mighty Meaty Beef Tenderloin 29
- Stuffed Porchetta 29
- Apple-injected Smoked Pork 29
- Beef Short Ribs 29
- Masterbuilt Smoker Cooker Corned Beef 30
- Sweet Cola Ribs 30
- Beef Jerky 30
- Smoked Flank Steak With Curried Pineapple (masterbuilt Electric Smoker) 31
- Chinese Style Lamb Shanks 31
- Crowd Pleasing Meatloaf 31
- Chimichurri Smoked Loin Chops 31
- Brown Sugar & Mustard Glazed Ham ... 32
- Indian Pork Roast 32
- Smoked Pastrami 32
- Smoked "onion Soup" Pork 33
- Wisconsin Beer Brats 33
- Sirloin Tip Roast 33
- Smoked Pork Shoulder 33
- Smoked Pork Loin With Sweet Habanero Rub (masterbuilt Electric Smoker) 34
- Smoked Rack Of Lamb 34
- Smoked Flank Steak With Peanut Oil Marinade (masterbuilt Electric Smoker) 34
- Smoked Bologna 34
- Succulent Tri-tip Roast 35
- Hungarian Pulled Pork Sandwich 35
- Smoked Asian Style Pork Tenderloin (masterbuilt Electric Smoker) 35
- Smoked Pork Ribs With Teriyaki Sauce (masterbuilt Electric Smoker) 36
- Smoked Lamb Kabobs 36
- Fiery Pork Loin With Blueberry Chutney 36
- Tri-tip Roast 36
- Smoked Ham With Glaze 37
- Perfectly Smoked Pork Butt 37

Smoked Dry Mustard Beef Round Steak (masterbuilt Electric Smoker) 37
Slow Smoked Pork Ribs 37
Smoked Ribeye With Herb Rubs (masterbuilt Electric Smoker)................................38
Smoked French Sour Lamb Cutlets (masterbuilt Electric Smoker)................38
Smoked Pork Loin 38
Saucy Beef Back Ribs 38
Simple Pulled Pork Butt................................39
Smoked Pork Ribs With Fresh Herbs (masterbuilt Electric Smoker) 39
Cross-rib Beef Roast 39
Smoked Lamb Chops With Fresh Herbs (masterbuilt Electric Smoker) 40
Chicago Rib Tips 40
Cherry Memphis Pork Ribs 40
Moroccan Lamb Ribs 40
Ultimate Chuck Roast 41
Baby Back Ribs With Bbq Sauce................. 41
Smoked Chorizo Queso 41
Decadent Rump Roast 41
Irish-style Lamb 42
Sticky Smoky Meatloaf................................42
Tenderloin Kebabs 42
Simple Pulled Pork....................................42
Smoked Pork Belly 43
Asian Honey Pork Chops 43
Meats Combo Meatloaf................................43
World's Most Tender "3-2-1 Ribs" 43
Smoked Sour Baby Ribs (masterbuilt Electric Smoker) 44
Smoked Leg Of Lamb................................44
Savory And Sweet Pork Ribs........................44
Basic Brisket 45
Smoked Ultimate Flank Steak 45
Delicious Maple Glazed Smoked Bacon 45
Delicious Smoked Pork Belly........................45
Mole-mole Baby Back Ribs 46
Glazed Pork Tenderloin 46
Smoked Prime Rib 46
Smoked Loin Chops 46
Flavorful Beef Brisket 47
Smoked Pastrami Burgers 47
Glazed Meatloaf 47
Bbq Pulled Pork..48
Hot-stuffed Pork Chop................................48
Sweet And Savory Classical Pork................48
Apple Smoked Pork Loin 49
Smoked Apple Ribs 49
Glorious Lamb Shoulder............................49
Smoked Beef Brisket With White Wine Marinade (masterbuilt Electric Smoker) 49
Smoked Molasses Lamb Chops 50
Smoked Molasses Ribeye Beef Steak (masterbuilt Electric Smoker) 50
Rosemary Lamb Chops 50
Bbq Lamb Chops 50
Smoked Short Ribs.................................... 51
Bacon-wrapped Fatty.................................. 51
Smoked Tri-tip Roast 51
Beefy Jalapeno Fatty.................................. 51

Poor Man's Burnt Ends 52
Welcoming Pork Shoulder 52
Memphis Bbq Spaghetti.............................. 52
Kansas City Burnt Ends.............................. 53
Perfect Smoked Beef Burgers 53
Smoked Pork Loin With Beer-anise Marinade (masterbuilt Electric Smoker)..................... 53
Triple Smoked Burger 54
Deviled Ham Crackers 54
New York Strip Steak With Bourbon Butter 54
Pit Smoked Pork Shoulder 54
Cider Brined Pulled Pork.............................55
Smoked Hamburgers...................................55
Smoked Goat Ribs With Garlic (masterbuilt Electric Smoker) 55
Smoked Steak Strips...................................55
Lip-smackin' Short Ribs 56
Perfectly Smoked Beef Ribs........................ 56
Seasoned Chuck Roast................................ 56
Ribeye Steaks 56
Texan Beef Brisket 57
Hearty Ribeye Steaks...................................57
Country Style Pork Ribs 57
Smoked Coconut Aminos Marinated Flank Steak (masterbuilt Electric Smoker).............57
Molasses Lamb Chops 58
Smoked Lamb Lollipops.............................. 58
Smoked Cheesy Burgers 58
Smoked Hot Pepper Pork Tenderloin (masterbuilt Electric Smoker) 58
Perfectly Smoked Pork Spare Ribs.............. 59
Smoked Chuck Roast.................................. 59
Summer Spiced Sausage 59
Smoked Lamb Breast.................................. 59
Simple Beef Roast 60
Tex Mex Pulled Pork Taco Filling 60
Best-ever Pork Chops 60
Dry Rubbed Pork Chops 60
Masterbuilt Beef Brisket..............................61
Smoked Burgers With Seared Avocado 61
Smoked Beef Brisket...................................61
Crazy Smoked Pork Spare Ribs 62
Rosemary Garlic Pork Tenderloins.............. 62
South Carolina Pulled Pork 62
Masterbuilt Smoked Seasoned Chuck Roast 63
Garlic Sauce And Lamb Chops 63
Smoked Hamburger Jerky 63
Smoked Loin Chops With Cherry Chutney.. 64
Pastrami 64
Hickory Smoked Burgers 64
Smoked Pork Ribs 64
Smoked Herb Marinated Lamb Skewers..... 65
Perfectly Smoked Filet Mignon.................... 65
Smoked Lamb Shoulder Chops 65
Masterbuilt Smoked Lamb Shank................ 65
Southwestern Smoked Chili 66
Paprika Herb Rub Garlic & Onion Tenderloin66
German Pork Hock 66
Basic Smoked Burgers 66
Smoked Pork Ribs With Avocado Oil (masterbuilt Electric Smoker)..................... 67
Spiced Pork Loin.. 67

East Texas Pulled Pork 67
Cowboy Omelet 68
Smoked Meatballs..68
Pulled Pork Hoagie 68
Basic Smoked Beef Jerky Recipe..................68
Basic Smoked Burgers 69
Dry Rubbed and Smoked Tri-Tip Roast
Recipe 69
Glaze (double for extra sauce) 69
Herb Rubbed Smoked Rack of Veal 70
Marinated Smoked Beef Short Ribs 70
Smoked Beef Braciole Finished in Tomato
Sauce Recipe 71
Smoked Beef Tenderloin with Horseradish
Sauce Recipe 71
Smoked Brisket 72
Smoked Dry Rubbed Bottom Round Roast . 72
A Little Spicy Smoked Lamb Sausage Recipe73
Basic Smoked Beef Jerky Recipe 73
Homemade Smoked Maple Cured Bacon 74
Savory and Sweet Smoked Ribs with Classic
BBQ Sauce 74
Smoked Blueberry and Maple Glazed Baby
Back Ribs 75
Smoked Boston Butt Recipe for Pulled Pork76
Smoked Ham Hocks Recipe 76
Smoked Ham with Maple & Mustard Glaze
Recipe 77
Smoked Porchetta with Fresh Herbs 77
Smoked Whole Bologna Roll 78
Fish and Seafood Recipes 79
Smoked Fish Spread 79
Smoked Asian Trout 79
Masterbuilt Smoked Mackerel 79
Perfectly Cured Salmon 79
Masterbuilt Smoked Trout 80
Masterbuilt Electric Smoker Shrimp Kabobs80
Succulent Trout 80
Butterflied Lobster Tails 80
Marinated Smoked Oysters 81
Smoked Clams 81
Enticing Salmon.. 81
Scrambled Smoked Fish Bowls 81
Smoked Lobster With Herbed Butter
(masterbuilt Electric Smoker) 82
Smoked Catfish 82
Simple Smoked Salmon 82
Zesty Tuna 82
Smoked Eel..82
Omega-3 Rich Salmon 83
Fancy Appetizers 83
Tuna Steaks 83
Easy Smoked Tuna.......................................83
Marinated Trout...83
Herbed Shrimp..84
Simple Salt & Pepper Smoked Salmon.........84
Smoked Red Fish Fillets 84
Simple Brined Trout 84
Shrimps 85
Smoked Sweet Salmon 85
Delicious Lobster Tail 85

Smoked Halibut Fillets (masterbuilt Electric
Smoker) 85
Smoked Scallops 86
Whole Snapper 86
Stuffed Salmon..86
Delicious Scallops 86
Spicy Cuban Catfish 87
Smoked Jumpers 87
Smoked Salmon Chowder 87
Honey Glazed Cod 87
Bacon-wrapped Scallops 88
Alaskan Candied Salmon 88
Smoked Trout 88
Cape Cod Lobster Rolls 88
Bacon Wrapped Smoked Scallops.................89
Halibut With Homemade Tartar Sauce 89
Cured Salmon 89
Creamy Shrimp Pasta Salad 89
Maple Smoked Salmon Steaks 90
Gourmet Snapper 90
Peach-smoked Ahi Tuna Steaks 90
Smoked Lobster 90
Smoked Savory Sardine (masterbuilt Electric
Smoker)..91
Smoked Lobster Tails 91
Ale-brined Catfish With Cilantro Lemon
Dipping Sauce 91
Honey Mustard Halibut Fillets 91
Smoked Lemony Catfish Fillets (masterbuilt
Electric Smoker) 92
Smoked Cod 92
Smoked Tilapia 92
Smoked Salmon With Peppercorn Crust 92
Smoked Snow Crab Legs 93
Honey Chipotle Salmon With Pineapple Salsa93
Lemon Pepper Tuna 93
Stunning Sardine 93
Poultry Recipes 94
Smoked Buffalo Chicken Wings 94
Chicken And Guacamole 94
Smoked Turkey With Flavors Of Mixed Herbs94
Let It Cool For 15 Minutes And Serve
Standing Smoked Chicken 95
Honey Smoked Turkey 95
Special Dinner Turkey 95
Spicy Chicken Wings 96
Spicy Honey-apple Bbq Wings 96
Simple Smoked Chicken Wings 96
Bacon Wrapped Chicken Lollipops............... 96
Honey Brined Turkey 97
Turkey In The Electric Smoker 97
Pool Party Wings 97
Thanksgiving Party Turkey 97
Inspired Turkey Breast 98
Fully Smoked Herbal Quail 98
Sweet And Spicy Chicken Wings.................. 98
Stuffed Chicken Breast In Masterbuilt Smoker99
Cola Glazed Chicken Breasts 99
Christmas Dinner Duck................................ 99
Herb-rubbed Apple Smoked Turkey.......... 100
Seasoned Drumsticks 100
Turkey With Chimichurri........................... 100

Sweet Bbq Wings.................................101
Smo-fried Cajun Turkey 101
Grandma's Whole Smoked Chicken............101
Smoked Herbed Chicken Breasts 101
Asparagus Stuffed Smoked Chicken Breasts102
Smoked Chicken Breasts With Rosemary
(masterbuilt Electric Smoker) 102
Well-seasoned Drumsticks 102
Supremely Smoked Alderwood Turkey Breast102
Spiced Chicken Thighs................................103
Romain Chicken Breasts 103
Lemon Pepper Chicken Quarters 103
Smoked Turkey Breast................................103
Smoked Turkey 104
Rotisserie Chicken 104
Get-together Chicken Wings......................104
Red Hot Chicken Wings 104
Smoked Soy Chicken Legs 105
Smofried Chicken Wings 105
Utterly Delicious Duck Breast 105
German Style Turkey Breast 105
Apple-smoked Duck....................................106
Sweet 'n' Spicy Chicken Wings 106
White Wine Turkey Dogs............................106
Basic Smoked Chicken 106
Smoked Chicken Thighs In Red Pepper
Marinade (masterbuilt Electric Smoker) ... 107
Spicy Chicken Wings With Dipping Sauce. 107
Alabama Chicken Sandwiches With White
Bbq Sauce 107
Supreme Chipotle Wings 108
Turkey Breast 108
Bacon-wrapped Chicken Lollipops.............108
Cajun Style Chicken Breasts 108
Smoked Chicken Legs 108
Smoked Chicken Breast In Coffee Marinade
(masterbuilt Electric Smoker) 109
Old Fashioned Barbecue Chicken 109
Chicken With Western Kentucky Mop & Dip109
Smoked Garlicky Chicken Breast (masterbuilt
Electric Smoker)..110
Beer Smoked Chicken In Masterbuilt Smoker110
Simple Turkey Breast.................................110
Versatile Chicken Breasts 110
Tender Sweet Sriracha Bbq Chicken 111
Bbq Chicken Legs 111
Easy Smoked Turkey...................................111
Smoked Turkey Breast With Orange-onion
Marinade (masterbuilt Electric Smoker) 111
Authentic Citrus Smoked Chicken 112
Weekend Dinner Chicken 112
Smoked Whole Chicken 112
County Fair Turkey Legs.............................112
Smoked Apple Curry Chicken Breast
(masterbuilt Electric Smoker) 113
Orange Smoked Chicken.............................113
Smoked Turkey Cocktail Bites (masterbuilt
Electric Smoker)..113
Citrus Goose Breast....................................113
Marinated Chicken Breasts.........................114
Smoked Chicken Patties (masterbuilt Electric
Smoker) 114

Moist Wrapped Chicken Tenders............... 114
Chicken Breast 114
Orange Crispy Chicken 115
Tandoori Chicken 115
Chipotle Turkey Legs 115
Cheesy Turkey Meatballs........................... 116
Smoky Wrap Chicken Breasts 116
Easiest Bbq Smoked Turkey Wings 116
Smoked Chicken Cutlets In Strawberries -
Balsamic Marinade (masterbuilt Electric
Smoker)... 116
Spicy Jamaican Jerk 117
Smoked Chicken Tenders 117
Smoked White Wings 117
Smoked Blue Wings 117
Smoked Sweet And Spicy Chicken Wings... 117
Smoked Chicken Thighs............................. 118
Smoked Chicken Breast With Dark Sauce
(masterbuilt Electric Smoker) 118
Amazing Mesquite Maple And Bacon Chicken118
Apple Brined Smoked Duck Breast............ 118
Brined and Smoked Bone-in Chicken Breasts119
Brined and Smoked Pheasant with a Honey
Glaze Recipe 119
Herb Rubbed Smoked Turkey Recipe........ 120
Savory Herb Rubbed and Aromatic Stuffed
Smoked Turkey Recipe............................... 120
Seasoned & Smoked Chicken Drumsticks .. 121
Smoked Chicken Breasts with Creamed
Spinach Filling... 121
Smoked Marinated Chicken Skewers 122
Sweet and Spicy Smoked Chicken Wings with
Yogurt Dipping Sauce 122
Games Recipes 123
Smoked Up Pheasant..................................123
Boar Shoulder 123
Whole Quail 123
The Great Boar Shoulder............................124
Smoked Duck 124
Bacon Wrapped Dove 124
Delicious Smoked Rabbits..........................124
Smoked Wild Goose Breast In Beer Marinade
(masterbuilt Electric Smoker)....................125
Smoked Wild Boar Chops (masterbuilt
Electric Smoker) 125
Smoked Rabbit With Rosemary Wine
Marinade (masterbuilt Electric Smoker)....125
Masterbuilt Electric Smoker Goose Jerky ..125
Masterbuilt Electric Smoker Venison 126
Masterbuilt Smoked Rabbit 126
Sauces, Mobs & Rubs.................................127
Sweet Spice Rub...127
Green Salsa 127
Paprika Bbq Rub..127
Black Bean & Sesame Sauce 127
Exotic Rub Mix 127
Texas Style Brisket Rub..............................127
Teriyaki Sauce 128
Easy Mustard Sauce....................................128
Cheesy Cowboy Butter................................128
Hot Pepper And Vinegar Bbq Sauce 128
Sesame & White Bean Sauce 128

Memphis Rub.. 129
The Great Chimichurri Sauce 129
Creative Smoked Salt 129
Chili Chipotle Sauce 129
Montreal Steak Rub 129
Smoked Red Peppercorns.......................... 129
Carolina Barbeque Rub.............................. 130
Lovely Chicken Spice Rub.......................... 130
Gentle Alabama White Sauce 130
Cheese & Nuts 131
Christy's Smoked Pimento Cheese Appetizer131
Splendid Cheeseburger Patty 131
Smoked Brie With Roasted Peppers & Garlic131
Smoked Brie Cheese....................................131
Smoked Rosemary Cashews 132
Smoked Gouda Cheese................................ 132
Smoked Cheese Crisps 132
Garlic And Cayenne Almonds.................... 132
Smoked Mozzarella 132
Hamburger Recipes 133
Smoked Yummy Chicken Burgers
(masterbuilt Electric Smoker) 133
Smoked Classic Burgers (masterbuilt Electric
Smoker) 133
Smoked Turkey Burgers With Mayo And
Mustard (masterbuilt Electric Smoker) 133
Smoked "spicy Trio" Burgers (masterbuilt
Electric Smoker)... 133
Smoked Hamburgers With Panko
(masterbuilt Electric Smoker) 133
Other Recipes 134
Asparagus And Onion Mix........................ 134
Hearty Jalapeno Peppers............................ 134
Rosemary Smoked Cashews 134
Apple-brined Smoked Turkey 134
Sweet And Spicy Smoked Pecans 134
Festival Turkey Legs 135
Smoked Cherries 135
The Original Smoked Cauliflower 135
Smoked Cabbage Steaks With Dijon
Vinaigrette.. 135
Smoked Chorizo With Mustard-caper Sauce
(masterbuilt Electric Smoker) 135

Smoked Deer Sausages (masterbuilt Electric
Smoker)..136
Mexican Stuffed Cornbread 136
Smoked Eggs...136
Smoked Vegetables.....................................136
Smoked Up Peaches 136
Mixed Veggie Combo 137
Smoked Cocktail Peanuts 137
Smoked Salmon Cucumbers 137
Smoked Almonds..137
Smoked Paprika Roasted Potatoes 137
Country Smoked Christmas Ham 138
Tamarind Smoked Turkey Sausages
(masterbuilt Electric Smoker).....................138
Smoked Maple Butter Soaked Apples.........138
Cold Smoked Nuts......................................138
Thanksgiving Garlic Smoked Turkey.........138
Smoked Chicken Sausages With Fennel
Dressing (masterbuilt Electric Smoker) 139
Properly Smoked Mushrooms.....................139
Roasted Broccoli 139
Cold Smoked Tomato Salsa........................139
Smoked Brussel Sprouts.............................139
Lemon Rosemary Turkey Breasts 140
Smoked Cabbage.. 140
Smoked Bananas 140
Smoke Roasted Sweet Potatoes.................. 140
Amazing Corn 140
Smoked Oysters With Olive Relish 141
Smoked Stuffed Turkey With Vegetables ... 141
Smoked Corn Recipe 141
Go-to-summer Side Dish............................ 141
Marinated and Smoked Venison Tenderloin141
Provencal Style Marinated and Smoked
Rabbit...142
Smoked Classic Deviled Eggs 142
Smoked Mac and Cheese with Two Cheeses
Recipe...143
Smoked Potato, Ham, and Cheese Casserole
Recipe...143
Smoked Sweet and Sour Tofu Skewers Recipe144
Smoking Hard and Semi-hard Cheeses 144
Twice Smoked Cheese and Bacon Potatoes 145
Appendix : Recipes Index 146

INTRODUCTION

Almost everybody loves a barbeque, but nothing compares to that rich smoking flavor. If you really are serious about smoking food, you need a high-quality smoker. This is where Masterbuilt comes in. They are not the first to enter the industry, but they are known to create some of the best smokers in the market. They offer a wide range of them, from cutting-edge digital charcoal models to small and simple ones. They are well-designed, reasonably priced. No matter what you need, there is a Masterbuilt Smoker for you. The only downside is that you have to choose yours out of the whole product line.

What you can do with your smoker is as varied as the offerings from Masterbuilt. Consider this 500-recipe cookbook the ultimate and definitive guide on how you could use your smoker to its utmost potential.

Why Masterbuilt?

Masterbuilt is not the first manufacturer to enter the market. Even so, it is one of the leading brands in the industry. It started out about 45 years ago and sold many types of smokers and grills. Masterbuilt sells many high-quality products at a low price. Recently, there is a noticeable increase in quality and they keep releasing new products with innovative features. People love Masterbuilt for many reasons such as:
- Insulation: The insulation performance from Masterbuilt smokers is better than that of their competitors at a similar price. Insulation helps maintain a stable internal temperature, thus saving fuel and simplify the cooking process. This also means that Masterbuilt smokers still work well in cold or windy conditions.
- Size-to-cost ratio: Not many people care to measure this, but it is something to think about. You get more cooking space per dollar on Masterbuilt smokers compared to their competitors.
- User-friendly: Masterbuilt designs the smokers in a way that makes them very easy to use, especially for beginners.
- Intuitive features: All Masterbuilt Smokers come with various features that make them just better than other products. Some include wheels, flexible racks, digital panel and control, mobile apps, and more.

Types of Smoker

That said, where to begin? There are many types of smokers out there, each with their own strengths and weaknesses. Although there are many Masterbuilt smokers, they can be classified into the following types:

Charcoal Smoker

The classic charcoal smokers come in various shapes and sizes. That includes Masterbuilt Bullet Smoker. They are the best of the bunch in terms of flavor, but the worst in terms of maintenance. They are a bit more labor-intensive compared to gas or electric smokers as you need to set it up, then babysit, then clean the smoker after use.

When wood is heated up to around 1,000 °F, most of the non-carbon organic compounds are burnt off. The char that is left behind does not produce a lot of smoke and burns cleanly. The char is then used to form little briquettes that we call charcoal.

Burning charcoal produces chemicals such as carbon dioxide, carbon monoxide, and nitrogen oxide, adding flavor to the food. You can also set wood chips above the charcoal to smolder if you want more smoke and smokey flavor. The heat and smoke travel upward, cooking the food that is suspended above.

The air intakes near the charcoals are used to control the heat. The more air you let into the firebox, the hotter the charcoal burns. The trick here is to manage the airflow and smoke inside. Too much air and your food will end up dry and tough. Too little air and your food will become bitter from the smoke and ash.

If you want a real smokey flavor, then you should get a charcoal smoker. It might take some getting used to and it is time-consuming to smoke food with it, but it is the best smoker to get that special flavor.

Pros:
- The best smoker if you want that smokey flavor
- Comes in various shape and sizes

Cons:
- Need more babysitting, practice, and know-how
- It takes time to start smoking
- Lots of cleaning up after smoking

Propane/Gas Smoker

As the name suggests, gas smokers heat your food with gas. It's worth pointing out that gas or propane smokers are the same things. Sometimes, you may see the word Liquefied Petroleum Gas (LPG), which also means the same thing.

A gas smoker can be hooked up to an external gas bottle or a gas line in your home if you have it. If you're going to cook outdoors, you need a gas bottle, which you can find at most gas stations and outdoor stores.

Many gas smokers you see have the burner and vents at the bottom and the dampers and chimney at the top. The gas goes from the bottle through a pipe to the cooking section, where it is ignited as it comes out of the valves. Gas cookers do not produce smoke naturally, so you will need to use wood chips to create that smokey flavor.

If you want a little more flavor than an electric cooker, but still want that convenience and control, then a gas smoker is your best bet. Its portability and ease of maintenance make it the perfect option in most cooking scenarios, be it outdoors or indoors.

Pros:
- Easy to use
- Fuel is widely available
- Easy temperature control
- Takes only about 15 minutes to get from cold to cooking

Cons:
- More flavor than electric grill, but some say that gas smokers make everything taste like bacon
- You might need to use two gas bottles, just to be sure that you don't run out halfway

Electric Smoker

If you don't care too much about the smokey flavor and just want a "set and forget" smoking solution, then electric smokers are for you. You don't have to deal with managing airflow and smoke from wood or charcoal, or fuel from your gas tank, let alone cleaning everything up once you're done. You are good to go as long as you have electricity. This makes it perfect for those who cannot use gas, wood, or charcoal smokers for whatever reasons.

With an electric smoker, all you need to do is to set the temperature and timer, which can be done on the smoker itself or remotely from a mobile app. That depends on the model you use. Then, just sit back with a beer and wait. You do not have to worry about checking up on your food every 30mns constantly. The smoking process is completely automated.

Electric smokers do not use combustion to heat your food. They use a heating element, powered by electricity. Since there is no burning involved, there is no smoke unless you use wood chips, which are suspended above the heating element.

The heat burns the wood chips, which creates smoke. Above the wood chips is a water pan, and then the food racks. The heat boils the water, creating vapor that, with the smoke from the wood chips, enhances the smokey flavor of the food. Moreover, the water pan shields the food from the direct heat of the heating element, keeping the temperature low, and the smoking time slow.

Pros:
- Very easy to use
- No other fuel source needed
- The smoking process is automated

Cons:
- Smokey flavor from the electric smoker is different from other smokers
- Your food won't form a smoke ring, due to the lack of combustion
- The moist atmosphere inside the smoker means it is harder to achieve a crisp crust on ribs or chicken skin

Pellet Smoker

A pellet smoker is another compromise between a charcoal smoker and an electric smoker. It combines the combustion power of a charcoal cooker and the convenience of an electric cooker. The best thing about the pellet smoker is that it is an all-in-one solution as you can use it as a grill, an oven, and a smoker.

As the name suggests, pellet smokers use wood pellets as a source of fuel. These wood pellets are made from sawdust, which is compressed into little pellets that look like chicken feed. These pellets are placed inside a hopper on the side of the smoker and are then fed into the firebox by the auger drill. The firebox houses a heated metal rod, which ignites the wood pellets, creating smoke and heat in the cooking chamber.

Pellet smokers have built-in thermometers that regulate the temperature in the chamber. It automatically adjusts the airflow and number of pellets being fed into the firebox to ensure that the heat remains consistent.

Overall, a pellet smoker is for those who want to combine the power of a charcoal smoker and an electric cooker without much compromise. It's versatile and convenient, but it does not come cheap.

Pros:
- Combustion means you get an authentic smokey flavor
- The cooking system allows you to set it and forget it
- Versatile can be used as an oven, grill, and smoker
- Not much cleaning up to do because pellets leave almost nothing behind after burning

Cons:
- Pricey
- You still need electricity, since the heating rod, the fans, and the drill run on electricity
- Wood pellets are not easy to find and it can be expensive to stockpile

Digital Charcoal Smoker

If you are willing to spend a lot of money, Masterbuilt offers a smoking solution that brings the authentic smokey flavor and the convenience of an electric smoker together. It works similarly to a pellet smoker, except it uses charcoal instead of wood pellet.

Pros:
- The no-compromise solution between a charcoal smoker and an electric smoker
- Easy to clean
- Large cooking area

Cons:
- Large and clunky
- Very expensive

How to use a Smoker

Different smokers will have different ways to operate, but they generally follow the same guideline. If you are using an electric smoker, a pellet smoker, or a digital charcoal smoker, then it's just a simple matter of adding fuel, setting the timer and temperature, adding the food, and wait.

Season your smoker

It sounds silly, but it helps enhances the flavor. It works similarly to seasoning the cutting board. Your food absorbs seasoning well before it is cooked.

Light It up

Next, prepare the fuel. It's a simple matter of dumping in the wood pellet or attaching the gas if you use a pellet or gas smoker. For a manual charcoal smoker, you need to dump the charcoal in a chimney starter and light it up. Wait until it starts to ash over, which takes about 15 minutes. Then, add coal to the smoker. Make sure to fully open the intake and chimney baffles before adding the charcoal. Wait until the temperature reaches the desired level before adding meat.

Maintaining the Temperature

At this point, make sure to keep the smoker and firebox doors closed as much as possible so that the temperature remains constant. When you see that the temperature has reached the desired level, quickly add the meat to the smoker and close the door again.

That is where you work the baffles to control the flow of oxygen. The intake baffle controls the heat and the chimney baffle controls the flow of the smoke. You can keep the chimney baffle wide open and keep the intake baffle closed at least halfway, and adjust it as the temperature fluctuates.

Add Wood Chunks

Even though charcoal smokers can achieve that smokey flavor, it is recommended to still add wood chunks to enhance it. Some even go as far as to add wood chunks from different trees to give their food that extra fragrance. Consider using fruitwoods, nutwoods, or hardwoods that are intended for smoking as they deliver the best flavor. Also, use larger wood chunks instead of small chips since larger chunks mean they smolder more slowly and consistently.

Add Moisture

Moisture helps your food absorb that smokey flavor. There are two ways to do this. You can put a metal rack over the coals and put a water pan on it. That way, the smoke becomes humidified as it enters the grilling chamber. You can also spray some water on your food, but don't overdo it to the point that you wash away the smoke coating.

Wait and Cleaning Afterwards

From that point, it's just a matter of waiting until it is done. Make sure to clean your smoker after every use. Masterbuilt recommends making a mixture of 50/50 hot water and apple cider vinegar in a spray bottle. Spray and clean with a sponge. The use of harsh chemicals is not recommended.

Safety Tips

Do:
- Keep the smoker as far as possible from any potential fire hazard or your home. The minimum distance is 10 feet. This distance rule also applies to garages, porches, and carports. Watch out for decorations like baskets, pillows, etc, as they can easily catch on fire. Always smoke your food outside.
- Clean your smoker regularly. Try to make a habit of cleaning it after cooking. Grease and fat can cause sudden flare-ups if you let them build up as they are flammable.
- If you use a gas smoker, make sure that there is no gas leak. One way to do this is by mixing liquid dish soap with water and apply the solution on the hoses and connections. If you see large bubbles when you turn on the gas, then there's a leak. Check to see if there are holes or whether the connections are tight enough.
- Have a spray bottle of water nearby. There might be flare-ups, so you want to calm it as soon as possible. It won't ruin your food. In addition to this, have a fire extinguisher in case things go south.

Don't:
- Turn on the gas while the lid is still closed. It causes a gas buildup and you will get a fireball in your face when you light it and open it.
- Ignore your grill: This only applies to smokers that cannot automate the cooking process. Fire spreads very quickly, so you should prepare everything else first so you can keep a close eye on your smoker.
- Overload: Never pack too much food in your smoker, especially fatty meats. It slows the cooking process down and the fat from the meat can cause a flare-up.

Vegan and Vegetarian Recipes

Smoked Eggplant
Serves: 4
Cooking Time: 20 Minutes.
Ingredients:
- 2 medium eggplant
- Olive oil

Directions:
Preheat your smoker to 200°F/93°C and soak your wood chips for an hour. Remove the woodchips from the liquid then pat dry before using. Then carefully peel your eggplant then slice into rounds of around ¼"/1cm thick. Brush each of these rounds with olive oil then place directly into the smoker. Smoke for approximately an hour until soft and tender. Serve and enjoy!

Smoked Watermelon
Serves: 5
Cook Time: 45 Minutes
Ingredients:
- 1 Seedless watermelon
- Balsamic vinegar
- Wooden skewers, soaked into water

Directions:
Chop the ends off of the seedless watermelon; then let it stand aside over a cutting board and slice the skin and the white rind off Slice the watermelon into small cubes; then put the cubes into a large bowl Drizzle with the balsamic vinegar over the watermelon cubes Toss the ingredients with both your hands Preheat your Masterbuilt electric smoker to a temperature of about 22F with the top of the vent open. Add the water to about half full into the bottom of the bowl Add the wood chips to the side tray While the Masterbuilt electric smoker is heating up, place about cubes of watermelon over each of the soaked skewers Place the skewers into the Masterbuilt electric smoker; and smoke for about 45 minutes Make sure to replenish the wood chips when needed Serve the skewers and enjoy its delicious taste!

Smoked Portobello Mushrooms With Herbs De Provence
Serves: 4
Cooking Time: 10 Minutes
Ingredients:
- 12 large Portobello mushrooms
- 1 tbsp. Herbs de Provence
- ¼ c. extra virgin olive oil
- Sea salt
- Black pepper

Directions:
Preheat smoker to 200°F and add wood chips (recommended oak wood chips). In a bowl, mix Herbs de Provence, olive oil, salt, and pepper to taste. Clean the mushrooms with a dry cloth or paper towel. Rub the mushrooms all over with herbs mixture. Place the mushrooms, cap side down, directly on the top grill rack. Smoke for approximately 2 hours. Remove carefully so the herbal liquid in the cap remains in place. Serve whole and enjoy!

Herby Smoked Cauliflower
Serves: 4   Cooking Time: 20 Minutes
Ingredients:
- 1 head cauliflower
- Olive oil
- Salt
- Pepper
- 2 tsps. dried oregano
- 2 tsps. Dried basil

Directions:
Start by soaking your woodchips for about an hour and preheating your smoker to 200°F/93°C. Remove the woodchips from the liquid then pat dry before using. Then take your cauliflower and chop into medium-sized pieces, removing the core. Place the pieces of cauliflower onto a sheet pan and then drizzle with the olive oil. Sprinkle the seasonings and herbs over the cauliflower then pop into the smoker. Smoke for 2 hours, checking and turning often. Serve and enjoy!

Smoked Potato Salad
Serves: 4   Cooking Time: 30 Minutes
Ingredients:
- 3 eggs, hard-boiled
- 2 tbsps. cider vinegar
- 1 lb. russet potatoes
- 1 tbsp. Dijon mustard
- ½ c. red onion
- ⅓ c. light mayonnaise
- Salt
- Black pepper

Directions:
Preheat the electric smoker to 225°F. Put prepared wood chips in the wood tray — use mesquite chips for the best result. Put peeled potatoes in a saucepan and cover with water. Put on the lid and bring to a boil. Cook for 20 minutes. Pat potatoes dry, and put them on paper towels. Directly smoke potatoes on the racks for 2 hrs. as you add extra wood chips in a cycle of 4minutes. Remove potatoes, let them cool. Chop them well for the preparation of the salad. Combine boiled eggs, onion, mayonnaise, pickles, mustard, pepper, salt, and vinegar. Mix all these ingredients well. Add potatoes to the prepared mixture. Put in the fridge for several hrs. covered

Smoky Corn On The Cob
Serves: 5
Cooking Time: 10 Minutes
Ingredients:
- 10 ears sweet corn
- ½ c. butter
- Salt
- Black pepper

Directions:
Preheat your smoker to 225°F and add wood chips (recommended oak or hickory). Put the ears of corn on the top racks of the smoker and smoke for 2 hours. Rotate the corn every minutes. Serve hot with butter, salt, and pepper.

Delicious Portobello Mushrooms
Serves: 4
Cooking Time: 2 Hours
Ingredients:
- 12 large Portobello mushrooms
- 1 tablespoon Herbs de Provence
- ¼ cup extra virgin olive oil
- Salt and pepper to taste

Directions:
Take your drip pan and add water, cover with aluminum foil. Pre-heat your smoker to 200 degrees F Take a bowl and mix in Herbs de Provence, olive oil, salt, and pepper Clean mushrooms using a dry cloth Rub mushrooms al over with herbs mixture, transfer mushrooms, cap side down on top grill rack Use water fill water pan halfway through and place it over drip pan. Add wood chips to the side tray Smoke for 2 hours Remove carefully and serve, enjoy!

Squash Casserole
Serves: 10
Cooking Time: 45 Minutes
Ingredients:
- 2 ½ pounds boiled yellow squash, mashed
- 1 yellow onion, chopped
- 1 package Velveeta cheese
- ¼ cup herb cheese spread
- ¼ cup mayonnaise
- ¼ teaspoon Cajun seasoning
- Salt and pepper to taste
- 2 eggs, beaten
- ½ cup butter

Directions:
Preheat the smoker to 2250F. Place water in the water pan and add hickory wood chips into the side tray. Place all Ingredients: in a casserole dish and give a good stir well to combine all Ingredients:. Put the casserole dish inside the smoker and cook for minutes.

Smoked Potato Salad
Serves: 4
Cooking Time: 30 Minutes
Ingredients:
- 3 eggs, hard-boiled
- 2 tbsps. cider vinegar
- 1 lb. russet potatoes
- 1 tbsp. Dijon mustard
- ½ c. red onion
- ⅓ c. light mayonnaise
- Salt
- Black pepper

Directions:
Preheat the electric smoker to 225°F. Put prepared wood chips in the wood tray — use mesquite chips for the best result. Put peeled potatoes in a saucepan and cover with water. Put on the lid and bring to a boil. Cook for 20 mins. Pat potatoes dry, and put them on paper towels. Directly smoke potatoes on the racks for 2 hrs. as you add extra wood chips in a cycle of 4mins. Remove potatoes, let them cool. Chop them well for the preparation of the salad. Combine boiled eggs, onion, mayonnaise, pickles, mustard, pepper, salt, and vinegar. Mix all these ingredients well. Add potatoes to the prepared mixture. Put in the fridge for several hrs. covered.

Smoked Squash Casserole
Serves: 2
Cooking Time: 40 Minutes
Ingredients:
- 2½ lbs. yellow squash
- 2 tbsps. parsley flakes
- 2 eggs, beaten
- 1 medium yellow onion
- 1 sleeve saltine crackers
- 1 package Velveeta cheese
- ½ c. Alouette Sundried Tomato
- Basil cheese spread
- ¼ c. Alouette Garlic and Herb cheese spread
- ¼ c. mayonnaise
- ¾ tsp. hot sauce
- ¼ tsp. Cajun seasoning
- ½ c. butter
- ¼ tsp. salt
- ¼ tsp. black pepper

Directions:
Preheat the electric smoker to 250°F. Combine squash and onion in a large saucepan and add water to cover. Boil on medium heat until tender. Drain and to this hot mixture, add Velveeta cheese, Alouette cheese, mayonnaise, parsley flakes, hot sauce, Cajun seasoning, salt, and pepper to taste. Stir all together well. Cool a little, add eggs and stir until mixed. Melt butter in a saucepan. Add crushed crackers to the butter and stir well. Combine ½ cup of butter-cracker mix with the squash mixture. Stir thoroughly. Pour into a disposable aluminum foil pan. Top the squash with remaining butter and crackers. Cover the pan tightly with aluminum foil. Put on the lower rack of the smoker and cook for 1 hr. Put one small handful of prepared wood chips in the wood tray for the best result use hickory. After an hour, remove the foil from the casserole and cook for another 15 minutes.

Twice Pulled Potatoes

Serves: 4
Cooking Time: 30 Minutes.
Ingredients:
- 1 lb. pulled pork
- 2 russet potatoes
- 1/3 c. sour cream
- 4 oz. cream cheese
- 1/3 c. cheddar cheese
- Chives
- BBQ sauce, to taste

Directions:
Preheat the electric smoker to 225°F. Smoke washed potatoes for 2 hours. Mix potato flesh, cheddar cheese, sour cream, cream cheese, pulled pork and BBQ sauce in a bowl and stir well. Put prepared mixture back into potatoes skins. Smoke for another mins. Season with more BBQ sauce, if desired. Sprinkle some cheddar cheese and chives on the top.

Smoked Portobello Mushrooms With Herbs De Provence

Serves: 4
Cooking Time: 10 Minutes
Ingredients:
- 12 large Portobello mushrooms
- 1 tbsp. Herbs de Provence
- ¼ c. extra virgin olive oil
- Sea salt
- Black pepper

Directions:
Preheat smoker to 200°F and add wood chips (recommended oak wood chips). In a bowl, mix Herbs de Provence, olive oil, salt, and pepper to taste. Clean the mushrooms with a dry cloth or paper towel. Rub the mushrooms all over with herbs mixture. Place the mushrooms, cap side down, directly on the top grill rack. Smoke for approximately 2 hours. Remove carefully so the herbal liquid in the cap remains in place. Serve whole and enjoy!

Smoked Green Beans With Lemon

Serves: 4
Cooking Time: 20 Minutes
Ingredients:
- 2 lbs. fresh green beans, trimmed and soaked
- 2 tbsps. Apple vinaigrette dressing
- 1 lemon

Directions:
Place beans in a colander. Preheat smoker to 140°F and add wood chips (recommended Oak wood chips). Place the beans in the pan in a single layer and lightly coat with the dressing. Place the beans on the upper shelf of the smoker and smoke for 1 hour. Remove from the heat, cover with foil and let rest for 1minutes. Pour lemon juice, sprinkle with the lemon zest and serve.

Smoked Brussels Sprouts

Serves:6-8
Cooking Time:2 Hours 15 Minutes
Ingredients:
- Brussels sprouts, rinsed and trimmed (1-lbs, 0.45-kgs)
- Extra-virgin olive oil – 2 tablespoons
- 2 cloves garlic, minced
- Sea salt – 1 teaspoon
- Freshly cracked black pepper – ½ teaspoon
- Water, to fill
- Preheat your electric smoker to 250°F (120°C)
- Add the wood chips
- Fill the water bowl to halfway

Directions:
First, cut the Brussels sprouts in half, lengthwise. Add the sprouts to a glass bowl and on high, microwave for 3 minutes. Set aside to cool for 3 minutes. Add the olive oil, garlic, salt, and pepper in a mixing bowl and whisk until incorporated. Add the sprouts to the bowl and toss to coat evenly. Add the sprouts to an ovenproof frying pan or cast iron skillet. Position the skillet on the upper rack of your smoker and smoke for approximately 2 hours, until fork tender. Check the cooking progress after 1½ hours. Serve and enjoy.

Smoked Summer Vegetables

Serves: 4
Cooking Time: 30 Minutes
Ingredients:
- Summer squash
- 2 zucchini
- 1 onion
- 2 cups mushrooms
- 2 cups French-cut green beans

Directions:
Wash thoroughly and slice squash, onion, and zucchini, mushrooms, and green beans. Combine all these ingredients and mix well. Preheat the electric smoker to 250°F. Make cup-shaped containers from heavy duty aluminum foil. Put vegetables in these cups. Add herbs and spices to taste. Pinch the top of foil cups together. Make several holes in the foil so that the smoke can circulate around the vegetables. Smoke for 1 hr. at 220°F.

Smoked Volcano Potatoes

Serves: 2
Cooking Time: 15 Minutes.
Ingredients:
- 2 russet potatoes
- ¾ c. sour cream.
- 1 c. cheddar cheese
- 2 tbsps. green onion
- 8 bacon strips
- 4 tbsps. butter
- 2 tbsps. olive oil
- Salt

Directions:
Preheat the electric smoker to 250°F. Wash potatoes, pierce using the fork. Take the oil and salt and rub on the potatoes. Wrap the potatoes in foil and put in the smoker. Smoke potatoes for 3 hrs. Cut off the top of each potato and remove the potato flesh, leaving the shell empty. Fry and crumble the bacon. Combine potato flesh with bacon, butter, sour cream, and cheese in a bowl. Put the prepared filling in the potatoes, add some cheese on the top. Wrap the potato with 2 bacon slices — for securing use toothpicks. Smoke for another 1 hr. Add green onions with a little sour cream on top (sour cream will give a special flavor to the potato).

Smoked Volcanic Potatoes

Serves: 4
Cooking Time: 3 Hours
Ingredients:
- 2 russet potatoes
- ¾ cup sour cream
- 1 cup cheddar cheese
- 2 tablespoons green onion
- 8 bacon strips
- 4 tablespoons butter
- 2 tablespoons olive oil
- Salt as needed

Directions:
Take your drip pan and add water, cover with aluminum foil. Pre-heat your smoker to 200 degrees F Use water fill water pan halfway through and place it over drip pan. Add wood chips to the side tray Take oil and salt, rub on potatoes and wrap potatoes in foil Transfer to smoker Smoke for 3 hours, cut off the top each potato and remove potato flesh, leave shell empty Fry and crumble the bacon, add potato flesh with bacon, butter, sour cream, cheese in a bowl Add prepared filling into the potatoes, add cheese on

top Wrap potato with 2 bacon slices, secure with a toothpick Smoke for 1 hour more Add green onions with little sour cream, on top Serve and enjoy!

Smoked Lemony-garlic Artichokes

Serves: 4
Cooking Time: 20 Minutes
Ingredients:
- 4 artichokes
- 4 minced garlic cloves
- 3 tbsps. Lemon juice
- ½ c. virgin olive oil
- 2 parsley sprigs
- Sea salt

Directions:
Put a large pot on your stove with a metal steaming basket inside. Fill with water just to the bottom of the basket and bring to a boil. Cut the artichoke tail and take out the toughest leaves. With cooking shears, clip the pointy ends off of the outermost leaves. Cut the artichokes in half lengthwise. Remove the hairy choke in the center. Put the halves, stem side down, in the steamer basket. Reduce the heat to a rolling simmer. On the pot, cover and steam for about 20 to 25 minutes, until the inside of the artichoke is tender. Prepare a dressing: place in a mortar the garlic, lemon juice, olive oil, parsley, and salt. Take away the basket and let the artichokes come to room temperature. Preheat your smoker to 200°F. Place the artichokes in aluminum foil packets and brush garlic mixture all over the artichokes. Smoke the artichoke halves for approximately 1 hour. Serve hot.

Smoked Salsa

Serves: 2
Cooking Time: 30 Minutes
Ingredients:
- 3 tomatoes, diced
- 4 jalapeno, diced
- ½ onion, diced
- 4 cloves of garlic, minced
- 1 tablespoon cilantro
- 1 lime, juiced
- Salt to taste

Directions:
Preheat the smoker to 2250F. Place water in the water pan and add apple wood chips into the side tray. Combine all Ingredients: and place in an aluminum pan. Smoke for 30 minutes. Chill before serving with tortilla chips.

Smoked Green Beans With Lemon
Serves: 4
Cooking Time: 20 Minutes
Ingredients:
- 2 lbs. fresh green beans, trimmed and soaked
- 2 tbsps. Apple vinaigrette dressing
- 1 lemon

Directions:
Place beans in a colander. Preheat smoker to 140°F and add wood chips (recommended Oak wood chips). Place the beans in the pan in a single layer and lightly coat with the dressing. Place the beans on the upper shelf of the smoker and smoke for 1 hour. Remove from the heat, cover with foil and let rest for 1minutes. Pour lemon juice, sprinkle with the lemon zest and serve.

Smoked Volcano Potatoes
Serves: 2
Cooking Time: 15 Minutes
Ingredients:
- 2 russet potatoes
- ¾ c. sour cream.
- 1 c. cheddar cheese
- 2 tbsps. green onion
- 8 bacon strips
- 4 tbsps. butter
- 2 tbsps. olive oil
- Salt

Directions:
Preheat the electric smoker to 250°F. Wash potatoes, pierce using the fork. Take the oil and salt and rub on the potatoes. Wrap the potatoes in foil and put in the smoker. Smoke potatoes for 3 hrs. Cut off the top of each potato and remove the potato flesh, leaving the shell empty. Fry and crumble the bacon. Combine potato flesh with bacon, butter, sour cream, and cheese in a bowl. Put the prepared filling in the potatoes, add some cheese on the top. Wrap the potato with 2 bacon slices — for securing use toothpicks. Smoke for another 1 hr. Add green onions with a little sour cream on top (sour cream will give a special flavor to the potato).

Groovy Smoked Asparagus
Serves: 4
Cooking Time: 5 Minutes
Ingredients:
- 1 bunch asparagus
- 2 tbsps. Olive oil
- 1 tsp. chopped garlic
- Kosher salt
- ½ tsp. black pepper

Directions:
Prepare the water pan of your smoker accordingly Pre-heat your smoker to 5 degrees Fahrenheit/135 degree Celsius Fill a medium-sized bowl with water and add 4 handfuls of woods and allow them to soak Add the asparagus to a grill basket in a single layer Drizzle olive oil on top and sprinkle garlic, pepper, and salt Toss them well Put the basket in your smoker Add a few chips into the loading bay and keep repeating until all of the chips after every 20 minutes Smoke for 60- minutes Serve and enjoy!

Smoked Apples with Maple Syrup
Servings: 6
Cooking Time: 1-1/2 to 2 hours
Ingredients:
- 6 crisp and sturdy apples
- 1/4 cup raisins
- 1/4 cup pure maple syrup
- 1/4 cup (4 TBS) cold butter
- Hickory wood chips
- Disposable foil baking pan, about 1 to 2 inches deep, just large enough to hold the apples

Directions:
Set up your smoker by filling the water bowl 1/2 way and adding wood chips to the tray. Preheat to 250°F with the door or top closed and the vent open. This will take 5 to 10 minutes. Using a small melon baller, core the apples leaving the bottom intact so the filling won't leak out. Place the apples inside the pan so they are standing up with the cavity facing you. Place an equal amount of raisins in the cavity of each apple. Pour an equal amount of maple syrup into each apple to cover the raisins. Top each cavity with a spoonful or pat of butter. Place the baking dish of apples inside the smoker. Cook for 1-1/2 to 2 hours, checking at 1 hour. You want the apples to be soft when squeezed but not collapsing. Check the water and wood chips every 45 minutes. Continue smoking the apples until the right texture is achieved. Serve the apples in bowls with spoons. A scoop of vanilla ice cream is nice with smoked apples.

Smoked Baked Beans
Servings: 6 to 8
Cooking Time: 2 to 3 hours
Ingredients:
- 6 slices bacon, cut widthwise into 1/4" pieces
- 1 large yellow or white onion, finely chopped
- 1 red or green bell pepper, chopped into small bite size pieces
- 2 cloves garlic, minced
- Three 15 ounce cans of Great Northern beans, drained and rinsed
- 1/3 cup packed dark brown sugar
- 1/3 cup ketchup
- 1/4 cup dark molasses
- 2-1/2 TBS apple cider vinegar, preferably unfiltered
- 2 TBS Worcestershire sauce
- 1-1/2 TBS Dijon mustard
- Salt and freshly ground black pepper
- 3/4 cup dark beer or water (not added all at once)

Directions:
In a heavy oven-proof pot or Dutch oven, sauté the bacon over medium heat until just cooked through, approximately 5 minutes. Drain off all but 2 tablespoons of the bacon fat. Add the onion, bell pepper, and garlic and cook until soft, approximately 5 minutes. Stir in the beans, sugar, ketchup, molasses, vinegar, Worcestershire sauce, and mustard. Add salt and pepper to taste. Stir in some of the beer or water until just moist, not soupy. Reserve the rest for adding later, if needed. Preheat your smoker to 225°F with the top vent open. Add water to half full in the bottom bowl. Add wood chips (hickory or maple work well) to the side tray. Place the pot on a rack inside the smoker, uncovered. Smoke until thick and richly flavored, approximately 2 to 3 hours. Stir occasionally and add more beer or water as needed if the beans are drying out too much. Remember to replenish the wood chips and water as needed, approximately every 60 minutes.

Smoked Bananas for Sundaes and Smoothies
Servings: 6 to 12
Cooking Time: 30 to 60 minutes
Ingredients:
- 6 whole ripe bananas
- Apple or maple wood chips

Directions:
Set up your smoker by filling the water bowl 1/2 way and adding wood chips to the tray. Preheat to 200°F with the door or top closed and the vent open. This will take approximately 5 minutes. Using a sharp fork, prick a few holes in the banana peels to just pierce them for any steam to release – approximately 4 pricks. Place the bananas on a rack inside the smoker. Set a timer for 30 minutes.

Check the bananas at the 30 minute time. The skin should be starting to brown and the bananas should start to feel slightly soft when gently squeezed. Continue to smoke until the texture is achieved. Set the bananas aside while you fill some bowls with ice cream and toppings. Peel the bananas, slice with a very sharp paring knife, and place on top of the ice cream. Or, use the bananas in a fruit and yogurt smoothie that is thick and creamy enough to eat with a spoon.

Smoked Brussels Sprouts
Servings: 6
Cooking Time: 45 minutes
Ingredients:
- 1-1/2 lbs Brussels sprouts
- 2 cloves of garlic minced
- 2 TBS extra virgin olive oil
- Sea salt and cracked black pepper

Directions:
Rinse the sprouts under cold running water in a colander and allow them to drain. Trim the brown bottoms off of the sprouts and remove any discolored outer leaves. Place the damp sprouts in a large bowl and coat with the olive oil, minced garlic, and salt & pepper to taste. Transfer to your foil pan. Smoke in a preheated electric smoker on the upper rack with any wood chips and water or apple cider in the smoker bowl at 250°F for approximately 45 minutes until fork tender.

Smoked Curried Almonds
Servings: 6 to 8
Cooking Time: 1 to 2 hours
Ingredients:
- 1 lb raw almonds with skins on
- 2 TBS butter, melted
- 1-1/2 TBS turbinado or raw sugar
- 2 tsps curry powder
- 1 tsp sea salt
- 1/4 tsp ground cayenne pepper
- Disposable foil sheet pan or foil lined sheet pan

Directions:
Preheat your smoker to 225°F with the top vent open. Add water to half full in the bottom bowl. Add wood chips (pecan or oak work well) to the side tray. In a large bowl, combine the butter, sugar, curry powder, salt, and cayenne. Add the nuts and toss to coat evenly. Place the nuts on a disposable sheet pan in a single layer. Smoke for approximately 60 minutes until crunchy and lightly browned with smoke. Check the nuts at 60 minutes. Leave in for up to 2 hours, if necessary for to achieve a good toasted texture. Be mindful that nuts can burn if overcooked and will become bitter. Remember to replenish the water and wood chips if needed. Allow the nuts to cool and store them in air-tight containers or sealable baggies.

Smoked Watermelon Skewers

Servings: 4 to 6
Cooking Time: 45 to 90 minutes
Ingredients:

- 1 small seedless watermelon
- Balsamic vinegar
- Wooden skewers that have been soaked in water

Directions:
Cut the ends off of the watermelon. Stand it up on a cutting board and slice the skin and white rind off. Slice the watermelon into 1" cubes. Place the cubes in a large bowl and drizzle a small amount of balsamic vinegar over the cubes. Toss with your hands to just coat slightly. Preheat your smoker to 225°F with the top vent open. Add water to half full in the bottom bowl (Water is optional for this recipe. I found it helpful.). Add wood chips to the side tray. While the smoker is heating up, place approximately 8 cubes of watermelon on each soaked skewer. Place the skewers directly on a smoker rack. Smoke for 45 minutes and check for taste and texture. Continue smoking until you get the results that are to your liking. Remember to replenish the wood chips if needed. Serve the skewers as is or remove the cubes and use them in a refreshing cocktail. You can also make a classic watermelon and feta cheese salad.

Smoked Summer Vegetables

Serves: 6
Cooking Time: 1 Hour
Ingredients:

- 2 summer squash, sliced and seeds removed
- 2 zucchini, sliced
- 1 onion, sliced
- 2 cups mushrooms sliced
- Salt and pepper to taste
- 3 tablespoons olive oil

Directions:
Toss all Ingredients: in a bowl. Place in a baking sheet. Preheat the smoker to 2250F. Place water in the water pan and add maple wood chips into the side tray. Put the vegetables in the smoker. Cook for 1 hour.

Smoked Lemony-garlic Artichokes

Serves: 4
Cooking Time: 20 Minutes
Ingredients:

- 4 artichokes
- 4 minced garlic cloves
- 3 tbsps. Lemon juice
- ½ c. virgin olive oil
- 2 parsley sprigs
- Sea salt

Directions:
Put a large pot on your stove with a metal steaming basket inside. Fill with water just to the bottom of the basket and bring to a boil. Cut the artichoke tail and take out the toughest leaves. With cooking shears, clip the pointy ends off of the outermost leaves. Cut the artichokes in half lengthwise. Remove the hairy choke in the center. Put the halves, stem side down, in the steamer basket. Reduce the heat to a rolling simmer. On the pot, cover and steam for about 20 to 25 minutes, until the inside of the artichoke is tender. Prepare a dressing: place in a mortar the garlic, lemon juice, olive oil, parsley, and salt. Take away the basket and let the artichokes come to room temperature. Preheat your smoker to 200°F. Place the artichokes in aluminum foil packets and brush garlic mixture all over the artichokes. Smoke the artichoke halves for approximately 1 hour. Serve hot.

Side Dishes, Snacks & Desserts Recipes

Smoked Yellow Squash
Serves: 4
Cooking Time: 25 Minutes
Ingredients:
- 4 medium yellow squash
- 1/2 cup extra virgin olive oil
- 2 cloves garlic, crushed
- salt and pepper to taste

Directions:
Cut your squash horizontally. Cut it into ¼ inch and ½ inch slices.   In a small pan heat up some garlic clove and olive oil over medium heat. Do this until the garlic starts to sizzle. Brush each slice of squash with this garlic oil. Add salt and pepper to taste.   Place the squash in the smoker on a rack. Flip it on its other side halfway through. Continue to brush with the garlic oil as needed.   Serve while still warm.

Kimchi Coleslaw
Serves: 6
Cooking Time: 10 Minutes
Ingredients:
- 5 scallions, finely sliced
- 1 head Napa cabbage, cut in half lengthwise
- 1 English cucumber, julienned
- ½ cup vegetable oil
- ¼ cup rice wine vinegar
- 2 Tbsp sambal
- 1 tsp salt

Directions:
Preheat smoker to 80°F.   In a large bowl, combine rice wine vinegar, sambal, and salt and stream in oil while whisking the dressing.   Add scallions and cabbage but do not toss.   Place cabbage halves directly on the smoker grates and smoke for 10 minutes.   Thinly slice the cabbage and add to the dressing mixture.   Toss the salad together and allow it to sit for 20-30 minutes before serving.

Mixed Vegetables
Serves: 8
Cooking Time: 2 Hours
Ingredients:
- 1/3 cup olive oil
- 2 tablespoons balsamic vinegar
- 2 teaspoons Dijon mustard
- 1 garlic clove (minced)
- Salt and freshly ground black pepper, to taste
- 2 medium zucchini (sliced 3/4" thick)
- 2 medium yellow squash (sliced 3/4" thick)
- 1 red onion (cut into wedges)
- 1 green bell pepper (cut into 1" chunks)
- 1 red bell pepper (cut into 1" chunks)
- 6 red potatoes (cut into 1" chunks)
- 8 ounces white mushrooms (halved)
- Chopped fresh herb leaves (for garnish)

Directions:
For the dressing, whisk olive oil, vinegar, mustard and garlic and season to taste with salt and pepper. Spread vegetables in a single layer on a rimmed baking pan, drizzle with the dressing and season to taste with salt and pepper. Place pan on top grate of Masterbuilt smoker preheated to 5°F and smoke until vegetables are fork-tender, about 2 hours, turning occasionally.   Transfer vegetables to a large bowl and garnish with chopped herbs to serve. Enjoy!

Deviled Eggs
Serves: 6
Cooking Time: 15 Minutes
Ingredients:
- 6 hard boiled eggs (peeled)
- 1/4 cup mayonnaise
- 1 teaspoon apple cider vinegar
- 1/2 teaspoon dried mustard
- 1/4 teaspoon salt
- White pepper, to taste
- Sweet paprika, for garnish

Directions:
Arrange eggs on the top grate of Masterbuilt smoker preheated to 225°F with hickory wood chips. Smoke eggs for about minutes. Remove eggs from smoker and let cool.   Halve eggs and scoop out yolks. Mash yolks with mayonnaise, vinegar, mustard, salt and pepper until smooth. Transfer yolk mixture to a plastic zip-top bag, snip off a corner of the bag and pipe yolk mixture into hollowed egg whites.   Arrange deviled eggs on a platter, cover and refrigerate until chilled through, about 1 hour. Just before serving, sprinkle eggs with paprika. Enjoy!

Smoked Sweet Onions
Serves: 6
Cooking Time: 3 Hours
Ingredients:
- 6 large sweet onions, peeled and de-stemmed
- 2 teaspoons ginger powder
- 1 teaspoon sea salt
- 1 teaspoon ground black pepper
- 2 teaspoons red chili powder
- 2 teaspoons allspice
- 2 teaspoons dried thyme
- 3 tablespoons olive oil

Directions:
Plug in the smoker, fill its tray with hickory woodchips and water pan halfway through, and place dripping pan above the water pan. Then open the top vent, shut with lid and use temperature settings to preheat smoker at 0 degrees F. In the meantime, stir together all the ingredients except for onions until combined and then brush all over the onions. Place onions on smoker rack, then shut with lid and set the timer to smoke for 3 hours or until done. Check vent of smoker every hour and add more woodchips and water to maintain temperature and smoke. Slice onions and serve.

Maple-glazed Nuts
Serves: 6
Cooking Time: 30 Minutes
Ingredients:
- 2 tablespoons butter
- 1/2 cup pure maple syrup
- 1 teaspoon vanilla extract
- 1/2 teaspoon ground cinnamon
- 1/2 teaspoon salt
- 2 cups shelled pecan or walnut halves

Directions:
Melt butter in a large saucepan. Add maple syrup, vanilla, cinnamon and salt and heat to a simmer. Remove mixture from heat, add nuts and stir to coat. Spread nuts in a single layer on a rimmed metal baking sheet. Place baking sheet on the top grate of Masterbuilt smoker preheated to 5°F with hickory wood chips. Smoke nuts for about 15 minutes, stir and smoke about 15 minutes more. Remove nuts from smoker and stand until hardened and thoroughly cooled, about 2 hours. Serve as desired and enjoy!

Smoked Peaches Drowning In Rum With Ice Cream
Serves: 4

Cooking Time: 20 Minutes
Ingredients:
- 2 peaches
- 1/3 cup Dark Rum
- 1 tbsp. lemon or lime juice
- 1 tbsp. vanilla
- 2 tsp. maple syrup
- 1/4 cup sugar
- 4 scoops vanilla ice cream

Directions:
In a sauce pan pour in sugar, booze, molasses, lemon juice, and vanilla. Melt all of this over high heat. Stir the mixture, and boil it for minutes. Allow it to cool afterward. Cut each of the peaches in half, and remove the pits. Place them in the smoker. The skin should slide off. In a bowl add a scoop of ice cream. Pour the mixture from the pan over it. Top it off with the peaches. Serve this immediately.

Smoked Portobello Mushroom
Serves: 10
Cooking Time: 1 Hour 40 Minutes
Ingredients:
- Portobello mushroom (1-lb., 0.5-kg)
- The Spice
- Worcestershire sauce – ¼ cup
- Melted butter – ¼ cup
- Garlic powder – 3 tablespoons
- Salt – 2 tablespoons
- Pepper – 2 teaspoons
- The Heat
- Use Apple wood chips for smoking.

Directions:
Turn an electric smoker on and set the time to 225°F (7°C) Wash and clean the mushrooms then cut the stems. Set aside. Place Worcestershire sauce and melted butter in a bowl then stir until incorporated. Stir the mushrooms into the Worcestershire mixture then toss until the mushrooms are completely coated with the sauce mixture. Sprinkle garlic powder, salt, and pepper over the mushrooms then stir well. Once the smoker has reached the desired temperature, arrange the seasoned mushrooms on the smoker's rack. Set the time to an hour and a half and smoke the mushrooms. In the last 10 minutes of smoking, brush the smoked mushrooms with the remaining butter mixture and continue smoking. Once it is done, take the smoked mushrooms out of the smoker and transfer to a serving dish. Serve and enjoy.

Roasted Pears

Serves: 8
Cooking Time: 1 Hours.
Ingredients:
- 8 large pears, halved lengthwise, cored
- ½ teaspoon nutmeg, grated
- 10 tablespoons butter, at room temperature
- 1 teaspoon ground cinnamon
- 10 tablespoons ground hazelnuts
- 1 teaspoon ground cloves
- 2 teaspoons vanilla extract
- Juice of a lemon
- 2 cups Poire Williams (Pear Brandy)
- 10 tablespoons brown sugar
- 1 teaspoon lemon zest, grated
- 2 tablespoons rum

Directions:
Brush cut part of the pear with lemon juice. Add sugar and butter into a bowl and beat until fluffy. Add vanilla, lemon zest, cloves, graham cracker crumbs, nutmeg, and cinnamon then beat until well combined. Fill this mixture in the pears in the cavity of the core. Place the stuffed apples in a greased disposable aluminum foil pan. Preheat the smoker to 5°F following the manufacturer's instructions. Place the disposable pan in the smoker. Smoke until the apples are soft. It should take 45-60 minutes. But keep a check. Remove from the smoker. Remove the pears from the disposable pan and place on a fireproof platter. Pour Poire Williams in a saucepan and place the saucepan over medium heat. Warm it and remove from heat. Light a matchstick and touch it to the brandy. It will catch fire. Pour the brandy along with the flame on the pears and serve.

Burnt End Baked Beans

Serves: 8
Cooking Time: 2 Hour
Ingredients:
- 8 ounces Smoked Bacon, finely diced
- 2 cups Quick Barbecue 2 cups burnt ends from Smoked Brisket, finely chopped
- 2 15-ounce cans of pinto beans, drained and rinsed
- 3 cloves garlic, finely chopped

Directions:
Place bacon in a large, cold skillet and turn the heat on low. When the bacon begins to crisp, add onion and garlic and cook until vegetables are translucent. In a disposable aluminum pan, combine onion and bacon mixture, barbecue sauce, burnt ends, beans, broth, honey and brown sugar.

Preheat smoker to 275°F. Smoke the beans for 2 hours, stirring once halfway through. Serve hot.
Tip: These beans can be cooked in a 350°F for 1 hour oven or in a slow cooker on low for 4-hours.

Pork Belly Burnt Ends

Serves: 15
Cooking Time: 1 Hours. 45 Minutes.
Ingredients:
- Sauce:
- 3 tbsp. unsalted butter
- 1 c. barbecue sauce
- 2 tbsp. honey
- Pork:
- 5 lb. pork belly – in chunks
- 1 c. dry rub
- 3 tbsp. Extra Virgin Olive Oil
- Suggested Wood Chips: Cherry

Directions:
Warm up the smoker ahead of time between 225-250°F. Trim away the fat and slice into 2-inch cubes. Pour the olive oil into a large bowl with the meat. Use the dry rub and arrange on a wire rack or right on the smoker rack. Prepare uncovered for 3 hours. Remove and place in an aluminum pan. Prepare the sauce and pour over the pork. Cover with some foil and put back on the smoker rack for 90 minutes (0°F internal temp.) Remove the foil and close the cover lid. Smoke 15 additional minutes, remove and serve.

Jalapeno Poppers

Serves: 4
Cooking Time: 1 Hours.
Ingredients:
- 8 oz. onion & chive cream cheese
- 12 jalapenos – split and canoed
- 4 oz. sour cream
- ½ c. shredded cheddar & Colby cheese
- Pinch of kosher salt
- Black pepper
- Thin bacon
- Garlic powder
- Chosen Wood Chips: Hickory

Directions:
Combine all of the fixings (omit the bacon and jalapenos for now). And place in a freezer bag. Split and remove the seeds from the jalapenos. Spread or pipe (cut a hole in the corner of the bag) the filling into the peppers and cover with a slice of bacon. Secure with toothpicks. Smoke one hour at 275°F.

Cheesy Potatoes
Serves: 8
Cooking Time: 1 Hour
Ingredients:
- 4 tablespoons butter
- 1/4 cup flour
- 1 sweet onion (diced)
- 1 red bell pepper (diced)
- 3 garlic cloves (minced)
- 2 cups milk
- 8 ounces cheddar cheese (shredded)
- 1 cup sour cream
- 1 teaspoon kosher salt
- 1/2 teaspoon freshly ground black pepper
- 1 bag (32 ounces) frozen hash brown potatoes

Directions:
For the sauce, melt butter in a large saucepan and sauté onion and bell pepper until softened, 3 to 4 minutes, stirring occasionally. Add garlic and sauté about minute more, stirring constantly. Whisk flour into butter mixture until smooth. Add milk in a thin stream, stirring constantly, and heat to a boil. Reduce heat and simmer until thickened, about 2 minutes, stirring constantly. Remove sauce from heat, add cheese, sour cream, salt and pepper and stir until cheese melts. Spray a large foil pan with nonstick cooking spray. Place potatoes and cheese sauce in pan and stir gently until combined. Place pan on top grate of Masterbuilt smoker preheated to 275°F and smoke until potatoes are tender, about 1 hour. Remove pan from smoker and let stand for about 5 minutes before serving. Enjoy!

Smoked Avocados With Strawberry-mango Salsa
Serves: 4
Cooking Time: 9 Minutes
Ingredients:
- 4 not-fully-ripe avocados, just turning soft
- 1/4 cup honey
- 1/4 cup olive oil
- 1 medium mango, peeled, pitted, and cut into 1/2" cubes
- 1/2 lb. strawberries, cut into 1/2" cubes
- 1 tbsp. balsamic vinegar
- 1/3 cup orange juice
- 2 tsp. lemon juice
- Lettuce leaves, for serving

Directions:
Slice each of the avocados lengthwise. Remove the seeds. Get a small bowl, and with a whisk mix together the olive oil and honey. Brush this on the exposed parts of the avocados. Cover it up with plastic wrap and set aside. Get a medium bowl and mix together lemon juice, mango, orange juice, strawberries, and vinegar. Place the avocados in the smoker. Brush with the oil mixture and flip them over. Place each avocado on a bed of lettuce. Fill each of the seed cavities with the fruit salsa you made earlier. Serve as is.

Smoked Pineapple With Honey
Serves: 6
Cooking Time: 10 Minutes
Ingredients:
- 1 whole, fresh pineapple
- 2 limes, zested and juiced
- ¼ cup honey

Directions:
Cut the top and bottom from the pineapple and stand it on its bottom. Using a sharp knife, remove the outer skin from the pineapple. Cut the pineapple into six spears, removing the most fibrous part of the core. Arrange pineapple spears onto a small sheet tray. Preheat the smoker to 1°F. In a small bowl, combine honey, lime juice and lime zest. Smoke the pineapple spears in their sheet tray for 10 minutes. Arrange the pineapple on a platter and drizzle with the honey-lime mixture. Serve.

Naan
Serves: 6
Cooking Time: 6 Minutes
Ingredients:
- 1 (.25 ounce) package active dry yeast
- 1 cup warm water
- 1/4 cup white sugar
- 3 tsp. milk
- 1 egg, beaten
- 2 tsp. salt
- 4 1/2 cups bread flour
- 2 tsp. minced garlic (optional)
- 1/4 cup butter, melted

Directions:
Get a large bowl, and dissolve the yeast in some warm water. Leave it to stand for ten minutes. Add in the flour, sugar, salt, egg, and milk. This will make the dough. Knead it for eight minutes on a surface that has been lightly floured. Now place the dough in a boil that was rubbed with oil. Cover the top with a damp cloth, and place it aside. Allow the dough to rise for one hour. Punch down on your dough. Knead in the garlic. Begin to pinch off handfuls of the dough. Roll them to the size of golf balls, and put on a tray. Cover them up with a towel, and allow them to rise for half an hour. Once the dough is done rising place the dough in the smoker. It should be browned lightly. Brush the uncooked side with some butter. Turn the dough over halfway through. Repeat step 4 until all the Naan is smoked.

Beef Jerky
Serves: 4
Cooking Time: 8 Hours.
Ingredients:
- 2 lb. sirloin
- 1 tbsp. cider vinegar
- 1 c. soy sauce
- 4 tbsp. freshly cracked black pepper
- 1 dash of each:
- Worcestershire sauce
- Hot pepper sauce

Directions:
Slice the sirloin into ½-inch slices. Whisk the Worcestershire sauce, pepper sauce, vinegar, pepper, and soy sauce in a large mixing container. Toss in the slices of meat, refrigerate and marinate overnight. Set the cooker on low heat and lightly oil the cooking grate. Lay the strips in a single layer and smoke for 6-8 hours. It's done when the edges look dry with a small amount of moisture in the center of each jerky treat.

Applesauce
Serves: 6
Cooking Time: 1 Hour
Ingredients:
- 9 medium apples (about 3 pounds)
- 4 tablespoons butter (cut into cubes)
- 1/2 cup red wine
- 1/4 cup water
- 1/2 cup sugar
- 1 teaspoon ground cinnamon
- 1/2 teaspoon ground nutmeg
- 1/4 teaspoon salt

Directions:
Peel, quarter and core apples and place on the top grate of Masterbuilt smoker preheated to 225°F with mild fruit wood chips. Smoke apples for about 30 minutes. Remove apples from smoker, cut into thin slices and place in a large saucepan with the butter, wine, water, sugar, cinnamon, nutmeg and salt. Heat apple mixture to a boil, then reduce heat to low, cover pan and simmer until apples are very soft, 15- minutes. Mash applesauce to desired consistency with a potato masher or fork, or puree in a blender or food processor until smooth. Serve applesauce immediately, or let cool to room temperature, or refrigerate until chilled through. Enjoy!

White Chocolate Bread Pudding
Serves: 15
Cooking Time: 1 Hours. 30 Mins
Ingredients:
- 2 pounds brioche, cubed
- 4 cups whole milk
- 1/8 teaspoon salt
- 16 ounces white chocolate, coarsely chopped
- 4 large egg yolks
- 8 large eggs
- 2 teaspoons pure vanilla extract (use 4 teaspoons extract if not using vanilla beans)
- 2 vanilla beans (optional), halved, scrape the seeds

- 6 cups heavy whipping cream
- Butter for greasing
- 3 cups sugar
- Smoked ice cream to serve

Directions:
Preheat the smoker to 250°F following the manufacturer's instructions. Take a large disposable aluminum foil and place the bread cubes in it in a single layer. Place the pan in the smoker and smoke for 30-45 minutes until the bread cubes are toasted. Meanwhile, add eggs, yolks, vanilla extract and salt in a large heatproof bowl and whisk until well combined. Place a heavy saucepan over medium heat. Add milk, cream, sugar and vanilla bean as well as its seeds. Heat for a few minutes until hot and the sugar is dissolved. Remove from heat. Add half the chocolate and stir constantly until it melts. Cool for a while. Add about ½ cup of this mixture into the bowl of eggs and whisk constantly. Continue this process until all the milk mixture is added to the egg mixture, whisking each time. Add vanilla essence if using and whisk again. Add the toasted bread cubes into it and stir. Grease a cast iron skillet with butter. Pour the entire mixture into the skillet. Sprinkle remaining chocolate pieces on it. Preheat the smoker to 275°F following the manufacturer's instructions. Place the skillet in the smoker. Smoke for around minutes to 1-½ hours (depending on what temperature you have set the smoker) or until set. Remove from the smoker and serve hot with smoked ice cream.

Southern Smoked Potato Salad
Serves: 8
Cooking Time: 1 To 2 Hours
Ingredients:
- 3 pounds russet potatoes (halved)
- 1 cup mayonnaise
- 1/4 cup yellow mustard
- 1/4 cup sweet pickle relish
- 1 tablespoon apple cider vinegar
- 1 tablespoon sugar
- 1/2 teaspoon onion powder
- 1/2 teaspoon garlic powder
- 1/4 teaspoon celery salt
- Salt and freshly ground black pepper, to taste
- 4 hard boiled eggs (chopped)
- 2 celery stalks (diced)
- Sweet paprika (for garnish)

Directions:
Place potatoes on top grate of Masterbuilt smoker preheated to 225°F and smoke until tender, to 2 hours. While potatoes are smoking, prepare the dressing. Mix mayonnaise, mustard, pickle relish and vinegar until thoroughly combined. Add sugar, onion powder, garlic powder and celery salt, season to taste with salt and pepper and stir until sugar is dissolved. Set dressing aside. Peel potatoes, cut into bite-size pieces and place in a large bowl with eggs and celery. Add dressing, season to taste with salt and pepper and stir gently to coat. Cover bowl with plastic wrap and refrigerate potato salad for at least hours. Sprinkle potato salad with paprika just before serving. Enjoy!

Cornbread
Serves: 8
Cooking Time: 1 Hour
Ingredients:
- 1 1/2 cups white cornmeal
- 1/2 cup flour
- 2 tablespoons sugar
- 1 tablespoon baking powder
- 1 teaspoon baking soda
- 1/2 teaspoon salt
- 1 cup buttermilk
- 1 egg (beaten)
- 1/4 cup sour cream
- 6 tablespoons butter (melted)
- 1 tablespoon bacon drippings

Directions:
In a medium bowl, mix cornmeal, flour, sugar, baking powder, baking soda and salt until combined and set aside. In a separate bowl, whisk buttermilk, egg and sour cream until thoroughly combined. Add buttermilk mixture to cornmeal mixture and stir just until combined. Add butter and stir just until combined. Melt bacon drippings in a medium cast iron skillet, swirl to coat and remove from the heat. Evenly spread batter into skillet. Place skillet on top grate of Masterbuilt smoker preheated to 250°F and smoke until cornbread tests done with a toothpick, minutes to 1 hour. Remove skillet from smoker and let cornbread stand for about 1minutes. Cut cornbread into wedges to serve. Enjoy!

Hamburger Jerky
Serves: 8
Cooking Time: 4 Hours.
Ingredients:
- 2 lb. lean ground beef
- 1 tbsp. allspice
- 1 minced garlic clove
- 2 t. grated ginger
- ½ c. soy sauce
- Suggested Wood Chips – Hickory or Mesquite

Directions:
Make strips from flattened hamburger – ½-inches wide and 5 inches long with a thickness of about ¼-inch. Add a layer of the strips in a dish to marinate. For the Marinade: Add the ingredients in a small dish, blending well. Shake it over the meat, flip, and shake the other side well. Add the strips to the dish, making sure to coat each slice evenly. Cover the bowl and let them rest for 6-10 hours in the fridge. Shuffle the meat several times for even flavoring. Smoke at 140ºF for four hours.

Smoke Roasted Apple Crisp
Serves: 12
Cooking Time: 15 Minutes
Ingredients:

- 12 sweet apples
- 3 tbsps. Lemon juice
- 3 tbsps. Arrowroot
- 12 tbsps. Butter
- ¾ tsp. lemon zest, grated
- 1½ c. sugar
- 1/8 tsp. salt
- 3 tsp. ground cinnamon
- ¾ c. granola
- ¾ c. flour
- ¾ c. brown sugar.
- Apple ice cream of cinnamon ice cream to serve

Directions:
Place apples in a glass bowl Add lemon juice and lemon zest and toss well. Add 2/c. sugar, 2 tsp. ground cinnamon and arrowroot and toss well. Taste and adjust the sugar if required. Transfer into a cast iron skillet and set aside. Add rest of the ingredients except ice cream into the food processor bowl and pulse until the mixture is coarse in texture. Do not pulse for long. Sprinkle this mixture over the apples in the skillet. Preheat the smoker to 275°F following the manufacturer's instructions. Place the cast iron skillet in the smoker. Smoke until the mixture is crisp and golden brown on top. It should take 45-60 minutes. Remove from the smoker and cool for a while. Serve warm as it is or with ice cream.

Smoked Cabbage
Serves: 3
Cooking Time: 2 Hours
Ingredients:
- 1 small head of green cabbage
- 1/2 teaspoon sea salt and more as needed
- 1/2 teaspoon ground black pepper and more as needed
- 1 tablespoon apple cider vinegar
- 2 tablespoons butter
- 2 tablespoons olive oil

Directions:
Plug in the smoker, fill its tray with hickory woodchips and water pan halfway through, and place dripping pan above the water pan. Then open the top vent, shut with lid and use temperature settings to preheat smoker at 5 degrees F. In the meantime, remove the core of cabbage, then fill it with vinegar, season with salt and black pepper and rub with butter. Season exterior of cabbage with salt and black pepper and place it in a foil pan. Place cabbage on smoker rack, then shut with lid and set the timer to smoke for 1 hour and 30 minutes. Check vent of smoker every hour and add more woodchips and water to maintain temperature and smoke. Then smoke cabbage directly in the smoker for 30 minutes and then cut into wedges to serve.

Pizza Jalapeño Poppers

Serves: 6

Cooking Time: 20 Minutes

Ingredients:

- 12 Jalapeño peppers
- 8 oz. Cream cheese
- 4 oz. Cheddar cheese
- 4 oz. Mozzarella cheese
- 2 Bread heel slices
- 12 Bacon slices

Directions:

Preheat your smoker to 200°F/93°C and soak your wood chips for an hour. Remove the woodchips from the liquid then pat dry before using. Pop the cheeses into the food processor and hit the button. Blend until smooth. Next cut the stems off the peppers, scoop out the seeds and fill the inside of the pepper with the cheese mixture. Tear out a small piece of bread from the crusts and pop them into the end of the pepper to prevent the cheese to ooze out when it warms. Now wrap the bacon around the pepper and hold in place with toothpicks. Place directly into your smoker and cook for an hour. Check after the half an hour and turn. Leave longer if required.

Alligator Eggs

Serves: 6

Cooking Time: 30 Minutes

Ingredients:

- 12 thin slices bacon
- 8 ounces cream cheese, softened
- 6 jalapenos
- 1 cup sharp cheddar cheese

Directions:

Slice jalapenos in half and remove seeds. Set aside. In a small bowl, combine cheddar cheese and cream cheese until mixed. Stuff 2 Tbsp of the cream cheese mixture into each jalapeno half. Wrap each jalapeno half in one strip of bacon, securing with a toothpick. Place jalapenos on a sheet tray. Preheat the smoker to 275°F. Smoke the alligator eggs on the sheet tray for 30 minutes or until the bacon is crisp. Serve immediately.

Teriyaki Smoked Venison Jerky

Serves: 6

Cooking Time: 6 Hours.

Ingredients:

- 1 lb. venison loin or roast
- ¼ c. dry – red wine
- 1/3 cup honey
- 1/3 cup soy sauce
- 1 tbsp. rice wine vinegar – mirin
- 1 tsp. minced ginger
- 1 minced garlic clove
- ½ tsp. salt
- ½ tsp. pepper
- Unsweetened apple juice
- Wood Chip Suggestion: Soaked apple or cherry

Directions:

Warm up the smoker to 5°F and fill the water tray with a concentration of ½ water and ½ juice and add the soaked chips. Toss all of the marinade fixings in a sealable plastic baggie or large baking dish. Prepare the venison by slicing 1-inch wide x ¼-inch wide strips and lay them against the grain. Pound each piece several times and add to the bag. Place in the fridge for up to 12 hours. Discard the marinade and pat dry the meat with paper towels. Add to the smoker racks and smoke for 4-6 hours. After ½ hours., replenish the water and wood chips. When done, let cook, serve, and enjoy!

Smoked Caesar Salad

Serves: 6

Cooking Time: 10 Minutes

Ingredients:

- 2 heads romaine lettuce, split lengthwise in half
- 3 garlic cloves
- 3 anchovy fillets
- 2 lemons, juiced
- 1 cup grated Parmesan cheese
- 2 Tbsp Dijon mustard
- Extra-virgin olive oil
- Kosher salt
- 4 slices day old Italian bread, cubed

Directions:

In a blender or food processor, combine dressing ingredients, minus olive oil and salt. Gradually stream in olive oil until the dressing reaches your desired consistency. Taste and season with salt, if necessary. Preheat oven to 0°F. Toss bread cubes with olive oil, a pinch of salt and a pinch of black pepper. Bake the bread for 8-10 minutes or until golden brown. Preheat the smoker to 80°F. Place romaine halves directly on the smoker's grate and smoke for 10 minutes. Remove the romaine from the smoker and cut into bite sized pieces. Toss lettuce with dressing, croutons, and shredded Parmesan. Serve immediately.

Bacon & Endive Salad
Serves: 6
Cooking Time: 10 Minutes
Ingredients:
- Bacon Candy
- Candied Walnuts
- 2 heads endive
- 2 cups frisee
- 1 bunch spinach, cleaned and stems removed
- ¼ cup dried cranberries
- 1/4 cup olive oil
- 2 Tbsp Dijon Mustard
- 1 Tbsp honey
- 1 shallot, finely minced

Directions:
Cut the heads of endive in half, set aside. Preheat smoker to 80°F. In the bottom of a large bowl, combine mustard, honey, shallot, lemon juice and olive oil. Season with salt and pepper. Add frisee, spinach, cranberries, bacon candy, and walnuts. Arrange the endive directly on the smoker grates. Smoke for 10 minutes and remove. Slice the endive into thin strips and add to the rest of the salad. Toss and serve.

Smoked Banana Foster
Serves: 10
Cooking Time: 10 Minutes
Ingredients:
- 10 overripe bananas, peeled, halved lengthwise
- Rum and raisin sauce to serve

Directions:
Preheat the smoker to 250°F following the manufacturer's instructions. Take a large disposable aluminum foil and place the bananas on it in a single layer. Smoke for 15-20 minutes. Serve with rum and raisin sauce.

Four Cheese Smoked Mac 'n' Cheese
Serves: 4
Cooking Time: 1 Hour
Ingredients:
- (16-ounce) package elbow macaroni
- 1/4 cup butter
- 1/4 cup all-purpose flour
- 3 cups milk
- 1 (8-ounce) package cream cheese, cut into large chunks
- 1 tbsp. salt
- 1/2 tbsp. black pepper
- 2 cups (8 ounces) extra sharp Cheddar cheese, shredded
- 2 cups (8 ounces) Gouda cheese, shredded
- 1 cup (4 ounces) Parmesan cheese, shredded

Directions:
Be sure to cook the pasta first according to the directions. Get a medium saucepan, melt the butter, and then be sure to whisk the flour with the butter. Allow it to cook over a medium heat for only two minutes. Whisk in the milk. Bring it all to a boil for five minutes. Add in the cream cheese, stirring until the entire mixture has become smooth. Next, add in the pepper and salt. Get a large bowl. Mix together cream sauce, 1 cup cheddar, 1 cup gouda cheese, pasta, and parmesan cheese. Transfer the mixture to an aluminum roasting pan. Sprinkle all the leftover gouda and cheddar cheese on top of the mixture. Place the mac 'n' cheese in the smoker. It should turn brown and be bubbly once done. Serve while still warm.

Tangerine Smoked Flans
Serves: 10
Cooking Time: 15 Minutes
Ingredients:
- For caramel:
- ½ c. water
- 2 c. sugar
- For flan:
- 1 c. sugar
- 4 large egg yolks
- 6 large eggs
- 1/8 tsp. salt
- 2 c. half and half
- 2 tsps. Vanilla extract
- 2 cinnamon sticks
- 2 ½ c. whole milk
- 12 strips tangerine zest

Directions:
To make caramel: Place a heavy saucepan over high heat. Add sugar and water and stir. Cover and cook for 2 minutes. Lower heat to medium and uncover. Cook until the sugar caramelizes and is golden brown in color. Do not stir during this process. Remove from heat and pour into 10-12 ramekins. Wear kitchen gloves and swirl the ramekins so that the caramelized sugar coats the bottom as well as the sides. Set aside the ramekins to cool. It will harden. Set your ramekins on a baking sheet that is rimmed. Meanwhile make the flan as follows: Add eggs, yolks, sugar and salt in a large heatproof bowl and whisk until well combined. Place a heavy saucepan over medium heat. Add milk, half and half, tangerine zest, cinnamon and vanilla bean. Heat for a few minutes until warm. Remove from heat. Add about ½ cup of this mixture into the bowl of eggs and whisk. Continue this process until all the milk mixture is added to the egg mixture, whisking each time. Add vanilla essence if using and whisk again. Cool for a while and pour into the ramekins Preheat the smoker to 250°F following the manufacturer's instructions. Place the baking sheet with ramekin cups in the smoker. Smoke for around 1 ½ hours or until the flan is set. Remove from the smoker and cool completely. Chill for 5-6 hours in the refrigerator. To serve: Run a knife around the edges of the flan. Invert onto a plate and serve.

Smoked Peaches
Serves: 6
Cooking Time: 10 Minutes
Ingredients:
- 6 fresh peaches.
- 1 c. wood chips of your choice

Directions:
Preheat your smoker to 200°F/93°C and soak the wood chips for an hour. Remove the wood chips from the liquid then pat dry before using. Place the peaches directly into your smoker and cook for minutes – the first 20 with the skin down, the final 10 with the skin up. Remove from the smoker, and serve warm with meats, in salads or even as a special way to round off your meal.

Bananas Calypso
Serves: 4
Cooking Time: 12 Minutes
Ingredients:
- 1/3 cup sugar
- ¼ cup unsalted butter, melted
- 2 tbsp. lime juice
- 1 tsp. ground cinnamon
- 4 firm bananas, peeled
- 1/3 dark rum
- 4 scoops ice cream

Directions:
Combine the cinnamon, sugar, lime juice, and melted butter in a small bowl. Brush each of the banana's with only ¼ cup of this butter mixture. Place the bananas in the smoker. Turn the bananas over halfway through the smoking process. Once the bananas are done smoking, put them on a dish that is flameproof. Slice the bananas up, and pour the last of the butter mixture into the dish. Put the dish back in the smoker. Allow the bananas to smoke for the rest of the time. After you remove the bananas from the smoker pour the rum over them. Immediately serve the bananas with ice cream.

Stuffed Cabbage
Serves: 4
Cooking Time: 5 Hours
Ingredients:
- 1 medium head green cabbage
- 4 tablespoons butter (divided)
- 1 small onion (diced)
- 2 garlic cloves (minced)
- 2 plum tomatoes (seeded, diced)
- 2 tablespoons chopped fresh oregano
- 2 tablespoons chopped fresh basil

- 1/2 cup finely grated Parmesan cheese (divided)
- Salt and freshly ground black pepper, to taste
- 1/4 cup panko bread crumbs

Directions:
Core cabbage and hollow out the center, leaving a shell about to 2 inches thick. Remove stem and shred cabbage removed from the center. For the filling, melt 3 tablespoons butter in a medium nonstick skillet and sauté onion until softened, about 4 minutes, stirring frequently. Add garlic and sauté about minute more. Add shredded cabbage, tomatoes, oregano, basil and about 1/3 cup Parmesan cheese and season to taste with salt and pepper. Stir filling until thoroughly combined and stuff into cabbage. Melt remaining butter and stir in bread crumbs and remaining Parmesan cheese. Spread bread crumb mixture over filling in cabbage. Wrap stuffed cabbage in heavy-duty aluminum foil and place on top grate of Masterbuilt smoker preheated to 225°F. Smoke cabbage until tender, about 5 hours. Remove cabbage from smoker, remove from foil and remove blackened leaves if necessary. Cut cabbage into four wedges and serve immediately. Enjoy!

Smokey Pimento Cheese Appetizer
Serves: 8
Cooking Time: 1 Hours.
Ingredients:
- 1 container (12.oz.) pimento cheese spread
- 1 lb. kielbasa sausage
- Sliced jalapeno peppers
- Saltine crackers

Directions:
Warm up the smoker to 225ºF in advance. When ready, just add the sausage for 45 min. to hours. Remove from the smoker. Arrange the crackers – salt-side down – with 1 teaspoon of cheese spread. Slice the smoked sausage into ½-inch segments and add along with a jalapeno slice. Enjoy!

Smoky Okra
Serves: 4
Cooking Time: 10 Minutes
Ingredients:
- 1 lb. Okra
- Smoked Paprika
- 1tbsp. vegetable oil
- ¾ tsp. salt

Directions:
Place the okra in a large bowl, and toss it with the oil, salt, and paprika. Put the okra on wooden skewers. Place the okra on the smoker. Turn the okra over halfway through smoking. Once done eat it while it's still warm.

Smoked Trout Potato Skins

Serves: 4
Cooking Time:2 Hours, 5 Minutes
Ingredients:
- 8 (3-inch-long) russet potatoes (about 2 1/4 lb.s), scrubbed and thoroughly dried
- 2 tsp. unsalted butter (1/4 stick), melted
- Kosher salt
- Freshly ground black pepper
- 1 tbsp. grapeseed or vegetable oil
- 1/2 tbsp. lime juice
- 2 cups baby arugula, washed and dried
- 1 cup Smoked Trout Pâté

Directions:
Be sure to pierce each potato with a fork. Place on the rack in the smoker, and allow them to smoke for two hours. Once they're done, place they on a wire rack. Allow them to cool for ten minutes so you can handle them. Cut each potato lengthwise. Scoop out all the flesh of the potato, leaving only ¼ inch of the meat inside intact. Coat the insides of the potato with melted butter, pepper, and salt. Do the same for the skin of the potato on both sides. Place potatoes back in the smoker, and allow them to smoke for about six to ten minutes. In a medium bowl mix together lime juice and oil. Add in the arugula at this point. Mix it with the mixture. Divide this mixture among the skins. Top each one off with a tbsp. of the trout pate. Place back in the smoker, and smoke for an additional 5 minutes. Serve afterwards.

Smoky Beans Barbecue

Serves: 10
Cooking Time: 50 Minutes
Ingredients:
- Canned beans (1-lb., 0.4-kg)
- The Spice
- Barbecue sauce – ¾ cup
- Brown sugar - ¾ cup
- Ketchup – ½ cup
- Water – ½ cup
- Molasses – ¼ cup
- Chili powder – 2 tablespoons
- Black pepper – 2 teaspoons
- The Heat
- Use Apple wood chips for smoking.

Directions:
Turn an electric smoker to 225°F (7°C). Place the entire ingredients in a pan then stir well. Bring to boil over medium heat. Once the mixture is boiled, stir and remove from heat. Let it warm. Transfer the boiled beans to a disposable aluminum pan then spread evenly. When the smoker is ready, place the aluminum pan with beans in the smoker. Cover the smoker and set the time to 45 minutes. Once it is done, remove from heat and let the smoked beans warm for a few minutes. Transfer to a serving dish then enjoy!

Pork Tenderloin Appetizers

Serves: 4
Cooking Time: 2 Hours.
Ingredients:
- 1 (1 ½ lb.) pork tenderloin
- Freshly cracked black pepper
- Sea salt to taste
- Garlic salt
- Pimento cheese dip
- Bruschetta toast
- 1 jar mild jalapeno peppers
- Wood Choice: Hickory

Directions:
Warm up the smoker ahead of time to 225°F. and add the chips. Combine the garlic salt, sea salt, and black pepper to season the tenderloin. Arrange in a pan —unwrapped— and smoke to 1 ½ hours (150ºF. internal temp.) Remove and wrap with heavy-duty foil. Place back in the cooker for another 30 minutes (165ºF internally). When it's done, just slice into ¼ to 3/8-inch medallions and slice into halves. Arrange on Platter. Place the toast, cheese dip, and pepper to serve and enjoy.

Hasselback Potatoes

Serves: 4
Cooking Time: 1 Hour
Ingredients:
- 4 Yukon Gold potatoes
- 4 tablespoons butter (melted, divided)
- Salt and freshly ground black pepper, to taste
- 1/4 cup freshly grated Parmesan cheese
- Chopped fresh parsley, for garnish

Directions:
Scrub potatoes and with a sharp knife, cut slits all the way across the potatoes 8" to 1/4" apart, being sure not to cut all the way through. Brush potatoes with about tablespoons butter and season to taste with salt and pepper. Place potatoes on a sheet of aluminum foil on the top grate of Masterbuilt smoker preheated to 225°F and smoke for about minutes. Brush potatoes with remaining 2 tablespoons butter and continue smoking until tender, about 30 minutes more. Sprinkle cheese and parsley over potatoes and serve immediately. Enjoy!

Smoked Chocolate Bread Pudding
Serves: 15
Cooking Time: 20 Minutes
Ingredients:
- 2 lbs. brioche
- 4 c. whole milk
- 1/8 tsp. salt
- 16 oz. bittersweet chocolate
- 4 large egg yolks
- 8 large eggs
- 2 tsp. vanilla extract
- 2 vanilla beans
- 6 c. heavy whipping cream
- Butter
- 3 c. sugar
- Smoked ice cream

Directions:
Preheat the smoker to 250°F following the manufacturer's instructions. Take a large disposable aluminum foil and place the bread cubes in it in a single layer. Place the pan in the smoker and smoke for 30-45 minutes until the bread cubes are toasted. Meanwhile, add eggs, yolks, vanilla extract and salt in a large heatproof bowl and whisk until well combined. Place a heavy saucepan over medium heat. Add milk, cream, sugar and vanilla bean as well as its seeds. Heat for a few minutes until hot and the sugar is dissolved Remove from heat. Add half the chocolate and stir constantly until it melts. Cool for a while. Add about ½ cup of this mixture into the bowl of eggs and whisk constantly. Continue this process until all the milk mixture is added to the egg mixture, whisking each time. Add vanilla essence if using and whisk again. Add the toasted bread cubes into it and stir. Grease a cast iron skillet with butter. Pour the entire mixture into the skillet. Sprinkle remaining chocolate pieces on it. Preheat the smoker to 275°F following the manufacturer's instructions. Place the skillet in the smoker. Smoke for around 45 minutes to 1-½ hours (depending on what temperature you have set the smoker) or until set. Remove from the smoker and serve hot with smoked ice cream.

Pecan Tassies
Serves: 4
Cooking Time: 30 Minutes
Ingredients:
- 3 ounces (1 small brick) full fat cream cheese
- 1 stick salted butter (8 tsp.) at room temp
- 1 cup all-purpose flour
- 1/3 cup pecans, coarsely chopped
- 1 egg
- 3/4 cup dark brown sugar
- 1/2 tbsp. vanilla
- 1 tbsp. salted melted butter

Directions:
Mix together the flour, cream cheese, and butter in a bowl. Make balls that are 1 inch tall and place in a mini muffin pan. Be sure to press the balls down into the pan. Whisk the melted butter, eggs, vanilla, and brown sugar. Pour this into the cups so it's 2/full. Place in the smoker. Allow to cool for a few minutes before serving.

Bacon Wraps
Serves: 20
Cooking Time: 2 Hours. 30 Minutes.
Ingredients:
- 1 pkg. (16 oz.) cocktail sausages
- 1 lb. pkg. bacon
- 13 c. packed brown sugar
- Wood Suggestion: Hickory

Directions:
Set the temperature of the smoker at 275ºF. Slice the bacon lengthwise into 3 segments. Wrap each piece around the sausage. Roll each one in the brown sugar and secure with a toothpick. Arrange on a baking tin. Place on the rack and smoke 2 to 2 ½ hours until crispy.

Beef, Pork & Lamb Recipes

Mighty Meaty Beef Tenderloin
Serves: 12
Cooking Time: 4-6 Hours
Ingredients:
- 4 lb. beef tenderloin roast
- Barbecue Beef Mop

Directions:
Using a paper or kitchen towel, pat-dry the tenderloin roast. Place the roast into cups of Barbecue Beef Mop in a zip top bag. Refrigerate overnight. The next day, remove the roast from the marinade and pat dry. Let it sit at room temperature while preheating the smoker to 275°F. Place the tenderloin directly on the smoker's grates. Smoke to an internal temperature of 135°F for medium rare. Allow the meat to rest for 20-30 minutes before carving. Slice the roast and serve.

Stuffed Porchetta
Serves: 12
Cooking Time: 20 Minutes
Ingredients:
- 6 pounds pork belly, fat trimmed
- 12-ounce sundried tomato spread
- 2 cups giardiniera, Chicago styled
- 1 cup bacon jam
- ½ cup dry rub

Directions:
Plug in the smoker, fill its tray with oak woodchips and water pan halfway through, and place dripping pan above the water pan. Then open the top vent, shut with lid and use temperature settings to preheat smoker at 5 degrees F. In the meantime, rinse pork, pat dry and then season with dry rub on all sides until evenly coated. Place seasoned pork on a cutting board or clean working space spread tomato spread on top, layer with giardiniera and tomato spread, then roll pork and tie with kitchen twines. Place stuffed pork on smoker rack, insert a meat thermometer, then shut with lid and set the timer to smoke for 2 to 3 hours or more until meat thermometer registers an internal temperature of 19degrees F. Check vent of smoker every hour and add more woodchips and water to maintain temperature and smoke. When done, transfer porchetta to a cutting board, let rest for 15 minutes and then slice to serve.

Apple-injected Smoked Pork
Serves: 12
Cooking Time: 6 Hours
Ingredients:
- 2 cups apple cider
- 2 tsp. dry rub seasoning
- 2 tsp. apple cider vinegar
- 2 tsp. honey
- 1/2 tbsp. cayenne pepper
- 1/4 cup orange juice
- 1/2 cup lemon juice
- Dash Worcestershire sauce
- 2 tsp. kosher salt
- 1 (6 to 8-lb.) pork butt

Directions:
Get a large bowl, and whisk together all ingredients for your marinade. Place your pork in a large casserole dish. Use a syringe to inject your marinade ¾ of the way inside of the pork. You're going to want to do this several times in a different place each time on your eat. Cover the pork in plastic wrap and store in the fridge between 4-12 hours. Place pork in the smoker. Drain off any liquid that has remained on the meat, and be sure to pat it dry. Season the pork with your dry rub seasoning so it has a better taste. You're going to want to cover both sides. Allow the pork to cool for a few minutes before serving.

Beef Short Ribs
Serves: 6
Cooking Time: 5 To 6 Hours
Ingredients:
- 12 beef short ribs (about 6 pounds, about 5" long)
- 1 cup yellow mustard
- 2 tablespoons soy sauce
- 2 tablespoons apple cider vinegar
- 1 tablespoon lime juice
- 2 tablespoons kosher salt, plus more to taste
- 2 tablespoons freshly ground black pepper, plus more to taste
- 2 tablespoons brown sugar
- 2 tablespoons garlic powder
- 1 tablespoon sweet paprika

Directions:
Pour about 2 cups water into the Masterbuilt smoker's water pan. Place pecan or cherry wood chips in the smoker's wood tray and preheat smoker to 225°F. Remove silver skin from ribs if necessary, trim fat if desired and score ribs along the bones with a sharp knife. Mix mustard, soy sauce, vinegar and lime juice and rub all over ribs. Mix salt, pepper, brown sugar, garlic powder and paprika and rub all over ribs. Let ribs stand for about 15 minutes. Place ribs bone-sides down on smoker grate and smoke until tender and the internal temperature of the meat reaches 190°F, 5 to 6 hours. Add wood chips to the wood tray as necessary. Remove ribs from smoker, cover loosely with aluminum foil and let rest for about 15 minutes. Cut ribs into individual pieces and serve with barbecue sauce if desired. Enjoy!

Masterbuilt Smoker Cooker Corned Beef

Serves: 5
Cook Time: 1 Hour
Ingredients:

- 4 Rib eye steaks of approximately 1 and ½ inches of thickness
- 1 Tablespoon of extra virgin olive oil
- 1 Pinch of Kosher salt
- 1 Pinch of cracked black pepper
- Garlic powder
- Onion
- Seasoning rub
- Cherry wood chips

Directions:

Place the steaks over a clean cutting board Season the steaks with the pepper, the salt and any other dried seasoning of your choice Remove a rack from the Masterbuilt electric smoker and place the beef steaks on the rack for some time to rest while you preheat your smoker. Place the steaks on the rack inside your smoker Add the wood chips to the baking tray of your smoker. Place the water in a large bowl; then preheat your smoker to a temperature of about 220°F. Put the rack with the prepared seasoned steaks in the smoker Smoke the meat for about 45 minutes Serve and enjoy your delicious dish!

Sweet Cola Ribs

Serves: 4
Cooking Time:1 Hour, 15 Minutes
Ingredients:

- Sweet Cola Barbecue Sauce:
- 1 tbsp. vegetable oil
- 1 medium onion, finely chopped
- 3 cloves garlic, finely chopped
- 2 cups ketchup
- 1 can cola
- 1/2 cup apple cider vinegar
- 2 tsp. brown sugar
- 1/2 tbsp. fresh ground black pepper
- 1/2 tbsp. onion powder
- 1/2 tbsp. ground mustard
- 1/2 tbsp. lemon juice
- 1 tbsp. Worcestershire sauce
- Dry Rub:
- 2 tsp. salt
- 2 tsp. brown sugar
- 2 tsp. garlic powder
- 2 tsp. onion powder
- 1 tbsp. ground cumin
- 1 tbsp. chili powder
- 1 tbsp. black pepper

- 2 racks pork spare ribs (about 3 lb. each)

Directions:

Head up a medium saucepan over medium heat. Add in the oil. Once it's heated up, add onion and garlic. Sauté them until they become tender. Add the rest of the sauce ingredients, and bring it all to a boil. Reduce the heat, and then allow it to simmer for one hour and fifteen minutes. In a small bowl, combine all the dry rub ingredients. Rinse the ribs off. Be sure to dry them. Pull off any excess membrane or fat from the ribs. Season both sides as much as you please with the dry rub and sauce. Be sure to store the ribs in the fridge for four to twelve hours. Place the ribs in the smoker. Flip them a couple of times while they're smoking. Serve ribs while still warm.

Beef Jerky

Serves: 6
Cooking Time: 7 To 9 Hours
Ingredients:

- 2 pounds lean beef top round or flank steak
- 3/4 cup apple cider vinegar
- 3/4 cup soy sauce or teriyaki sauce
- 2 tablespoons kosher salt
- 1 tablespoon smoked paprika
- 1 tablespoon brown sugar
- 1 tablespoon molasses
- 2 teaspoons freshly ground black pepper, plus more to taste
- 1 teaspoon red pepper flakes
- 1 teaspoon garlic powder
- 1 teaspoon onion powder

Directions:

Using a very sharp knife, trim as much fat as possible from beef and cut into slices 4" thick (wrap beef in plastic wrap and freeze for 30 minutes if desired to make slicing easier). Combine remaining ingredients in a glass baking dish, add beef and toss gently to coat Cover dish and refrigerate 8 to 12 hours. Place hickory wood chips in the Masterbuilt smoker's wood tray and preheat smoker to 175°F. Remove beef strips from marinade and pat dry with paper towels. Arrange strips in a single layer on smoker grates, open top vent and smoke until the beef strips are dry and leathery, 7 to 9 hours. Add wood chips to the wood tray as necessary. When jerky is dried as desired, let cool completely in the smoker. Cut jerky strips into smaller pieces with a kitchen shears and serve immediately, or store in a zip-top plastic bag or covered glass jar in the refrigerator for up to 2 weeks, or in the freezer for up to 3 months. Enjoy!

Smoked Flank Steak With Curried Pineapple (masterbuilt Electric Smoker)

Serves: 4
Cooking Time: 2 Hours

Ingredients:
- 4 flank steaks
- 1/4 cup olive oil
- 8 oz pineapple chunks in juice
- 3 tsp curry powder
- 1 Tbsp red currant jelly
- 1/2 tsp salt, or to taste

Directions:
Place the flank steak in a shallow dish. In a bowl, combine olive oil, pineapple chunks in juice, curry powder, red currant jelly and salt and pepper. Pour the mixture over flank steak. Cover and refrigerate for hours. Bring the meat to room temperature 30 minutes before smoking. Preheat Masterbuilt Electric Smoker. Allow the smoker temperature to reach 225 degrees Fahrenheit. When it is ready, add some water to the removable pan that is usually on the bottom shelf. Fill the side "drawer" with dry wood chips. Place steak in your smoker, and smoke until tender. For 3 flank steaks (essentially double/triple the recipe) smoke for 1 1/2 hours. Remove flank steak from the grill and let cool for 10 minutes.

Chinese Style Lamb Shanks

Serves: 2
Cooking Time: 10 Hours

Ingredients:
- 2 (1¼lb) lamb shanks
- 1-2 cups water
- ½ cup brown sugar
- ½ cup rice wine
- ½ cup soy sauce
- 3 tbsp dark sesame oil
- 4 (1½x½-inch) orange zest strips
- 2 (3-inch long) cinnamon sticks
- 1½ tsp Chinese five spice powder

Directions:
Soak apple wood chips in water for at least hour. Preheat the smoker to 5-250 degrees F, using charcoal and soaked apple wood chips. With a sharp knife, pierce each lamb shank at many places. In a bowl, add remaining all ingredients and mix until sugar is dissolved. In a large roasting pan, place lamb shanks and top with sugar mixture evenly. In a foil pan, transfer the lamb shanks with sugar mixture. Place the foil pan into the smoker and cook for about 8-10 hours, flipping after every 30 minutes. (If required, add enough water to keep the liquid ½-inch over. Serve hot.

Crowd Pleasing Meatloaf

Serves: 6
Cooking Time: 4 Hours

Ingredients:
- For Meatloaf:
- 2 lbs ground beef
- ½ cup panko bread crumbs
- 2 eggs, lightly beaten
- ¼ cup milk
- ½ medium red onion, grated
- 2 garlic cloves, minced
- 2 tbsp whiskey
- 1 tbsp Worcestershire sauce
- 1 tbsp steak rub
- 6-ounce pepper jack cheese, cut into strips
- For Sauce:
- ½ cup ketchup
- 1/3 cup brown sugar
- ¼ cup whiskey
- 1 tbsp steak rub
- 2 tsp red pepper flakes, crushed

Directions:
Preheat the smoker to 225 degrees F. Soak oak wood chips in water for at least 1 hour. For meatloaf: in a large bowl, add all ingredients and mix until well combined. Place half of meat mixture in the bottom of a grill basket. Place the cheese over meatloaf, leaving about 1-inch on all sides. Place the remaining meat mixture on top and press the edges together to seal completely. For sauce: in a small bowl, add all the ingredients and mix until well combined. Spread the sauce on top of meatloaf evenly. Place the meatloaf into the smoker and cook, covered for about 4 hours. Transfer the meatloaf onto a wire rack for about 5 minutes before slicing. Cut into desired sized slices and serve.

Chimichurri Smoked Loin Chops

Serves: 6
Cooking Time: 1 Hour

Ingredients:
- 6 loin chops, cut 2 inches thick
- 4 cups crushed ice
- 4 cloves garlic, whole
- 2 limes, halved
- ½ gallon hot water
- ½ cup Kosher Salt
- ½ cup brown sugar
- 3 cloves garlic
- 2 Tbsp red wine vinegar
- 1 bunch curly parsley
- ¾ cup extra-virgin olive oil

Directions:
In a large, non-reactive bowl, combine water, salt and sugar and stir until dissolved. Add crushed ice, limes, and garlic to the brine. Add pork chops when the ice has melted. Allow to sit in the refrigerator for at least 1 hour and up to overnight. Preheat the smoker to 225°F. Remove the chops from the brine, pat dry and allow to sit at room temperature for 30 minutes before smoking. In a food processor, pulse parsley, garlic, red pepper flake, and salt until chopped. Add vinegar. With the food processor running, stream in the olive oil. This sauce gets better the longer it sits. Place the loin chops directly on the smoker grates. Smoke the chops until the internal temperature reaches 145°F. Remove the chops from the smoker and allow them to rest 15 minutes before serving. Spoon chimichurri over the pork chops when serving.

Brown Sugar & Mustard Glazed Ham

Serves:10-12
Cooking Time:6 Hour 30 Minutes
Ingredients:

- Bone-in, pre-cooked ham (8-lbs, 3.65-kgs)
- Onion powder – 2 teaspoons
- Garlic powder – 1 teaspoon
- Dried rosemary leaves – 1 teaspoon
- Dried thyme leaves – 1 teaspoon
- Sweet paprika – 2 teaspoons
- Kosher salt – ½ teaspoon
- Freshly ground black pepper – ½ teaspoon
- Brown sugar – 2 tablespoons
- Olive oil – 1-2 tablespoons
- Honey mustard, to brush
- Orange juice – 1 cup
- Pineapple juice – 1 cup
- Runny honey – ½ cup
- Honey mustard – ¼ cup
- Ground cloves – ¼ teaspoon
- Ground ginger – 1 teaspoon
- Firmly packed brown sugar – 2 cups
- Preheat smoker to 225°f (107°c)
- Add the wood chips, refilling when needed

Directions:
Take the ham out of the fridge and using kitchen paper towels, pat dry. Place the ham on a baking sheet. In a bowl, combine the onion powder together with the garlic powder, rosemary, thyme, paprika, salt, pepper, brown sugar and 1 tbsp of olive oil. Whisk thoroughly to achieve a silky smooth paste. You may add additional oil if needed. Rub the surface of the ham with the paste and set aside to rest for 60 minutes at room temperature. In a pan, combine the orange juice, pineapple juice with the honey, mustards, cloves, ginger, and cardamom. Heat over moderate to low heat. Stirring frequently until the mixture is entirely blended and warmed through. Turn the heat down to low. Brush the ham with the honey-mustard mixture and transfer to the smoker, cooking for minutes, without lifting the smoker's lid. After 60 minutes, open the smoker and baste the ham with a little of the glaze. Close the smoker lid and continue cooking for between 4-6 hours, remembering to baste every 45 minutes. When the internal temperature of the ham registers 125°F (50°C), combine 3-4 tablespoons of the remaining glaze with the brown sugar to create a honey-like consistency. Whisk until entirely smooth. Brush the paste over the top of the ham, allowing it to drip down the sides of the ham, covering the majority of the surface. Continue smoking until the ham reaches an internal temperature of 145°F (63°C).

There should be a sweet crust on the surface of the ham. Remove from the smoker and set aside for half an hour before slicing.

Indian Pork Roast

Serves: 12
Cooking Time: 10 Hours
Ingredients:

- 4-star anise
- 1 teaspoon cumin
- 1 teaspoon coriander
- ½ teaspoon cardamom seeds
- ½ teaspoon black peppercorns
- 1 teaspoon turmeric
- 1 teaspoon salt
- 4 tablespoons canola oil
- 6 pounds pork roast

Directions:
Combine all Ingredients: in a mixing bowl and allow to marinate in the fridge overnight. Preheat the smoker to 50F. Place water in the water pan and add hickory wood chips into the side tray. Place the pork roast on the middle tray. Adjust the cooking time to 10 hours. Constantly, brush the meat with the marinade.

Smoked Pastrami

Serves: 8
Cooking Time: 8 Hours
Ingredients:

- 4 pounds corned Beef
- 2 tablespoons Italian seasoning
- Corned beef seasoning packet
- 3 tablespoons mustard paste
- Water as needed

Directions:
Place beef in a large container with lid, pour in water to cover it, then cover with a lid and let soak in the refrigerator for 8 hours. Then plug in the smoker, fill its tray with hickory woodchips and water pan halfway through, and place dripping pan above the water pan. Then open the top vent, shut with lid and use temperature settings to preheat smoker at 2 degrees F. In the meantime, remove beef from water, pat dry, then coat with mustard and season with Italian seasoning and corned beef seasoning. Place seasoned beef on smoker rack, place meat thermometer, then shut with lid and set the timer to smoke for 6 to 8 hours or until meat thermometer register an internal temperature of 200 degrees F. Check vent of smoker every hour and add more woodchips and water to maintain temperature and smoke. Serve straightaway.

Smoked "onion Soup" Pork
Serves: 6
Cooking Time: 4 Hours 30 Minutes
Ingredients:
- A rack of pork spare ribs
- 2 packs of onion soup mix
- Barbecue pork rib rub (with salt, garlic powder, pepper and paprika)
- 4 cups of water

Directions:
Remove the white membrane off the pork meat and trim off any excess fat Pre-heat your smoker to 0 degree Fahrenheit Prepare your rub mixture by mixing salt, garlic powder, pepper and paprika in a bowl Rub the rib with the mixture Transfer to the smoker and smoker for 2 hours Blend 2 packs of onion soup with 4 cups of water Once smoking is complete, take a heavy aluminum foil and transfer the meat to the foil, pour the soup mix all over Seal the ribs Smoke for another 1 and a ½ hours Gently open the foil and turn the rib, seal it up and smoke for 1 hour more Slice and serve!

Wisconsin Beer Brats
Serves: 6
Cooking Time: 2 Hours
Ingredients:
- 2 cans (12 ounces each) American-style premium lager beer, such as Pabst Blue Ribbon
- 4 tablespoons butter (melted)
- 1 yellow onion (thickly sliced)
- 12 uncooked brats (bratwurst-style sausages)
- 6 hard rolls or Kaiser rolls

Directions:
Pour beer and butter into the Masterbuilt smoker's water pan and add onions. Place hickory wood chips in the smoker's wood tray and preheat smoker to 225°F. Arrange bratwursts on smoker grate and smoke until the internal temperature of the meat reaches 160°F, about hours. If more wood chips are needed in the wood tray, use mesquite. Strain onions from water pan. Arrange two bratwursts on each roll and top with some of the onions. Serve immediately and enjoy!

Sirloin Tip Roast
Serves: 6
Cooking Time: 20 Minutes
Ingredients:
- 2 lbs. sirloin tip roast
- For marinade:
- ½ tsp. black pepper
- 1 tsp. chili powder

- 1 tbsp. minced onion
- 1 tsp. minced garlic
- ½ c. brown sugar
- ½ c. soy sauce
- ½ c. Worcestershire sauce
- 1 tsp. salt

Directions:
Add roast into the ziplock bag. Combine together all marinade ingredients and pour into the ziplock bag. Seal bag and place in refrigerator for hours. Preheat the smoker at 250 F/121 C. Place marinated roast into the smoker and cook for 4 hours or until internal temperature reaches 1 F/68 C. Serve and enjoy.

Smoked Pork Shoulder
Serves: 12
Cooking Time: 8 Hours
Ingredients:
- 8-pound pork shoulder roast, bone-in, and fat trimmed
- 2 teaspoons onion powder
- 2 teaspoons garlic powder
- 2 teaspoons celery salt
- 4 teaspoons salt
- 2 teaspoons ground black pepper
- 1/4 cup brown sugar
- 1/2 teaspoon cayenne pepper
- 1/2 cup paprika
- 2 teaspoons dry mustard

Directions:
Rinse pork shoulder, pat dry completely with paper towels and place roast in a foil pan. Stir together remaining ingredients until mixed and then season roast with the spice mixture until evenly coated. Cover pan tightly with plastic wrap and let marinate in the refrigerator for 8 hours. Then remove pork from refrigerator and let rest for 1 hour at room temperature. Meanwhile, plug in the smoker, fill its tray with hickory woodchips and water pan halfway through, and place dripping pan above the water pan. Then open the top vent, shut with lid and use temperature settings to preheat smoker at 225 degrees F. Place pork on smoker rack, insert a meat thermometer, then shut with lid and set the timer to smoke for 8 hours or more until meat thermometer registers an internal temperature of 190 degrees F. Check vent of smoker every hour and add more woodchips and water to maintain temperature and smoke. When done, transfer pork to a cutting board, cover with aluminum foil and let rest for 30 minutes. Then remove bone from the pork, slice thinly and serve.

Smoked Pork Loin With Sweet Habanero Rub (masterbuilt Electric Smoker)
Serves: 8
Cooking Time: 1 Hour And 25 Minutes
Ingredients:
- 4 lbs pork loin
- Sauce
- Mandarin Habanero Seasoning or any other hot sauce
- 1 cup honey
- 1 cup mustard
- 1 Tbsp Salt and white pepper to taste

Directions:
Combine the Habanero seasoning, honey, mustard and tamari sauce in a mixing bowl. Generously rub the spice mix all over the meat. Preheat your electric smoker to 225°F. When it is ready, add some water to the removable pan that is usually on the bottom shelf. Fill the side "drawer" with dry wood chips (hickory or maple). Place meat in the smoker and smoke till the internal temperature is 145F, about 2 1/2 to 3 hours. When the meat reaches an internal temperature around 145 degrees F, pull it off, cover it and let it rest for 5 to 10 minutes. Slice and serve hot.

Smoked Rack Of Lamb
Serves: 6
Cooking Time: 3 Hours
Ingredients:
- 1 rack of lamb, frenched
- For Marinade:
- 2 tablespoons lemon juice
- 1/4 cup olive oil
- 2 tablespoons Dijon mustard
- 1 teaspoon dried rosemary, crushed
- ½ teaspoon ground black pepper
- 1 teaspoon minced garlic
- For Rub:
- 1 teaspoon dried mint
- 1 teaspoon salt
- 1 teaspoon dried rosemary
- ¼ teaspoon cayenne pepper
- 1 teaspoon dried parsley
- 1 teaspoon garlic powder
- 1 tablespoon Dijon mustard
- 1 teaspoon dried oregano
- 1 teaspoon onion powder
- ¼ cup olive oil
- 1 teaspoon dried basil
- Balsamic reduction

Directions:
Stir together all the ingredients for the marinade, then add into a large plastic bag, place rack of lamb in it, seal the bag and turn it upside down to evenly coat it. Place the rack of lamb into the refrigerator to marinate for to 3 hours. Then remove the lamb from marinade, brush to coat lamb with mustard and sprinkle with garlic powder, onion powder, and cayenne pepper. Stir together remaining ingredients of rub except for oil and balsamic reduction, then rub the spice mixture on all sides of lamb and drizzle with oil. Plug in the smoker, fill its tray with hickory woodchips and water pan halfway through, and place dripping pan above the water pan. Then open the top vent, shut with lid and use temperature settings to preheat smoker at 225 degrees F. Place rack of lamb on smoker rack, insert a meat thermometer, then shut with lid and set the timer to smoke for 2 hours or more until meat thermometer registers an internal temperature of 145 degrees F. Check vent of smoker every hour and add more woodchips and water to maintain temperature and smoke. When done, cover the lamb with aluminum foil for 10 minutes, then slice and drizzle with balsamic reduction. Serve straightaway.

Smoked Flank Steak With Peanut Oil Marinade (masterbuilt Electric Smoker)
Serves: 6
Cooking Time: 1 Hour
Ingredients:
- 3 lbs beef steak, preferably flank
- 1/2 cup peanut oil
- 2 Tbsp fresh mint leaves finely chopped
- Fresh thyme to taste finely chopped
- 1/2 tsp cumin seeds
- 1 tsp sea salt coarse

Directions:
Rub the beef steaks with sea salt and place in a large dish. Combine peanut oil, fresh mint, thyme, and cumin. Pour the peanut oil mixture over the beef. Cover and refrigerate for 4 hours. Bring the meat to room temperature 30 minutes before smoking. Preheat your electric smoker to 22F. When it is ready, add some water to the removable pan that is usually on the bottom shelf. Fill the side "drawer" with dry wood chips. Arrange steak in smoker rack and smoke 45 to 1 hour per pound: 45 minutes if you want medium-rare to medium, and closer to 1 hour if you want medium to well done. Remove the steaks from the smoker and let it rest for 10 -15 minutes. Serve.

Smoked Bologna
Serves: 12
Cooking Time: 4 Hours
Ingredients:
- 3 pounds bologna roll
- 2 tablespoons ground black pepper
- 3/4 cup brown sugar
- 1/4 cup yellow mustard

Directions:
Plug in the smoker, fill its tray with apple woodchips and water pan halfway through, and place dripping pan above the water pan. Then open the top vent, shut with lid and use temperature settings to preheat smoker at 5 degrees F. In the meantime, score bologna with ¼ inch deep diamond pattern, then coats with mustard and season with black pepper and sugar. Place bologna on smoker rack, insert a meat thermometer, then shut with lid and set the timer to smoke for 3 to hours. Check vent of smoker every hour and add more woodchips and water to maintain temperature and smoke. When done, transfer bologna to a cutting board, let cool for 15 minutes and then cut into ½ inch thick slices. Serve bologna slices as sandwiches.

Succulent Tri-tip Roast

Serves: 4
Cooking Time: 2 Hours
Ingredients:

- 3 pounds tri-tip roast
- 1 teaspoon onion powder
- 1 teaspoon black pepper
- 1 teaspoon brown sugar
- ½ teaspoon garlic powder
- 2 teaspoons salt
- 1 and ½ teaspoon red chili powder
- 1 teaspoon espresso powder

Directions:

Rinse your roast well and dry using paper towels, score about ¼ inch deep diamond patterns on top Take a bowl and stir in all the ingredients and rub the mixture well, all over the meat Let it sit for 1 hour at room temperature Take your drip pan and add water, cover with aluminum foil. Pre-heat your smoker to 250 degrees F Use water fill water pan halfway through and place it over drip pan. Add wood chips to the side tray Transfer meat to a smoker (Fat side up) and let it smoke or 2 hours until the internal temperature reaches 130 degrees F Once done, transfer to a cutting plater and cover with a tent foil, let it rest for 20 minutes Slice and enjoy it!

Hungarian Pulled Pork Sandwich

Serves: 15
Cooking Time: 8-10 Hours
Ingredients:

- 4 ½ lbs. pork shoulder, bone-in, Boston-butt
- 1 Tbsp Spanish smoked paprika
- 1 tsp Hungarian sweet paprika
- 1 Tbsp light brown sugar, firmly packed
- 1 tsp onion powder
- 1 tsp salt
- 1 tsp black pepper, freshly ground
- 1 tsp dry mustard
- 1 tsp red pepper, ground
- 2 cups apple cider vinegar
- ¾ cup ketchup
- 2 Tbsp granulated sugar
- 1 Tbsp hot pepper sauce
- 1 tsp salt
- 1 tsp dried red pepper, crushed
- ½ tsp black pepper, freshly ground
- 15 hamburger buns
- 1 (16-oz.) pack shredded coleslaw mix

Directions:

In a large bowl, combine all rub ingredients. Coat the prepared rub onto the Boston-butt and place the meat in a separate large bowl. Refrigerate the pork butt, covered, for at least 8 hours or overnight, for best results. After chilling, remove the meat from the fridge and let it sit for 30 minutes at room temperature as the smoker preheats to 225°F. In a microwave-safe bowl, mix together all sauce ingredients except the coleslaw mix. Microwave the mixture on high setting for 2-3 minutes until the sugar is completely dissolved. Set aside to cool. Coleslaw In a large bowl, mix together ½ cup of the cooled, prepared sauce and the coleslaw mix. Toss the mixture properly and set aside. Set the pork butt directly on the smoker grate. Smoke it for 8-hours or until the internal temperature reaches 200°F. Let it sit for a 30 minutes before carving. Using 2 forks, shred the meat. Discard the fat and bone. In a large bowl, mix together 2 cups of the prepared sauce and the shredded pork. Toss well. Lay the bottom halves of the hamburger buns in a tray or large serving platter. Spoon 5-6 Tbsp of the meat and⅓ cup of the coleslaw on each bun half. Place the upper halves of the burger buns to finish off the burgers. Serve them with additional sauce for dipping.

Smoked Asian Style Pork Tenderloin (masterbuilt Electric Smoker)

Serves: 10
Cooking Time: 3 Hours And 45 Minutes
Ingredients:

- 1 cup brown sugar
- 1/4 cup tamari sauce
- 1 cup Apple Cider Vinegar
- 1 tsp fresh ginger grated
- 1 tsp Salt and black pepper to taste
- 5 lbs pork tenderloin

Directions:

Whisk brown sugar, tamari sauce, apple cider vinegar, grated ginger and salt and pepper to taste in mixing bowl. Place the tenderloin in a large container and pour apple cider mixture; toss well. Place in fridge for 4 - 5 hours (preferably overnight). Preheat your electric smoker to 225°F. When it is ready, add some water to the removable pan that is usually on the bottom shelf. Fill the side "drawer" with dry wood chips. Remove tenderloin from fridge and pat dry on kitchen paper. Place pork in a smoker, and smoke for 2 1/2 - 3 hours, or until internal temp reaches 150°F. Remove from smoker and wrap with aluminum foil. Place back into smoker for an additional 30 minutes, or until internal temp reaches 145°F. When ready let cool for 15 minutes before slicing and serving.

Smoked Pork Ribs With Teriyaki Sauce (masterbuilt Electric Smoker)
Serves: 10
Cooking Time: 4 Hours And 45 Minutes
Ingredients:
- 1/2 cup teriyaki sauce
- 3 Tbsp dry red wine
- 1/4 cup water
- 2 garlic cloves, minced
- 5 lbs pork ribs

Directions:
Cut the ribs into serving-size portions. Combine the teriyaki sauce, red wine, water and minced garlic in a large plastic bag; stir. Add ribs, close bag tightly and shake several times. Refrigerate for 6 hours or overnight. Drain ribs and reserve marinade. Preheat your electric smoker to 22F. When it is ready, add some water to the removable pan that is usually on the bottom shelf. Fill the side "drawer" with dry wood chips. Place the ribs in a smoker, and smoke for 3 hours at 225° F. After 3 hours, remove ribs, baste generously with reserved marinade and wrap in aluminum foil. Return to smoker and cook for an additional 1 to 1 1/2 hours, or until internal temperature reaches 160° F.

Smoked Lamb Kabobs
Serves: 4-5
Cook Time: 60 Minutes
Ingredients:
- For the marinade
- ½ Cup of olive oil
- ¼ Cup of red wine vinegar
- 2 Tablespoons of grated orange rind
- 1 Tablespoon of lemon juice
- 1 Chopped spring onion
- ½ Teaspoon of ground cloves
- ¼ Teaspoon of ground cinnamon
- 1 Trimmed lamb fillet, chopped into cubes

Directions:
Start by combining the ingredients of the marinade in a large shallow dish. Add the lamb to the marinade and let refrigerate for about 4 to 6 hours Prepare your Masterbuilt electric smoker cooker by preheating it to a temperature of about 2° F Drain the lamb and reserve the marinade; then pour the remaining quantity of the marinade into a pan and bring the mixture to a boil for about 1 minute Arrange the lamb onto the lamb skewers; then smoke cook the lamb skewers over with the lid closed for about 4to 60 minutes basting the marinade once during the process of smoking Remove the kabobs from the Masterbuilt electric smoker cooker Serve and enjoy your kabobs!

Fiery Pork Loin With Blueberry Chutney
Serves: 8-10
Cooking Time: 2 ½-3 Hours
Ingredients:
- 1 (3-4 lb.) boneless pork loin
- 3 Tbsp Grill Seasoning
- 2 Tbsp whole-grain mustard
- 2 Tbsp red wine vinegar
- 2 jalapenos, seeded and finely diced
- 2 garlic cloves, minced
- 1 Tbsp olive oil
- 1 medium red onion, finely chopped
- 1 lb. fresh blueberries
- ⅓ cup sugar

Directions:
Rinse the pork loin and pat-dry with a paper towel. Spread the loin with the whole-grain mustard and sprinkle with grill seasoning. Let it sit at room temperature while preheating the smoker to 250°F. Blueberry Chutney In a small saucepan, saute the onion, garlic, and ginger in olive oil over medium heat for 4-minutes or until the onion becomes translucent. Stir in the blueberries and jalapeno and cook for another 4 minutes. Pour the vinegar and add in the sugar, bring to a boil. Once boiling, reduce the heat and let the mixture simmer for 10 minutes, stirring from time to time. Remove from heat and set aside. Set the loin directly on the smoker grate. Smoke the loin for 2 hours or until the loin reaches an internal temperature of 145°F. Cover the loin with aluminum foil and allow the meat to rest for 20-25 minutes before carving. Upon serving, slice the loin into ½ inch slices and top each with a spoonful of blueberry chutney. Serve.

Tri-tip Roast
Serves: 6
Cooking Time: 2 Hours
Ingredients:
- 3-pound tri-tip roast
- 1 teaspoon onion powder
- 1 teaspoon ground black pepper
- 1 teaspoon brown sugar
- 1/2 teaspoon garlic powder
- 2 teaspoons sea salt
- 1 ½ teaspoon red chili powder
- 1 teaspoon espresso powder

Directions:
Rinse roast, pat dry using paper towels and then score about ¼ inch deep diamond pattern on it. Stir together remaining ingredients, then rub on all sides of roast until evenly coated and let marinate for 1 hour at room temperature. Then plug in the smoker, fill its tray with hickory woodchips and water pan halfway through, and place dripping pan above the water pan. Then open the top vent, shut with lid and use temperature settings to preheat smoker at 225 degrees F. Place roast on smoker rack, fat-side up, insert a meat thermometer, then shut with lid and set the timer to smoke for 2 hours or more until meat thermometer registers an internal temperature of 130 degrees F. Check vent of smoker every hour and add more woodchips and water to maintain temperature and smoke. When done, transfer roast to a cutting board, cover with aluminum foil and let rest for 20 minutes. Slice roast into ½ inch thick pieces and serve.

Smoked Ham With Glaze
Serves: 20
Cooking Time: 4 Hours And 30 Minutes
Ingredients:
- 16 pounds baked ham shoulder, bone-in
- 1/2 cup maple syrup
- 1/2 cup cane sugar
- 2 tablespoons brown mustard
- 1/4 cup sweet apple cider

Directions:
Rinse ham, pat dry with paper towels, place it on a foil pan and let rest for 45 minutes at room temperature. Then plug in the smoker, fill its tray with apple woodchips and water pan halfway through, and place dripping pan above the water pan. Then open the top vent, shut with lid and use temperature settings to preheat smoker at 0 degrees F. In the meantime, use a sharp knife to score pork about ½ inch deep diamond pattern. Place pork on smoker rack, insert a meat thermometer, then shut with lid and set the timer to smoke for 1 to 1 ½ hour or more until meat thermometer registers an internal temperature of 130 degrees F. Check vent of smoker every hour and add more woodchips and water to maintain temperature and smoke. Meanwhile, prepare the glaze and for this, place a small saucepan over medium heat, add remaining ingredients, stir well and cook for 5 to 10 minutes or until slightly thick. When done, transfer pork onto a cutting board, let cool for 15 minutes and then brush with prepare glaze until evenly coated on all sides. Return ham into the smoker and cook for another 2 to 3 hours or until meat thermometer register an internal temperature of 140 degrees F. Transfer ham to a cutting board, cover with foil, let rest for 15 minutes and then slice to serve.

Perfectly Smoked Pork Butt
Serves: 8-10
Cooking Time: 8-16 Hours
Ingredients:
- 8-10 lbs. pork shoulder roast, preferably Boston Butt roast
- 2 cups Basic Barbecue

Directions:
Dry the pork butt with a paper towel. Liberally apply the Basic Barbecue Rub to all surfaces of the meat. Refrigerate the roast for 4-6 hours or overnight. After chilling, remove the roast from the fridge and let it sit at room temperature for 30 minutes while preheating the smoker to 225°F. Set the roast directly on the smoker grate. Use the water pan for extra moist roast. Smoke the roast until the internal temperature reaches 200°F. Remove the roast from the smoker and allow it to rest for 30 minutes before handling. Using two forks, shred the meat and serve with your favorite barbecue sauce. To use the Texas Crutch: Smoke the roast for 4-6 hours, or until the internal temperature of the roast reads 150°F. Remove the roast from the smoker. Wrap the roast tightly in a double layer of heavy-duty aluminum foil with a splash of apple juice or beer inside the foil. Return the roast back to smoker. Remove the roast from the smoker once the internal temperature of the meat reaches 200°F. Unwrap the roast and allow it to sit for 30 minutes until it is cool enough to handle. Gently use two forks to shred the meat. Serve with preferred barbecue sauce.

Smoked Dry Mustard Beef Round Steak (masterbuilt Electric Smoker)
Serves: 4
Cooking Time: 2 Hours
Ingredients:
- 2 lbs beef top round steak, cut 3/4 inch thick
- 1/2 tsp salt
- 1/2 cup mustard
- 2 Tbsp packed brown sugar
- 1 Tbsp white wine vinegar (good quality)
- 1/2 tsp pepper flakes, (optional)

Directions:
Rub salt all around the steak. Preheat Masterbuilt Electric Smoker. Allow the smoker temperature to reach 5 degrees Fahrenheit. When it is ready, add some water to the removable pan that is usually on the bottom shelf. Fill the side "drawer" with dry wood chips. Place the meat directly on racks of your Masterbuilt Smoker. Smoke at about for 30 minutes per pound, checking the temperature at 4minutes with a meat thermometer. Remove from heat when the internal temperature is at 135 degrees using a meat thermometer. Remove the meat from the smoker and let rest for 10 minutes. Meanwhile, combine mustard, brown sugar, white wine vinegar and pepper flakes and a pinch of salt. Pour the mustard mixture over beef and serve.

Slow Smoked Pork Ribs
Serves: 8
Cooking Time: 4 Hours
Ingredients:
- 8 lbs pork loin baby back ribs
- 1/4 cup yellow honey mustard
- 1/4 cup brown sugar
- 1/3 cup paprika
- 1/4 cup onion powder
- 1/4 cup granulated garlic powder
- 2 tsp. dried parsley flakes
- 1 -2 tbsp. chipotle chili pepper flakes
- 1 tbsp. black pepper
- 2 tsp. chili powder
- 1 tbsp. ground cumin
- 1 tbsp. salt
- Spicy BBQ sauce

Directions:
Bring your ribs up to room temperature. Mix all the rub ingredients together. Rub this mustard mixture over every surface of your ribs. Place your ribs on the smoker. When their halfway done wrap them up in heavy duty foil. Smoke for the remaining time. Un-wrap the ribs for one hour afterward. You can eat these ribs with spicy BBQ sauce.

Smoked Ribeye With Herb Rubs (masterbuilt Electric Smoker)

Serves: 6
Cooking Time: 2 Hours And 20 Minutes
Ingredients:
- 1/4 cup parsley, fresh and chopped
- 1/4 cup oregano leaves, fresh an chopped
- 2 Tbsp basil, fresh and chopped
- 2 Tbsp rosemary leaves, fresh and chopped
- Salt and pepper to taste
- 3 lbs. beef ribeye

Directions:
Season beef ribeye with salt and pepper. Combine all herbs and generously rub the herb spice mix all over the meat. Preheat Masterbuilt Electric Smoker. Allow the smoker temperature to reach 225 degrees Fahrenheit. When it is ready, add some water to the removable pan that is usually on the bottom shelf. Fill the side "drawer" with dry wood chips. Place the ribeye in the Masterbuilt and cook until the internal temperature is 120 degrees F for a medium rare steak. The smoking time took about 50 minutes (the thinner the steak, the faster it will reach a higher internal temperature). Remove meat from smoker and let it rest for 10 minutes, slice and serve.

Smoked French Sour Lamb Cutlets (masterbuilt Electric Smoker)

Serves: 8
Cooking Time: 4 Hours
Ingredients:
- 6 cloves garlic peeled minced
- 2 Tbsp apple cider vinegar
- 1/2 cup water
- 1/4 cup extra-virgin olive oil
- Pinch salt and black ground pepper to taste
- 4 lbs. lamb cutlets

Directions:
Combine all Ingredients: for the marinade. Brush generously lamb cutlets with marinade and refrigerate for 4 hours. Remove out of the refrigerator just 45 minutes before you want to smoke it. Preheat Masterbuilt Electric Smoker. Allow the smoker temperature to reach 225 degrees Fahrenheit When it is ready, add some water to the removable pan that is usually on the bottom shelf. Fill the side "drawer" with dry Hickory wood chips. Place the meat in the top rack and give smoke until internal temperature reach 150 degrees F (about 4 hours). Remove the chops and let cool 15 minutes before serving. Serve.

Smoked Pork Loin

Serves: 8-10
Cooking Time: 2 ½-3 Hours
Ingredients:
- 1 (3-4 lb.) boneless pork loin
- 3 Tbsp Grill Seasoning
- 2 Tbsp whole-grain mustard

Directions:
Rinse the pork loin and pat-dry with a paper towel. Spread the loin with the whole-grain mustard and sprinkle with grill seasoning. Let it sit at room temperature while preheating the smoker to 250°F. Set the loin directly on the smoker grate. Smoke the loin for 2 hours. Insert a meat thermometer at the thickest portion of the meat halfway before the smoking time is done. Remove the loin from the smoker once the internal temperature reaches 145°F. Cover the loin with aluminum foil and allow the meat to rest for 20-25 minutes before carving. Upon serving, slice the loin into ½ inch slices and serve.

Saucy Beef Back Ribs

Serves: 8
Cooking Time: 6 Hours Plus 1 Hour Resting
Ingredients:
- 4 racks center cut beef back ribs (about 2 pounds each)
- 1 cup yellow mustard
- 1/4 cup kosher salt, plus more to taste
- 2 tablespoons freshly ground black pepper, plus more to taste
- 2 tablespoons garlic powder
- 2 tablespoons smoked paprika
- 2 tablespoons chili powder
- 2 teaspoons chipotle chili powder
- 2 teaspoons cayenne pepper
- 3/4 cup apple juice (divided)
- 1/2 cup honey
- 1/2 cup ketchup

Directions:
Pour about 2 cups water into the Masterbuilt smoker's water pan. Place oak or pecan wood chips in the smoker's wood tray and preheat smoker to 225°F. Remove silver skin from ribs and rub ribs all over with mustard. Mix salt, pepper, garlic powder, paprika, chili powders and cayenne pepper. Set aside about tablespoons of the spice mixture for the sauce. Rub remaining spice mixture all over the ribs and let stand for about 15 minutes. Place ribs bone-sides down on smoker grate and smoke for about hours, spritzing with apple juice every hour. Meanwhile, for the sauce, whisk remaining 1/2 cup apple juice with honey and ketchup. Add reserved spice mixture to sauce, whisk to combine and divide sauce into two separate portions. Baste ribs all over with half of the sauce, wrap in foil and continue smoking until the internal temperature of the meat reaches 200°F, about 3 hours more. Add wood chips to the wood tray as necessary. Remove wrapped ribs from smoker and let rest for about 1 hour. Unwrap ribs and cut into portions as desired. Serve ribs with the remaining sauce and enjoy!

Simple Pulled Pork Butt

Serves: 8
Cooking Time: 8 Hours
Ingredients:

- 8 pounds pork butt roast
- 6 tablespoons jarred mustard
- ½ cup brown sugar
- ¼ cup of salt
- 2 tablespoons garlic powder
- 2 tablespoons onion powder
- 1 tablespoon dried thyme
- 1 tablespoon dried oregano
- 1 tablespoon paprika
- 1 tablespoon cracked pepper
- Unsweetened apple juice
- Soft rolls and BBQ sauce for serving

Directions:
Cut the upper fat from your meat and trim them making sure to leave just ¼ inch layer of fat, thoroughly wash them well and pat them dry using clean paper   Gently rub mustard all over the meat   Take ab owl and add all the dry ingredients and mix well, coat the meat with the dry rub   Transfer the meat to your fridge and let it sit for about 12 hours.   Take your drip pan and add water, cover with aluminum foil. Pre-heat your smoker to 22degrees F   Use water fill water pan halfway through and place it over drip pan. Add wood chips to the side tray.   Transfer meat to the smoker and smoke for about 8 hours, making sure to keep replenishing the wood chips and liquid (apple juice) from time to time   Once the internal temperature reaches 190 degrees F, the meal is ready   Take it out and let it cool for 20 minutes   Slice and enjoy it!

Smoked Pork Ribs With Fresh Herbs (masterbuilt Electric Smoker)

Serves: 6
Cooking Time: 5 Hours And 15 Minutes
Ingredients:

- 1/2 cup olive oil
- 1 tsp fresh parsley finely chopped
- 1 tsp fresh sage finely chopped
- 1 tsp fresh rosemary finely chopped
- Salt and ground black pepper to taste
- 3 lbs. bone-in pork rib roast

Directions:
Combine the olive oil, garlic, parsley, sage, rosemary, salt, and pepper in a bowl; stir well. Generously rub the herbs mix all over the meat. Preheat your electric smoker to 225°F.   When it is ready, add some water to the removable pan that is usually on the bottom shelf.   Fill the side "drawer" with dry wood chips (Hickory and mesquite). Smoke your ribs directly on the racks for 3 hours at 225 degrees Fahrenheit.   Remove the ribs from

the racks and tightly wrap them in aluminum foil. Place them back in the smoker for 2 hours. Transfer to a serving platter; let it rest 10 - 15 minutes before serving.

Cross-rib Beef Roast

Serves: 6
Cooking Time: 4 Hours
Ingredients:

- ¼ cup olive oil
- 3 pounds cross-rib beef roast, boneless and fat trimmed
- For Rub:
- 3 teaspoons garlic powder
- 1 ½ tablespoon salt
- 1 tablespoon ground black pepper
- 1 tablespoon paprika
- 2 teaspoons cumin
- ¼ teaspoon dried sage
- 2 teaspoons crushed rosemary
- 1 tablespoon Worcestershire
- For Injection:
- 1/8 teaspoon ground black pepper
- 1/8 teaspoon salt
- 1/8 teaspoon dried rosemary
- 1/2 teaspoon minced garlic
- 1/2 stick of salted butter, melted
- 1/2 teaspoon dried sage
- 2 teaspoons Worcestershire sauce
- Water as needed

Directions:
Place all the ingredients for the rub in a bowl and stir until mixed.   Brush oil on all side of the roast, rub with the prepared spice mixture until evenly coated, then cover with plastic wrap and marinate in the refrigerator for 6 hours.   Then place all the ingredients for injection in a food processor and pulse for 1 minute or until grind.   Fill this mixture into injection and inject into marinated roast as deep as possible.   Cover roast again with plastic wrap and place in the refrigerator for 40 minutes. Meanwhile, plug in the smoker, fill its tray with oak woodchips and water pan halfway through, and place dripping pan above the water pan.   Then open the top vent, shut with lid and use temperature settings to preheat smoker at 235 degrees F.   Place roast on smoker rack, place meat thermometer, then shut with lid smoke until meat thermometer registers an internal temperature of 140 degrees F.   Check vent of smoker every hour and add more woodchips and water to maintain temperature and smoke.   When done, wrap roast with aluminum foil and let rest for 20 minutes.   Then slice roast across the grain and serve.

Smoked Lamb Chops With Fresh Herbs (masterbuilt Electric Smoker)
Serves: 6
Cooking Time: 4 Hours
Ingredients:
- 12 lamb chops
- Salt and ground pepper to taste
- 3 garlic cloves
- 3 tsp basil leaves
- 3 tsp marjoram leaves
- 3 tsp thyme leaves

Directions:
Sprinkle lamb chops lightly with salt and pepper. In a bowl mix herbs and mashed garlic; generously rub the spice mix all over the meat. Wrap in a foil, and refrigerate for at least 4 hours. Remove out of the refrigerator just 45 minutes before you want to smoke it. Preheat Masterbuilt Electric Smoker. Allow the smoker temperature to reach 225 degrees Fahrenheit. When it is ready, add some water to the removable pan that is usually on the bottom shelf. Fill the side "drawer" with dry Hickory wood chips. Place the meat in the top rack and smoke until internal temperature reaches 150 degrees F (about 4 hours). Remove the chops and let cool 15 minutes before serving.

Chicago Rib Tips
Serves: 6
Cooking Time: 4 To 4 1/2 Hours
Ingredients:
- 1/2 cup packed brown sugar (divided)
- 3 tablespoons kosher salt
- 2 tablespoon chili powder
- 1 tablespoon freshly ground black pepper
- 1 teaspoon cayenne pepper
- 1 teaspoon celery salt
- 1 teaspoon rubbed sage
- 1 teaspoon onion powder
- 1/4 teaspoon ground nutmeg
- 1/4 teaspoon ground cinnamon
- 1 /4 teaspoon ground ginger
- 4 pounds pork rib tips
- 1/3 cup ketchup
- 1/3 cup pineapple juice
- 2 tablespoons apple cider vinegar
- 2 tablespoons white sugar
- 1 tablespoon chili powder

Directions:
Thoroughly mix 4 cup brown sugar with salt, chili powder, black pepper, cayenne pepper, celery salt, sage, onion powder, nutmeg, cinnamon and ginger, breaking up any clumps. Reserve about 2 tablespoons spice mixture for the sauce. Rub remaining spice mixture over rib tips, wrap in aluminum foil and refrigerate for 1 to 8 hours.

Place oak or hickory wood chips in the smoker's wood tray and preheat smoker to 0°F. Set foil pouch of rib tips on smoker grate. Pierce several holes in pouch and smoke rib tips for about 1/2 hours. Meanwhile, for the sauce, in a small saucepan over medium heat whisk ketchup, pineapple juice, vinegar, sugar, chili powder and Worcestershire sauce with remaining brown sugar and spice rub. Heat sauce to a boil, stirring occasionally. Reduce heat and simmer, uncovered, until thickened to desired consistency, about 30 minutes, stirring occasionally. Baste rib tips all over with sauce and continue smoking until the meat easily pulls from the bones, 30 minutes to 1 hour more. Chop rib tips into pieces between the bones and serve immediately with the remaining sauce. Enjoy!

Cherry Memphis Pork Ribs
Serves: 2
Cooking Time: 10 Hours
Ingredients:
- 2 baby back ribs
- A packet of your favorite BBQ rub
- Dr. Pepper Cherry cola

Directions:
Place all Ingredients: in a Ziploc bags and allow to marinate in the fridge overnight. Preheat the smoker to 50F. Place water in the water pan and add cherry wood chips into the side tray. Place the ribs in the smoker. Adjust the cooking time to 10 hours or until meat falls off the bone. Constantly, brush the meat with the marinade.

Moroccan Lamb Ribs
Serves:4
Cooking Time:3 Hours 20 Minutes
Ingredients:
- 2 racks of lamb, membrane removed
- Paprika – 2 tablespoons
- Coriander seeds – ½ tablespoon
- Kosher salt – ½ tablespoon
- Cumin seeds – 1 teaspoon
- Ground allspice- 1 teaspoon
- Powdered lemon peel – 1 teaspoon
- Ground black pepper – ½ teaspoons
- Preheat the smoker to 250°f (121°c) for indirect cooking
- Add your choice of wood chips

Directions:
Combine the paprika followed by the coriander seeds, kosher salt, cumin seeds, ground allspice, lemon peel, and black pepper and using a pestle and mortar grind the seasonings into a powder. Season both sides of the lamb liberally with the rub. Transfer to your smoker, cover and cook for hours until tender. Remove from the smoker and serve.

Ultimate Chuck Roast

Serves: 6
Cooking Time: 4-5 Hours
Ingredients:

- 1 whole 4-5 pound chuck roast
- ¼ cup of olive oil
- ¼ cup of firmly packed brown sugar
- 2 tablespoon of Cajun seasoning
- 2 tablespoon of paprika
- 2 tablespoon of cayenne pepper

Directions:
Pre-heat your smoker to 225 degree Fahrenheit using oak wood   Rub chuck roast all over with olive oil   Take a small bowl and add brown sugar, paprika, Cajun seasoning, cayenne   Coat the roast well with spice mix   Transfer the transfer the chuck roast to smoker rack and smoke for 4-hours   Once the internal temperature reaches 1 degree Fahrenheit, take the meat out and slice   Enjoy!

Baby Back Ribs With Bbq Sauce

Serves: 4
Cooking Time: 5 Hours
Ingredients:

- Apple juice for basting
- ½ a teaspoon cayenne pepper
- 2 teaspoons garlic powder
- 2 teaspoons onion powder
- 1 tablespoon pepper
- 1 and ½ tablespoons salt
- ¼ cup smoked paprika
- ½ cup brown sugar
- 2 slabs baby back ribs
- For Sauce
- ½ teaspoon pepper
- 2 tablespoons salt
- 2 tablespoons apple cider vinegar
- 2 tablespoons Worcestershire sauce
- ¼ cup molasses
- 28 ounces tomato sauce
- 2 cups of water
- 2 tablespoons yellow mustard
- 6 ounces tomato paste
- 3 garlic cloves, minced
- 1 small onion, diced
- 2 tablespoons canola oil

Directions:
Take your ribs and transfer to a clean surface with the meat side facing down   Gently remove the membrane by slicing with a paring knife   Take a bowl and add all of the dry ingredients, rub the meat with the mixture   Let it sit for 30 minutes   Take your drip pan and add water, cover with

aluminum foil. Pre-heat your smoker to 22degrees F   Use water fill water pan halfway through and place it over drip pan. Add wood chips to the side tray   Add ribs to the smoker (meat side up) and smoke for 3 hours, add more wood chips if needed   For the sauce, take a large-sized pan and place it over medium heat, add oil and heat it up   Add onions and Saute for 5 minutes, add garlic and cook for 1 minute more   Add 2 cups water, molasses, sauce, Worcestershire, salt, vinegar, pepper, cayenne and whisk well   Simmer for 2 hours on low heat   Pour mixture over beef, enjoy! Enjoy once done!

Smoked Chorizo Queso

Serves:4
Cooking Time:1 Hours 10 Minutes
Ingredients:

- Chorizo (1-lbs, 0.45-kgs)
- Processed cheese, cubed (1-lbs,0.45-kgs)
- Cream cheese, cubed – ½ cup
- Canned tomatoes and chili (10-ozs, 285-gms)
- Tortilla chips, to serve
- Preheat your electric smoker to 250°F (121°C)
- Add apple wood chips

Directions:
In a skillet or frying pan, cook the chorizo and drain the grease.   In a disposable aluminum, tray combine the processed cheese with the cream cheese, canned tomatoes, and cooked chorizo. Smoke in the smoker for 60 minutes, until entirely melted, mixing every 20 minutes.   Serve with tortilla chips.

Decadent Rump Roast

Serves: 8
Cooking Time: 6 Hours
Ingredients:

- 3 lb beef rump roast
- 1 tsp smoked paprika
- 1 tsp onion powder
- 1 tsp garlic powder
- Salt and freshly ground black pepper, to taste
- 2-4 tbsp Worcestershire sauce

Directions:
Preheat the smoker to 200 degrees F, using charcoal.   In a bowl, mix together all spices.   Coat the rump roast with Worcestershire sauce evenly and then rub generously with spice mixture.   Place the roast into the smoker and cook for about 5-6 hours.   Transfer the roast onto a cutting board and set aside for about 10-1minutes before serving. With a sharp knife, cut the roast in desired sized slices.   Sprinkle with a little salt and serve.

Irish-style Lamb
Serves: 6
Cooking Time: 4 Hours
Ingredients:
- 1 lamb leg, fat trimmed and boneless
- 2 teaspoons minced garlic
- 2 tablespoons salt
- 2 tablespoons ground black pepper
- 3 tablespoons rosemary, fresh

Directions:
Plug in the smoker, fill its tray with hickory woodchips and water pan halfway through, and place dripping pan above the water pan. Then open the top vent, shut with lid and use temperature settings to preheat smoker at 5 degrees F. In the meantime, rinse leg of lamb, pat dry and then use a knife to butterfly its flesh. Stir together remaining ingredients until combined, then place half of the spice mixture into the lamb, rub remaining spice mixture on all over the lamb and secure with kitchen twine. Place leg of lamb on smoker rack, place meat thermometer, then shut with lid and set the timer to smoke for 4 hours or more until meat thermometer registers an internal temperature of 16degrees F. Check vent of smoker every hour and add more woodchips and water to maintain temperature and smoke. Serve straightaway.

Sticky Smoky Meatloaf
Serves: 3-4
Cooking Time:3 Hours 30 Minutes
Ingredients:
- Lean ground beef (2-lbs, 0.9-kgs)
- 1 red pepper, minced
- 1 yellow onion, peeled and minced
- 2 cloves garlic, peeled and minced
- BBQ sauce - ⅔ cup
- 1 egg, beaten
- Breadcrumbs – ½ cup
- Salt – 1 teaspoon
- Black pepper – ½ teaspoon
- Cayenne pepper – ¼ teaspoon
- BBQ rub – 3 tablespoons
- Add a bowl of water to the bottom of the smoker and add hickory wood chips. Preheat to 250°f (120°c).

Directions:
Using clean hands, combine the beef, pepper, onion, garlic, half of the BBQ sauce, egg, breadcrumbs, salt, pepper, and cayenne. Shape the mixture into a loaf and season with BBQ rub. Place in the smoker and cook for approximately hours. At this point, brush the meatloaf with the remaining BBQ sauce. Continue to cook until the internal temperature registers 160°f (70°c). The wood chips or water may need to be replenished during this time.

Tenderloin Kebabs
Serves: 4-6
Cooking Time: 30-60 Minutes
Ingredients:
- 2 lbs beef tenderloin, trimmed and cubed into 2 inch cubes
- Double batch of North African
- 2 Zucchini, cut into 1 inch rounds
- 1 lb button mushrooms
- 2 bell peppers, cut into 2 inch pieces
- 1 onion, cut into 2 inch pieces
- 8 oz cherry tomatoes
- Skewers, soaked in water

Directions:
Place cold tenderloin chunks and half of the rub in a large zip top bag. Massage thoroughly and allow to sit for 30 minutes. In a separate zip top bag, combine the remaining rub and vegetables and allow to sit for 30 minutes. Preheat the smoker to 275°F. Thread meat onto skewers, leaving a space between the chunks. On separate skewers, thread alternating vegetables. Place the skewers on the smoker grates and smoke until the meat registers 135°F. Remove the skewers and serve immediately.

Simple Pulled Pork
Serves: 16
Cooking Time: 12 To 15 Hours
Ingredients:
- 2 cups apple cider
- 1 bone-in pork shoulder roast (8 to 10 pounds)
- 3 tablespoons yellow mustard
- 3 tablespoons brown sugar
- 1 tablespoon kosher salt
- 1 tablespoon smoked paprika
- 2 teaspoons onion powder
- 2 teaspoons freshly ground black pepper
- 2 teaspoons garlic powder
- 1/2 teaspoon cayenne pepper

Directions:
Pour apple cider into the Masterbuilt smoker's water pan. Place hickory wood chips in the smoker's wood tray and preheat smoker to 225°F. Brush mustard over pork roast. Mix brown sugar, salt, paprika, onion powder, black pepper, garlic powder and cayenne pepper and rub over roast. Place pork roast fat-side up on smoker grate and smoke until the internal temperature of the roast reaches 205°F, 12 to 15 hours. Add wood chips to the wood tray as necessary. Remove pork roast from smoker, cover loosely with aluminum foil and let rest for about 30 minutes. Remove bone from roast and pull meat apart with two forks, removing gristle and fat as necessary. Serve as desired and enjoy!

Smoked Pork Belly

Serves: 5
Cook Time: 4 Hours
Ingredients:

- 2 Pounds of pork belly
- For the Pork Dry Rub
- 2 Tablespoons of kosher salt
- ½ Cup of packed brown sugar
- 1 Tablespoon of smoked paprika
- 1 Tablespoon of Dark chili powder
- ½ Tablespoon of ground black pepper

Directions:
Prepare the pork belly meat and dry rub it Mix all of your ingredients of the prepared dry rub together in a bowl and whisk with a fork Prepare the pork meat by removing its skin; then slice the scores through the fat; but be careful not to score slices into the flesh This process is very easy to do it when the pork belly is cold Put the cold belly over a sheet pan or on top of a baking dish and sprinkle with a certain amount of rub on top of the belly Cover the meat and refrigerate it for about 24 hours Remove the pork belly from the refrigerator one hour before smoking it to bring it to the room temperature Bring the temperature up to about 225° F; then add the wood chips to start the smoke Place an aluminium drip pan with a quantity of water that doesn't exceed a few inches under the grates so that it can catch drippings Put the pork belly on the grate with the fat side and smoke the meat for about 3 to 4 hours Remove the pork from the smoker and let rest on top of a wire rack for about 15 minutes You can whether serve the pork belly immediately, or you can let it rest for about 15 minutes Enjoy your dish!

Asian Honey Pork Chops

Serves: 8
Cooking Time: 2 Hours
Ingredients:

- 2-4 pork chops, 1/2 inch to 3/4 inch thick
- 1 tbsp toasted sesame seed oil or olive oil
- 1/2 cup chicken broth
- 1/2 cup honey
- 1/4 cup soy sauce
- 2 tsp. ketchup
- 1/4 tbsp. crushed red pepper flakes
- 1/4 tbsp. garlic salt

Directions:
Sprinkle your chops with oil and garlic salt. Place the chops in a greased pan. Mix the rest of the remaining ingredients, and pour these over the chops. Smoke your chops. Save the extra sauce for some rice on the side.

Meats Combo Meatloaf

Serves: 6

Cooking Time: 4 Hours
Ingredients:

- 1½ lbs ground pork
- 1½ cups BBQ sauce, divided
- 2 lbs ground beef chuck
- 2 roasted bell peppers, chopped
- 1/3 cup onion, chopped finely
- 4 garlic cloves, minced
- 2 eggs, beaten
- ¾ cup fresh breadcrumbs
- 1 tbsp dried oregano, crushed
- Salt and freshly ground black pepper, to taste

Directions:
Preheat the smoker to 225 degrees F, using charcoal. In a large bowl, add ½ cup of BBQ sauce and remaining all ingredients and mix until well combined. Arrange a 24-inch piece of foil in a small baking sheet, doubling it over by folding it half. Mold the sides of foil upwards to make a loaf pan. Place the meat mixture in loaf pan and press to form a meatloaf Place the loaf pan over smoker rack and cook for about 3-4 hours. In the last hour of coking, coat the meatloaf with the remaining BBQ sauce. Transfer the meatloaf onto a wire rack for about 5 minutes before slicing. Cut into desired sized slices and serve.

World's Most Tender "3-2-1 Ribs"

Serves: 6
Cooking Time: 6 Hours
Ingredients:

- 2 (~4 lb.) racks pork spare ribs, trimmed
- ⅓ cup Big Bold Barbecue ¼ cup yellow mustard
- ½ cup apple juice

Directions:
Rinse the spare ribs under cold water and pat-dry with a paper towel. Put them on a cutting board, bone side up. Coat both sides of the ribs with the mustard, and then sprinkle evenly with the rub. Let it sit at room temperature while preheating the smoker to 225°F. Set the ribs directly on the smoker grate, bone side down. Smoke the ribs for 3 hours. Remove the ribs from the smoker and set each rack in its own large piece of heavy-duty aluminum foil. Pour ½ cup of the apple juice in each rack and immediately close the foil tightly around the ribs. Return back to the smoker and smoke for another 2 hours. After 2 hours, remove the ribs from the smoker and discard the foil. Place them back to the smoker, directly on the smoker grate, and smoke for another hour. Once done, remove from the smoker and allow to rest for 5-10 minutes before carving. Note: Smoking the ribs directly on the smoker grate for another hour after smoking them with foil ensures that the ribs will have a crispy outer layer while the meat on the inside is tender enough to "fall right off the bone."

Smoked Sour Baby Ribs (masterbuilt Electric Smoker)
Serves: 8
Cooking Time: 4 Hours And 25 Minutes
Ingredients:
- 4 lbs slabs of baby back ribs
- 1 Tbsp brown sugar - (packed)
- 2 Tbsp garlic & onion powder
- Kosher salt and ground black pepper to taste
- 1/2 cup Stout red wine vinegar (basting)

Directions:
Mix all of the dry rub Ingredients: together in a bowl or measuring cup. Rub into the tops, bottoms, and sides of the ribs. Set the ribs aside to rest and come to room temperature for about 45 minutes. Preheat your electric smoker to 225°F. When it is ready, add some water to the removable pan that is usually on the bottom shelf. Fill the side "drawer" with dry wood chips. After 3 hours, place the aluminum foil under the ribs and baste generously with stout red wine vinegar to moisten. Wrap the ribs completely in the foil and cook for an additional 1 to 1-1/2 hours, or until the internal temperature reaches 160 degrees. Serve hot.

Smoked Leg Of Lamb
Serves: 8
Cooking Time: 5 Hours
Ingredients:
- 6 pounds leg of lamb
- 1 tablespoon minced garlic
- 1 teaspoon sea salt
- 1 teaspoon ground black pepper
- 1 teaspoon dried rosemary
- 1 teaspoon dried marjoram
- ½ cup wine vinegar
- ½ cup dry white wine
- ½ cup olive oil

Directions:
Rinse lamb, pat dry with paper towels and place in a large plastic bag. Place remaining ingredients in a blender, pulse for 1 minute or until smooth, then pour this mixture into the bag containing lamb and seal the bag. Turn the plastic bag upside down to coat lamb with the spice mixture and then place in the refrigerator for 6 hours. When ready to smoke, plug in the smoker, fill its tray with hickory woodchips and water pan halfway through, and place dripping pan above the water pan. Then open the top vent, shut with lid and use temperature settings to preheat smoker at 22degrees F. In the meantime, remove the lamb from marinade and add marinade in the water pan of the smoker. Place lamb on smoker rack, insert a meat thermometer, then shut with lid and set the timer to smoke for 4 to 5 hours or more until meat thermometer registers an internal temperature of 150 degrees F. Check vent of smoker every hour and add more woodchips and water to maintain temperature and smoke. Serve straightaway.

Savory And Sweet Pork Ribs
Serves: 8
Cooking Time: 4 Hours And 30 Minutes
Ingredients:
- 2 racks baby back ribs, each about 2 pounds
- 1/2 cup brown sugar
- 1/4 cup smoked paprika
- 1 ½ tablespoon salt
- 1 tablespoon ground black pepper
- 2 teaspoons garlic powder
- 2 teaspoons onion powder
- ½ teaspoon red chili powder
- Apple cider vinegar as needed for basting

Directions:
Use a paring knife to peel and remove the membrane from ribs, rinse well and pat dry with paper towels. Stir together all the ingredients except for the vinegar, then rub this mixture on all sides of ribs and let rest at room temperature for 30 minutes. When ready to cook, plug in the smoker, fill its tray with hickory woodchips and water pan halfway through, and place dripping pan above the water pan. Then open the top vent, shut with lid and use temperature settings to preheat smoker at 250 degrees F. Place seasoned ribs on smoker rack, insert a meat thermometer, then shut with lid and set the timer to smoke for 3 hours. Check vent of smoker every hour and add more woodchips and water to maintain temperature and smoke. After 3 hours of smoking, baste ribs with vinegar, wrap them completely in aluminum foil and continue smoking for 1 to 1 ½ hour or until meat thermometer registers an internal temperature of 160 degrees F. Serve straightaway.

Basic Brisket
Serves: 12
Cooking Time: 8 To 9 Hours Plus 1 To 2 Hours Resting
Ingredients:
- 1 full "whole packer" beef brisket (12 to 15 pounds)
- 1/2 cup brown sugar (divided)
- 1/4 cup chili powder
- 1/4 cup sweet paprika
- 1/4 cup kosher salt, plus more to taste
- 2 tablespoons garlic powder
- 2 tablespoons onion powder
- 2 tablespoons ground cumin
- 1 tablespoon ancho chili powder
- 1 tablespoon freshly ground black pepper, plus more to taste
- 1 teaspoon cayenne pepper, plus more to taste
- 4 tablespoons butter (melted)
Directions:
Pour 2 cups water into the Masterbuilt smoker's water pan. Place a mixture of hickory and apple wood chips in the smoker's wood tray and preheat smoker to 250°F. Thoroughly rinse brisket with cold water and pat dry with paper towels. Trim brisket as necessary to about 1/4" fat and trim fat between the flat and the deckle (separate portions if necessary to fit in smoker). Mix 1/4 cup brown sugar with chili powder, paprika, salt, garlic powder, onion powder, cumin, ancho chili powder, black pepper and cayenne pepper and rub all over brisket. Place brisket fat-side down on smoker grate and smoke until the internal temperature of the meat reaches 165°F, about 6 hours. Add wood chips to the wood tray as necessary. Mix butter and remaining 1/4 cup brown sugar and brush all over brisket. Wrap brisket in two layers of aluminum foil and continue smoking until the internal temperature of the meat reaches 200°F, 2 to 3 hours more. Remove brisket from smoker and let rest for 1 to 2 hours. Slice brisket against the grain and serve with barbecue sauce as desired. Enjoy!

Smoked Ultimate Flank Steak
Serves: 3
Cooking Time:1 ½ Hours
Ingredients:
- 1 1/2-2 lbs flank steaks
- 1/4 cup madeira wine
- 1/4 cup olive oil
- 1 tbsp. lemon pepper
- 1/2 tbsp. black pepper
- 1 tbsp. sea salt or 1 tbsp. kosher salt
- 1/8 cup soy sauce or 1/8 cup Worcestershire sauce
- 3 garlic cloves, crushed
- 1/2 tbsp. marjoram

Directions:
Put the steak in a bag. Add in the rest of the ingredients, and shake around to coat the steak evenly. Allow the steak to marinate for 6 to 1hours. During the time it's marinating, be sure to turn the steak over at least four times. Smoke the steak. Once done serve with preferred sides.

Delicious Maple Glazed Smoked Bacon
Serves: 6
Cooking Time: 15 Hours
Ingredients:
- 1 and a ½ gallons of water
- 2 tablespoon of sodium nitrate
- 1 cup of sugar based curing mix
- 2 cups of coarse salt
- 1 cup of brown sugar
- 1 , 14 pound whole pork belly
Directions:
Take a large sized kettle and add water, sodium nitrate, brown sugar, curing salt and maple syrup Mix well and bring the whole mixture to a boil over high-heat Cook for 15 minutes until everything is dissolved Pour the mixture into a 5 gallon plastic bucket and allow it to cool down to room temperature Cut the pork belly against the grain into 4-6 slabs and transfer to your bring bucket, place a weight on top if needed to fully submerge them Cover and allow them to refrigerate for 7 days When ready to smoke, remove the pork from the brine mix and rinse under cold water Allow the pieces to stand under open air/fan for 1-2 hours until dry Smoke the slabs at 110 degree Fahrenheit for 8-12 hours, making sure to keep adding more chips after every 1 hour Remove, slice and serve!

Delicious Smoked Pork Belly
Serves: 10
Cooking Time: 15 Minutes
Ingredients:
- 5 lbs. pork belly
- 1 c. dry rub
- 3 tbsps. olive oil
- For sauce:
- 2 tbsps. honey
- 3 tbsps. butter
- 1 c. BBQ sauce
Directions:
Preheat the smoker to 250 F/1 C. Add pork cubes, dry rub, and olive oil into the bowl and mix well. Place pork cubes into the smoker and smoke uncover for hours. Remove pork cubes from smoker and place on foil pan. Add honey, butter and BBQ sauce and stir well. Cover pan with foil and place back into the smoker. Cook pork for another 90 minutes. After 90 minutes remove the foil. Close the lid to the smoker and smoke for 15 minutes or until sauce thickens. Serve and enjoy.

Mole-mole Baby Back Ribs

Serves: 9
Cooking Time: 10 Hours
Ingredients:
- 3 racks baby back ribs
- 2 tablespoons extra virgin olive oil
- 2 tablespoons garlic, minced
- 1 cup honey,½ cup balsamic vinegar
- ¼ cup soy sauce
- ½ cup espresso
- 1 tablespoon celery salt
- 2 tablespoons garlic powder
- 2 tablespoons oregano, ground
- ½ tablespoons cocoa powder

Directions:
Place all Ingredients: in a mixing bowl and allow to marinate in the fridge overnight.Preheat the smoker to 2250F. Place water in the water pan and add your favorite wood chips into the side tray. Put the meat–marinate and all–in a heat-proof dish and place in the smoker.Adjust the cooking time for 10 hours. Constantly, brush the meat with the marinade.

Glazed Pork Tenderloin

Serves: 6
Cooking Time: 2 1/2 Hours
Ingredients:
- 1 cup apple cider
- 1 1/2 cups orange juice (divided)
- 2 teaspoons rubbed sage (or 1 teaspoon ground sage)
- 2 tablespoons butter (melted)
- 1 teaspoon kosher salt (divided)
- 1/2 teaspoon freshly ground black pepper (divided)
- 1 pork tenderloin (4 to 5 pounds)
- 1/4 cup honey

Directions:
Pour apple cider and cup orange juice into the Masterbuilt smoker's water pan. Place maple or apple wood chips in the smoker's wood tray and preheat smoker to 225°F. Mix sage into butter, brush over tenderloin and season with about half of the salt and pepper. Place tenderloin on smoker grate and smoke for about 1 hour. Mix honey and remaining 1/2 cup orange juice, brush over tenderloin and season with remaining salt and pepper. Continue smoking tenderloin until the internal temperature of the meat reaches 145°F, about 1 1/2 hour more. Add wood chips to the wood tray as necessary. Remove tenderloin from smoker, cover loosely with aluminum foil and let rest for about 30 minutes. Slice tenderloin as desired to serve. Enjoy!

Smoked Prime Rib

Serves: 12
Cooking Time: 8 Hours
Ingredients:
- 6 tablespoons salt
- 3 tablespoons black pepper
- 2 tablespoons brown sugar
- 2 tablespoons garlic powder
- 8 pounds prime rib roast

Directions:
Preheat the smoker to 2500F. Add water to the water pan and the preferred wood chips into the side tray. In a bowl, mix all the Ingredients: and make sure that the prime rib roast is evenly coated with the spice rub. Place on the middle rack and adjust the cooking timer to 8 hours. Once cooked, remove from the smoker and allow to cool before slicing.

Smoked Loin Chops

Serves: 6
Cooking Time: 1 Hour
Ingredients:
- 6 loin chops, cut 2 inches thick
- 4 cups crushed ice
- ½ gallon hot water
- ½ cup Kosher Salt
- ½ cup brown sugar

Directions:
In a large, non-reactive bowl, combine water, salt and sugar and stir until dissolved. Add crushed ice to chill brine and pork chops when the ice has melted. Allow to sit in the refrigerator for at least 1 hour and up to overnight. Preheat the smoker to 225°F. Remove the chops from the brine, pat dry and allow to sit at room temperature for 30 minutes before smoking. Place the loin chops directly on the smoker grates. Smoke the chops until the internal temperature reaches 145°F. Remove the chops from the smoker and allow them to rest 10-15 minutes before serving.

Flavorful Beef Brisket

Serves: 12
Cooking Time: 8½ Hours
Ingredients:
- 1 (8-10lb) brisket, untrimmed
- 3 tbsp ancho chili powder
- 2 tbsp kosher salt
- 1 tbsp dried oregano, crushed
- 1 tbsp celery seeds
- 1 tbsp ground allspice
- 1 tbsp ground coriander
- 1 tbsp garlic powder
- 1 tbsp ground mustard
- 1 tbsp smoked Spanish paprika
- 1 tbsp freshly ground black pepper
- 2 cups apple juice

Directions:
In a bowl, add all ingredients except brisket and apple juice, mix well. Rub the brisket with the spice mixture generously. With a plastic wrap, cover the brisket and refrigerate 8-24 hours. Soak pecan wood chips in water for at least 1-2 hours. Remove the brisket from the refrigerator and set aside in room temperature for about 1 hour before cooking. Preheat the smoker to 225 degrees F, using charcoal and pecan wood chips. In a spray bottle, place the apple juice and set aside. Place the brisket on the smoker, fat-side and cook, covered for about 4 hours, spraying the brisket with apple juice after every 2 hours. Now, wrap the brisket with a piece of foil and cook for about 3½-4½ hours. Transfer the brisket onto a cutting board and set aside for about 20 minutes before serving. With a sharp knife, cut the brisket in desired sized slices and serve.

Smoked Pastrami Burgers

Serves: 2
Cooking Time: 20-30 Minutes
Ingredients:
- 1 lb ground chuck or other 80/20 ground beef
- 2 tsp Basic Beef 4 oz thinly sliced pastrami
- 2 hamburger buns
- 4 Tbsp mayonnaise
- 2 Tbsp ketchup
- 1 tsp pickle relish
- 2 slices Swiss cheese
- 1-2 leaves of lettuce
- 2 slices tomato

Directions:
Preheat the smoker to 250°F. Form hamburger into two patties and place in a shallow aluminum pan and season both sides with Basic Beef Rub. Place the pan in the smoker and cook 15-20 minutes or until the internal temperature reaches 150°F. Remove the burgers from the smoker and top with pastrami. Return to the smoker until the internal temperature of the hamburgers reaches 160°F. Remove from smoker and top with cheese. Cover lightly with aluminum foil and allow the burgers to rest for 5 minutes. In a small bowl, combine mayonnaise, ketchup and relish. Spread the mayonnaise mixture on all of the toasted buns. Top bottom bun with burger, garnishes of your choice, and the remaining bun.

Glazed Meatloaf

Serves: 12
Cooking Time: 3 Hours
Ingredients:
- 1/2 cup milk
- 1 cup quick-cooking oats
- 1/4 cup ketchup
- 1/4 cup barbecue sauce
- 1 tablespoon apple cider vinegar
- 1 tablespoon soy sauce
- 1 teaspoon chipotle chili powder
- 2 teaspoons garlic powder
- 2 teaspoons onion powder
- 1 tablespoon barbecue sauce
- Kosher salt and freshly ground black pepper, to taste
- 2 pounds ground chuck
- 1 pound ground pork
- 1 onion (finely chopped)
- 2 eggs (lightly beaten)
- 2 tablespoons Worcestershire sauce
- 4 garlic cloves (minced)

Directions:
Place hickory wood chips in the Masterbuilt smoker's wood tray and preheat smoker to 275°F. Pour milk over oats and let stand for about 10 minutes. Whisk ketchup, barbecue sauce, vinegar, soy sauce and chipotle chili powder until smooth and season to taste with salt and pepper. Divide mixture in half and set aside. Crumble ground beef and ground pork in a large bowl. Add eggs, Worcestershire sauce, garlic and oat mixture and knead together by hand until thoroughly combined. Form meat mixture into a tightly packed loaf and set on a well-greased rimmed baking sheet. Brush meatloaf with half of the ketchup mixture and season to taste with salt and pepper. Place baking sheet on smoker grate and smoke for about 90 minutes. Brush meatloaf with remaining ketchup mixture and continue smoking until the internal temperature of the meat reaches 160°F, about 90 minutes more. Add wood chips to the wood tray as necessary. Remove baking sheet from smoker, cover meatloaf with aluminum foil and let rest for about 10 minutes. Cut meatloaf into slices as desired to serve. Enjoy!

Bbq Pulled Pork
Serves: 16
Cooking Time: 8 Hours
Ingredients:
- 8-pound pork butt roast, fat trimmed
- 2 tablespoons onion powder
- 2 tablespoons garlic powder
- 1/4 cup sea salt
- 1/2 cup brown sugar
- 1 tablespoon ground black pepper
- 1 tablespoon paprika
- 1 tablespoon dried thyme
- 1 tablespoon dried oregano
- 6 tablespoons yellow mustard
- BBQ sauce for serving
- Burger rolls for serving

Directions:
Rinse pork, pat dry and then rub with mustard. Stir together remaining ingredients and sprinkle the spice mixture all over the pork until evenly coated. Transfer pork roast into a foil pan, fat-side up, cover with plastic wrap and let marinate in the refrigerator for 8 to 12 hours. Then remove pork from the pan and let rest at room temperature for 30 minutes. In the meantime, plug in the smoker, fill its tray with hickory woodchips and water pan halfway through, and place dripping pan above the water pan. Then open the top vent, shut with lid and use temperature settings to preheat smoker at 225 degrees F. Place pork on smoker rack, insert a meat thermometer, then shut with lid and set the timer to smoke for 8 hours or more until meat thermometer registers an internal temperature of 190 degrees F. Check vent of smoker every hour and add more woodchips and water to maintain temperature and smoke. When done, transfer pork to a cutting board, let rest for 20 minutes and then shred with two forks. Evenly divide shredded pork on buns, top with BBQ sauce and serve.

Hot-stuffed Pork Chop
Serves: 6
Cooking Time: 6 Hours
Ingredients:
- 1 cup cooked rice
- 1-pound pork sausages
- ½ teaspoon Cajun seasoning
- ½ teaspoon black pepper
- 6 pork chops, center cut into ¾ inch thick resembling a butterfly

Directions:
Mix cooked rice and sausages. Season with Cajun seasoning and black pepper. Stuff the pork chop pockets with the rice and sausage mixture. Preheat the smoker to 2250F. Place water in the water pan and add your favorite wood chips into the side tray. Line the middle tray with aluminum foil and place the pork chop on top. Adjust the cooking time to hours.

Sweet And Savory Classical Pork
Serves: 8
Cooking Time: 4-5 Hours
Ingredients:
- 2 slabs baby back ribs
- ½ cup brown sugar
- ¼ cup smoked paprika
- 1 and ½ tablespoons salt
- 1 tablespoon ground garlic powder
- 2 teaspoons garlic powder
- 2 teaspoons onion powder
- ½ teaspoon cayenne pepper
- Apple liquid for basting

Directions:
Wash the meat well and lay the slabs of meat on a clean surface Take a bowl and add the dry ingredients, mix well Generously sprinkle the mixture all over the meat and coat them well Let them sit for 30 minutes Take your drip pan and add water, cover with aluminum foil. Pre-heat your smoker to 22degrees F Use water fill water pan halfway through and place it over drip pan. Add wood chips to the side tray. Transfer meat to smoker and smoke for 3 hours While the meat is being cooked, take a small bowl and make the sauce and add in the wet ingredients Once done, transfer to meat to a foil tent and let it cool While the meat is cooling, make sure to keep basting it with the prepared sauce Wrap the meat using foil and transfer to the smoker, smoke for t to 1 and ½ hours more until the internal temperature reaches 160 degrees F Serve and enjoy! Enjoy!

Apple Smoked Pork Loin
Serves:8
Cooking Time:4 Hours 50 Minutes
Ingredients:
- Whole boneless pork loin (6.0-lbs, 2.72-kgs)
- Chines 5-spice powder – 1 tablespoon
- Sea salt – 2 teaspoons
- Freshly cracked black pepper – 1 teaspoon
- Garlic powder – ½ teaspoon
- Nutmeg _ ¼ teaspoon
- Safflower oil – 1 tablespoon
- Preheat smoker to 225°f (107°c) using oak wood chips
- Add a 50/50 apple juice and water mix in the bowl of our smoker base.
- Add apple wood chips to the tray

Directions:
First, rinse the pork loin in cool water. Pat dry with kitchen paper towels. Trim off excess fat or silver skin leaving a ¼ -ins (0.6cms) of fat on the meat. Transfer the loin to a sheet pan. In a bowl, combine the Chinese 5-spice powder with the sea salt, cracked black pepper, garlic powder, nutmeg, and oil. Rub the spice mix all over the pork loin and allow the meat to rest at room temperature for up to 1 hour. Put the pork inside the smoker on the middle rack, fat side facing upwards. Close the door and set the timer for 3 hours. When the pork has been smoking for 2 hours, check the meat. It needs to read an internal temperature of 155°F (68°C). Check the pork every 45 minutes, adding additional wood chips as necessary. When the pork is smoked to the correct temperature, transfer it to a chopping board and tent with foil. Set the meat aside to rest for 20 minutes. Slice, and serve with slaw.

Smoked Apple Ribs
Serves: 2
Cooking Time: 10 Hours
Ingredients:
- 2 full racks of ribs
- 2 bags of brown sugar
- 1 small bottle of apple juice

Directions:
Combine all Ingredients: in a Ziploc bag and allow to marinate in the fridge overnight. Preheat the smoker to 50F. Place apple juice in the water pan and add hickory wood chips into the side tray. Place the ribs in the middle tray. Adjust the cooking time to 10 hours. Constantly, brush the meat with the marinade.

Glorious Lamb Shoulder
Serves: 10
Cooking Time: 7 Hours
Ingredients:

- 1 (7lb) boneless lamb shoulder, excess fat trimmed
- 1½ tbsp ancho chili powder
- ½ tbsp dried oregano
- ½ tbsp dry mustard powder
- ½ tbsp ground allspice
- ½ tbsp ground coriander
- ½ tbsp garlic powder
- ½ tbsp celery salt
- ½ tbsp smoked sweet paprika
- 2 tbsp canola oil
- 1-2 cups BBQ sauce
- Salt and freshly ground black pepper, to taste

Directions:
In a bowl, add all the ingredients except the lamb, canola oil and BBQ sauce and mix well. Rub the lamb shoulder with the spice mixture generously. Roll the meat and with kitchen string, tie at 1-inch intervals. Cover the lamb shoulder and refrigerate overnight. Remove the lamb shoulder from refrigerator and coat with oil evenly. Set aside in room temperature for about 30 minutes before cooking. Preheat the smoker to 225 degrees F, using charcoal and cherry wood chips. Place the lamb shoulder into the smoker, fat side up and cook for about 6-7 hours. In the last 30 minutes of the cooking, coat the shoulder with some of the BBQ sauce. Transfer the lamb shoulder onto a cutting board and and discard the kitchen twine. Set aside for about 20 minutes before serving. With a sharp knife, cut the leg of lamb in desired sized slices and serve.

Smoked Beef Brisket With White Wine Marinade (masterbuilt Electric Smoker)
Serves: 8
Cooking Time: 3 Hours And 40 Minutes
Ingredients:
- MARINADE
- 1 1/4 cups dry white wine
- 2/3 cup soy sauce
- 1/4 cup brown sugar
- 1/2 tsp garlic powder
- 4 lbs. beef brisket

Directions:
Combine all Ingredients: in a shallow container. Place the beef, toss, cover and marinate overnight. Remove from marinade and pat dry on a kitchen towel. Preheat your electric smoker to 225°F. When it is ready, add some water to the removable pan that is usually on the bottom shelf. Fill the side "drawer" with dry wood chips. Smoke at about 2 degrees for 30 minutes per pound, checking the temperature at 45 minutes with a meat thermometer. Remove from heat when the internal temperature is at 135 degrees using a meat thermometer. Remove from Smoker and let cool for 10 - 15 minutes. Slice and serve.

Smoked Molasses Lamb Chops
Serves: 4
Cooking Time: 10 Minutes
Ingredients:
- ½ c. dry white wine
- 1 c. molasses or honey
- 4 tbsp. minced fresh mint
- Salt
- Pepper
- 2 lbs. lamb

Directions:
Combine molasses, wine, fresh mint, salt, and pepper to taste in a bowl. Season cut side of boned lamb with salt and pepper, then spread with molasses mixture; roll and tie lamb. Brush outer surface with molasses mixture. Preheat smoker to 225°F. Lay your meat on the top of rack then give smoke until internal temperature reaches 1°F. Remove the chops and let cool 15 minutes before serving.

Smoked Molasses Ribeye Beef Steak (masterbuilt Electric Smoker)
Serves: 6
Cooking Time: 1 Hour And 20 Minutes
Ingredients:
- 3 lbs beef steak grass fed
- 1 cup beef broth
- 3 Tbsp molasses
- 2 Tbsp red wine vinegar
- 2 Tbsp balsamic vinegar
- Salt and ground pepper

Directions:
Sprinkle the beef steak with salt and pepper, and rub well from all sides. Mix the beef broth, molasses, red wine vinegar and balsamic vinegar in a bowl. Pour the molasses mixture over the beef steak. Cover and refrigerate for hours or overnight. Remove meat from fridge and pat dry on a kitchen paper. Preheat your electric smoker to 225°F. When it is ready, add some water to the removable pan that is usually on the bottom shelf. Fill the side "drawer" with dry wood chips. Place the ribeye in the Masterbuilt and cook until the internal temperature is 120 degrees F for a medium rare steak. The smoking time took about 50 minutes, but remember the thinner the steak, the faster it will reach a higher internal temperature. Remove from the smoker and let rest for 10 - 15 minutes before serving.

Rosemary Lamb Chops
Serves: 12
Cooking Time: 50 Minutes
Ingredients:

- 12 lamb loin chops
- 3 teaspoons salt
- 1 tablespoon rosemary, chopped
- ¼ cup olive oil
- ¼ cup Jeff's rub

Directions:
Sprinkle salt on top of chops and place in the refrigerator for 2 hours. Meanwhile, stir together oil and rosemary and let sit for 1 hour. After 2 hours, brush rosemary mixture on lamb chops and then sprinkle with the rub. Plug in the smoker, fill its tray with hickory woodchips and water pan halfway through, and place dripping pan above the water pan. Then open the top vent, shut with lid and use temperature settings to preheat smoker at 22degrees F. Place lamb chops on smoker rack, insert a meat thermometer, then shut with lid and set the timer to smoke for 50 minutes or more until meat thermometer registers an internal temperature of 1 degrees F. When done, wrap lamb chops in aluminum foil for 10 minutes and then serve.

Bbq Lamb Chops
Serves: 4
Cooking Time: 2 Hours And 30 Minutes
Ingredients:
- 4 lamb chops
- ½ teaspoon garlic powder
- 1 ½ teaspoon salt
- ½ teaspoon ground black pepper
- 1 tablespoon paprika
- 1 ½ teaspoon mustard powder
- ¼ cup apple cider vinegar
- ½ cup BBQ sauce

Directions:
Pour vinegar in a large baking dish, add lamb chops and let soak for 30 minutes. Then drain the chops and sprinkle with remaining ingredients except for BBQ sauce until evenly coated on all sides. Plug in the smoker, fill its tray with mesquite woodchips and water pan halfway through, and place dripping pan above the water pan. Then open the top vent, shut with lid and use temperature settings to preheat smoker at 225 degrees F. Place chicken on smoker rack, place meat thermometer, then shut with lid and set the timer to smoke for 2 hours or more until meat thermometer register an internal temperature of 130 degrees F. Check vent of smoker every hour and add more woodchips and water to maintain temperature and smoke. Then brush BBQ sauce on all sides of lamb chops and continue smoking or until the internal temperature of lamb chops reach to 140 degrees F. Serve straightaway.

Smoked Short Ribs
Serves: 6
Cooking Time: 20 Minutes
Ingredients:
- 3 lbs. short ribs
- ½ c. dry rub
- ¼ c. olive oil
- ½ c. ground black pepper
- ½ c. kosher salt
- For spritz:
- 1/3 c. Worcestershire sauce
- 1/3 c. dry red wine
- 1/3 c. beef broth
- For braising:
- 2 tbsps. butter
- 1 tbsp. rub
- 1 c. beef broth
- 1 c. dry red wine

Directions:
Heat your smoker to 225 F/7 C with wood chips. Season meat with black pepper and salt. Place seasoned ribs into the smoker for 2 hours. After 2 hours spritz ribs after every 30 minutes for 2 hours. Combine together all braising ingredients into the aluminum pan. Add ribs to the aluminum pan and cover the pan with foil. Place pan in the smoker and cook for about 2 hours. Once internal temperature reaches 205 F/96 C then removes meat from smoker and set aside for 15 minutes. Remove ribs from pan and serve.

Bacon-wrapped Fatty
Serves: 12
Cooking Time: 2 1/2 Hours
Ingredients:
- 1 pound sliced bacon
- 1 pound ground beef
- 8 ounces ground pork
- 1/4 cup finely minced onion
- 4 ounces sliced Colby or mild cheddar cheese
- 1 teaspoon kosher salt, plus more to taste
- 1/2 teaspoon freshly ground black pepper, plus more to taste

Directions:
Place hickory wood chips in the Masterbuilt smoker's wood tray and preheat smoker to 250°F. On a rimmed baking sheet lined with aluminum foil, tightly weave bacon into a square mat. Mix ground beef, ground pork, salt and pepper and spread over bacon weave. Sprinkle onion up the center of the ground meat and top with cheese slices, leaving a border of about 1" at the ends. Season entire surface of ground meat to taste with salt and pepper. Roll ground beef into a log in the center of the bacon weave, pressing ends and seam to seal. Roll up bacon weave to cover the ground beef, tucking in ends as much as possible. If desired, tie fatty with kitchen twine. Place baking sheet on smoker grate and smoke until the internal temperature of the meat reaches 165°F, about 2 1/2 hours. Add wood chips to the wood tray as necessary. Remove baking sheet from smoker, cover fatty loosely with aluminum foil and let rest for about 10 minutes. Remove kitchen twine from fatty as necessary. Cut fatty into slices as desired to serve. Enjoy!

Smoked Tri-tip Roast
Serves: 6-8
Cooking Time:3 Hours 20 Minutes
Ingredients:
- Tri-tip roast, no fat cap (2.5-lbs, 1.13-kgs)
- Chili powder – 1½ teaspoons
- Sea salt – 2 teaspoons
- Brown sugar – 1 teaspoon
- Black pepper – 1 teaspoon
- Onion powder – 1 teaspoon
- Espresso powder – 1 teaspoon
- Garlic powder – ½ teaspoon
- Add a bowl of water to the bottom of the smoker and add cherry wood chips to the side tray. Preheat to 225°f (107°c).

Directions:
First, prepare the rub. Combine the chili powder, salt, sugar, pepper, onion powder, espresso powder, and garlic powder. Cover the outside of the roast with the rub, set aside to rest for 45 minutes. Arrange the roast in the center of the smoker and arrange a drip pan on the rack below. Close the door, open the vent and smoke for a couple of hours until the internal temperature registers 135°f (57°c). The wood chips or water may need to be replenished during this time. Take the roast out of the smoker and tent with aluminum foil, set aside for half an hour. Thinly slice and serve.

Beefy Jalapeno Fatty
Serves: 6
Cooking Time: 45 Minutes
Ingredients:
- 1-pound ground beef
- ½ cup cream cheese
- ½ cup jalapeno
- Salt and pepper to taste
- 2 packs bacon

Directions:
In a mixing bowl, add the ground beef, cream cheese, jalapeno, salt and pepper. Mix until well combined. Use your hands to form logs with the beef mixture. Wrap bacon around the beef logs. Place in the fridge for about hours to solidify. Preheat the smoker to 2250F. Add apple juice in the water pan and put hickory wood chips into the side tray. Place the beef jalapeno fatty in the rack and smoke for 4minutes.

Poor Man's Burnt Ends

Serves: 9
Cooking Time: 8 Hours
Ingredients:
- 3 pounds beef chuck roast
- 2 teaspoons salt
- 2 teaspoons black pepper
- 1 cup commercial barbecue sauce

Directions:
In a mixing bowl, combine all Ingredients: and marinate in the fridge for at least an hour. Preheat the smoker to 50F. Add apple cider vinegar to the water pan and mesquite wood chips into the side tray. Place the marinated chuck roast on the middle of the smoker. Adjust the cooking time to 8 hours.

Welcoming Pork Shoulder

Serves: 16
Cooking Time: 8 Hours
Ingredients:
- For Roast:
- 1 (8lb) pork shoulder roast
- 4 cups apple cider
- 1 chopped onion
- For Rub:
- 5 tbsp light brown sugar
- 5 tbsp white sugar
- 2 tbsp paprika
- 1 tbsp garlic powder
- 1 tbsp onion powder
- 1 tbsp freshly ground black pepper
- Salt, to taste

Directions:
In a bowl, mix together all the rub ingredients. In a large bowl, add about ¼ cup of rub mixture and apple cider and ix well. Add pork shoulder and coat with mixture evenly. Refrigerate, covered for about 12 hours. Soak apple wood chips in water for at least 1 hour. Preheat the smoker to 210 degrees F, using apple wood chips. Remove pork shoulder from bowl. In water pan of smoker, add cider marinade, onion and about ¼ cup of rub mixture. Rub the pork shoulder with remaining rub mixture evenly. Arrange pork shoulder on the center of smoker and cook for about 8 hours.

Transfer the pork shoulder onto a cutting board and set aside for about 30 minutes before serving. With 2 forks, shred the pork shoulder and serve.

Memphis Bbq Spaghetti

Serves: 8
Cooking Time: 2 1/2 Hours
Ingredients:
- 2 tablespoons vegetable oil
- 1 medium yellow onion (diced)
- 1 red bell pepper (diced)
- 2 garlic cloves (minced)
- 2 teaspoons sweet paprika
- 1 teaspoon kosher salt, plus more to taste
- 1/2 teaspoon freshly ground black pepper, plus more to taste
- 1/2 teaspoon ground allspice
- 1/2 teaspoon ground cinnamon
- 1/2 teaspoon ground mustard
- 1 can (28 ounces) crushed tomatoes
- 1 can (6 ounces) tomato paste
- 2 cups water
- 1/4 cup brown sugar
- 1/4 cup red wine vinegar
- 1 pound (about 2 cups) leftover smoked pulled pork
- 1 package (1 pound) dried spaghetti

Directions:
Heat oil in a large saucepan or nonstick skillet over medium-high heat and sauté onion and bell pepper until softened, stirring occasionally, about 5 minutes. Add garlic and cook about minute more, stirring constantly. Add paprika, salt, pepper, allspice, cinnamon and ground mustard and stir to coat. Add tomatoes, tomato paste, water, brown sugar and vinegar to onion mixture and season to taste with salt and pepper. Heat sauce to a boil, stirring occasionally. Reduce heat and simmer for about hours, uncovered, adding more water if necessary (sauce should remain thin). Prepare spaghetti according to package directions and drain. Add pulled pork to sauce and stir until heated through. Divide spaghetti among 8 bowls and top with the sauce. Serve immediately and enjoy!

Kansas City Burnt Ends

Serves: 6
Cooking Time: 6 To 7 Hours
Ingredients:
- 1 brisket point (4 to 5 pounds)
- 1/2 cup brown sugar
- 1/2 cup white sugar
- 1/4 cup kosher salt, plus more to taste
- 1/4 cup chili powder
- 1/4 cup coarsely ground black pepper, plus more to taste
- 3 tablespoons paprika
- 3 tablespoons ground cumin
- 2 teaspoons cayenne pepper, plus more to taste
- 1 tablespoon garlic powder
- 1 tablespoon onion powder
- 1 tablespoon butter
- 1/4 cup minced onion
- 4 garlic cloves (minced)
- 1 cup ketchup
- 1 cup tomato sauce
- 3/4 cup red wine vinegar
- 1/4 cup molasses
- 1 teaspoon hickory-flavored liquid smoke, plus more to taste
- Dash cinnamon or ginger

Directions:
Pour 2 cups water into the Masterbuilt smoker's water pan. Place hickory or cherry wood chips in the smoker's wood tray and preheat smoker to 225°F. Thoroughly rinse brisket point with cold water, pat dry with paper towels and trim fat to 1/4". Mix brown sugar, white sugar, salt, chili powder, black pepper, paprika, cumin and cayenne pepper. Set aside about 1/3 of the spice mixture to make the sauce. Add garlic powder and onion powder to remaining spice mixture and rub over brisket. Place brisket fat-side down on smoker grate and smoke until the internal temperature of the meat reaches 175°F, about 5 hours. Add wood chips to the wood tray as necessary. Wrap brisket in aluminum foil and continue smoking until the internal temperature of the meat reaches 200°F, 1 to 2 hours more. Add wood chips to the wood tray as necessary. Meanwhile, for the sauce, melt butter in a medium saucepan over medium-low heat and sauté onion until tender, about minutes, stirring frequently. Add garlic and sauté about 1 minute more, stirring constantly. Add ketchup, tomato sauce, vinegar, molasses, liquid smoke and reserved spice mixture and season to taste with salt and pepper. Heat sauce to a boil, stirring occasionally. Reduce heat and simmer to thicken to desired consistency, stirring occasionally, 10 to 15 minutes. Remove wrapped brisket from smoker and let rest for about 30 minutes. Remove foil from brisket, saving the cooking juices. Chop brisket into 1" chunks and toss with the cooking juices. Serve burnt ends with the sauce and enjoy!

Perfect Smoked Beef Burgers

Serves: 6
Cooking Time: 1 Hour 30 Minutes
Ingredients:
- 2 pounds ground beef
- 2 teaspoons salt
- 1 and ½ teaspoon ground black pepper
- 6 slices American Cheese
- 6 burger rolls, halved

Directions:
Take your drip pan and add water, cover with aluminum foil. Pre-heat your smoker to 250 degrees F Use water fill water pan halfway through and place it over drip pan. Add wood chips to the side tray Take a bowl and add ground beef, salt, and pepper. Mix well and prepare 6 patties Transfer patties to smoker rack and smoke for about 1 and ½ hours until the internal temperature reaches 160 degrees F Top each patty with cheese and let it smoke for 1minutes more until cheese melts Serve in burger rolls and enjoy!

Smoked Pork Loin With Beer-anise Marinade (masterbuilt Electric Smoker)

Serves: 6
Cooking Time: 3 Hours And 15 Minutes
Ingredients:
- MARINADE
- 1/4 cup honey
- 1 1/2 cups dark beer
- 2 tsp Anise seeds
- 1Tbs fresh thyme finely chopped
- Salt and pepper to taste
- PORK
- 3 lbs pork loin

Directions:
Combine all Ingredients: for the marinade in a bowl. Place the pork with marinade mixture in a resealable plastic bag. Refrigerate for several hours, or overnight. Place the water in the pan at the bottom of your smoker. Fill the drawer or tray with wood chips. Preheat your smoker (use a 2-zone or Indirect setup) to about 225°F. Remove the pork from marinade (reserve marinade for later) and place on kitchen towel. Place meat in the smoker and smoke till the internal temperature is 145F, about 2 1/2 to 3 hours. Remove the meat and let rest for 10 minutes before slicing. Serve hot or cold.

Triple Smoked Burger
Serves: 1
Cooking Time: 12 – 15 Minutes
Ingredients:
- 1/2 cup mayonnaise
- 1 1/2 tsp. Dijon mustard
- 2 tsp. minced chipotle in adobo, including some sauce, divided
- 8 bacon slices
- 1 1/2 lb.s ground beef chuck (not lean)
- 2 tsp. sweet smoked paprika
- 1 large red onion, cut into 4 (1/2-inch) thick rounds, each stuck with a wooden pick to keep it together
- 1 firm-ripe avocado, quartered lengthwise, peeled, and cut lengthwise into 1/3-inch thick slices
- Olive oil for brushing on onion and avocado
- 4 hamburger buns, grilled or toasted

Directions:
Puree your mayo, tbsp. of chipotle, and mustard in a blender. Place in a small bowl. Cook the bacon in a small skillet over some medium heat. Transfer the bacon to some paper towels to drain once they're crispy. Mix the beef with 1 tsp. of salt, 1 tbsp. chipotle, and paprika. Do the exact same for the other patties. Brush some olive oil on the avocado and onion. Do this for both sides. Place avocado slices on the rack of the smoker. Turn them only once, giving each of Place the patties on the smoker. Halfway through flip them over. Spread some sauce on the buns and top with cilantro, lettuce, avocado, bacon, onion, and the patties.

Deviled Ham Crackers
Serves: 24
Cooking Time: 30 Minutes Plus 1 Hour Refrigerating
Ingredients:
- 12 ounces (about 1 1/2 cups) leftover cubed smoked ham
- 1/4 cup mayonnaise
- 1 tablespoon minced sweet onion
- 1 garlic clove (minced)
- 1 tablespoon yellow or Dijon mustard
- 1 teaspoon smoked paprika, plus more for garnish
- 1/2 teaspoon freshly ground black pepper, plus more to taste
- Milk, as needed
- 1 celery stalk (diced)
- 24 cocktail crackers
- 6 cherry tomatoes (halved)
- Celery leaves, for garnish

Directions:
Pulse ham, mayonnaise, onion, garlic, mustard, paprika and pepper in a food processor to desired consistency. Add milk while processing as needed. Stir celery into spread and refrigerate until chilled through, about 1 hour. Scoop spread onto crackers, sprinkle with paprika and garnish with cherry tomato halves or celery leaf sprigs. Serve immediately and enjoy!

New York Strip Steak With Bourbon Butter
Serves: 2
Cooking Time:1 Hour 30 Minutes
Ingredients:
- 2 New York strip steaks
- Salted butter, room temperature – ½ cup
- Fresh parsley, chopped – 1 tablespoon
- 1 green onion top, minced
- Bourbon – 2 tablespoons
- Smoked paprika – 1 teaspoon
- Steak rub
- Preheat smoker to 225°f (107°c) using pecan wood chips

Directions:
First, prepare the butter. Combine the butter, parsley, green onion, bourbon, and paprika in a small bowl. Transfer to a piece of plastic wrap, shape into a log and roll tightly. Chill until ready to use. Season the steaks with steak rub and place in the smoker. Cook for approximately 60 minutes until the internal temperature registers 130°f (55°c), for medium-rare. Place a skillet over high heat. When the steak is cooked to your liking, sear each piece on both sides in the skillet. Top with a couple slices of bourbon butter and serve straight away.

Pit Smoked Pork Shoulder
Serves: 6
Cooking Time: 12 Hours
Ingredients:
- 2 pork shoulder, roasts
- Shoulder Rub:
- 1/4 cup brown sugar
- 1/2 cup white sugar
- 1/2 cup paprika
- 1/3 cup garlic powder
- 2 tsp. white salt
- 1 tbsp. chili powder
- 1 tbsp. cayenne pepper
- 2 tsp. black pepper
- 1 tbsp. dried oregano
- 1 tbsp. cumin
- Injection Liquid:
- 3/4 cup apple juice
- 1/2 cup water
- 1/2 cup sugar
- 3 tsp. salt
- 2 tsp. Worcestershire sauce

Directions:
Mix all of your spices together in a small bowl. In a medium sized bowl, whisk together your ingredients for the injector. You want the salt and sugar to be completely dissolved. Take your roasts out of the fridge. Inject both roasts with your liquid. Pat your roasts with the dry rub you made. Allow the roasts to sit for one and a half hours. Place pork roasts in the smoker. Once they're done, shred finely to make pulled pork.

Cider Brined Pulled Pork

Serves: 16
Cooking Time: 12 To 15 Hours
Ingredients:

- 1 bone-in pork shoulder roast (8 to 10 pounds)
- 1 quart apple cider, plus more if needed
- 1/3 cup white sugar
- 1/4 cup light brown sugar
- 2 tablespoons kosher salt
- 1 tablespoon freshly ground black pepper
- 1 tablespoon smoked paprika
- 1 tablespoon onion powder
- 1 tablespoon garlic powder
- 1 teaspoon chipotle chili powder
- 1 onion (chopped)
- 4 garlic cloves (minced)
- 2 tablespoons yellow mustard

Directions:
Place pork roast in a large plastic or glass container. Pour apple cider over roast to cover. In a small bowl, mix white sugar, brown sugar, salt, pepper, paprika, onion powder, garlic powder and chipotle chili powder. Add about 1/4 cup of the spice mixture to the container with the pork roast, reserving remaining spice mixture. Cover container and refrigerate for at least 1hours. Remove pork roast from brine, reserving brine. Pat roast dry with paper towels. Pour about 2 cups of the reserved brine into the Masterbuilt smoker's water pan and add onion and garlic. Place hickory wood chips in the smoker's wood tray and preheat smoker to 225°F. Brush mustard over pork roast and rub with reserved spice mixture. Stir any remaining spice mixture into the smoker's water pan. Place pork roast fat-side up on smoker grate and smoke until the internal temperature of the roast reaches 205°F, 12 to 15 hours. Add wood chips to the wood tray as necessary. Remove pork roast from smoker, cover loosely with aluminum foil and let rest for about 30 minutes. Strain juices from the water pan. Remove bone from roast and pull meat apart with two forks, removing gristle and fat as necessary. Stir strained juices into the pulled pork as desired to serve. Enjoy!

Smoked Hamburgers

Serves: 6
Cooking Time: 1 Hour And 30 Minutes
Ingredients:

- 2 pounds ground beef
- 2 teaspoons sea salt
- 1 ½ teaspoon ground black pepper
- 6 slices of American cheese
- 6 burger rolls, halved

Directions:
Plug in the smoker, fill its tray with hickory woodchips and water pan halfway through, and place dripping pan above the water pan. Then open the top vent, shut with lid and use temperature settings to preheat smoker at 5 degrees F. In the meantime, place ground beef into a large bowl, season with salt and black pepper and then shape mixture into 6 patties, each

about 6-ounce. Place patties on smoker rack, insert a meat thermometer, then shut with lid and set the timer to smoke for 1 to 1 ½ hour or more until meat thermometer registers an internal temperature of 160 degrees F. Check vent of smoker every hour and add more woodchips and water to maintain temperature and smoke. Then top each patty with a slice of cheese and continue smoking for 15 minutes or until cheese melts. Serve patties in burger rolls.

Smoked Goat Ribs With Garlic (masterbuilt Electric Smoker)

Serves: 6
Cooking Time: 4 Hours
Ingredients:

- 4 lbs. goat ribs, chopped into large pieces
- 8 cloves garlic finely chopped
- 1/4 cup olive oil
- 1/4 cup bone broth (preferably homemade)
- 2 tsp sweet paprika

Directions:
In a mortar pestle garlic with the salt. Place garlic in a large bowl together with remaining Ingredients:; toss goat to coat in marinade. Cover with plastic wrap and refrigerate overnight (the meat can be tough if it is not marinated well). Remove from fridge 1 hour before cooking. Preheat Masterbuilt Electric Smoker. Allow the smoker temperature to reach 22degrees Fahrenheit. When it is ready, add some water to the removable pan that is usually on the bottom shelf. Fill the side "drawer" with dry wood chips. Smoke it at 225 F until internal temperature reaches 150 F. Remove ribs from smoker and foil them in an aluminum foil. Place them again in a smoker, and smoke until the internal temperature reaches 170 F.

Smoked Steak Strips

Serves: 6
Cooking Time:1 Hour, 15 Minutes
Ingredients:

- 2 tsp. freshly ground black pepper
- 1 tbsp. garlic powder
- 1/2 tbsp. salt
- 1/4 tbsp. dry mustard
- 2 (12-ounce) New York strip or sirloin strip steaks, trimmed
- 2 tsp. Worcestershire sauce

Directions:
Combine the mustard, pepper, salt, and garlic powder all in one small bowl. Rub this on both sides of the steak strips. Place these coated pieces in a plastic bag. Toss in the Worcestershire sauce. Seal to coat the sauce all over the steak strips, and seal. Allow them to marinate in the fridge for half an hour. Arrange the steaks on the rack of the smoker. In a spare pan pour two cups of water into it, and place it in the smoker over a place that doesn't have direct heat. Close the lid of the smoker and allow steaks to smoke. Once the steaks are done serve over rice or with some steamed vegetables.

Lip-smackin' Short Ribs
Serves: 6
Cooking Time: 5 Hours
Ingredients:
- 6 lbs bone-in short ribs
- ¼ cup Basic Beef ¼ cup Worcestershire sauce

Directions:
Rinse the ribs and pat them dry with a paper towel. Trim any excess fat. Brush the ribs with the Worcestershire sauce. Coat the brushed ribs with the Basic Beef Rub. Refrigerate the ribs for at least 1 hour. After chilling, remove from the fridge and let it sit at room temperature for at least 30 minutes while preheating the smoker to 225°F. Set the ribs directly on the smoker grate, meat side up. Use the water pan for extra moist ribs. Smoke the ribs for 5 hours or until the internal temperature reaches 185°F Let it sit for a 15 minutes before serving. TIP: If you would like to sauce your beef short ribs, do so at the 3 hour mark to ensure the sauce has a chance to caramelize on the ribs.

Perfectly Smoked Beef Ribs
Serves: 4-6
Cooking Time: 5 Hours
Ingredients:
- 2 (3-4 lb.) racks beef back ribs
- 2 cups Basic Beef
- ½ cup of your favorite barbecue sauce, we like the Classic Texas Barbecue Sauce for this preparation

Directions:
Pat the ribs dry with a paper towel. With the bone side up, removing the membrane from the under-side of the beef ribs. This membrane is inedible and makes the beef ribs tough. Liberally season both sides of the ribs with the Basic Beef Rub. Let it sit for 30 minutes at room temperature while preheating the smoker to 225°F. Set the ribs on the smoker grate, rib side down. Smoke the ribs for 3 hours. Remove the ribs and wrap them in aluminum foil with 2 Tbsp of beer or apple juice in the foil. Return the ribs to the smoker for an additional 2 hours. Remove the wrapped ribs, unwrap them completely and discard the aluminum foil. Generously slather the smoked ribs with your favorite sauce. Return the ribs to the smoker for 1 hour or until the sauce caramelizes and the internal temperature reaches 185°F. Allow the ribs to rest 15 minutes before carving and serving.

Seasoned Chuck Roast
Serves: 12
Cooking Time: 6 Hours
Ingredients:
- 6 pounds chuck roast, boneless and fat trimmed
- 2 teaspoons onion powder
- 2 teaspoons garlic powder
- 1 ½ tablespoon sea salt
- 2 teaspoons ground black pepper
- 1 teaspoon brown sugar
- 1 teaspoon paprika
- 1/4 teaspoon cayenne

Directions:
Rinse roast, pat dry using paper towels and place in a large baking dish. Stir together remaining ingredients and rub this mixture on all sides of roast until evenly coated. Then plug in the smoker, fill its tray with hickory woodchips and water pan halfway through, and place dripping pan above the water pan. Then open the top vent, shut with lid and use temperature settings to preheat smoker at 250 degrees F. Place roast on smoker rack, insert a meat thermometer, then shut with lid and set the timer to smoke for 6 hours or until meat thermometer register an internal temperature of 160 degrees F. Check vent of smoker every hour and add more woodchips and water to maintain temperature and smoke. Then wrap roast completely with aluminum foil and let sit for 1 hour. Slice and serve roast as sandwiches.

Ribeye Steaks
Serves: 4
Cooking Time: 45 Minutes
Ingredients:
- 4 ribeye steaks, each about 1 ½ thick
- 1 ½ teaspoon garlic powder
- 2 teaspoons salt
- 2 teaspoon ground black pepper
- 1 teaspoon onion powder
- 4 tablespoons olive oil

Directions:
Rinse steak, pat dry with paper towels, then brush with oil and season well with garlic powder, onion powder, salt, and black pepper. Then plug in the smoker, fill its tray with cherry woodchips and water pan halfway through, and place dripping pan above the water pan. Then open the top vent, shut with lid and use temperature settings to preheat smoker at 220 degrees F. Place seasoned steaks on smoker rack, insert a meat thermometer, then shut with lid and set the timer to smoke for minutes or more until meat thermometer registers an internal temperature between 125 to 145 degrees F. When done, transfer steak to a cutting board, cover with aluminum foil and let rest for 10 minutes. Slice and serve.

Texan Beef Brisket
Serves:18
Cooking Time:16 Hours 30 Minutes
Ingredients:
- 1 whole packer brisket, chilled (12-lbs, 5.5-kgs)
- Garlic powder – 2 tablespoons
- Salt – 2 tablespoons
- Black pepper – 2 tablespoons
- Preheat smoker to 225°f (107°c) using hardwood smoke and indirect heat.

Directions:
Arrange the brisket so the point end is underneath. Cut away and discard any excess fat. Trim down the crescent-shaped fat section to ensure a smooth transition between point and flat. Trim any excess fat from the point. Square the ends and edges of the flat. Flip the brisket and trim the fat cap down to a ¼-ins (0.6-cms) thick. In a small bowl, combine the garlic, salt, and pepper. Sprinkle the mixture over the whole brisket. Arrange the brisket in the smoker with the point end facing the heat source. Close the lid and cook for approximately 8 hours until the internal temperature registers 16f (73°c). Roll out a piece of butcher paper and arrange the brisket in the center. Wrap the paper around the brisket securely so that it is leak-proof. Return the parcel to the smoker and arrange seam side down. Close the smoker lid and continue to cook until the internal temperature registers 200°f (93°c). This will take approximately 7 hours. Allow the cooked meat to rest for an hour before slicing and serving against the grain.

Hearty Ribeye Steaks
Serves: 4
Cooking Time: 45 Minutes
Ingredients:
- 4 ribeye steaks, each of 1 and ½ inch thickness
- 1 and ½ teaspoons garlic powder
- 2 teaspoon salt
- 2 teaspoons ground black pepper
- 1 teaspoon onion powder
- 4 tablespoons olive oil

Directions:
Rinse the steak thoroughly underwater using paper towels and brush them well with oil, season with garlic powder, onion powder, salt, and pepper Take your drip pan and add water, cover with aluminum foil. Pre-heat your smoker to 0 degrees F Use water fill water pan halfway through and place it over drip pan. Add wood chips to the side tray Transfer seasoned steak to your smoker rack and smoke for about minutes until the internal

temperature reaches 125 degrees F Once done, transfer to a cutting board and cover with aluminum foil, let it rest for 10 minutes Slice and serve, enjoy!

Country Style Pork Ribs
Serves: 4
Cooking Time: 3-4 Hours
Ingredients:
- 2 lbs. meat strips
- ¼ cup Cajun Dry
- 2 cups of your favorite barbecue sauce (We love the Quick Barbecue Sauce for an easy weeknight meal.)

Directions:
Rinse the meat strips under cold water and pat-dry with a paper towel. Sprinkle the strips with the Cajun Dry Rub. Set aside. Let it sit at room temperature while preheating the smoker to 240°F. Set the strips directly on the smoker grate. Smoke the strips for 1 hour. Remove them from the smoker and set the strips on an aluminum pan. Pour the barbecue sauce over the strips and cover them with a heavy-duty aluminum foil. Return back to the smoker and smoke for another 2-3 hours or until the internal temperature reaches 1°F. Serve with more barbecue sauce on the side.

Smoked Coconut Aminos Marinated Flank Steak (masterbuilt Electric Smoker)
Serves: 6
Cooking Time: 3 Hours
Ingredients:
- 3/4 cup coconut aminos*
- 3 Tbsp coconut oil, melted (or olive oil)
- 3 garlic cloves, minced
- 2 Tbsp lime juice
- Salt and black pepper freshly ground
- 4 lbs flank steak

Directions:
Combine coconut aminos, melted coconut oil, garlic, lime juice and salt and pepper. Generously rub the spice mix all over the meat, cover and refrigerate overnight. Preheat Masterbuilt Electric Smoker. Allow the smoker temperature to reach 250 degrees Fahrenheit. When it is ready, add some water to the removable pan that is usually on the bottom shelf. Fill the side "drawer" with dry wood chips. Place the steak in the smoker and smoke your steak until it reaches an internal temperature of 12degrees F (rare) to 145 degrees F (medium). The general rule of thumb is that for every 1.5 lbs. of meat, an hour of smoking is necessary; however, the real determinant is the temperature. Slice the steak and serve.

Molasses Lamb Chops
Serves: 4
Cooking Time: 3 Hours
Ingredients:
- ½ cup dry white wine
- 1 cup molasses for honey
- 4 tablespoons molasses
- 4 tablespoon fresh mint, minced
- Salt and pepper to taste
- 2 pounds lamb

Directions:
Take a bowl and add molasses, wine, fresh mint, salt and pepper   Season cut side of the boned lamb with salt and pepper, spread molasses mixture and roll and tie the lamb   Brush outer surface with molasses mixture   Take your drip pan and add water, cover with aluminum foil. Pre-heat your smoker to 225 degrees F   Use water fill water pan halfway through and place it over drip pan. Add wood chips to the side tray   Lay meat on top rack and smoke until the internal temperature reaches 150 degrees F   Remove chops and let it cool for 15 minutes   Serve and enjoy!

Smoked Lamb Lollipops
Serves: 4
Cooking Time: 1 Hour
Ingredients:
- 1 rack of lamb, fat trimmed
- 2 tablespoons shallots, peeled and chopped
- 1 teaspoon minced garlic
- ½ teaspoon salt
- ½ teaspoon ground black pepper
- 2 tablespoons rosemary, fresh
- 2 tablespoons sage, fresh
- 1 tablespoon thyme, fresh
- 1 tablespoon honey
- ¼ cup olive oil

Directions:
Rinse lamb, pat dry and place in a baking dish. Add remaining ingredients in a food processor, pulse for 1 minute or until smooth, then tip the mixture on lamb and rub well until evenly coated. Cover dish with plastic wrap and marinate in the refrigerator for 24 hours.   When ready to smoke, plug in the smoker, fill its tray with hickory woodchips and water pan halfway through, and place dripping pan above the water pan.   Then open the top vent, shut with lid and use temperature settings to preheat smoker at 22degrees F.   Place the marinated rack of lamb on smoker rack, insert a meat thermometer, then shut with lid and set the timer to smoke for 1 hour or more until meat thermometer registers an internal temperature of 120 degrees F.   When done, transfer lamb to a cutting board, let rest for 5 minutes and then slice to serve.

Smoked Cheesy Burgers
Serves: 2
Cooking Time: 20-30 Minutes
Ingredients:
- 1 lb ground chuck or other 80/20 ground beef
- 2 tsp Basic Beef
- 1 onion, thinly sliced
- 1 Tbsp extra-virgin olive oil
- 2 oz. cream cheese, softened
- 2 oz shredded sharp cheddar cheese
- 1 Tbsp blue cheese, crumbled
- 2 hamburger buns, toasted
- 2 slices bacon, cooked
- 2 Tbsp choice of barbecue sauce

Directions:
Preheat the smoker to 250°F.   In a medium skillet, heat olive oil over medium heat. Add onions and cook slowly until onions turn translucent then caramelize, around minutes.   In a bowl, combine cream cheese, sharp cheddar cheese, and blue cheese.   Form hamburger into four patties of equal size.   Place half of the cheese mixture the center of one patty. Top with an additional patty and seal around the edges. Repeat for the other hamburger. Season both hamburgers with the basic beef rub and place in a shallow aluminum foil pan.   Place the pan on the preheated smoker.   Smoke the burgers until they reach an internal temperature of 155°F.   Remove the burgers from the smoker and allow to rest for 5 minutes. The internal temperature will continue to increase to 160°F. Spread barbecue sauce over the top of each hamburger bun.   Place hamburgers on the toasted bottom bun. Top with bacon and the other bun. Devour next to a pile of napkins.

Smoked Hot Pepper Pork Tenderloin (masterbuilt Electric Smoker)
Serves: 6
Cooking Time : 3 Hours And 25 Minutes
Ingredients:
- 3/4 cup chicken stock
- 1/2 cup tomato-basil sauce
- 2 tsp hot red chili pepper (or to taste)
- 1 Tbsp oregano
- Salt and pepper to taste
- 2 lb pork tenderloin

Directions:
Whisk together the chicken stock, tomato-basil sauce, hot red chili pepper, oregano, and salt and pepper.   Brush generously all over the tenderloin. Preheat your electric smoker to 225°F.   When it is ready, add some water to the removable pan that is usually on the bottom shelf.   Fill the side "drawer" with dry wood chips.   Place meat in the smoker and smoke internal temperature of 145 degrees F, for about 2 1/2 - 3 hours.   Before slicing let it rest for 10 minutes.   Serve.

Perfectly Smoked Pork Spare Ribs

Serves: 8-10
Cooking Time: 5-6 Hours
Ingredients:
- 3 (4-5 lb.) racks pork spareribs, St. Louis style, trimmed
- 2 cups Basic Barbecue Rub, or another rub of your choice
- ¼ cup peanut oil
- 2 cups favorite barbecue sauce (We like the Kansas City Style Barbecue Sauce.)
- 2 Tbsp apple juice, for spraying

Directions:
Rinse the ribs and pat-dry with a paper towel. Rub or brush the spareribs with a the peanut oil. Next, rub the ribs with the Basic Barbecue Rub. Refrigerate overnight. Preheat the smoker to 225°F. Allow the ribs to come to room temperature for 30 minutes before smoking. Set the ribs directly on the smoker grate, bone side down. Use the water pan for extra moist ribs. Smoke the ribs for 3 hours. Remove the ribs from the smoker and spritz with a generous amount of apple juice. Wrap them tightly in a double layer of heavy-duty aluminum foil. Return them to the smoker, meat side down, and smoke for another 2 hours. After 2 hours, remove them from the smoker and uncover. Discard the liquid together with the foil. Brush 1-2 coats of your preferred barbecue sauce onto the ribs. Smoke the ribs for another 45 minutes - 1 hour or until the sauce is set and the ribs reach an internal temperature of 185°F Once done, remove from the smoker and let them rest for 10-minutes before carving. When serving, cut in-between bone to separate the ribs and serve with the remaining barbecue sauce.

Smoked Chuck Roast

Serves: 10
Cooking Time: 9 Hours Plus 1 To 2 Hours Resting
Ingredients:
- 1 boneless chuck roast (about 5 pounds)
- 1/4 cup kosher salt, plus more to taste
- 1/4 cup coarsely ground black pepper, plus more to taste
- 1/4 cup garlic powder
- 3 cups beef stock (divided)
- 1 onion (sliced)

Directions:
Rinse roast with cold water and pat dry with paper towels. Mix salt, pepper and garlic powder and rub all over roast. Tie roast into a roll with kitchen twine. Place roast in a plastic or glass container, cover and refrigerate for 8 to hours. Pour cups water into the Masterbuilt smoker's water pan. Place hickory or oak wood chips in the smoker's wood tray and preheat smoker to 225°F. Place roast fat-side up on smoker grate and smoke for hours, spraying with stock every hour. Add wood chips to the wood tray as necessary. Increase smoker temperature to 250°F. Place roast in an aluminum baking pan and add remaining 2 cups stock and onion slices. Place uncovered pan on smoker grate and continue smoking roast until the internal temperature of the meat reaches 165°F, about 3 hours more. Add wood chips to the wood tray as necessary. Cover pan with aluminum foil and continue smoking until the roast is falling-apart tender and the internal temperature of the meat reaches 200°F, about 3 hours more. Add wood chips to the wood tray as necessary. Remove covered pan from smoker and let roast rest for about 30 minutes. Remove roast from pan and cut kitchen twine from roast. Shred roast with two forks and moisten with pan juices, or slice roast and use pan juices to make gravy. Serve and enjoy!

Summer Spiced Sausage

Serves:18
Cooking Time:8 Hours 30 Minutes
Ingredients:
- Lean hamburger meat (5-lbs, 2.25-kgs)
- Meat cure – 5 teaspoons
- Sugar cure – 2 tablespoons
- Liquid smoke -2 teaspoons
- Mustard seeds – 2 teaspoons
- Garlic powder – 1 teaspoon
- Peppercorns – 2 teaspoons
- Red pepper, crushed – 2 teaspoons
- Coarse pepper – 2 teaspoons
- Preheat smoker to 225°f (107°c)

Directions:
Combine the meat, meat cure, sugar cure, liquid smoke, mustard seeds, garlic, peppercorns, red pepper, and coarse pepper. Transfer the mixture to a resealable container and chill for 2-3 days. Mix the meat at least twice every day. Form the mixture into ins (5-cms) and place in the smoker. Cook for approximately 8 hours until the internal temperature registers 160°f (70°c). Plus days standing time.

Smoked Lamb Breast

Serves: 6
Cooking Time: 2 Hours And 30 Minutes
Ingredients:
- 2 pounds lamb breast, bone-in
- ½ cup apple cider vinegar
- ¼ cup yellow mustard
- ½ cup Barbecue Rub

Directions:
Plug in the smoker, fill its tray with hickory woodchips and water pan halfway through, and place dripping pan above the water pan. Then open the top vent, shut with lid and use temperature settings to preheat smoker at 0 degrees F. In the meantime, rinse lamb with vinegar, then coat with mustard and sprinkle with BBQ rub. Place lamb on smoker rack, insert a meat thermometer, then shut with lid and set the timer to smoke for 2 to 2 ½ hours or more until meat thermometer registers an internal temperature of 165 degrees F. Check vent of smoker every hour and add more woodchips and water to maintain temperature and smoke. When done, cover the lamb with aluminum foil and let rest for 10 minutes. Slice to serve.

Simple Beef Roast
Serves: 6
Cooking Time: 15 Minutes
Ingredients:
- 2 lbs. beef roast
- 1 tbsp. ground black pepper
- 1 tbsp. salt
- 1 tbsp. olive oil

Directions:
Heat your smoker to 225 F/7 C. Coat beef roast with olive oil and season with pepper and salt. Place in smoker for 60 minutes or until internal temperature reaches 1 F/54 C. Wrap meat in foil and set aside for 30 minutes. Cut into strips and serve.

Tex Mex Pulled Pork Taco Filling
Serves: 12
Cooking Time: 9 To 12 Hours Plus 1 To 4 Hours Resting
Ingredients:
- 2 cups pork, chicken or vegetable stock
- 1 onion (chopped)
- 4 garlic cloves (minced)
- 3 tablespoons green chili powder
- 2 teaspoons kosher salt
- 1 teaspoon garlic powder
- 1 teaspoon onion powder
- 1 teaspoon freshly ground black pepper
- 1 teaspoon ground cumin
- 1 teaspoon ancho chili powder
- 1 bone-in pork shoulder roast (6 to 7 pounds)

Directions:
Pour stock into the Masterbuilt smoker's water pan and add onion and garlic. Place mesquite wood chips in the smoker's wood tray and preheat smoker to 250°F. Mix green chili powder, salt, garlic powder, onion powder, black pepper, cumin and ancho chili powder and rub over pork roast. Place pork roast fat-side up on smoker grate and smoke until the internal temperature of the roast reaches 205°F, 9 to 12 hours. Add wood chips to the wood tray as necessary. Remove pork roast from smoker and wrap tightly in aluminum foil. Cover wrapped roast with a towel, place in an empty cooler, cover cooler and let roast rest for 1 to hours (the pork will be more tender the longer it rests). Unwrap roast, remove bone and shred meat with two forks, removing gristle and fat as necessary. Serve pulled pork with your favorite taco fixings and enjoy!

Best-ever Pork Chops
Serves: 4
Cooking Time: 1 Hour 10 Minutes
Ingredients:
- 4 (1lb) bone-in, center cut pork chops
- 2 tbsp dried thyme, crushed
- 2 tbsp dark brown sugar
- 1 tbsp cayenne pepper
- 1 tbsp onion powder
- 1 tbsp garlic powder

Directions:
In a bowl, mix together all ingredients except pork chops. Generously rub the pork chops with spice mixture. With a plastic wrap, cover the pork chops and refrigerate overnight. Arrange the roast in a large plate and refrigerate for about 6 hours. Soak apple wood chips in water for at least 1 hour. Preheat the smoker to 275 degrees F, using charcoal and apple wood chips. Place the chops into the smoker and cook, covered for about minutes. Serve hot.

Dry Rubbed Pork Chops
Serves: 12
Cooking Time: 1 And ½ To 2 Hours
Ingredients:
- 4 pork chops, 1- ½ inch thick
- 1 and ½ tablespoons salt
- 1 tablespoon brown sugar
- 1 tablespoon smoked paprika
- 1 tablespoon onion powder
- 2 teaspoon garlic powder
- 2 teaspoons fresh ground pepper
- 2 tablespoons mustard
- 2 tablespoons extra virgin olive oil

Directions:
Take a large bowl and add salt, sugar, onion powder, paprika, garlic powder, pepper and mix well Take another bowl and mix mustard and olive oil Wash beef under water and pat them dry, coat well with the mustard mixture Slather the whole sugar and onion mixture all over the meat Take your drip pan and add water, cover with aluminum foil. Pre-heat your smoker to 2 degrees F Use water fill water pan halfway through and place it over drip pan. Add wood chips to the side tray. Transfer meat to smoker and smoke for 1 and 1/2 hours until the internal temperature reaches 145 degrees F Once an internal temperature of 145 degrees F is reached, let it smoke for 30 minutes more Once done, transfer to meat to a foil tent and let it cool Shred and serve Enjoy!

Masterbuilt Beef Brisket

Serves: 8
Cook Time: 8 Hours
Ingredients:
- 1 Whole packer brisket of about 12 to 14 pounds
- 2 Tablespoons of coarse kosher salt
- 2 Tablespoons of coarse ground black pepper
- 2 Tablespoons of garlic powder

Directions:
Store the brisket in the refrigerator until it is the right time to trim it Flip the brisket over so that the point end is underneath it Remove any excess of fat from the flat muscle Trim down the crescent moon shaped fat part until you see a smooth transition between the flat and the point Square the ends and the edges of the flat; then flip the brisket over and trim the top fat to ¼ inches of thickness across the surface of the brisket In a large mixing bowl or an empty container, combine all together the pepper with the garlic and the salt and rub over the brisket in order to evenly distribute the spices on all sides Preheat your Masterbuilt electric smoker to a temperature of about 225°F by using an indirect source of heat and with hardwood smoke Place the brisket on top of your smoker with the ending point facing the main source of heat Lock the lid and smoke the meat for about hours or until the internal thermometer reads about 165° F On top of a large working surface, roll out a piece of butcher paper and center the brisket in the middle Wrap the meat brisket by folding an edge over an edge and create a kind of leak proof seal Place the brisket back into the smoker with the seam side down Lock the lid of the smoker and maintain a temperature of about 225 degrees F; then continue to cook until the internal temperature of the meat brisket reaches about 202° F Remove the beef brisket to a cutting board and let rest for about 1 hour before slicing it Slice both the flat and the point of the beef meat against the grain with a sharp knife and serve it immediately!

Smoked Burgers With Seared Avocado

Serves: 2
Cooking Time: 20-30 Minutes
Ingredients:
- 1 lb ground chuck or other 80/20 ground beef
- 2 tsp Basic Beef
- 1 Tbsp olive oil, for brushing on avocado
- ½ of a firm-ripe avocado, pitted, peeled, and cut lengthwise into 4 (⅓ inch thick) slices
- 2 hamburger buns
- 2 Tbsp mayonnaise

- 1 tsp Sriracha
- 2 slices bacon, cooked
- 1-2 leaves of lettuce
- 2 slices tomato

Directions:
Preheat the smoker to 250°F. Form hamburger into two patties and place in a shallow aluminum pan and season both sides with Basic Beef Rub. Place the pan in the smoker and cook 20- minutes or until the internal temperature reaches 160°F. Remove the burgers from the smoker and allow to rest for 5 minutes. Heat a small skillet over medium-high heat. Brush both sides of the avocado slices with olive oil. Season with salt and pepper. Place avocado in the skillet and sear for 1-2 minutes on each side. In a small bowl combine mayonnaise and sriracha. Spread one bun with sriracha mayonnaise mixture. Top with a hamburger, desired garnishes, and the remaining bun.

Smoked Beef Brisket

Serves: 6
Cook Time: 9 Hours
Ingredients:
- ¼ Cup of packed brown sugar
- 1 Teaspoon of onion powder
- 1 Tablespoon of garlic powder
- 1 Tablespoon of smoked paprika
- 1 Tablespoon of seasoning salt
- 2 Teaspoons of ground black pepper
- 1 Teaspoon of oregano leaves dried
- ½ Teaspoon of cumin
- 10 Pounds of Brisket

Directions:
Place the beef brisket in a large dish; then take each of the ingredient; except for the brisket and combine very well with a spoon Once the ingredients are perfectly mixed; rub the into the brisket Cover the dish with the meat inside it with an aluminium foil and let sit in the refrigerator for about 12 to 24 hours Soak the wood chunks for about 1 hour before smoking the meat Once the wood chunks are wrapped, place it in the tray within your smoker Prepare the water tray by wrapping it with aluminum foil and drop in 3 tablespoons of liquid smoke into the tray of the water Turn on your Masterbuilt smoker and pre-heat it to 225° F. When it is the right time to put the brisket on the smoker, lay it with the fat side down. Put an electric meat thermometer in the brisket and close the smoker door. Smoke on low until the inner temperature reaches about 170° F for about 9 hours Let the meat rest for about 5 minutes Serve and enjoy your dish!

Crazy Smoked Pork Spare Ribs
Serves: 6
Cooking Time: 4 Hours
Ingredients:
- 6 pound of pork spareribs
- For Dry Rub
- ½ a cup of packed brown sugar
- 2 tablespoon of chili powder
- 1 tablespoon of paprika
- 1 tablespoon of freshly ground black pepper
- 2 tablespoon of garlic powder
- 2 teaspoon of onion powder
- 2 teaspoon of kosher salt
- 2 teaspoon of ground cumin
- 1 teaspoon of ground cinnamon
- 1 teaspoon of jalapeno seasoning salt
- 1 teaspoon of Cayenne pepper
- For Mop Sauce
- 1 cup of apple cider
- ¾ cup of apple cider vinegar
- 1 tablespoon of onion powder
- 1 tablespoon of garlic powder
- 2 tablespoon of lemon juice
- 1 jalapeno pepper finely chopped up
- 3 tablespoon of hot pepper sauce
- Kosher salt as needed
- Black pepper as needed
- 2 cups of soaked wood chips

Directions:
Take a medium sized bowl and add brown sugar, chili powder, 2 tablespoon of garlic powder, 2 teaspoon of onion powder, cumin, cinnamon, kosher salt, cayenne pepper, jalapeno seasoning Mix well and rub the mixture over the pork spare ribs Allow it to refrigerate for 4 hours Heat up your smoker to 250-degree Fahrenheit Take a medium bowl and stir in apple cider, apple cider vinegar, 1 tablespoon of onion powder, jalapeno, 1 tablespoon of garlic powder, salt, pepper and lemon juice Add a handful of soaked wood chips and transfer the ribs to your smoker middle rack Smoke for 3-4 hours making sure to keep adding chips after every hour Take the meat out and serve!

Rosemary Garlic Pork Tenderloins
Serves: 8
Cooking Time: 2 Hours
Ingredients:
- 2 cups chicken stock
- 1 onion (chopped)
- 4 garlic cloves (minced, divided)
- 2 tablespoons olive oil
- 3 tablespoons dried rosemary
- 1 tablespoon kosher salt
- 1 teaspoon freshly ground black pepper
- 2 pork tenderloins (about 3 pounds each)

Directions:

Pour stock into the Masterbuilt smoker's water pan and add onion and about half of the garlic. Place pecan, peach or hickory wood chips in the smoker's wood tray and preheat smoker to 250°F. Mix olive oil, rosemary, salt, pepper and remaining garlic and rub over pork tenderloins. Place tenderloins on smoker grate and smoke until the internal temperature of the meat reaches 145°F, about 2 hours. Add wood chips to the wood tray as necessary. Remove tenderloins from smoker, cover loosely with aluminum foil and let rest for about 30 minutes. Slice tenderloins as desired to serve. Enjoy!

South Carolina Pulled Pork
Serves: 16
Cooking Time: 9 To 12 Hours
Ingredients:
- 3/4 cup water
- 1/4 cup Worcestershire sauce
- 1 1/4 cup apple cider vinegar (divided)
- 1 onion (sliced)
- 1 1/4 cup yellow mustard (divided)
- 1 bone-in pork shoulder roast (6 to 7 pounds)
- 1/4 cup brown sugar
- 2 tablespoons kosher salt, plus more to taste
- 1 tablespoon paprika
- 1 tablespoon garlic powder
- 1 tablespoon chili powder
- 2 teaspoons freshly ground black pepper, plus more to taste
- 1/4 cup Dijon mustard
- 1/4 cup cider vinegar
- 2 tablespoons soy sauce
- 1/2 teaspoon cayenne pepper

Directions:
Pour water, Worcestershire sauce and cup vinegar into the Masterbuilt smoker's water pan and add onion. Place hickory wood chips in the smoker's wood tray and preheat smoker to 225°F. Brush about 1/4 cup mustard over pork roast. Mix brown sugar, salt, pepper, paprika, garlic powder, chili powder and black pepper. Set aside about tablespoons spice mixture. Rub remaining spice mixture over pork roast. Place pork roast fat-side up on smoker grate and smoke until the internal temperature of the roast reaches 205°F, 9 to 12 hours. Add wood chips to the wood tray as necessary. Meanwhile, for the sauce, in a small saucepan over medium heat, whisk Dijon mustard, Worcestershire sauce and cayenne pepper with remaining 1 cup yellow mustard and 1/cup apple cider vinegar and season to taste with salt and pepper. Heat sauce to a boil, reduce heat and simmer until thickened, stirring occasionally, about 20 minutes. Remove pork roast from smoker, cover with aluminum foil and let rest for about 30 minutes. Remove bone from roast and shred meat with two forks, removing gristle and fat as necessary. Sprinkle reserved spice mixture over pulled pork and toss gently to coat. Serve pulled pork with the sauce and enjoy!

Masterbuilt Smoked Seasoned Chuck Roast

Serves: 5-6
Cook Time: 5 Hours
Ingredients:
- 5 to 6 Pounds of boneless chuck roast
- 1 and ½ tablespoons of sea salt
- 2 Teaspoons of cracked black pepper
- 2 Teaspoons of onion powder
- 2 Teaspoons of garlic powder
- 1 Teaspoon of paprika
- 1 Teaspoon of brown sugar
- ¼ Teaspoon of cayenne
- 2 Bottles of dark beer
- Heavy duty aluminum foil

Directions:
Give the roast a very quick rinse under cool water and pat it dry with clean paper towels   Trim the meat roast of any excess of fat   Set the meat aside while you are preparing the rub   In a large baking tray; combine your dry ingredients and with both your hands mix very well   Add the pork roast to the tray and coat all the sides with the prepared rub and pat it dry very well   Set the roast while you prepare your Masterbuilt electric smoker by adding the wood chips to the baking dish and add the water with ¼ cup of beer   Preheat your smoker to a temperature of about 225° F and 250° F   Open the top of the vent and when the smoker is ready; put the beef on top of the rack and place it in your smoker   Smoke the pork roast for about 5 hours, 1 hour per hour   Replenish the chips of wood each 45 to 60 minutes and the mixture of water and beer   When you reach the desired temperature; then place 2 sheets of the foil over a cutting board; then place the roast into a foil and cover it; make sure to seal the seams tightly   Put the sealed roast with the seam side up in the smoker once more   Smoke for about 1 hour or until the inner temperature reaches about 190° F   Remove the roast to your cutting board and allow it to sit in the aluminum foil for about 30 minutes for the juices to be perfectly absorbed   Open the aluminum foil and place the roast on a cutting board; then discard the foil and slice the roast   Slice the pork roast; then serve and enjoy your dish!

Garlic Sauce And Lamb Chops

Serves: 4
Cooking Time: 3 Hours
Ingredients:
- 6 garlic cloves
- 2 tablespoons apple cider vinegar
- ½ cup of water
- ¼ cup extra virgin olive oil
- 1 teaspoon salt
- 1 teaspoon pepper
- 4 pounds lamb cutlets

Directions:
Take a bowl and add minced garlic, vinegar, water, olive oil, salt, and pepper   Rub the mixture thoroughly over lamb cutlets and transfer them to your fridge, let them chill for4 hours   Remove from fridge and let them sit for 45 minutes   Take your drip pan and add water, cover with aluminum foil.   Pre-heat your smoker to 225 degrees F   Use water fill water pan halfway through and place it over drip pan. Add wood chips to the side tray   Place meat on the top rack and smoke for 3 hours or until the internal temperature reaches 150 degrees F   Remove chops and let them cool for 15 minutes   Serve and enjoy!

Smoked Hamburger Jerky

Serves: 10
Cooking Time: 4 Hours
Ingredients:
- 2 pounds lean ground beef
- 2 teaspoons ginger, grated
- 1 tablespoon powdered all spice
- 4 tablespoons sugar
- 1 clove of garlic, minced
- ½ cup soy sauce

Directions:
Combine all Ingredients: in a mixing bowl.   Use your hands to form medium-sized patties using the mixture.   Place in the fridge and allow to set for at least hours.   Preheat the smoker to 10F.   Place water in the water pan and add mesquite wood chips into the side tray.   Place the hamburger in the middle tray of the smoker.   Adjust the cooking time to 4 hours.

Smoked Loin Chops With Cherry Chutney

Serves: 6
Cooking Time: 1 Hour
Ingredients:
- 6 loin chops, cut 2 inches thick
- 4 cups crushed ice
- ½ gallon hot water
- ½ cup Kosher Salt
- ½ cup brown sugar
- 2 cups fresh cherries, pitted (you can also use frozen that have been thawed)
- ¾ cup cherry preserves
- ⅔ cup chopped onion
- 3 Tbsp balsamic vinegar
- 1 Tbsp vegetable oil
- 1 tsp fresh thyme

Directions:
In a large, non-reactive bowl, combine water, salt and sugar until dissolved. Add crushed ice to the brine. Add pork chops when the ice has melted. Allow to sit in the refrigerator for at least 1 hour and up to overnight. Preheat the smoker to 225°F. Remove the chops from the brine, pat dry and allow to sit at room temperature for 30 minutes before smoking. In a medium saucepan, heat oil over medium heat. Add onion and saute for 8 minutes or until the onion is translucent. Add allspice, cayenne, and thyme to the oil and onion and allow the spices to become fragrant, about 1 minute. Add cherry preserves, balsamic vinegar, and fresh cherries. Stir and reduce the heat to low. Allow the sauce to simmer 10 minutes, or until the chutney is thick. Reserve ½ cup of the chutney for glazing and set the rest aside. Place the loin chops directly on the smoker grates. Smoke the chops until the internal temperature reaches 135°F. Remove the chops from the smoker and brush liberally with the reserved chutney. Return the chops to the smoker until the internal temperature reaches °F. Remove the chops from the smoker and allow them to rest 10-minutes before serving. Serve with the remaining chutney.

Pastrami

Serves: 6
Cooking Time: 10-12 Hours
Ingredients:
- 1 (12-lb.) whole beef brisket
- 2 Tbsp pickling spice
- 3 Tbsp garlic, granulated
- 2 Tbsp ground coriander
- ¼ cup curing salt
- 3 Tbsp black pepper, coarsely ground
- 1 Tbsp coriander seeds, toasted and ground
- 1 tsp garlic, granulated
- 1 cup water

Directions:
Wash the brisket and pat-dry. Trim the fat evenly across the surface of the brisket, leaving ½ inch of fat on the meat. In a bowl, combine all cure ingredients. Coat the brisket entirely with the cure. Place the cured brisket in a 2-gallon resealable bag. Refrigerate it for days, turning the brisket 1-2 times per day. After 4 days, remove the brisket from the bag. Wash it well and pat-dry. In a mixing bowl, mix together all of the rub ingredients. Coat the brisket evenly with the rub. Let it sit for at room temperature for 30 minutes while the smoker comes to temperature (250°F). Set the brisket directly on the smoker grate, fat side up. Smoke the meat for 4-5 hours, or until the internal temperature registers 165°F. Remove the brisket from the smoker. Wrap the brisket tightly in aluminum foil, adding 1 cup of water before sealing the foil. Place the pastrami back to the smoker and cook until the internal temperature registers 190°F. For best results, let the pastrami rest for 20-30 minutes before slicing.

Hickory Smoked Burgers

Serves: 12
Cooking Time: 20 Minutes
Ingredients:
- 2 lb.s lean ground round (can use ground turkey for a low-fat burger)
- 1 package dry onion soup mix
- 1/2 cup water
- 1 tbsp. hot sauce
- 3/4 cup bread crumbs (if desired)
- Worcestershire sauce

Directions:
Place all the ingredients in a large bowl and mix together. Roll the beef into patties it should yield 1to 14 of them. Place the patties in the smoker. Flip over halfway through smoking. When they're ready serve immediately.

Smoked Pork Ribs

Serves:8
Cooking Time:5 Hours 5 Minutes
Ingredients:
- Pork ribs (4-lbs, 1.8-kgs)
- Salt – ½ tablespoon
- Brown sugar – ¼ cup
- Chili powder- 2½ teaspoons
- Ground cumin – 1½ tablespoons
- Cayenne pepper – 2 teaspoons
- Freshly ground black pepper – 2 teaspoon
- Garlic powder – 2 teaspoons
- Onion powder – 2 teaspoons
- Preheat your electric smoker to 225°F (107°C)
- Add hickory wood chips to the smoker

Directions:
In a bowl, combine the salt, brown sugar, chili powder, cumin, cayenne pepper, black pepper, garlic powder, and onion powder. Rub the g mix all over the pork and set aside for hours, before smoking. This will also allow the meat to come to room temperature. Smoke the ribs in the smoker for hours, using the hickory chips for the first 2 hours only. After 3 hours have elapsed remove the ribs from the smoker and wrap in heavy aluminum foil and cook for an additional 1-1½ hours. Serve the ribs and enjoy.

Smoked Herb Marinated Lamb Skewers
Serves: 6
Cooking Time: 15 Minutes
Ingredients:
- Marinade
- 1/3 c. olive oil
- 2 crushed garlic cloves
- 1 lemon
- ½ tsp. cumin
- 1 tsp. fresh thyme
- 1 tsp. dried oregano
- 1 tsp. rosemary sprig
- Salt
- Pepper
- Meat
- 3 lbs. lamb legs

Directions:
To make the marinade whisk all the ingredients a large bowl, . Cut meat into chunks and set aside. Add meat and toss to coat. Take a plastic wrap and cover the bowl. Refrigerate overnight. Remove the meat from the bowl and pat dry on paper towel. Skewer the meat onto a metal branch. Place skewers in foil and wrap well. Preheat smoker to 225°F and add wood chips (hickory). Place the meat on the top stand and give smoke until internal temperature reaches 150°F. Serve hot.

Perfectly Smoked Filet Mignon
Serves: 12
Cooking Time: 2-3 Hours (30 Min Per Lb.)
Ingredients:
- 4 lb beef tenderloin, trimmed
- 2-3 sprigs fresh thyme
- 2 shallots, peeled and chopped
- ½ cup chives, chopped
- ½ cup your favorite barbecue sauce - we like our Balsamic Barbecue Sauce for this
- 2 Tbsp butter
- 2 tsp Worcestershire sauce

Directions:
Heat the butter in a small pan over medium heat till it melts. Toss in shallots and herbs into the warm butter. Add the barbecue sauce and reduce heat to low. Keep stirring the barbecue butter sauce to keep it from solidifying. 1. Cut ¾ of the way through the tenderloin to make steaks 1-2 inches thick. 2. Lay the partially sliced tenderloin across the bottom of an aluminum baking dish to let the strips open. 4. Gently pour the barbecue butter sauce into each flap to baste the tenderloin generously. 5. Let the basted tenderloin come to room temperature as the smoker preheats to 275°F. 1. Set the pan with the tenderloin directly on the smoker grate when the desired smoke temperature has been reached. 2. Smoke the meat until the internal temperature of the thickest steak comes to 135°F. 3. Let the meat rest for 5-10 minutes before carving.

Smoked Lamb Shoulder Chops
Serves:4

Cooking Time:4 Hours 30 Minutes
Ingredients:
- 4 thick lamb shoulder chops
- Olive oil
- Texas style rub of choice
- Buttermilk – 4 cups
- Cold water – 1 cup
- Coarse kosher salt – ¼ cup
- Preheat smoker to 240°f (115°c) with indirect heat
- Fill the smoker's water pan with hot water
- Add cherry or apple wood chips

Directions:
Prepare the brine: Add the buttermilk along with the water to a large jug. Add the salt and stir for 30 seconds until the salt is entirely dissolved. Add the chops to a Ziplock bag and pour the buttermilk mixture over the chops, to cover. Transfer the ziplock bag to the fridge for 4 hours. Remove the chops from the ziplock bag, discard the brine and rinse the chops with cold water. Set to one side. Drizzle a drop of oil over the top side of the chops, using a pastry brush to cover. Scatter a generous amount of Texas-style rub over the top side of the chops. Turn the meat over and repeat the oil and Texas rub process. Add the lamb chops to the smoker and smoke for approximately 25 minutes. Cooking time will depend on the thickness of the meat. The chops are sufficiently cooked when an internal thermometer registers 110°F (43°C) transfer to an extremely hot grill to finish.

Masterbuilt Smoked Lamb Shank
Serves: 7
Cook Time: 2 Hours
Ingredients:
- 3 to 4 Lamb Shanks
- For the Harissa Paste:
- 6 to 8 Bird's eye chilies or any other spicy chili pepper with the stems removed
- 1 Skinned Bulb of garlic
- 1 Tablespoon of coriander
- 1 Tablespoon of cumin
- 1 and ½ tablespoons of kosher salt
- 3 Tablespoons of chopped fresh mint
- ½ Cup of chopped fresh cilantro
- 1 Tablespoon of red wine vinegar or sherry
- The juice and the zest of a lemon
- ½ Cup of olive oil
- Bradley Flavor Bisquettes

Directions:
Blend all together all your ingredients for the Harissa paste into a blender or a food processor and process until your mixture becomes smooth Add in more oil to reach the perfect consistency you are looking for Rub the lamb shanks generously into Harissa paste and let the rub marinate for an overnight Preheat your Masterbuilt Electric Smoker to about 250°F Put the lamb shanks into your Masterbuilt electric smoker and smoke for about 3 hours or until the temperature reaches about 14 F Let rest for about 5 to 10 minutes; then serve and enjoy it!

Southwestern Smoked Chili

Serves: 6
Cooking Time: 45 Minutes
Ingredients:
- 1 Tbsp extra-virgin olive oil
- 1 ½ cups onion, diced
- 1 ½ cups green pepper, diced
- 1 tbs. minced garlic
- 3 cups water
- 2 Tbsp tomato paste
- 1 14.5-ounce can tomato sauce
- 2 lbs. perfectly smoked brisket, chopped
- 3 cans beans, any variety, rinsed and drained
- 1 Tbsp Chili

Directions:
In a large pot, heat oil over medium heat. Add onion and green pepper and cook until soft. Add minced garlic and tomato paste and cook until tomato paste turns brick red. Add water and stir. Add chili rub, tomato sauce, brisket and beans. Simmer uncovered for 30 minutes or until the chili begins to thicken.

Paprika Herb Rub Garlic & Onion Tenderloin

Serves: 8-10
Cooking Time: 4-6 Hours
Ingredients:
- 4 lbs. beef tenderloin
- 8 garlic cloves, chopped
- 1 large onion, roughly chopped
- ¼ cup black pepper, coarsely ground
- 2 Tbsp fresh lemon juice
- 1 tsp kosher salt
- ¼ tsp cayenne pepper
- 1 cup Jeff's Mop Water
- ¼ cup favorite barbecue sauce

Directions:
In a food processor, pulse rub ingredients together until a paste forms. Wash the tenderloin and pat dry. Cover the meat with the rub, place in a zip top bag, and refrigerate overnight, for best results. The next day, remove the meat from the fridge at least 30 minutes before smoking to allow the meat to come up to room temperature. Preheat the smoker to 27F. Set the tenderloin directly on the smoker grate. Smoke the meat until it reaches an internal temperature of 110°F. Baste the meat on both sides with Jeff's Mop Water. When the roast reaches 130°F, brush on your preferred barbecue sauce. Return the roast to the smoker until it reaches 135°F for medium rare. Remove from the smoker and let it sit for 15-20 minutes before carving. Serve.

German Pork Hock

Serves: 2
Cooking Time: 1 ½ Hours
Ingredients:
- 1 leek, well cleaned, diced
- 1 stalk celery, diced
- 1 carrot, diced
- 1 onion, diced
- 1 - 2 meaty pork hocks
- salt, peppercorns, cumin (if desired)

Directions:
Put your hocks, vegetables, tbsp. salt, and 1 tbsp. peppercorns l a pot. Add in some water and bring it all to a boil. Reduce the heat and allow it to simmer for 3 hours. Be careful not to overcook the hocks. Drain the hocks and vegetables. In a baking dish or pan add in your hocks, vegetables, and only a small amount of cooking oil. Smoke the pork hocks. Recommended you serve this dish with sauerkraut and potatoes.

Basic Smoked Burgers

Serves: 6
Cooking Time: 1 Hour
Ingredients:
- 2 pounds 80/20 ground beef
- 2 teaspoons garlic powder
- 2 teaspoons onion powder
- 1 tablespoon barbecue sauce
- Kosher salt and freshly ground black pepper, to taste

Directions:
Place hickory wood chips in the Masterbuilt smoker's wood tray and preheat smoker to 250°F. Crumble ground beef in a large bowl, add garlic powder and onion powder and mix until thoroughly combined. Form beef mixture into 6 patties, each about 1" thick. Brush patties with barbecue sauce and season both sides to taste with salt and pepper. Reduce smoker temperature to 225°F. Arrange patties on smoker grates and smoke for minutes. Flip patties and smoke until the internal temperature of the meat reaches 160°F, about 30 minutes more. Add wood chips to the wood tray as necessary. Serve burgers immediately with desired buns, condiments and toppings and enjoy!

**Smoked Pork Ribs With Avocado Oil
(masterbuilt Electric Smoker)**
Serves: 7
Cooking Time: 4 Hours And 30 Minutes
Ingredients:

- 1 cup avocado oil
- 1 tsp garlic salt, or to taste
- 2 tsp garlic and onion powder
- 1/2 cup fresh parsley finely chopped
- 4 lbs spare ribs

Directions:
Whisk avocado oil, garlic salt, garlic powder, onion powder, fresh chopped parsley in a mixing bowl. Put pork ribs in a shallow container and pour avocado mixture over; toss to combine well. Cover and refrigerate for at least 4 hours, or overnight. Preheat your electric smoker to 225°F. When it is ready, add some water to the removable pan that is usually on the bottom shelf. Fill the side "drawer" with dry wood chips. Remove pork ribs from marinade (reserve marinade) and arrange the pork chops on the rack. Smoke 1 1/2 hours at 225 degrees F. Remove the ribs, baste generously with reserved marinade, and wrap in heavy-duty aluminum foil. Return to smoker and cook for an additional 1 hour, or until internal temp reaches 160 degrees. Transfer pork chops on serving plate and let rest for 15 - 20 minutes before serving.

Spiced Pork Loin
Serves: 12
Cooking Time: 3 Hours
Ingredients:

- 6-pound pork loin, boneless
- 1/2 teaspoon garlic powder
- 2 teaspoons sea salt
- 1 teaspoon ground black pepper
- 1 tablespoon Chinese five spice powder
- 2 tablespoons olive oil

Directions:
Rinse pork, pat dry with paper towels and place on a foil pan. Stir together remaining ingredients until smooth paste form, then rub this paste on all sides of pork and let marinate for 60 minutes at room temperature. Meanwhile, plug in the smoker, fill its tray with oak woodchips and water pan halfway through, and place dripping pan above the water pan. Then open the top vent, shut with lid and use temperature settings to preheat smoker at 225 degrees F. Place pork on smoker rack, insert a

meat thermometer, then shut with lid and set the timer to smoke for 3 hours or more until meat thermometer registers an internal temperature of 1 degrees F. Check vent of smoker every hour and add more woodchips and water to maintain temperature and smoke. When done, transfer pork to a cutting board, cover with aluminum foil, and let rest for 30 minutes. When done, transfer pork to a cutting board, cover with aluminum foil, and let rest for 30 minutes. Slice pork into ½ inch thick pieces and serve.

East Texas Pulled Pork
Serves: 16
Cooking Time: 12 To 15 Hours
Ingredients:

- 1 cup apple juice
- 1/4 cup honey
- 1/4 cup white sugar
- 2 tablespoons salt
- 1 bone-in pork shoulder roast (8 to 10 pounds)
- 2 tablespoons brown sugar
- 1 teaspoon sweet paprika
- 1 teaspoon chili powder
- 1 teaspoon kosher salt
- 1/2 teaspoon cayenne pepper
- 1/2 teaspoon garlic powder
- 1/2 teaspoon onion powder
- 1/2 teaspoon freshly ground black pepper
- 1/4 cup yellow mustard

Directions:
Place pecan, oak, apple or cherry wood chips in the Masterbuilt smoker's wood tray and preheat smoker to 225°F. In a small bowl, mix apple juice, honey, white sugar and salt and stir until sugar and salt are dissolved. Using a meat injector, inject apple juice mixture into pork roast all over, about 1" deep at intervals. In another small bowl, mix brown sugar, paprika, chili powder, kosher salt, cayenne pepper, garlic powder, onion powder and black pepper. Brush mustard all over roast and rub with spice mixture. Place pork roast fat-side up on smoker grate and smoke until the internal temperature of the roast reaches 205°F, 12 to 15 hours. Add wood chips to the wood tray as necessary. Remove pork roast from smoker, wrap with foil and let rest for about 20 minutes. Remove bone from roast and shred meat with two forks, removing gristle and fat as necessary. Serve and enjoy!

Cowboy Omelet
Serves: 1
Cooking Time: 10 Minutes
Ingredients:
- 1 tablespoons butter (divided)
- 2 tablespoons minced onion
- 2 tablespoons minced bell pepper
- 2 eggs (lightly beaten)
- 2 tablespoons milk
- Salt and freshly ground black pepper, to taste
- 2 ounces (about 1/4 cup) leftover pulled pork
- 2 tablespoons shredded pepper jack cheese

Directions:
In a small non-stick skillet, melt 2 tablespoon butter and sauté onion and bell pepper until softened, stirring frequently, about 5 minutes. Remove onion mixture from skillet and set aside. Whisk eggs and milk, season to taste with salt and pepper. Melt remaining butter in skillet and swirl to coat. Add egg mixture to skillet and cook for about 1 minute. Lift cooked edges and tilt pan so uncooked egg runs underneath until top is nearly set. Cover skillet and let cook until top is set, about 1 minute more. Carefully flip omelet and spread onion mixture, cheese and pulled pork over half of the omelet. Cover pan until cheese is melted, about 2 minutes. Gently slide omelet out of skillet onto a plate and fold the omelet in half over the filling. Serve omelet with barbecue sauce if desired and enjoy!

Smoked Meatballs
Serves: 12
Cooking Time: 1 1/2 Hours
Ingredients:
- 2 pounds ground beef
- 1 pound ground pork
- 2/3 cup panko bread crumbs
- 1 egg (beaten)
- 1/3 cup finely grated Parmesan cheese
- 2 tablespoons milk
- 2 teaspoons garlic powder
- 2 teaspoons onion powder
- 2 teaspoons Kosher salt
- 1 teaspoon freshly ground black pepper

Directions:
Place hickory wood chips in the Masterbuilt smoker's wood tray and preheat smoker to 225°F. In a large bowl, mix all ingredients until thoroughly combined. Using a 1-tablespoon scoop, form mixture into about 60 meatballs. Arrange meatballs on racks, place in smoker and smoke until the internal temperature of the meat reaches 160°F, about 1 1/2 hours. Add wood chips to the wood tray as necessary. Serve meatballs immediately and enjoy!

Pulled Pork Hoagie
Serves: 3
Cooking Time: 2 Hours
Ingredients:
- 1 pound pulled pork
- 4 hoagie rolls
- 1 tomato, sliced
- 4 slices provolone cheese

Directions:
Preheat the smoker to 2250F. Add water to the water pan and add your favorite wood chips into the side tray. Place the pulled pork in a heat-proof dish and add hoagie rolls on top of the pulled pork. Add tomato slices on top and the sliced provolone cheese. Put in the smoker for 2 hours.

Basic Smoked Beef Jerky Recipe
Servings: 4
Cooking Time: 4 hour
Ingredients:
- 1 lb London broil, trimmed of fat, cut into 1/4-inch strips
- 3/4 cup unfiltered apple cider vinegar
- 2 TBsps sea salt
- 2 TBS brown sugar
- 2 TBS blackstrap molasses
- 1 TBS cracked black pepper
- 1 tsp garlic powder
- 1 tsp onion powder
- 1 bottle stout or dark beer (divided into 2)
- Hickory or mesquite wood chips, soaked in water

Directions:
Place the London broil in the freezer for approximately 30 minutes. Meanwhile, make your marinade: Combine all of the other ingredients, using only 1/2 of the beer in a large baking dish. Slice the semi-frozen beef into 1" wide x 1/4" thick strips. Place these in a baking dish and cover with the marinade. Cover the dish and place it in the refrigerator for 4 to 8 hours, or overnight. You can also do this in a sealable plastic baggie. Remove the beef strips from the marinade and pat them dry with paper towels. Remove the racks from the smoker and layer the beef on as many racks as you need, leaving a little air space around each strip. Fill the water pan with the remaining beer and some water to bring it to 1/2 full. Add wood chips to the bottom tray. Turn the smoker on to 180°F and set the timer for 3.5 hours. Place the racks with beef in the preheated smoker. Check the wood chips and liquid at 2 hours. Add more if needed. Allow the jerky to cool on the racks. Store in the refrigerator, or eat immediately!

Basic Smoked Burgers
Servings: 4
Cooking Time: 1 hour 15 minutes
Ingredients:
- 2 Lbs. ground beef chuck
- Sea salt
- Cracked black pepper
- Slices of provolone, cheddar, or American cheese (optional)
- Rolls for serving

Directions:
Remove 2 wracks from the smoker to place the burgers on. Prepare your smoker by adding wood chips to the tray and water to the bowl. Preheat the smoker to 225°F. Open the top vent. Form the ground beef into 1/2" thick patties that are approximately 5 to 6 ounces of meat each. Place the patties on the racks and generously season both sides with salt and pepper. Place the racks into the preheated smoker. Smoke the burgers for 60 to 90 minutes until they reach on internal temperature of 150 to 160°F. Check the burgers at 60 minutes. Add more wood chips and water if needed. If you want cheese on your hamburgers, place it on top of each patty when there is approximately 10 to 15 minutes of smoking time remaining. Smoke for the remaining minutes with the cheese on top. Serve the burgers with toppings, such as sliced onions, lettuce, tomatoes, ketchup, or mustard.

Dry Rubbed and Smoked Tri-Tip Roast Recipe
Servings: 6
Cooking Time: 3 hour
Ingredients:
- 2 to 3 pound tri-tip roast
- 2 tsps sea salt
- 1-1/2 tsps mild chili powder
- 1 tsp black pepper
- 1 tsp brown sugar
- 1 tsp espresso powder
- 1 tsp onion powder
- 1/2 tsp garlic powder
- Water for the smoker bowl
- Cherry wood chips (can substitute hickory or other fruit wood)
- Drip pan for beneath the roast
- Aluminum foil

Directions:
In a small bowl, mix together all of the rub ingredients. Place the roast on a cutting board. If the roast has a fat cap on it, score the fat diagonally about an inch apart with a sharp chef's knife. Turn it 90 degrees and score again to form a diamond pattern. While still on the cutting board, season the meat all over with the rub, pressing it into the roast. Place the roast aside and allow it come to room temperature for 30 to 60 minutes. Place the water in the bowl at the bottom of the smoker. Place the wood chips in the side tray. Preheat the smoker to 225°F. Place the tri-tip, fat side up, on the middle rack of the smoker. Place the drip pan on the rack below the roast. Use a foil sheet pan or line a sheet pan with foil for easier cleanup. Place the digital thermometer in the fatter end of the roast. Close the door and open the vent. Smoke for approximately 2 hours for medium rare. The internal temperature should read 130 to 135°F. Be sure to check the wood chips and water at 60 minutes. Add more if necessary. Remove the roast to a clean cutting board and tent loosely with foil for 20 minutes to allow the juices to be reabsorbed. Slice thinly and serve with a starchy side and a green vegetable. Recipe ideas follow.

Glaze (double for extra sauce)
Servings: 4
Cooking Time: 3 hour 20 minutes
Ingredients:
- 1/2 cup ketchup
- 2 TBS yellow mustard
- 2 TBS brown sugar

Directions:
In a large bowl, place the ground meat and allow it to rest so it comes to room temperature. Place your eggs in a separate bowl and beat them lightly. Allow the eggs to also come to room temperature. Prepare your smoker by filling the tray with wood chips of your choice. Fill the water bowl 1/2 way with plain water. Preheat the smoker to between 225°F and 250°F with the top vent cracked open. In a large sauté pan, heat the olive oil. Add the onions, bell pepper, herbs, salt, and pepper. Cook this mixture for approximately 6 minutes over medium-low heat, stirring occasionally, until the onions just start to wilt. Turn off the heat and allow the onion mixture to cool for a few minutes. Then, stir in the Worcestershire sauce, tomato paste, and broth or milk. Reserve a little broth or milk for mixing in later if needed. Add the onion mixture, eggs, and bread crumbs to the ground meat. Gently combine all of this using your hands. Try not to make it too mushy. It can be rustic so it isn't dense after smoking. If it feels too dry add some more broth or milk. Shape the meat into a large rectangular loaf or 2 smaller loaves. Place it inside your preheated smoker directly on the rack. If you are smoking sides to go with your loaf, place the meat on the lower rack to avoid any raw juices dripping into your sides. Make the glaze by whisking all of the ingredients together in a bowl. Check the wood chips and water every 60 minutes, or when you don't see enough smoke coming through the vent. Replenish as needed. After 2 hours, brush enough glaze all over the meatloaf and return it to the smoker for approximately 1 more hour. The loaf is ready when the internal temperature reaches 160°F. Serve with some sides and a bit of warmed up glaze.

Herb Rubbed Smoked Rack of Veal
Servings: 4
Cooking Time: 3 hour 40 minutes
Ingredients:
- 4 pound veal rack
- 4 TBS Kosher or coarse salt
- 3 TBS brown sugar
- 2 TBS dried thyme
- 1 TBS dried rosemary
- 1 TBS paprika
- 1 TBS garlic powder
- 1 TBS freshly cracked pepper
- 1/4 tsp cayenne pepper
- 3 TBS extra virgin olive oil
- Water
- Hickory or apple wood chips

Directions:
In a small bowl, combine the salt, sugar, thyme, rosemary, paprika, garlic, pepper, and cayenne. Trim any silver skin off of the rack. Remove all but 1/4" of the fat cap (optional). Place the veal ribs on a baking sheet or in a baking dish and brush olive oil on all surfaces. Pat the dry rub all over the veal. Cover with plastic wrap and place the pan in the refrigerator for 4 hours. Remove the veal from the refrigerator 45 minutes prior to smoking it. Preheat your MB smoker to 225°F. Fill the water bowl 1/2 way. Place wood chips in the side tray. Open the top vent. Place the veal directly on the middle grill rack of the smoker, fat side up. Smoke for 3 to 4 hours or until the internal temperature reaches approximately 155°F when checked with a digital or probe meat thermometer. While the veal is cooking, prepare your root vegetables for smoking during the final 2 hours. Check the water bowl and wood chip tray every 60 minutes and replenish as needed. Remove the rack of veal to a clean cutting board and cover loosely with foil. Allow the veal to rest for 15 minutes before slicing. Slice between the rib bones and serve the chops with lemon wedges, smoked root vegetables, and a tomato salad. Recipes follow.

Marinated Smoked Beef Short Ribs
Servings: 4
Cooking Time: 9 hour 10 minutes
Ingredients:
- 3 to 4 lbs beef chuck short ribs
- 1/2 cup soy sauce
- 1/2 cup water
- 1/2 cup honey
- 3 TBS rice wine vinegar
- 2 TBS peanut oil
- 2 TBS sesame oil
- 2 TBS grated fresh ginger
- 2 TBS minced garlic
- 1 TBS chili paste
- Water and apple juice
- Apple, cherry, or oak wood chips

Directions:
In a large bowl, whisk together all of the marinade ingredients until well combined. Taste the mixture to be sure it has the correct amount of saltiness, sweetness, acidity, and heat. Adjust if necessary. Place the ribs in large sealable plastic bags. Pour enough marinade over the ribs to cover them. Seal the bags and massage gently to coat the ribs. Place the bags in a baking dish and put in the refrigerator for 4 to 12 hours. Remove the dish from the refrigerator 40 minutes before placing the ribs in the smoker. Place wood chips in the tray of your smoker. Fill the water bowl half with water and half with apple juice. Preheat the smoker to 250°F with the top vent open. Place the slab of ribs, or individual ribs, on the smoker rack. Cook for 8 to 10 hours until the internal temperature reaches 200°F and the meat has started to pull away from the bone. Replenish the wood chips and liquid approximately every 60 minutes. Remove the ribs from the smoker and wrap them in foil. Allow to rest for 30 to 60 minutes before serving. Serve the ribs with an Asian style barbeque sauce on the side, a crunchy cabbage slaw, and plenty of napkins.

Smoked Beef Braciole Finished in Tomato Sauce Recipe

Servings: 4
Cooking Time: 1 hour 55 minutes

Ingredients:

Beef

- 1-1/2 pound flank steak
- 4 TBS extra virgin olive oil (EVOO), divided
- 3 or 4 slices prosciutto
- 3 or 4 slices provolone cheese
- 1/2 cup Italian seasoned bread crumbs
- 1 garlic clove, minced
- 2/3 cup grated parmesan cheese
- 2 TBS minced fresh flat leaf parsley
- 1/2 tsp sea salt
- 1/2 tsp freshly ground black pepper
- Salt and pepper for seasoning the exterior

Sauce

- 1/2 cup EVOO
- 1 small onion, chopped
- 2 cloves garlic, sliced thinly
- 1 carrot, grated
- 2 tsps dried oregano
- 1/2 cup dry red wine
- 2 quarts of good quality canned, crushed tomatoes
- 6 fresh basil leaves, rolled and sliced thinly
- 2 bay leaves
- Sea salt and freshly ground black pepper to taste

Directions:

Beef

Place the flank steak between 2 sheets of plastic wrap on a cutting board. Using the smooth face of a meat mallet, pound the flank steak so that it is between 1/8 and 1/4 inch thick. Brush one side of the beef with 1 tablespoon of EVOO. Add a layer of prosciutto to cover the steak. Then, add one layer of provolone cheese. In a medium bowl, mix together the bread crumbs, parmesan cheese, garlic, parsley, salt, and pepper. Stir in 2 tablespoons of EVOO. Sprinkle the bread crumb mixture evenly over the provolone cheese. Starting at 1 short end, carefully roll the steak to enclose the filling completely. Using butcher's or kitchen twine, tie the steak roll at 1 inch intervals to secure. Coat the exterior of the roll with the remaining tablespoon of EVOO. Season with salt and pepper. Prepare your smoker by filling the water bowl 1/2 way with a mixture of water and dry red wine. Fill the tray with wood chips. I used oak for this recipe. Preheat to 250°F with the top vent open and the door closed. Place the beef roll, seam side down on a rack inside the smoker. Cook for at least 1 hour and up to 2 hours. You want the internal temperature of the braciole to be between 145°F and 165°F. Prepare the sauce while the beef is smoking. Remove the beef from the smoker and submerge it in the simmering tomato sauce for 20 minutes and up to 60 minutes, turning as needed. Remove the braciole from the sauce and slice it into 1/2 inch thick portions, remembering to remove the twine as you go along. Serve the beef rolls either alone with sauce spooned over the top or with cooked penne pasta and some extra parmesan cheese. Sautéed escarole is a nice side dish. Sauce In a large sauce pot or Dutch oven over medium-high, heat the EVOO. Add the onion and sauté for 5 minutes until the onion starts to become translucent. Stir in the garlic, carrots, and oregano. Cook until the garlic and oregano are fragrant, approximately 3 to 5 minutes. Add the wine and stir to deglaze the pan, approximately another 3 minutes. Add the tomatoes, basil, and bay leaves and bring to a low boil. Turn the heat down to a slow simmer. Cover the pot and allow the sauce to simmer for 45 to 60 minutes, stirring every 10 minutes. You want the sauce to thicken so that it isn't watery. If too thick, you can always add a little bit of water. Taste the sauce and season with salt and pepper to your liking. Add the smoked braciole and simmer it in the sauce as directed above in the "Beef" section of the recipe. You may have some leftover sauce. It will freeze very well in 1 cup portions in sealable plastic baggies or small freezer-proof containers for weeknight meals. It should last for up to 6 months.

Smoked Beef Tenderloin with Horseradish Sauce Recipe

Servings: 10
Cooking Time: 1 hour 45 minutes

Ingredients:

- 1 whole beef tenderloin, trimmed (approximately 6 pounds)
- 2 TBS extra virgin olive oil
- 2 TBS kosher salt
- 1-1/2 TBS freshly ground black pepper
- 1 cup sour cream
- 3/4 cup prepared horseradish
- 1/4 cup Dijon mustard
- 1/4 cup good mayonnaise
- 1/4 cup chopped chives
- Water or water and red wine
- Oak or hickory wood chips

Directions:

Tie the roast as described above. Set it aside to come to room temperature. Fill the water bowl of your smoker half way with water, or 1/2 water and 1/2 red wine, and place the wood chips in the tray. Open the top vent. Preheat your smoker to 275°F. Coat the tenderloin with olive oil. Season it all over with the salt and pepper. Place the beef directly on the smoker rack. If there is a probe thermometer attached, place it in one end of the roast. Smoke the tenderloin for 1-1/2 hours and check the internal temperature. You are looking for 125°F to 130°F. Continue to smoke for up to 2 hours, checking the temperature every 15 minutes. Remember to check the water and wood chips every 45 minutes and replenish as needed. Make the sauce while the beef is smoking. In a medium mixing bowl, whisk together the sour cream, horseradish, mustard, mayonnaise, and chives. Cover and refrigerate until ready to serve. Remove the cooked beef tenderloin to a clean cutting board and tent loosely with foil. Allow the meat to rest for at least 15 minutes before slicing. Snip the twine off of the meat with kitchen shears and remove. Slice the beef into 1/2 inch thick portions. Serve with the horseradish sauce on the side.

Smoked Brisket
Servings: 12
Cooking Time: 11 hour
Ingredients:
- 12 pound uncured brisket
- 1/2 cup brown sugar
- 1/2 Cup smoked paprika
- 6 TBS chili powder
- 6 TBS kosher salt
- 4 TBS cracked black pepper
- 4 TBS ground cumin
- 2 TBS garlic or onion powder
- 2 TBS dried oregano
- 2 TBS ground coriander
- 2 tsps cayenne pepper (alter to your liking)
- Raw, unfiltered apple cider vinegar (ACV)
- Mesquite or hickory wood chips

Directions:
Remove the brisket from the package and pat dry with paper towels. Clean any connective tissue or silver skin from the lean side. Trim the fat cap down to approximately 1/4 inch thickness, leaving enough on for moisture and flavor. Place the brisket on a large sheet pan. Mix all of the dry seasonings together in a bowl. Generously coat all sides of the beef with the dry rub, patting it into the meat. With the fat side up, cover the meat with plastic wrap and place in the refrigerator for 15 minutes or up to 4 hours. (Make your side dishes while the meat marinates). Preheat the smoker to 225°F. Meanwhile, take the brisket out of the refrigerator and allow it to come slightly to room temperature but still cool. Fill the water bowl or pan 1/2 way with the apple cider vinegar. Add the wood chips to the side tray. Place the brisket directly on the middle rack with the fat side up. Insert the digital thermometer, if your smoker has one, into the thicker end of the meat. Close the door and set the timer for 10 hours. Check the water bowl a few times and refill with ACV as necessary. Check for smoke every hour and refill the wood chip tray as needed. Check the internal temperature of the meat after 9 hours. You are looking for between 190°F and 200°F. Remove the meat to a cutting board and cover it and the board to seal with aluminum foil. Let the meat rest covered for a minimum of 15 minutes and up to 2 hours before slicing and serving.

Smoked Dry Rubbed Bottom Round Roast
Servings: 10
Cooking Time: 2 hour
Ingredients:
- 3 pound bottom round roast of beef
- 1/4 cup prepared yellow mustard
- 1 TBS freshly ground black pepper
- 2 tsps garlic powder
- 2 tsps onion powder
- 1-1/2 tsps brown sugar
- 1 tsp paprika
- 1 tsp kosher or coarse sea salt
- Water and wood chips for the smoker

Directions:
Remove the bottom round roast from the refrigerator 40 minutes prior to cooking it so it can come to room temperature. In a mixing bowl, whisk together the pepper, garlic powder, onion powder, sugar, paprika, and salt. Using your hands, coat the entire roast with the mustard. Pat the dry rub into the layer of mustard to cover the roast. Set aside while you preheat your smoker. Fill the water bowl of your smoker half way and place the wood chips in the tray. Open the top vent. Preheat your smoker to 250°F. Place the roast directly on the smoker rack. If there is a probe thermometer attached, place it in one end of the roast. Smoke the beef for 90 minutes and check the internal temperature. You are looking for 130°F to 135°F. Continue to smoke for up to 1 hour and 45 minutes, checking the temperature every 20 minutes. Remember to check the water and wood chips every 45 minutes and replenish as needed. Remove the cooked bottom round roast to a clean cutting board and tent loosely with foil. Remember that the roast will continue to cook up to approximately 140°F. Allow the meat to rest for at least 15 minutes before slicing. You can allow the roast to cool down completely if using for sandwiches. Slice the smoked bottom round roast as thinly as possible and use to make classic roast beef sandwiches. See the recipe that follows. Or, serve with your favorite side dishes.

A Little Spicy Smoked Lamb Sausage Recipe
Servings: 8
Cooking Time: 2 hour
Ingredients:
- 2 pounds lamb shoulder, cubed
- 1/2 pound lamb or beef fat, cubed
- 1 TBS sea salt
- 1 tsp raw turbinado sugar
- 2 TBS dried rosemary
- 2 tsps dried thyme
- 2 tsps cracked black pepper
- 1 glove fresh garlic, minced
- 1 tsp hot paprika
- 1/4 cup dry red wine or dry sherry
- Collagen casings (approximately 7 to 10 feet)

Directions:
Place your hog casings in a large bowl with cool water to soak for an hour to remove the salt. Rinse the casings well with cold running water. Allow the water to run inside the casings. If using edible collagen, follow the manufacturer's packaging instructions for preparing. Grind the meat and fat on a course setting into a large bowl. Or, mix your pre-ground meat products together in a large bowl. Add the salt, sugar, seasonings, and liquid. With a non-latex glove, mix the ingredients well by hand to combine. You can also use a spoon, but your hand works best in my experience. Set up your appliance for stuffing, per the manufacturer's instructions. Place the open end of the casing over the nozzle. Tie off the other end to close it. Gently push the rest of the casing to cover the nozzle completely. Slowly push the meat mixture into the casing using one hand to help fill the casing and the other to regulate the speed. This may take some practice. You want the casing to be filled but not overstuffed to where it breaks. If a casing breaks, just remove that section and tie off the end. You can reuse the meat in the broken section or make breakfast patties with it. Here is a quick video showing one way to stuff sausage into casings with a stand mixer attachment. Tie off the sausage roll into individual links by twisting the casing every 4 to 6 inches. You can also leave the sausage in a single whole roll. Hang the linked or whole sausage to air dry for 1 to 3 hours in a cool area. You may have to be creative with this. A folding clothes drying rack works great. If you can't figure out where to hang the sausage, place the roll on paper towels and rotate often so that all surfaces dry. Place some paper towels in the bottom of a storage container large enough to hold all of the sausage. Layer the sausage, then more paper towel, then more sausage until the container is full. Place a top on the container. Put this in the refrigerator and chill for 12 to 24 hours.

Basic Smoked Beef Jerky Recipe
Servings: 4
Cooking Time: 4 hour
Ingredients:
- 1 lb London broil, trimmed of fat, cut into 1/4-inch strips
- 3/4 cup unfiltered apple cider vinegar
- 2 TBsps sea salt
- 2 TBS brown sugar
- 2 TBS blackstrap molasses
- 1 TBS cracked black pepper
- 1 tsp garlic powder
- 1 tsp onion powder
- 1 bottle stout or dark beer (divided into 2)
- Hickory or mesquite wood chips, soaked in water

Directions:
Place the London broil in the freezer for approximately 30 minutes. Meanwhile, make your marinade: Combine all of the other ingredients, using only 1/2 of the beer in a large baking dish. Slice the semi-frozen beef into 1" wide x 1/4" thick strips. Place these in a baking dish and cover with the marinade. Cover the dish and place it in the refrigerator for 4 to 8 hours, or overnight. You can also do this in a sealable plastic baggie. Remove the beef strips from the marinade and pat them dry with paper towels. Remove the racks from the smoker and layer the beef on as many racks as you need, leaving a little air space around each strip. Fill the water pan with the remaining beer and some water to bring it to 1/2 full. Add wood chips to the bottom tray. Turn the smoker on to 180°F and set the timer for 3.5 hours. Place the racks with beef in the preheated smoker. Check the wood chips and liquid at 2 hours. Add more if needed. Allow the jerky to cool on the racks. Store in the refrigerator, or eat immediately!

Homemade Smoked Maple Cured Bacon
Servings: 16
Cooking Time: 2 hour 35 minutes
Ingredients:
- 4 to 5 lb pork belly, skinned and trimmed (as described above)
- 1/3 cup maple sugar (can substitute brown sugar)
- 1/4 cup kosher salt
- 2 TBS coarsely ground black pepper
- 1 TBS celery salt
- 1 tsp pink curing salt (optional)

Directions:
Rinse the pork belly under cold water and pat dry with plenty of paper towels. Place the pork belly on a rimmed baking sheet. In a medium mixing bowl, place the sugar, salt, pepper, celery salt, and pink salt (if using). Mix well with a whisk to combine and break up any clumps. Use your hands if necessary. Sprinkle half of the dry cure on top of the belly and rub it into the meat with your hands. Turn the belly over and repeat. Place the pork belly and any excess dry rub in a large sealable plastic bag, or wrap completely to seal well in a couple of layers of plastic wrap. Clean the baking sheet with hot soapy water and place the wrapped pork on the pan. Place the pan in the refrigerator on the bottom shelf so that there is no chance of any raw juices leaking onto other food items. Cure the pork for 5 days, turning it over once each day to redistribute the accumulating liquid. Place the cured pork belly in a clean sink and rinse well under cold water. Pat the belly completely dry with paper towels. Clean the baking sheet, if necessary. And, clean the sink very well with hot soapy water. Place the belly on a wire rack that fits inside the sheet pan. Place the pan back in the refrigerator and allow the pork to continue to dry and cure uncovered for 4 to 8 additional hours. Take the pork belly out of the refrigerator 45 minutes before smoking. Prepare the smoker. Add the wood chips to the side tray. Fill the water pan half way with a combination of water and apple cider. Open the top vent and preheat the smoker to 175°F. Lay the pork belly, fat side up, directly on the middle rack of the smoker. Smoke the pork belly for approximately 2 to 3 hours or until the internal temperature reads 150°F. The exterior shell of the belly should be bronze in color and firm to the touch. Remember to check the water bowl and wood chip tray halfway through the smoking process and replenish if needed. Clean and dry the baking sheet and wire rack well while the belly is smoking. Transfer the whole smoked bacon to the wire rack inserted in the baking sheet. Allow it to cool to room temperature so that you can handle it easily. Tightly wrap it in plastic wrap and refrigerate for another 4 to 8 hours. Slice all the chilled bacon to your desired thickness. The bacon is not fully cooked at this point. Cook what you want to eat.

(See cooking instructions below). And, freeze what you aren't going to use within a couple of days in tightly sealed freezer storage bags.

Savory and Sweet Smoked Ribs with Classic BBQ Sauce
Servings: 6
Cooking Time: 5 hour
Ingredients:
- 2 slabs of baby back ribs (approximately 2 lbs each)
- 1/2 cup brown or raw turbinado sugar
- 1/4 cup smoked paprika
- 1-1/2 TBS kosher salt
- 1 TBS ground black pepper
- 2 tsps garlic powder
- 2 tsps onion powder
- 1/2 tsp cayenne pepper or chili powder (your preference)
- Basting liquid of either red wine vinegar, stout, or apple juice
- Water for smoker
- Hickory or apple wood chips

Directions:
Lay the ribs flat on a clean surface, meat side down. Remove the membrane that covers the rib bones by slicing it at one end with a paring knife. You should be able to grab the cut end with a paper towel and peel the layer of membrane off. Check out this video to see how it is done. Mix all of the dry rub ingredients together in a bowl or measuring cup. Sprinkle on and rub into the tops, bottoms, and sides of the ribs. Set the ribs aside to rest and come to room temperature for approximately 30 minutes. Preheat your electric smoker to 225°F. When it is ready, add some water to the removable pan that is usually on the bottom shelf. This is optional, but it keeps the ribs moist. Fill the side "drawer" with dry wood chips. For less intense smoke flavor you can use water soaked chips. Place rib, meat side up, on the smoker's wire racks. If too large for the size smoker you have, cut them in half and arrange so that they fit. Cook in the smoker for 3 hours. If you don't see smoke after an hour or so, add more wood chips. Keep watching for smoke and add chips as needed. Make the sauce while the ribs are smoking (recipe follows). Or use your favorite jarred sauce. After 3 hours, place 2 large sheets of heavy-duty aluminum foil on your flat surface. Place a rack of ribs on each sheet of foil. Baste with your liquid of choice to moisten. A spray bottle or a pastry brush works well for this step. Wrap the ribs completely in the foil. Place the wrapped ribs back in the smoker and cook for an additional 1 to 1-1/2 hours, or until the internal temperature reaches 160 degrees. Serve with sauce on the side. Optional step: If you prefer your ribs slathered in sauce, you can coat the top of the ribs with some sauce and place them back in the smoker for another hour. This is referred to as the 3-2-1 smoking method.

Smoked Blueberry and Maple Glazed Baby Back Ribs

Servings: 4

Cooking Time: 5 hour

Ingredients:

- 4 racks of baby back ribs, approximately 2 pounds each
- Dry rub
- 3 TBS maple or brown sugar
- 3 TBS course sea salt
- 3 TBS paprika
- 2 TBS freshly ground black pepper
- 1 tsp garlic powder
- 1 tsp onion powder
- 1 tsp dry mustard

Sauce

- 2 cups fresh or frozen blueberries
- 3/4 cup ketchup
- 1/2 cup apple cider vinegar, preferably unfiltered
- 1/2 cup good maple syrup
- 1 TBS molasses
- 1 tsp chili powder
- 1 tsp sea salt
- 1 tsp freshly ground black pepper
- 1/2 tsp Worcestershire sauce
- 1/4 cup water, if needed
- Maple or apple wood chips
- Apple cider in a spray bottle
- Water or water and dark beer for smoking

Directions:

Lay the ribs flat on a clean surface, meat side down. Remove the chewy membrane that covers the rib bones by slicing it at one end with a paring knife. You should be able to grab the cut end with a paper towel and peel the layer of membrane off. Check out this video to see how it is done. Or, ask your butcher to trim the ribs.   Mix all of the dry rub ingredients together in a bowl or measuring cup. Sprinkle on and rub into the tops, bottoms, and sides of the ribs. Set the ribs aside to rest and allow them to come to room temperature for approximately 30 minutes.   Make the barbeque sauce while the ribs rest. Combine all the sauce ingredients, except the water, in a pot over high heat. Bring to a boil and reduce to a low simmer. Stir while the sauce thickens, adding water as needed if it becomes too thick. When it is a desirable consistency, remove from the heat and allow to cool. Once cool, blend the sauce until it is smooth, adding a little water if necessary. Refrigerate until ready to use.   Prepare the smoker. a) Charcoal Smoker: Set your grill up for indirect smoking. Begin by soaking the wood chips in water for approximately 60 minutes. Light your coals using a charcoal chimney and place the hot coals on one side of the grill. This is the area where the meat will cook indirectly and take on the smoke. Add some of the soaked wood chips directly on top of the hot coals. Close the lid and open the top vent. Allow the smoker or grill to get up to 225°F to 250°F.   b) Electric Smoker: Add the maple or apple wood chips to the side tray of the smoker. Fill the water bowl halfway with a combination of dark beer and water. Close the door, open the top vent, and preheat the smoker to 225°F.   Place the ribs, meat side up, on the smoker's wire racks. If too large for the size smoker you have, cut them in half and arrange so that they fit. Cook in the smoker for a total of 3.5 hours. At every 45 minutes spray the ribs with apple cider. Add more coals to the fire, liquid to the bowl, and wood chips every 45 to 60 minutes or when you don't see any smoke coming through the vent.   After 3.5 hours, baste the rib meat with 1/2 the blueberry sauce and smoke for another hour or two until the meat has pulled back from the ends of the bones and is very tender. Remove the ribs to a clean cutting board, baste with the remaining sauce, and tent with foil. Allow the ribs to rest for several minutes, then cut and serve on a large platter with sides. See recipe ideas below for beans and slaw. Start the beans about an hour before the ribs so that they are finished at the same time.

Smoked Boston Butt Recipe for Pulled Pork

Servings: 10

Cooking Time: 18 hour

Ingredients:

- 8 pound bone-in Boston butt roast
- 5 TBS jarred yellow mustard
- 1/3 cup packed brown sugar
- 3 TBS sea salt
- 2 TBS paprika
- 1 TBS garlic powder
- 1 TBS onion powder
- 2 tsps cracked black pepper
- 1/2 tsp cayenne pepper
- Unfiltered apple cider vinegar (ACV) in a spray bottle
- Water for drip pan

Directions:

Place the roast on a clean cutting board. If your roast has skin and/or a fat cap, trim most of the fat off, leaving a 1/4 inch layer for extra flavor. After trimming the fat, rinse the roast under cold running water and pat completely dry with plenty of paper towels. Place the roast inside the disposable pan. Side note: When working with raw pork, be sure to meticulously clean any surface it comes in contact with, including your hands, the sink, and the cutting board. Toss the paper towels out immediately. Combine the dry rub ingredients in a bowl. Time to get your hands dirty (or wear disposable gloves). Rub the entire roast well with the mustard to coat. Generously apply the dry rub, pressing it into the mustard, to completely cover the butt. The mustard will help to hold the dry rub in place. Cover the pan tightly with plastic wrap or aluminum foil. Place the pan in the refrigerator for 8 to 12 hours, basically overnight. Anymore than 24 hours is too long, as it will draw too much moisture out of the meat. An hour before you fire up the smoker, remove the roast from the refrigerator so that it can come to almost room temperature. After it has rested for an hour, remove the wrap and pour off any of the accumulated liquid in the bottom of the pan. Add the hickory or apple wood chips to the smoker drawer. Fill the water pan half way. Preheat the smoker to 225 degrees F. Place the roast on the upper rack of the smoker. Thoroughly wash out the disposable pan and place it on the rack below the roast to catch any drippings. Alternatively, use a clean disposable pan, if you have one. If your smoker has a meat thermometer attached, insert it into the roast at one end. While the pork is smoking, make a side of coleslaw, pickled vegetables, or macaroni & cheese. (See suggestions below). Smoke for approximately 8 hours.* Because of the sugar the meat will form a dark caramelized crust. This is delicious crunchy stuff. Replenish the wood chips and liquid approximately every 60 minutes. If you don't see any smoke coming from the vent, it is time to replenish. At 2 hour intervals spray some ACV on the roast just to moisten it. It is okay to turn the roast over once, but not necessary.

Smoked Ham Hocks Recipe

Servings: 4

Cooking Time: 4 hour 45 minutes

Ingredients:

- 1 gallon of filtered water
- 1 cup kosher salt
- 1/2 cup brown sugar
- 2 bay leaves
- 1 tsp black peppercorns
- 2 to 4 large fresh ham hocks
- Hickory wood chips
- Water

Directions:

In a large stainless steel or enameled pot, bring the water to a boil. Add the salt, sugar, herbs, and spices. Turn off the heat. Stir to dissolve. Allow the water to come to room temperature. Place the ham hocks into 2 (or more) gallon size resealable plastic baggies inside a baking dish to catch any spills. Pour the cooled water mixture evenly over the hocks to cover and seal the bags tightly, releasing any air. Place the dish with bags in the refrigerator for 24 hours. Rinse the hocks under cool water and dry off with paper towels. Place on a wire rack inside of a sheet pan. Feel free to improvise with makeshift tin foil rolls inside any sheet pan to raise up the hocks for better air circulation. Place the pan of uncovered hocks back in the refrigerator to air chill/dry for another 24 hours. This helps the ham to dry smoke and not steam. We are going to cook these at a higher temperature than a slow smoke that is called for when using curing salt. Preheat the smoker to 250°F. Add hickory wood chips to the side tray and water to the bowl. Smoke the hocks on the upper rack for 2 hours with the vent open, replenishing the wood chips and liquid every 60 minutes. At 2 hours, check the internal temperature of the hocks with a reliable meat thermometer. You are looking for at least 160°F. Continue to smoke until the temperature is achieved. Depending on your smoker, this could take up to 5 hours.

Smoked Ham with Maple & Mustard Glaze Recipe

Servings: 16
Cooking Time: 4 hour

Ingredients:
- 10 to 16 pound bone-in baked ham (shoulder, butt, or shank)
- 1/2 cup pure maple syrup
- 1/2 cup raw turbinado cane sugar
- 1/4 cup sweet apple cider or pineapple juice
- 2 TBS spicy brown mustard

Directions:
Remove the ham form the packaging and give it a light rinse under cool water to remove any preservatives and excess seasoning. Pat it dry with paper towels. Place the ham, flat side down, on the lined sheet pan. Allow it to come to room temperature for 30 to 45 minutes. Optional: Score the ham at 45 degrees in a diamond pattern that penetrates approximately 1/2 inch into the ham at 1-1/2 inches apart. If using a spiral cut ham you don't need to do this. It just helps the glaze to stick better and infuse into the ham. Place the water in the pan at the bottom of your smoker. Fill the drawer or tray with wood chips. Preheat the smoker to 250°F. Place the ham in the lower section of the smoker, allowing room for the sides on the racks above. Place the digital thermometer in the thick portion of the ham. Open the top vent. Cook the ham until it reaches 130°F. This may take 60 to 90 minutes, depending on the size of the ham. You will need to check at 60 minutes. Replenish the wood chips and water approximately every 45 minutes, if needed. While the ham is smoking, prepare your glaze by whisking together and simmering the other ingredients in a saucepan until just slightly thickened so it will stick to a pastry brush and the ham. It should resemble a thick and slightly runny syrup that coats the back of a soup spoon. Remove the ham from the smoker at 130°F and completely coat it with the glaze using a pastry brush. Be generous. Return the ham to the hot smoker and cook until the internal temperature reaches 140°F and the glaze is dark but not burned. This should take an additional 60 to 90 minutes (approximately 2-1/2 to 3 hours). Remember that the ham is pre-cooked, so you are just heating it through and adding additional smoke flavor. This is also the time to smoke your sides. Remove the ham to a cutting board and tent it with foil for 10 to 15 minutes before slicing. Serve with smoked potatoes and pineapple rings. Recipes follow. You will want to place your potatoes and pineapples in the smoker right after the glaze goes on the ham.

Smoked Porchetta with Fresh Herbs

Servings: 10
Cooking Time: 4 hour

Ingredients:
- 5 lb pork belly, skin on
- 2 lb boneless center cut pork loin, trimmed of silver skin and excess fat
- 3 TBS fennel seeds
- 2 TBS minced fresh sage leaves
- 2 TBS minced fresh rosemary leaves
- 3 cloves garlic, minced
- Zest of 1 lemon
- Zest of 1 orange
- 2 tsps sea salt
- 1-1/2 tsps freshly ground black pepper
- 1 tsp red pepper flakes
- Salt and pepper for seasoning the outside of the roll
- Apple wood chips
- Water and orange slices

Directions:
Place the pork belly, skin side up, on a wire rack inserted into a sheet pan. Place the belly in the refrigerator uncovered overnight to allow it to air dry. Take the belly and loin out of the refrigerator 30 minutes before assembling the porchetta. In a medium bowl, whisk together the fennel seeds, sage, rosemary, garlic, lemon zest, orange zest, salt, pepper, and red pepper flakes. Set this aside. Pat the pork belly of any surface moisture with paper towels. Place the pork belly skin side up on a clean cutting board. With a sharp knife, score the skin in a 1" wide crosshatch pattern. Turn the belly over and cover the flesh side evenly with 2/3 of the herb mixture. Place the pork loin in the center of the belly and coat with the remaining herb mixture. Roll the pork belly tightly around the loin until the edges of the belly meet or overlap slightly. Tie the roll with kitchen twine at 1 inch intervals. Take a rack out of your smoker and place the porchetta on it, seam side down. Set aside while you prepare your smoker. Place water and orange slices in the bowl of the smoker. Add wood chips to the side tray. Place a foil lined sheet pan on the rack below the porchetta rack to catch drippings. Set the temperature to 235°F and preheat with the top vent open. Place the rack with the porchetta in the preheated smoker. Close the door and cook for 3 to 4 hours until the internal temperature at the center of the pork reaches 145°F and the skin has crisped and browned. Start checking at approximately 2 hours and 45 minutes. Remember to check the water bowl and wood chip tray periodically. Refill each as needed. Remove the smoked porchetta to a clean cutting board and loosely cover it with foil. Allow it to rest for 20 minutes before slicing. Slice the porchetta into 1/4 inch thick slices and serve with a hardy salad. Or, slice the porchetta as thinly as possible and serve on a grilled crusty roll with grainy mustard and shredded lettuce or pickled onions. A kale and dandelion greens salad recipe follows. Reminder: Don't forget to remove the twine as you slice the porchetta. No one wants to chew on a string.

Smoked Whole Bologna Roll
Servings:
Cooking Time: 3 hour 10 minutes
Ingredients:
- 3 lb whole bologna roll
- 1/4 cup yellow mustard
- 3/4 cup brown sugar
- 2 TBS fresh cracked black pepper (adjust to your liking)
- Wood chips, such as apple or hickory
- Brown ale (optional)

Directions:
Prepare the smoker. Add your favorite wood chips to the side tray. Fill the water pan half way with either just water or a combination of water and brown ale. Open the top vent and preheat the smoker to 225°F.   While the smoker is heating up, prepare the bologna: Combine the brown sugar with the pepper. Remove any plastic wrapper from the bologna. Score the entire bologna, not more than 1/4 inch deep, into 1 inch diamonds. Or, score into 1 inch squares. Coat the roll entirely with the mustard. Pat the sugar and pepper rub into the mustard to coat completely.   Place the whole bologna directly on the upper rack of the preheated smoker. Smoke for approximately 3 to 4 hours until the exterior is nicely caramelized and a little crispy. Replenish the wood chips and liquid approximately every 60 minutes.   Slice the bologna into 1/2 inch thick pieces, resembling burgers. Serve as sandwiches (recipe follows). Otherwise, cut the thick slices into bite size pieces and serve with toothpicks and an easy barbecue dipping sauce (recipe follows).

Fish and Seafood Recipes

Smoked Fish Spread
Serves: 12
Cooking Tmie: 20 Minutes Plus 1 Hour Refrigerating Time
Ingredients:
- 8 ounces cream cheese (softened)
- 1/4 cup sour cream
- 1/4 cup mayonnaise
- 1 lemon (zested, juiced)
- 1 tablespoon minced fresh dill
- 1 teaspoon horseradish
- 1/2 teaspoon kosher salt, plus more to taste
- 1/2 teaspoon freshly ground black pepper, plus more to taste
- 4 ounces (about 1/2 cup) smoked fish (skinned, flaked)

Directions:
In a medium bowl, beat cream cheese with an electric hand mixer until smooth. Add sour cream, mayonnaise, lemon zest, lemon juice, dill, horseradish, salt and pepper and beat until smooth. Add smoked fish to cream cheese mixture, stir until combined and season to taste with salt and pepper. Refrigerate spread until chilled through, about 1 hour. Sprinkle spread with minced dill just before serving. Enjoy!

Smoked Asian Trout
Serves: 6
Cooking Time: 2 Hours
Ingredients:
- 6 trout filets
- ¼ cup soy sauce
- ¼ cup teriyaki sauce
- ½ tablespoon salt
- 1 teaspoon lemon pepper
- A dash of dill seeds

Directions:
Combine all Ingredients: in a mixing bowl and allow to marinate in the fridge for at least 2 hours. Preheat the smoker to 00F. Place water in the water pan and add hickory wood chips into the side tray. Put the salmon in the middle tray. Cook for 2 hours. Baste the salmon with the sauce every 30 minutes

Masterbuilt Smoked Mackerel
Serves: 6
Cook Time: 4-5 Hours
Ingredients:
- 5 to 7 pounds of mackerel
- To prepare the Brine:
- 2 and ½ Gallons of water
- ½ Cup of white sugar
- ½ Cup of Brown Sugar
- ½ Cup of salt
- 2 Tablespoons of Garlic Powder
- 2 Tablespoons of Chili Powder
- 3 Tablespoons of Lemon Juice

Directions:
Place the mackerel into a glass cooking dish and pour in the brine; then coat the sides very well with the brine Refrigerate the fish for about 8 hours Remove the mackerel from the refrigerator and rinse it with cold water. Pat the mackerel dry and preheat your Masterbuilt electric smoker to a temperature of 225° F Smoke the mackerel for about 4 to hours and when the fish is perfectly done, remove it from the smoker and season with salt and fresh lemon Serve and enjoy your smoked mackerel!

Perfectly Cured Salmon
Serves: 4
Cooking Time: 6 Hours
Ingredients:
- 1 and ½ pounds salmon fillet, skinless and boneless
- 1 bunch fresh dill, chopped
- ½ lemon, thinly sliced
- ¼ cup of salt
- ¼ cup brown sugar
- 2 tablespoons ground pepper

Directions:
Take a bowl and add salt, pepper, sugar and rub the mix all over salmon Place seasoned salmon into a shallow baking dish and top with lemon slices, add dill and wrap with plastic wrap Transfer to fridge ad let it sit for 8-12 hours Was and pat them dry, let it sit for 2 hours at room temperature Take your drip pan and add water, cover with aluminum foil. Pre-heat your smoker to 160 degrees F Place tuna steaks on plate and season with salt and sugar, add seasoned steaks in a sealed pack, let it chill for 4 hours. Use water fill water pan halfway through and place it over drip pan. Add wood chips to the side tray. Transfer fish to smoker and smoke for 3-6 hours until internal temperature reaches 130 degrees F Make sure to keep adding woodchips and water after every hour to maintain heat Serve and enjoy!

Masterbuilt Smoked Trout

Serves: 5
Cook Time: 30 Minutes
Ingredients:

- ½ Teaspoon of Garam Masala
- 1 Pinch of dried red chili flakes
- 1 Tablespoon of olive oil
- 3 and ½ oz of trout
- To prepare the raita
- 2 Tablespoons of plain yoghurt
- 1 Tablespoon of chopped fresh mint
- The juice of half a lime
- ½ Thinly sliced and chopped cucumber
- 6 Chopped radishes
- 1 Pinch of salt

Directions:
Start by making the raita and in order to do that, mix the yoghurt with the mint and add a squeeze of lime juice in a separate bowl; then season it with salt   Add in the cucumber and the radishes; then place in the refrigerator until you can use it   Preheat your Masterbuilt electric smoker cooker to 225° F   In a bowl, mix the Garam Masala with the chili and the olive oil; then spread over the mackerel   Place the trout over the baking tray and place it on top of the smoker and close the smoker with a lid   Smoke the trout for about 30 minutes   Remove the trout from the smoker and set aside for about 5 minutes   Serve and enjoy the smoked trout with the raita!

Masterbuilt Electric Smoker Shrimp Kabobs

Serves: 5
Cook Time: 35 Minutes
Ingredients:

- 1 to ½ pounds of large shrimps; Thawed
- 1/3 Cup of good extra virgin olive oil
- 4 Minced garlic cloves
- 2 Tablespoons of minced fresh basil leaves
- ½ Teaspoon of sea salt
- ½ Teaspoon of cracked black pepper
- Dry white wine for the smoking process
- Lemon for serving

Directions:
Place the olive oil, the garlic, the basil, the salt, and the pepper in a large mixing bowl   Whisk your ingredients together; then clean the shrimp by removing its shells and by taking the intestinal tract out of the back part of the shrimp.   Add the shrimp to the mixing bowl and toss very well to coat the ingredients with the dressing; then set it aside while you soak the skewers and you prepare the smoker   Remove one rack from the smoker in order to place the skewers on it; then prepare your smoker by adding the wood chips to the tray with half the water and half the quantity of white wine to the bowl; then preheat the smoker to a temperature of about 225° F; then open the vent   Place about 6

shrimps on each of the skewers by piercing the tail end and the head end   Place the skewers over the rack and put it inside the smoker   Squeeze some quantity of lemon over the shrimp   Smoke for about 35 minutes   Serve and enjoy your dish!

Succulent Trout

Serves: 6
Cooking Time: 3 Hours
Ingredients:

- 1 (5-7lb) whole lake trout, butterflied
- Kosher salt, to taste
- ½ cup fresh rosemary, chopped
- 3 tbsp fresh orange zest, grated

Directions:
Season the trout with the salt generously.   Sprinkle the rosemary and orange zest over the meat side of trout evenly.   Place the fish in a large container and refrigerate for about 6—7 hours.   Remove the trout from container and with paper towels, pat dry it.   Set aside at room temperature for about 2 hours before cooking.   Soak oak wood chips in water for at least 1 hour.   Preheat the smoker to 225 degrees F, using oak wood chips.   Place the trout onto smoker and cook for about 1½-3 hours or until desired doneness.   Serve hot.

Butterflied Lobster Tails

Serves: 4
Cooking Time: 45 Minutes
Ingredients:

- 4 lobster tails
- 4 tablespoons butter (melted)
- 4 garlic cloves (minced)
- 4 tablespoons lemon juice
- Kosher salt and freshly ground black pepper, to taste

Directions:
Pour 2 cups water into the Masterbuilt smoker's water pan. Place apple wood chips in the smoker's wood tray and preheat smoker to 275°F.   To butterfly-cut a lobster tail, cut the upper back shell with a kitchen shears down the center and spread shell halves open. Starting at the flipper end, run your finger between the meat and the shell to loosen the meat, leaving meat attached to the flipper. Remove meat, turn over and place back in shell. Repeat with remaining lobster tails.   Mix butter, garlic and lemon juice and brush about half over exposed lobster meat. Season meat to taste with salt and pepper, place tails on smoker grate and smoke for about 20 minutes. Baste meat with remaining butter mixture and continue smoking lobster tails until the internal temperature of the meat reaches 140°F, about 25 minutes more (meat may appear pink from smoking). Serve lobster tails immediately with additional butter as desired for dipping. Enjoy!

Marinated Smoked Oysters

Serves: 4
Cooking Time: 30-45 Minutes
Ingredients:
- 48 medium-sized oysters (about 5-7" in the shell), shucked
- Brine
- ½ gallon water
- ½ cup brown sugar
- ¼ cup Kosher salt
- 1 bay leaf
- 1 tsp garlic powder
- 1 tsp black pepper
- 4 cloves garlic, lightly mashed
- 2 cups extra-virgin olive oil
- 1 tsp crushed red pepper flakes

Directions:
In a small saucepan, heat olive oil, garlic, and red pepper flakes over low heat for 20 minutes. Set aside to cool. In a large, nonreactive bowl, stir brine ingredients together until salt and sugar dissolves. Add 4 cups of ice and oysters to the brine and refrigerate for -40 minutes. Preheat smoker to 225°F. Remove oysters from the fridge and rinse under cold water to remove any remaining seasoning or sediment. Place the oysters on sheet trays so they are not touching and slide the trays into the smoker. Smoke the oysters at 225°F until the edges begin to curl, around 30-45 minutes. Remove the oysters from the smoker and immediately pour into a large plastic container filled with the infused olive oil mixture. Stir to combine. Note: Allow the oysters to marinate in the olive oil, in the fridge, for 1-2 hours before serving. They will only get better as they sit. Serve with crackers, or use in any of the smoked oyster recipes in this book.

Smoked Clams

Serves: 4
Cooking Time: 20 Minutes
Ingredients:
- 36 fresh clams
- 5 cloves of garlic
- 4 tbsp. of butter
- Beer

Directions:
Soak the all the clams in some water for two hours. Be sure to scrub the clams as well under some cold water after soaking them. Mince the butter, garlic, and one twelve ounce beer. Arrange the clams on a metal tray. Add this mixture to the tray. Place the tray inside the smoker. Cook your clams for only 20 minutes in the smoker, or until they have opened. Once the clams are done, add in your preferred sauce and serve.

Enticing Salmon

Serves: 4
Cooking Time: 10 Hours
Ingredients:
- 4 (6-ounce) salmon fillets
- 2 cups low-sodium soy sauce
- 1 cup dry white wine
- 1 cup water
- ½ tsp Tabasco sauce
- 1/3 cup sugar
- ¼ cup salt
- ½ tsp garlic powder
- ½ tsp onion powder
- Freshly ground black pepper, to taste

Directions:
In a large bowl, add all ingredients except salmon and stir until sugar is dissolved. Add salmon fillets and coat with brine well. Refrigerate, covered for overnight. Remove salmon from bowl and rinse under cold water. With paper towels, pat dry the salmon fillets. Place the salmon fillets onto cooling rack, skin side down and set aside to cool for about 1 hour. Preheat the smoker to 165 degrees F, using charcoal. Arrange the salmon fillets onto smoker rack, skin side down and cook for about 3-5 hours or until desired doneness. Serve hot.

Scrambled Smoked Fish Bowls

Serves: 2
Cooking Time: 10 Minutes
Ingredients:
- 1 tablespoon butter
- 2 scallions (white and green ends separated, sliced)
- 2 ounces (about 1/4 cup) flaked smoked fish
- 4 eggs (lightly beaten)
- 2 tablespoons milk
- Salt and freshly ground black pepper, to taste
- 2 tablespoons crumbled feta cheese

Directions:
In a small bowl, whisk eggs and milk, season to taste with salt and pepper and set aside. Melt butter in a medium nonstick skillet and sauté white scallion slices until softened, about 5 minutes, stirring occasionally. Add smoked fish and stir until combined. Pour egg mixture into skillet, tilt to coat evenly and let cook for about 1 minute. Lift cooked edges and tilt pan, then stir and break up eggs until nearly cooked through. Sprinkle feta cheese over egg mixture and stir until incorporated and melted. Spoon eggs into two bowls and sprinkle with green scallion slices to serve. Enjoy!

Smoked Lobster With Herbed Butter (masterbuilt Electric Smoker)
Serves: 6
Cooking Time: 1 Hour And 5 Minutes
Ingredients:
- 4 frozen lobster tails, thawed
- 3 Tbsp butter with salt
- 2 tsp fennel bulb
- 2 tsp tarragon
- 2 tsp fresh parsley (chopped)

Directions:
Preheat Masterbuilt Electric Smoker. Allow the smoker temperature to reach 225 degrees Fahrenheit. When it is ready, add some water to the removable pan that is usually on the bottom shelf. Fill the side "drawer" with dry wood chips. Combine butter, fennel, tarragon, and parsley. Brush the butter mixture on both sides of the lobsters and set them bottom side down on the smoking grates. Smoke for about 45 minutes. Remove the lobsters from the grill and let cool for a few minutes. Serve warm.

Smoked Catfish
Serves: 4
Cooking Time: 1 Hour
Ingredients:
- 2 lbs of catfish fillets
- 1 quart of cold water
- 1 cup non-iodized salt
- Coarse black pepper

Directions:
Stir salt and water together until the salt has dissolved. Place the fillets in a freezer safe bag. Add in the brine you just made, and place the fillets in the fridge for an hour. Take the catfish fillets out of the bag and give them a rinse. Be sure to pat them dry. Add coarse black pepper to each side of the fillets. Press your black pepper into the fish so it won't fall off while smoking. Smoke the catfish. Once the flesh begins to flake, the fish is done.

Simple Smoked Salmon
Serves: 4
Cooking Time: 1 Hour
Ingredients:
- 2 skin-on boneless salmon fillets (about 8 ounces each)
- 2 teaspoons salt
- 2 teaspoons lemon pepper
- 1 lemon (thinly sliced)
- 1 red onion (thinly sliced)
- Dill sprigs, for garnish

Directions:
Place apple or cherry wood chips in the Masterbuilt smoker's wood tray and preheat smoker to 5°F.

Rinse salmon fillets with cold water and pat dry. Season fillets all over with salt and lemon pepper. Place fillets skin-sides down on a rimmed baking sheet and cover with onion slices and lemon slices. Place baking sheet on smoker grate and smoke until fillets are flaky, about 1 hour. Remove onion and lemon slices from salmon fillets. Arrange fillets on a serving platter, garnish with dill sprigs and serve immediately. Enjoy!

Zesty Tuna
Serves: 6
Cooking Time: 20 Minutes
Ingredients:
- 3 lbs tuna fillets
- ¾-1 cup butter
- 4 tbsp fresh lemon juice
- 4 tbsp fresh lime juice
- ½ tsp fresh lemon zest, grated finely
- ½ tsp fresh lime zest, grated finely
- 3 tsp garlic powder
- 1 tbsp mustard
- Salt and freshly ground black pepper, to taste

Directions:
Soak five large hickory chunks in water. Preheat the smoker to 300 degrees F, using charcoal. In a microwave-safe dish, add all ingredients except the tuna fillets microwave on 59% power for about 5 minutes, stirring after every 1½ minutes. Remove from microwave and stir the mixture well. Grease the grater and add hickory chunks to coals and wait for about minutes. Coat the tuna fillets with butter mixture evenly. Place the tuna fillets onto smoker, skin side down and top with the remaining butter mixture evenly. Cook for about 20 minutes or until desired doneness. Serve hot.

Smoked Eel
Serves: 2
Cooking Time: 3 Hours
Ingredients:
- 10 cups warm water
- 1-½ cup salt
- ½ cup brown sugar
- 4 lemons, halved
- 2 sprigs fresh thyme
- Other Ingredients:
- 2 fillets whole eel, cleaned and washed

Directions:
First, prepare the brine by mixing all the brine ingredients in a large pot, and place eel in it for hours. Next day, pat dry the eel and let it dry. Now, preheat the electric smoker to 5 degrees F and add wood chips. Smoke the eel for about hours. Once the skins get crisp, the eel is ready to be served. Enjoy.

Omega-3 Rich Salmon

Serves: 6

Cooking Time: 1 Hour

Ingredients:

- 2 lbs fresh salmon, pat dried
- 1 tsp fresh dill, minced
- 2 tbsp brown sugar
- Salt and freshly ground black pepper, to taste

Directions:

Soak cherry wood chips in water for at least hour. Preheat the smoker to 0-275 degrees F, using charcoal and cherry wood chips. In a bowl, add all ingredients except salmon and mix well Coat the salmon with mixture generously. Place the salmon into the smoker and cook for about 1 hour or until desired doneness. Serve hot.

Fancy Appetizers

Serves: 8

Cooking Time: 22 Minutes

Ingredients:

- 24 jumbo sea scallops, pat dried
- ½ cup butter
- 1 garlic clove, minced
- Salt and freshly ground black pepper, to taste
- 12 thin-cut bacon slices, halved crosswise

Directions:

In a small frying pan, melt the butter and sauté the garlic for about minute. Remove from the heat and set aside to cool slightly. In a large bowl, place the scallops, garlic butter, salt and pepper and mix well. Wrap a scallop with a bacon piece and secure each with a toothpick. Preheat the smoker to 400 degrees F, using charcoal and. Place the scallops onto the grill and cook for about 15-20 minutes. Serve hot.

Tuna Steaks

Serves: 6

Cooking Time: 1 Hour

Ingredients:

- 6 cups water, plus more as needed
- 1/2 cup brown sugar
- 1/2 cup kosher salt, plus more to taste
- 6 yellowfin tuna steaks (about 8 ounces each)
- 2 tablespoons teriyaki sauce
- Freshly ground black pepper, to taste

Directions:

For the brine, mix water, brown sugar and salt until sugar and salt are dissolved. Place tuna steaks in a single layer in a glass baking dish, add brine and turn steaks over to coat. Add more water to baking dish as needed to fully submerge the tuna steaks. Cover baking dish and refrigerate for 8 to hours. Place apple or cherry wood chips in the Masterbuilt smoker's wood tray and preheat smoker to 0°F. Carefully rinse tuna steaks with cold water and pat dry with paper towels. Brush tuna steaks with teriyaki sauce and season to taste with salt and pepper. Place tuna steaks on smoker grate and smoke for about 30 minutes. Turn steaks over and continue smoking until flaky and the internal temperature of the meat reaches 160°F, about 30 minutes more. Serve immediately and enjoy!

Easy Smoked Tuna

Serves: 4

Cooking Time: 7 Hours

Ingredients:

- 4 tuna steaks
- 1 ¼ cup sugar
- 1 teaspoon salt
- 1 teaspoon pepper
- ¼ teaspoon garlic
- ¼ cup honey

Directions:

Place all Ingredients: in a Ziploc bag and allow to marinate in the fridge for 3 hours. Preheat the smoker to 1400F. Add water to the water pan and add maple wood chips into the side tray. Put the tuna steaks in the middle tray. Cook for 7 hours. Baste the tuna with the sauce every hour.

Marinated Trout

Serves: 8

Cooking Time: 3 Hours

Ingredients:

- 4 pounds trout fillets
- 1/2 cup salt
- 1/2 cup brown sugar
- 2 quarts water

Directions:

Pour water in a large container with lid, add salt and sugar and stir until salt and sugar are dissolved completely. Add trout, pour in more water to submerge trout in brine and refrigerate for 4 to 8 hours, covering the container. Then remove trout from brine, rinse well and pat dry with paper towels. Place trout on a cooling rack, skin side down, and cool in the refrigerator for 2 hours or until dried. Then remove trout from the refrigerator and bring to room temperature. In the meantime, plug in the smoker, fill its tray with maple woodchips and water pan halfway through, and place dripping pan above the water pan. Then open the top vent, shut with lid and use temperature settings to preheat smoker at 160 degrees F. In the meantime, Place trout on smoker rack, insert a meat thermometer, then shut with lid and set the timer to smoke for 2 ½ to 3 hours or more until meat thermometer registers an internal temperature of 145 degrees F. Check vent of smoker every hour and add more woodchips and water to maintain temperature and smoke. Serve straightaway.

Herbed Shrimp
Serves: 4
Cooking Time: ¾ Hour
Ingredients:
- 1 lb fresh shrimp, peeled and deveined
- 2 tbsp olive oil
- 1 tbsp dried basil
- 1 tbsp dried oregano
- 1 tsp garlic powder
- Salt, to taste

Directions:
Soak alder wood chips in water for at least hour. Preheat the smoker to 5 degrees F, using charcoal and alder wood chips. In a large bowl, add all the ingredients and toss to coat well. Place the shrimp onto the foil covered smoker and cook for about 30- minutes. Serve hot.

Simple Salt & Pepper Smoked Salmon
Serves: 2
Cooking Time: 2 Hours
Ingredients:
- 2 pounds fresh salmon fillets
- 4 tablespoons melted butter
- 2 tablespoons lemon juice
- Salt and pepper

Directions:
Preheat the smoker to 225 degrees F. Add wood chips to begin the smoke. Now brush the butter over the fillets. Pour lemon juice over the fillets. Sprinkle the generous amount of pepper and salt to taste. Place salmon into the electric smoker. Cook for 2 hours. Once the fillets temperature reaches 150 degrees Fahrenheit, it's done. Serve and enjoy.

Smoked Red Fish Fillets
Serves: 2
Cooking Time: 1 Hour
Ingredients:
- 2 fillets of redfish with skin, each about 12 ounces
- 1 teaspoon garlic powder
- 1/2 cup salt
- 1 teaspoon ground black pepper
- 1/2 cup brown sugar
- 1 teaspoon dried lemon zest
- 1 lemon, sliced

Directions:
Stir together garlic powder, salt, black pepper, sugar, and lemon zest until combined. Take a glass baking dish, spread 1/3 of prepared spice mixture in the bottom, then later with one fillet, skin-side down and press lightly. Sprinkle half of remaining spice mixture over the fillet in pan, then top with another filet, flesh-side down and then sprinkle remaining spice mixture on top of it and around the side of fish. Cover the dish with plastic wrap and let marinate in the refrigerator for 8 to 12 hours. Remove marinated fish from the dish, rinse well, and pat dry using paper towels. Return fish into the refrigerator for 2 to 3 hours or until dried and then bring fish to room temperature for 45 minutes. When ready to cook, plug in the smoker, fill its tray with hickory woodchips and water pan halfway through, and place dripping pan above the water pan. Then open the top vent, shut with lid and use temperature settings to preheat smoker at 120 degrees F. Place fish on smoker rack, insert a meat thermometer, then shut with lid and set the timer to smoke for 1 hour or more until meat thermometer registers an internal temperature of 140 degrees F. Check vent of smoker every hour and add more woodchips and water to maintain temperature and smoke. Serve straightaway.

Simple Brined Trout
Serves: 6
Cooking Time: 3 Hours
Ingredients:
- 4 cups water
- ½ cup salt
- 2 lbs skin on trout fillets, pin bones removed

Directions:
In a large bowl, add water and salt and stir until salt is dissolved. Add trout fillets and coat with brine well. Refrigerate, covered for about hours. Remove trout from bowl and rinse under cold water. With paper towels, pat dry the trout fillets. Arrange a cooling rack in a sheet pan. Place the trout fillets onto cooling rack, skin side down. Refrigerate for about 22-24 hours. Preheat the smoker to 150-160 degrees F, using charcoal. Arrange the trout fillets into the smoker. Cook for about 2½-3 hours or until desired doneness. Serve hot.

Shrimps
Serves: 6
Cooking Time: 30 Minutes
Ingredients:
- 2 pounds shrimp, peeled, deveined and rinsed
- 2 tablespoons lemon juice
- 2 tablespoons chopped parsley
- 2 tablespoons onion powder
- 2 tablespoons garlic powder
- ¼ cup sea salt
- 3 tablespoons paprika
- 3 tablespoons ground black pepper
- 2 teaspoons cayenne pepper
- 2 tablespoons dried thyme
- 2 tablespoons olive oil

Directions:
Take a large foil pan, grease with oil and then place shrimps in it. Stir together remaining ingredients except for lemon juice and sprinkle this mixture on all over shrimps until evenly coated. Then Plug in the smoker, fill its tray with hickory woodchips and water pan halfway through, and place dripping pan above the water pan. Then open the top vent, shut with lid and use temperature settings to preheat smoker at 250 degrees F. Drizzle 1 tablespoon lemon juice over shrimps, then place the pan on smoker rack, then shut with lid and set the timer to smoke for 30 minutes or until shrimps are opaque, stirring halfway through. When done, remove the pan from the smoker, drizzle remaining lemon juice over shrimps and serve.

Smoked Sweet Salmon
Serves: 4
Cooking Time: 2 Hours
Ingredients:
- 4 6-ounce salmon filets
- ½ cup soy sauce
- 1 cup honey
- 1 teaspoon salt
- 2 teaspoon ground black pepper

Directions:
Place all Ingredients: in a mixing bowl and allow to marinate for at least 2 hours in the fridge. Preheat the smoker to 1600F. Add water to the water pan and add oak wood chips into the side tray. Place the marinated fish on the middle tray. Cook for 3 hours or until the fish is flaky.

Delicious Lobster Tail
Serves: 4
Cooking Time: 20 Minutes
Ingredients:
- 6 lobster tails
- ¼ cup butter
- 4 garlic cloves

Directions:
Take your drip pan and add water, cover with aluminum foil. Pre-heat your smoker to 400 degrees F   Use kitchen scissors to open lobster tail s gently, loosen up the lobster meat and keep them inside the shell, transfer to a plate   Take a pan and add butter, let it melt, add garlic cloves and let it heat over medium-low heat   Add garlic butter mixture all over lobster tail meat and transfer meat to the smoker   Use water fill water pan halfway through and place it over drip pan. Add wood chips to the side tray   Smoke for 20 minutes until the internal temperature reaches 130 degrees F   Take the smoker lobster out and pull out lobster meat from shells, pour garlic butter over and enjoy!

Smoked Halibut Fillets (masterbuilt Electric Smoker)
Serves: 6
Cooking Time: 2 Hours And 15 Minutes
Ingredients:
- 1 cup of virgin olive oil
- 2 cloves garlic, cut into quarters
- 1 Tbsp fresh rosemary (chopped)
- 1/2 cup white vinegar
- 4 halibut fillets

Directions:
Whisk the olive oil, chopped garlic, fresh rosemary and white vinegar in a large container. Submerge halibut fillets and toss to combine well. Cover and marinate in the refrigerator for several hours or overnight. Remove halibut fillets from marinade and dry on paper towels for 30 minutes. Preheat Masterbuilt Electric Smoker. Allow the smoker temperature to reach 21degrees Fahrenheit. When it is ready, add some water to the removable pan that is usually on the bottom shelf. Fill the side "drawer" with dry wood chips. Smoke the fish for about 2 hours or more, until the internal temperature reaches 140 degrees F. Turn once during cooking to avoid having the halibut fall apart. Transfer to a large serving platter, pour a little lemon juice over the fish and serve.

Smoked Scallops
Serves: 4
Cooking Time: 20 Minutes
Ingredients:
- 6 cups water
- 1/3 cup kosher salt
- 1/4 cup sugar
- 36 sea scallops
- 2/3 lb. thinly sliced prosciutto
- 6 green onions, sliced

Directions:
Mix together the sugar, water, and salt together in a bowl. Do this until all the sugar and salt has dissolved. Rinse your scallops off thoroughly before placing them in the brine. Cover it up and chill them for one hour. Drain afterward. Place the scallops in one layer on a wire rack. Chill them for another hour. You will want to place a water pan in the smoker. Add water only up to the fill line. Be sure to wrap your strips of prosciutto around each scallop. Secure them with wooden picks. Put all the scallops on an upper rack in the smoker. Sprinkle the green onions onto your scallops. Don't worry if most fall into the water. Once done serve the scallops up.

Whole Snapper
Serves: 6
Cooking Time: 4 Hours
Ingredients:
- 5-pound whole snapper, gutted, scaled and rinsed
- 2 tablespoons butter, soften
- 2 tablespoons olive oil
- ½ of medium fennel bulb, cored and thinly sliced
- ½ of small white onion, peeled and thinly sliced
- 1 whole lemon, thinly sliced
- 1 ½ teaspoons sea salt
- 1 teaspoon ground black pepper

Directions:
Whisk together butter and oil until combined in a medium bowl, then stir in salt and black pepper until mixed. Then plug in the smoker, fill its tray with hickory woodchips and water pan halfway through, and place dripping pan above the water pan. Then open the top vent, shut with lid and use temperature settings to preheat smoker at 225 degrees F. In the meantime, coat snapper with butter mixture and stuff its cavity with fennel, onion and half of lemon slices. Place stuffed snapper between two sheets of aluminum foil, then turn up the foil edges and place on the smoker rack. Then shut with lid and set the timer to smoke for 3 to 4 hours or more until meat thermometer registers an internal temperature of 145 degrees F. Check vent of smoker every hour and add more woodchips and water to maintain temperature and smoke. Serve straightaway.

Stuffed Salmon
Serves: 2
Cooking Time: 4 Hours
Ingredients:
- 5 pounds Salmon
- ¼ cup chopped green onions,
- 1 cup chopped tomato, peeled
- ¼ cup chopped celery
- ½ teaspoon minced garlic
- ¼ teaspoon salt
- ½ teaspoon lemon pepper seasoning
- ¼ cup chopped fresh dill
- 3 tablespoons olive oil
- ½ cup dry bread cubes

Directions:
Place all the ingredients except for salmon and oil in a bowl and stir until mixed. Brush salmon with oil and then stuff with the prepared mixture. Plug in the smoker, fill its tray with hickory woodchips and water pan halfway through, and place dripping pan above the water pan. Then open the top vent, shut with lid and use temperature settings to preheat smoker at 225 degrees F. Place salmon on a foil pan, then place it on smoker rack, insert a meat thermometer, then shut with lid and set the timer to smoke for 3 to 4 hours or more until meat thermometer registers an internal temperature of 140 degrees F. Check vent of smoker every hour and add more woodchips and water to maintain temperature and smoke. Serve straightaway.

Delicious Scallops
Serves: 4
Cooking Time: 40 Minutes
Ingredients:
- 2 lbs sea scallops, pat dried
- 2 tbsp fresh lemon juice
- Salt and freshly ground black pepper, to taste

Directions:
In a large bowl, add all ingredients and toss to coat well. Soak apple wood chips in water for at least 1 hour. Preheat the smoker to 200 degrees F, using charcoal and soaked apple wood chips. Place the scallops into the smoker and cook for about 30-minutes. Serve hot.

Spicy Cuban Catfish
Serves: 6
Cooking Time: 2 Hours
Ingredients:
- 1 tablespoon paprika
- 1 tablespoon garlic powder
- 1 teaspoon ground cumin
- 1 teaspoon onion powder
- 1 teaspoon dried oregano or thyme
- 1 teaspoon freshly ground black pepper, plus more to taste
- 1 teaspoon kosher salt, plus more to taste
- 1/2 teaspoon cayenne pepper, plus more to taste
- 1/4 cup orange juice
- 2 tablespoons butter (melted)
- 1 lime (zested, juiced)
- 6 catfish fillets (about 6 ounces each)

Directions:
Place apple or cherry wood chips in the Masterbuilt smoker's wood tray and preheat smoker to 200°F. In a small bowl, thoroughly mix paprika, garlic powder, cumin, onion powder, oregano, pepper, salt and cayenne pepper and set aside. In a separate bowl, mix orange juice, butter, lime juice and lime zest. Add 1 tablespoon spice mixture and mix well. Rub spice mixture into catfish fillets and place on smoker grate. Smoke fillets for about 30 minutes and baste with orange juice mixture. Continue smoking fillets until flaky and the internal temperature of the meat reaches 160°F, about 1 1/2 hours more, basting about every 30 minutes with remaining orange juice mixture. Serve catfish fillets immediately and enjoy!

Smoked Jumpers
Serves: 4
Cooking Time: 2 Hours
Ingredients:
- 8 large frog legs (about 3 pounds)
- 2 cups buttermilk
- 2 tablespoons olive oil
- 1 teaspoon kosher salt
- 1 teaspoon freshly ground black pepper
- 1 teaspoon sweet paprika
- 1/2 teaspoon cayenne pepper
- 1/2 teaspoon red pepper flakes
- Honey mustard and ranch salad dressing as desired, for dipping

Directions:
Separate frog legs if necessary and place in a large zip-top plastic bag. Add buttermilk to bag, seal, toss to coat and refrigerate for to 24 hours. Place apple or pecan wood chips in the Masterbuilt smoker's wood tray and preheat smoker to 5°F. Rinse frog legs with cold water and pat dry with paper towels. Mix salt, black pepper, paprika, cayenne pepper and red pepper flakes. Brush frog legs with oil and rub all over with spice mixture. Place frog legs on smoker grate and smoke until the internal temperature of the meat reaches 160°F, about 2 hours. Serve frog legs immediately with

honey mustard and ranch dressings as desired. Enjoy!

Smoked Salmon Chowder
Serves: 6
Cooking Time:1 Hour And 30 Minutes
Ingredients:
- 8-ounce salmon, cut into thick pieces
- 2 tablespoons butter
- 1 cup onion, chopped
- 2 cloves of garlic
- 3 tablespoons all-purpose flour
- 6 cups water
- 2 chicken bouillon cubes
- ½ cup chopped celery
- 1-pound red potatoes, sliced and cubed
- 1 teaspoon tarragon
- 1 tablespoon fresh lemon juice
- Salt and pepper to taste
- 1 cup half and half

Directions:
Preheat the smoker to 2000F. Add water in the water pan and oak wood chips into the side tray. Put the salmon on the rack and smoke for 40 minutes. Set aside. Over medium heat, melt the butter in a stockpot and sauté the garlic and onion until fragrant. Add the all-purpose flour and continue stirring for 3 minutes to create a roux. Blend in the water and chicken cubes and continue stirring. Place the celery, potatoes, tarragon, and lemon juice. Season with salt and pepper to taste. Bring to a boil for 10 minutes until the potatoes are soft. Add the smoked salmon and the half-and-half. Let it boil for another 5 minutes.

Honey Glazed Cod
Serves: 6
Cooking Time: 3 Hours
Ingredients:
- 2 lbs skin-on black cod fillets
- ¼ cup sugar
- 1 cup kosher salt
- 2 tbsp garlic powder
- 1 cup honey
- 1/8 tsp sweet paprika

Directions:
In a bowl, mix together the sugar, salt and garlic powder. In a plastic tub, place the sugar mixture. Place the cod fillets, skin side down and massage with the salt mixture. Cover and refrigerate for about 2-3 hours. Remove the cod fillets from tub and rinse under cold running water. With paper towels, pat it dry completely. Arrange a cooling rack in a sheet pan. Place the cod fillets onto cooling rack and refrigerate overnight. Soak alder wood chips in water for at least 1 hour. Preheat the smoker to 160 degrees F, using charcoal and alder wood chips. Place the cod fillets onto smoker and cook for about 2-3 hours. After first hour of cooking, coat the fillets with honey after every hour. Remove from the smoker and place onto a wire rack. Immediately, coat with the honey and let it cool for about 1 hour. Dust with paprika and serve.

Bacon-wrapped Scallops
Serves: 12
Cooking Time: 1 Hour
Ingredients:
- 12 large sea scallops
- 2 tablespoons butter (melted)
- 1 tablespoon pure maple syrup
- 1 teaspoon sweet paprika
- 1 teaspoon kosher salt, plus more to taste
- 1/2 teaspoon freshly ground black pepper, plus more to taste
- 1/4 teaspoon chili powder
- 1/4 teaspoon garlic powder
- 1/4 teaspoon onion powder
- 1/4 teaspoon cayenne pepper, plus more to taste
- 12 slices smoked bacon

Directions:
Remove muscles from sides of scallops as necessary. Place scallops in a large bowl, drizzle with butter and maple syrup, toss to coat and set aside. Mix paprika, salt, black pepper, chili powder, garlic powder, onion powder and cayenne pepper. Sprinkle spice mixture over scallops and toss gently to coat. Cover bowl and refrigerate for about 1 hour. Wrap a bacon slice around the edge of each scallop and secure with toothpicks if necessary. Arrange wrapped scallops in a single layer on a rack and season to taste with salt, pepper and cayenne pepper. Place rack with scallops on smoker grate and smoke until the internal temperature of the scallops reaches 1°F, about 1 hour. Remove toothpicks from wrapped scallops as necessary and serve immediately. Enjoy!

Alaskan Candied Salmon
Serves: 12
Cooking Time: 6 Hours
Ingredients:
- 5 lbs skin-on salmon fillets, cut into 2-inch thick strips
- 1 lb brown sugar
- 1 lb kosher salt
- 1 cup maple syrup

Directions:
In a bowl, mix together the brown sugar and salt. In a larger Tupperware, place about ¼-inch deep layer of the salt mixture. Arrange half of salmon strips over the salt mixture, skin side up. Repeat the layers once, ending with the salt mixture. Refrigerate, covered for about 2 hours. Remove the salmon from the cure and rinse under cold running water. With paper towels, pat dry the salmon strips completely. Arrange a cooling rack in a sheet pan. Place the salmon strips onto cooling rack and refrigerate overnight. Preheat the smoker to 180-225 degrees F, using charcoal.

Place the salmon filets into the smoker and cook for about 4-6 hours, coating with the maple syrup after every 90 minutes. Remove from the smoker and place onto a wire rack. Immediately, coat with the maple syrup and let it cool completely before serving.

Smoked Trout
Serves: 6
Cooking Time: 1 Hour
Ingredients:
- 3 cups water, plus more as needed
- 1/4 cup white sugar
- 1/4 cup brown sugar
- 1/4 cup salt
- 1 tablespoon lemon juice
- 2 teaspoons garlic powder
- 2 teaspoons chili powder
- 4 skin-on boneless trout (about 2 pounds)
- 2 tablespoons vegetable oil

Directions:
For the brine, mix water, sugars, salt, lemon juice, garlic powder and chili powder in a large glass baking dish. Add trout to baking dish and pour more water over trout as necessary to submerge. Cover baking dish and refrigerate for 2 to 8 hours. Place hickory wood chips in the Masterbuilt smoker's wood tray and preheat smoker to 5°F. Rinse trout with cold water, pat dry and brush with vegetable oil. Place trout skin-sides down on smoker grate and smoke until flaky, about 1 hour. Serve trout immediately and enjoy!

Cape Cod Lobster Rolls
Serves: 2
Cooking Time: 5 Minutes
Ingredients:
- 1 smoked lobster tail (shell removed)
- 2 tablespoons mayonnaise
- 1 celery stalk (diced)
- 1/2 teaspoon lime juice
- 2 tablespoons butter
- 2 deli hot dog rolls
- 2 green lettuce leaves
- Paprika (for garnish)
- Minced chives (for garnish)

Directions:
Chop lobster meat and mix with mayonnaise, celery and lime juice. Season meat mixture to taste with salt and pepper, stir until thoroughly combined and set aside. Heat a nonstick griddle or large skillet over medium-low heat. Spread butter on cut sides of hot dog rolls and toast until golden brown, about minutes. Line toasted rolls with lettuce leaves mound lobster mixture into rolls. Garnish rolls with paprika and chives and serve immediately. Enjoy!

Bacon Wrapped Smoked Scallops
Serves: 1
Cooking Time: 45 Minutes
Ingredients:
- 1 dozen sea scallops
- ¼ cup Olive oil
- 1 tbsp. Preferred rub
- 1 lb of thin sliced bacon

Directions:
Place the scallops in a zip lock bag. Add in the olive oil, and roll it around to coat your scallops evenly in the oil. Toss the rub in, and seal the bag again. Roll it around so the scallops are now coated in the rub. Let the scallops sit in the fridge with the bag to marinate for one hour. Take the scallops out of the bag and roll them up in the bacon. Use a toothpick to keep the bacon in place on the scallops. Arrange the scallops on the grate of the smoker. Once the scallops are finished smoking serve and enjoy.

Halibut With Homemade Tartar Sauce
Serves:4
Cooking Time:7 Hours 15 Minutes
Ingredients:
- Halibut (2-lbs, 0.9-kgs)
- Brown sugar – ¼ cup
- Granulated sugar – ¼ cup
- Kosher salt – ½ cup
- Ground coriander – 1 teaspoon
- White onion, minced – 2 tablespoons
- Tomatoes, diced – ¼ cup
- Dill pickled, diced – 2 tablespoons
- Mayonnaise – ½ cup
- Jarred vinegar from hot pepper jar – 2 teaspoons
- Salt, to taste
- Preheat your electric smoker to 200°F (93°C)
- Add orange smoker wood chips

Directions:
First, in a bowl combine the brown sugar with the granulated sugar along with the kosher salt and coriander. Rub the seasoning all over the fish. Wrap the fish in kitchen wrap and arrange on a rimmed baking sheet and transfer to the fridge, to brine for hours. Remove the kitchen wrap and rinse the fish. Using kitchen paper towel, pat dry. Set the catfish on a drying rack set over a sheet pan and place in the fridge for 1-2 hours. Remove from the fridge and cook in the smoker until the internal temperature registers 140°F (°C) for approximately 2 hours. For the tartar sauce, combine the white onion with the tomatoes, dill pickle, mayonnaise, and pepper vinegar, and season with salt, to taste.

Cured Salmon
Serves: 3
Cooking Time: 6 Minutes
Ingredients:
- 1 ½ pound salmon filet, skinless and boneless
- 1 bunch of fresh dill, chopped

- 1/2 of lemon, thinly sliced
- 1/4 cup salt
- 1/4 cup brown sugar
- 2 tablespoons ground black pepper

Directions:
Stir together salt, black pepper, and sugar and rub this mixture all over the salmon filet. Place seasoned salmon into a shallow baking dish, top with lemon slices and with dill, and wrap top with plastic wrap and then the whole dish. Place this dish into the refrigerator to marinate salmon for 8 to 12 hours. Then remove the dish from the refrigerator, uncover it, rinse fillet well, pat dry and let rest at room temperature for 2 hours. When ready to cook, plug in the smoker, fill its tray with pecan woodchips and water pan halfway through, and place dripping pan above the water pan. Then open the top vent, shut with lid and use temperature settings to preheat smoker at 1 degrees F. Place salmon on smoker rack, insert a meat thermometer, then shut with lid and set the timer to smoke for 3 to 6 hours or until meat thermometer register an internal temperature of 130 degrees F. Check vent of smoker every hour and add more woodchips and water to maintain temperature and smoke. Serve straightaway.

Creamy Shrimp Pasta Salad
Serves: 6
Cooking Time: 45 Minutes
Ingredients:
- 2 pounds medium shrimp (peeled, deveined)
- 1/4 cup Italian salad dressing
- 1 tablespoon Creole seasoning
- Kosher salt and freshly ground black pepper, to taste
- 1/2 cup plain unsweetened yogurt
- 1/4 cup mayonnaise
- 1 lemon (zested, juiced)
- 1/2 teaspoon chili powder
- 1/4 teaspoon garlic powder
- 1 package (8 ounces) small shell pasta
- 2 celery stalks (diced)

Directions:
Toss shrimp, salad dressing and Creole seasoning in a medium bowl and season to taste with salt and pepper. Cover bowl and refrigerate for 30 minutes to hour. Place oak wood chips in the Masterbuilt smoker's wood tray and preheat smoker to 0°F. Remove shrimp from marinade and place on smoker grate. Smoke shrimp until browned and cooked through, about 45 minutes. Meanwhile, cook pasta according to package directions. Drain pasta, rinse with cold water and drain thoroughly. For the dressing, whisk yogurt, mayonnaise, lemon juice, chili powder and garlic powder until thoroughly combined. Add pasta and diced celery to dressing, toss to coat and set aside. Remove shrimp from smoker, let stand until cool enough to handle and cut into bite-size pieces. Add shrimp to pasta mixture and toss to coat. Refrigerate pasta salad until chilled through, about 1 hour. Garnish salad with lemon zest just before serving. Enjoy!

Maple Smoked Salmon Steaks
Serves: 4
Cooking Time: 2 Hours
Ingredients:
- ½ teaspoon salt
- 1 teaspoon black pepper
- ½ lemon, juiced
- 1 tablespoon basil, chopped
- 1 tablespoon brown sugar
- 4 salmon steaks, bones and skin removed

Directions:
In a Ziploc bag, put all the Ingredients: and allow to marinate in the fridge for at least 2 hours. Preheat the smoker to 1700F. Add water to the water pan and add maple wood chips into the side tray. Place marinated salmon on the middle tray. Adjust the cooking time to 2 hours. Serve with a salad.

Gourmet Snapper
Serves: 3
Cooking Time: 55 Minutes
Ingredients:
- 1 (1½lb) whole snapper, scaled and gutted
- 16 cups water
- ½ cup kosher salt
- 1/3 cup light brown sugar
- 1 tbsp whole black peppercorns, crushed
- 2 tbsp olive oil
- 1 tbsp fresh lemon juice
- 1 garlic clove, minced
- 1 tbsp fresh rosemary, minced

Directions:
In a large food bucket, add water, salt and brown surge and stir until salt and sugar are dissolved. With a sharp knife, cut slits into both sides of fish about 1-inch apart. In the bucket, add fish and crushed peppercorns. Cover and refrigerate for about 2 hours. Drain the brine and with paper towels, pat dry the fish. In a bowl, add remaining ingredients and mix well. Coat the fish with oil mixture generously. Soak pecan wood chips in water for at least 1 hour. Preheat the smoker to 225-250 degrees F, using pecan wood chips. Place the fish on the grate, away from the direct heat of the fire and cook for about 15-20 minutes. Carefully flip fish and cook for about 30 minutes or u til desired doneness. Serve hot.

Peach-smoked Ahi Tuna Steaks
Serves:6

Cooking Time:6 Hours 20 Minutes
Ingredients:
- 6 Ahi tuna steaks (6-ozs, 170-gms each)
- Kosher salt – 3 tablespoons
- Light brown sugar – 3 tablespoons
- Extra-virgin olive oil – ¼ cup
- Lemon pepper seasoning shake
- Ground garlic – 1 teaspoon
- 1 fresh lemon, cut into 12 thin slices
- Preheat your electric smoker to 190°F (88°C)
- Add water to your smoker pan and place peach woods chip in the smoker tray

Directions:
Coat the tuna with the salt and sugar on all sides and place in a ziplock bag. Transfer to the fridge for 4 hours. Remove the tuna steaks from the bag and wipe off the majority of the dry brine. Coat both sides of the tuna steaks with extra-virgin olive oil, lemon pepper seasoning and garlic powder. Place the steaks onto the smoker rack. Arrange 2 slices of fresh lemon on top of each steak. Return the rack to the smoker and smoke for 60-10minutes or until an internal thermometer registers a heat of 140°F (60°C). Remove the steaks to a chopping board and set aside to rest for 2-3 minutes. Serve and enjoy.

Smoked Lobster
Serves: 4
Cooking Time: 45 Minutes
Ingredients:
- 8 lobster tails
- 8 kebab skewers
- ½ cup (1 stick) butter, softened
- 1 clove garlic, finely minced
- 1 Tbs Money 1 Tbs chopped chives

Directions:
Preheat your smoker to 225°F In a small bowl, combine butter, garlic, Money Rub, and chives until thoroughly combined. Set aside. Using kitchen shears, cut along the back of the lobster tail shell. Use your fingers to carefully separate the meat from the back of the shell. Thread a kebab skewer through the underside of the tail from front to back. This keeps the lobster tail from curling during cooking. Place the skewered lobster tails directly on the smoker grate. Smoke until the lobster reaches 130°F. Carefully spoon 1 Tbsp of the butter mixture onto the tail meat of each lobster. Continue cooking until the lobsters reach 140°F.

Smoked Savory Sardine (masterbuilt Electric Smoker)
Serves: 4
Cooking Time: 3 Hours And 30 Minutes
Ingredients:
- 2 lbs sardines
- Sea salt to taste
- Fresh oregano to taste
- 1/4 cup lemon juice, freshly squeezed
- 1/4 cup olive oil
- 1 lemon, sliced

Directions:
Clean sardines remove that head and giblets and rinse them under cool water to remove any remaining scales; salt to taste and sprinkle with fresh oregano. Whisk lemon juice, oil olive, oregano and salt in a shallow container, and add your sardines. Marinate sardines in the fridge overnight. Take your sardines out of the marinade, rinse under cold water and pat dry on a paper towel for 1 hour. Preheat Masterbuilt Electric Smoker. Allow the smoker temperature to reach 120 degrees Fahrenheit. When it is ready, add some water to the removable pan that is usually on the bottom shelf. Fill the side "drawer" with dry wood chips. Smoke sardines for 4-5 hours over almond wood. Sardines are ready when internal temperature reaches 140 degrees. Sprinkle with olive oil and lemon juice and serve.

Smoked Lobster Tails
Serves: 2
Cooking Time: 1 Hour
Ingredients:
- 1 cup butter or margarine, melted
- 1/4 cup fresh lemon juice
- 1 tbsp. minced fresh parsley
- 1/2 tbsp. grated lemon rind
- Pinch salt
- 4 frozen lobster tails, thawed (about 2 lb.s)

Directions:
Mix together the salt, butter, lemon juice, parsley, and lemon rind. Brush this over the lobster tails. Place the lobster tails in the smoker. The flesh should be white and firm once done.

Ale-brined Catfish With Cilantro Lemon Dipping Sauce
Serves:3
Cooking Time:2 Hours 40 Minutes
Ingredients:
- 3 whole catfish, cleaned and headed
- Olive oil – 1 tablespoon
- Seafood seasoning, to taste
- Belgian triple ale – 1½ cups
- Kosher salt – ⅛ cup

- 1 fresh lemon
- Yellow mustard – 1 teaspoon
- Water – 2 cups
- Mayonnaise – 1 cup
- 1 green onion, top only
- Cilantro, chopped – 2 tablespoons
- Hot sauce – 1 teaspoon
- Freshly squeezed orange juice – 2 teaspoons
- Salt – ⅛ teaspoon
- Cracked black pepper – ⅛ teaspoon
- Preheat your electric smoker to 265°F (130°C)
- Add orange smoker wood chips

Directions:
First, prepare the brine by combining the ale with the salt and juice in a bowl, stirring until the salt is entirely dissolved. Add the mustard and stir. Transfer the catfish to a large ziplock bag. Add sufficient water to cover the fish, seal the bag and place in the fridge for 60 minutes. After 60 minutes have elapsed, remove the fish from the brine. Discard the brine. Using kitchen paper towel, pat the fish dry. Rub the oil all over the fish and season with the seafood seasoning. Place the fish in the smoker. While the fish smokes, prepare the dipping sauce. In a bowl, combine the mayonnaise with the onion, cilantro, hot sauce, freshly squeezed orange juice, salt, and black pepper. Transfer to the fridge until needed. Smoke the fish until it registers 145°F (63°C). This will take approximately 1 hour 5 minutes. Remove the fish from the electric smoker and allow to rest for 10 minutes. Serve the smoked catfish with a side order of dipping sauce.

Honey Mustard Halibut Fillets
Serves: 6
Cooking Time: 6 Hours
Ingredients:
- ⅓ cup kosher salt
- 1 cup brown sugar
- 4 tablespoons cumin
- 1 tablespoon dried bay leaves, crushed
- ½ gallon water
- Other
- 6 halibut fillets
- 1 cup honey mustard rub

Directions:
Combine and mix well all the brine ingredients in a large bowl and place the fish in it for 2 hours. Next, pat dry the fish and let it dry. Season the fish with the mustard rub and massage gently for fine coating. Place the fish on a rack inside the smoker and cook for 6 hours at 5 degrees F. The internal temperature of fish should be about 150°F at the end of cooking. Serve and enjoy.

Smoked Lemony Catfish Fillets (masterbuilt Electric Smoker)

Serves: 6
Cooking Time: 20 Minutes

Ingredients:
- 1/2 cup olive oil
- Juice of 4 lemons
- 2 Tbsp Dijon mustard
- 1/2 tsp salt
- Fresh rosemary chopped to taste
- 4 (6- to 8-oz.) catfish fillets, 1/2-inch thick (about 2 lbs)

Directions:
Whisk olive oil, lemon juice, mustard, salt, and chopped rosemary in a bowl. Brush both sides of each fish fillet with half of the olive oil-lemon mixture; season with salt and pepper to taste. Preheat Masterbuilt Electric Smoker. Allow the smoker temperature to reach 200 degrees Fahrenheit. When it is ready, add some water to the removable pan that is usually on the bottom shelf. Fill the side "drawer" with dry wood chips. Smoke fish for 2 hours or until the internal temperature reaches 1 degrees F. Remove fish fillets to a serving platter, sprinkle with rosemary and serve.

Smoked Cod

Serves: 2
Cooking Time: 2 Hours

Ingredients:
- 4 to 5 fresh cod fillets
- 2 gallons water
- 2 cups orange juice
- 4 cloves garlic, crushed
- 4 tbsp. pepper
- 1 tbsp. onion powder
- Kosher salt
- 1 cup paprika
- 2 tbsp. cayenne

Directions:
Lay the cod out on a few paper towels. Sprinkle your fish with some salt. Wait half and hour, and then rinse the cod off under some cold water. Mix the brine mixture in one gallon of water, tsp. of pepper and garlic, orange juice, ½ cup paprika, and ¼ cup salt. Allow the fish to soak in the brine for 45 minutes. Mix the paprika, cayenne, onion powder, and remaining pepper in a small bowl. Rub this mixture into the cod on both sides. Rub it in as best you can. If the cod has skin on it, only rub the spices where the meat is exposed. Place cod in the smoker. Once done allow it to cool for a few minutes before serving.

Smoked Tilapia

Serves: 5
Cooking Time: 2 Hours

Ingredients:
- 5 tilapia fillets
- Ground black pepper to taste
- Salt to taste
- 2 tsp. chopped fresh dill or basil
- 3 tsp. garlic and herb seasoning
- 1 tbsp. olive oil
- 1 lemon, sliced

Directions:
In a small bowl mix together your olive oil, black pepper, herb seasoning, salt, garlic, and basil. Rub this mixture into your tilapia on each side. Place your tilapia in the smoker. When the tilapia is done cooking, serve it with a slice of lemon or squeeze the lemon over it.

Smoked Salmon With Peppercorn Crust

Serves: 10
Cooking Time: 2 Hours

Ingredients:
- 1 cup packed brown sugar
- 6 tablespoons salt
- 1 tablespoon minced ginger
- 3 bay leaves
- 1 teaspoon crushed allspice
- 4 pounds salmon filets with skin
- 1 teaspoon honey
- ½ cup mixed whole peppercorns

Directions:
In a pan, bring 2 cups of water to a boil. Add sugar, salt, ginger, bay leaves, and all spice. Stir until dissolved. Let it cool. Place the salmon in the brine andmarinate for hours in the fridge. Pour the brine away and pat dry the fish. Brush with honey and sprinkle generously with peppercorns. Preheat the smoker to 1400F. Add water to the water pan and maple wood chips into the side tray. Place the fish on the middle rack. Cook for 2 hours.

Smoked Snow Crab Legs

Serves: 3
Cooking Time: 25 Minutes
Ingredients:

- 3-5 lb.s of snow crab legs
- 1 cup of butter
- 1/4 cup lemon juice
- 2 tsp. lemon pepper seasoning
- 2 tsp. garlic powder or minced garlic

Directions:
Put the garlic, butter, lemon pepper seasoning, and lemon juice in a small mixing bowl. Mix everything together and microwave it for only 30 seconds. Stir it all together. Place the crab legs in the smoker. Baste them with the mixture you just made once every 10 minutes. Once the snow crab legs are done, take them out of the smoker. Either eat with some butter to dip them into or eat the meat as is.

Honey Chipotle Salmon With Pineapple Salsa

Serves: 4
Cooking Time: 45 Minutes
Ingredients:

- 2 lbs salmon, cut into 4 pieces
- 2 Tbsp Classic American Brown Sugar ¼ cup Honey Chipotle Barbecue
- 1 cup fresh or canned pineapple, minced
- 1 cup red bell pepper, minced
- ½ cup red onion, minced
- ½ cup fresh lime juice
- 1 Tbsp cilantro, finely chopped
- 1 Tbsp extra-virgin olive oil

Directions:
In a small bowl, combine all salsa ingredients and set aside. Liberally apply Classic American Brown Sugar Rub to the flesh side of the salmon. Cover and refrigerate for 1 hour. Remove the salmon from the fridge and preheat the smoker to 225°F Place salmon, skin side down, on a piece of parchment that has been placed over the grates of the smoker. Smoke for 30 minutes or until the salmon has reached an internal temperature of 130°F. Remove the salmon from the smoker and brush liberally with Honey Chipotle Barbecue Sauce. Return the salmon to the smoker and continue cooking until it reaches an internal temperature of 140°F. Allow the salmon to sit for 10 minutes before topping with pineapple salsa and serving.

Lemon Pepper Tuna

Serves: 6

Cooking Time: 1 Hour
Ingredients:

- 6 tuna steaks, each about 6 ounces
- 3 tablespoons salt
- 3 tablespoons brown sugar
- 1/4 cup olive oil
- ¼ cup lemon pepper seasoning
- 1 teaspoon minced garlic
- 12 slices of lemon

Directions:
Season tuna with salt and sugar until evenly coated on all sides, then place in a dish and cover with plastic wrap. Place dish into the refrigerator for 4 hours or overnight, then rinse well and pat dry and coat well with garlic powder, lemon pepper seasoning, and oil. Plug in the smoker, fill its tray with peach woodchips and water pan halfway through, and place dripping pan above the water pan. Then open the top vent, shut with lid and use temperature settings to preheat smoker at 120 degrees F. In the meantime, Place seasoned tuna on smoker rack, insert a meat thermometer, then shut with lid and set the timer to smoke for 1 hour or more until meat thermometer registers an internal temperature of 140 degrees F. Check vent of smoker every hour and add more woodchips and water to maintain temperature and smoke. When done, transfer tuna to a cutting board, let rest for 10 minutes and then serve with lemon slices.

Stunning Sardine

Serves: 5
Cooking Time: 2 Hours
Ingredients:

- 2 lbs sardine fillets
- 1 tbsp paprika
- 1 tbsp onion powder
- 1 tbsp garlic powder
- ½ tbsp ground cumin
- Salt and freshly ground black pepper, to taste
- Nonstick cooking spray

Directions:
Soak cherry wood chips in water for at least hour. Preheat the smoker to 0 degrees F, using cherry wood chips. In a bowl, mix together all spices Spray the sardine fillets with cooking spray evenly and then, rub with spice mixture generously. Again, spray the sardine fillets with cooking spray evenly. Arrange the filets onto a soaked wooden plank and place into the smoker. Cook for about 2 hours. Serve hot.

Poultry Recipes

Smoked Buffalo Chicken Wings
Serves: 8
Cooking Time: 20 Minutes
Ingredients:
- 5 lbs. chicken wings
- Pepper
- Salt
- 2 tbsps. Butter
- 1 c. red hot sauce

Directions:
Place chicken wings into the refrigerator for 3 hours. Preheat the smoker to 5 F/107 C. Remove chicken wings from refrigerator and coat with little olive oil. Season chicken wings with pepper and salt. Place chicken wings in the smoker for 1 hour. After 1-hour increase temperature to 350 F/17C and smoke for another 30 minutes. In a bowl, combine together sauce ingredients. Add smoked chicken wings into the bowl and toss well. Serve and enjoy.

Chicken And Guacamole
Serves: 4
Cooking Time: 1 Hour
Ingredients:
- 2 chicken breasts
- 2 avocado, ripe
- 1 tomato, diced
- 1 lime
- 1 teaspoon salt
- 1 teaspoon garlic powder
- 1 teaspoon Cajun
- 4 multigrain bread, slices

Directions:
Take your drip pan and add water, cover with aluminum foil. Pre-heat your smoker to 225 degrees F Apply Cajun seasoning generously to your chicken breasts Use water fill water pan halfway through and place it over drip pan. Add wood chips to the side tray. Add chicken inside your smoker and smoke for 1 and ½ hours until internal temperature reaches 165 degrees F Once done, remove chicken and keep it on the side, let it rest for 10 minutes. Slice up Cut into avocado into halves and remove seeds, scoop out the flesh into a medium-sized bowl Squeeze half lemon into the avocado and mix we, spoon to remove all lumps and bring to a smooth mix Add in chopped tomatoes and onions and stir Pour rest of the lime juice over avocado mix and season with salt and pepper Take a slice of multigrain and place chicken and salad mix on top, top with another slice and enjoy!

Smoked Turkey With Flavors Of Mixed Herbs
Serves: 6
Cooking Time: 20 Minutes
Ingredients:
- 14 lbs. Turkey
- 2 tsps. Dried thyme
- 1 tsp. Powdered sage
- 2 tbsps. Dried oregano
- 2 tbsps. Paprika
- 2 tbsps. Sea salt
- 1½ tbsps. Black pepper
- 1 tsp. Dried rosemary
- 1 tsp. Onion
- 1 tsp. Garlic powder
- ½ orange
- ¼ c. Olive oil
- ½ c. Apple Cider
- ½ c. Water

Directions:
To prepare the smoked turkey, you will require a perfect size of Turkey that could fit in your electric smoker. Once you buy the turkey, you will require to thaw it nice and slow. Although, if you choose a refrigerated turkey, you will still have to leave it for 3 days to completely thaw. Once the process is complete, clean the turkey and remove giblets and neck. After cleaning it, rinse it with water and let it dry. Meanwhile, it is kept to dry, prepare the brine mixing ½ cup or sugar and salt to water. It should be measured every gallon until the turkey is fully submerged. Allow the turkey to rest for 1hours. After 14 hours, take the turkey out of the brine and rinse it. The rinsing should be done with cold water. As you have rinsed the turkey, dry it with the help of a paper towel and keep it aside. Meanwhile, prepare the Masterbuilt Smoker for direct heating at a temperature of 225 degrees F. As the smoker is heating, prepare the herb mixture by mixing all the herbs in a mixing bowl. With this prepared mix, rub the turkey all over the outside surface. For better flavor, force the dry rub on the skin of Turkey. Also, for the second layering of rub, add the EVOO and zest of an orange in the herb mix. Again, nicely apply the seasoning all over the outside surface and let the turkey rest. Meanwhile, you take a water pan and add cider vinegar with an equal quantity of water. Place the water pan in the bottom of Masterbuilt Smoker. The pan must be half filled. Also, place a drip just a shelf below Turkey so that it could collect all the juices and drippings during the smoking process. Last but not the least, add the Applewood chips in the box and the smoker is ready to place the turkey. Now, while it is the time to place the turkey in the smoker, you will have to tightly tuck the wings beneath the turkey. After tucking the wings, place it on the rack and seal the door. The timer of the smoker should be set at 6.5 hours. To check the doneness of the turkey, insert a thermometer probe in the thickest part and wait for it to display 165 degrees F. While the smoking process is on, check the turkey every hour for a smoke; if you see less smoke, add more Applewood chips. After 6.5 hours, when the meat thermometer reads 165 degrees F, remove the smoked turkey and let it rest on cutting board for 20 minutes. After 20 minutes, carve beautifully and juices pieces of turkey and serve. You can serve herb-smoked sweet potatoes as a side dish to this flavorful turkey.

Let It Cool For 15 Minutes And Serve Standing Smoked Chicken
Serves: 6
Cooking Time: 1 And ½ Hours – 2 Hours
Ingredients:
- 12 garlic cloves, minced
- 3 whole onions, quartered
- ½ of a quartered lemon
- 1 tablespoon of salt
- 1 teaspoon of black pepper
- 1 and a ½ tablespoon of ground sage
- 1 and a ½ tablespoon of dried thyme
- 1 and a ½ tablespoon of dried rosemary
- 1 teaspoon of paprika
- 1 whole chicken of 4-6 pounds
- 3 tablespoon of vegetable oil

Directions:
Remove one or two of the top racks from the smoker to make room for your standing chicken Smash 8 pieces of garlic cloves and add them into the water pan alongside the onion and lemon pieces Pre-heat your smoker to temperature of 250 degree Fahrenheit Finely mince up the rest of the garlic cloves and combine them in a small sized bowl with pepper, salt, sage, rosemary, thyme, paprika and set it aside for later use Remove the giblets from the cavity of the chicken and rinse up the bird finely Pat it dry and rub it up with oil and then with the seasoning mixture created previously Set your chicken in a vertical position on top of your smoker and add in just a handful of soaked chips in the chip loading area Keep adding the chips for every 30 minutes The chicken should be done after about 2 hours when the internal temperature registers 165 degree Fahrenheit

Honey Smoked Turkey
Serves: 7
Cooking Time: 6 Hours
Ingredients:
- 1 gallon of hot water
- 1 pound of kosher salt
- 2 quarts of vegetable broth
- 8 ounce jars of honey
- 1 cup of orange juice
- 7 pound bag of ice cubes
- 15 pound of whole turkey with giblets and neck removed
- ¼ cup of vegetable oil
- 1 teaspoon of poultry seasoning
- 1 granny smith apples cored and cut up into large chunks
- 1 celery stalk cut up into small chunks
- 1 small sized onion cut up into chunks
- 1 quartered orange

Directions:
Take a 54 quart cooler and add kosher salt and hot water Mix them well until everything dissolves Add vegetable broth, orange juice and honey Pour ice cubes into the mix and add the turkey into your brine, keeping the breast side up Lock up the lid of your cooler and let it marinate overnight for 12 hours Make sure that the brine temperature stays under 40 degree Fahrenheit Remove the turkey from the brine and discard the brine Dry the turkey using a kitchen towel Take a bowl and mix vegetable oil and poultry seasoning Rub the turkey with the mixture Place apple, onion, celery and orange pieces inside the cavity of the turkey Pre-heat your smoker to a temperature of 400 degree Fahrenheit and add 1 cup of hickory wood chips Set your turkey onto your smoker and insert a probe into the thickest part of your turkey breast Set the probe for 160 degree Fahrenheit Smoke the turkey for 2 hours until the skin is golden brown Cover the breast, wings and legs using aluminum foil and keep smoking it for 2-3 hours until the probe thermometer reads degree Fahrenheit Make sure to keep adding some hickory chips to your heat box occasionally Remove the vegetables and fruit from the cavity of your Turkey and cover it up with aluminum foil Let it rest of 1 hour and carve it up!

Special Dinner Turkey
Serves: 14
Cooking Time: 5¼ Hours
Ingredients:
- 1 (15lb) whole turkey, neck and giblets removed
- ¼ cup olive oil
- Salt and freshly ground black pepper, to taste
- 1 cup chicken broth
- 2 tbsp apple cider vinegar
- 2 tbsp honey

Directions:
Soak apple wood chips in water for at least 4 hours. Preheat the smoker to 5 degrees F, using charcoal and apple wood chips. Arrange a rack in a large roasting pan. Place turkey over rack in roasting pan. Coat the turkey with oil generously and then season with salt and black pepper evenly. Place the roasting pan into the smoker and cook for about 45 minutes. Meanwhile, in a bowl, mix together remaining ingredients. After 45 minutes, coat the turkey with honey mixture. Cook for about 3½-4½ hours, coating with honey mixture after every 45 minutes. Transfer the turkey onto a cutting board and set aside for about 20 minutes before carving. With a sharp knife, cut the turkey in desired sized pieces and serve.

Spicy Chicken Wings
Serves: 6
Cooking Time: 1 Hour
Ingredients:
- For Chicken Wings:
- 5 pounds chicken wings
- 1 teaspoon onion powder
- 1 teaspoon garlic powder
- 2 ½ teaspoons sea salt
- ½ teaspoon ground black pepper
- ¼ cup paprika
- 1 ½ teaspoon cayenne pepper
- ½ cup brown sugar
- For Dipping Sauce:
- 3 tablespoons minced chives
- ½ teaspoon salt
- ½ teaspoon ground pepper
- 1-pint yogurt
- ¾ cup crumbled blue cheese

Directions:
Plug in the smoker, fill its tray with hickory woodchips and water pan halfway through, and place dripping pan above the water pan. Then open the top vent, shut with lid and use temperature settings to preheat smoker at 0 degrees F. In the meantime, rinse chicken wings, pat dry and cut off wing tips. Stir together onion powder, garlic powder, salt, black pepper, paprika, cayenne pepper, and sugar until mixed and then rub this spice mixture on all sides of chicken wings until evenly coated. Place chicken wings on smoker rack, insert a meat thermometer, then shut with lid and set the timer to smoke for 1 hour or until meat thermometer register an internal temperature of 16degrees F. In the meantime, prepare dipping sauce and for this, whisk together all the ingredients for dipping sauce and whisk well until smooth. Serve chicken wings with dipping sauce.

Spicy Honey-apple Bbq Wings
Serves: 6
Cooking Time: 1-1½ Hours
Ingredients:
- 5 lbs chicken wings
- ¼ cup Big Bold Barbecue
- 2 cups Honey Chipotle Barbecue ¼ cup apple jam or apple butter

Directions:

In a large zip top bag, combine chicken wings and rub. Allow the wings to sit in the refrigerator for a minimum of 1 hour and up to overnight. Remove the wings from the fridge and preheat the smoker to 250°F. Set the wings slices directly on the smoker grate. Smoke them for 1-1 ½ hours or until the internal temperature reaches 16F. Meanwhile, combine barbecue sauce and apple jam in a medium saucepan and warm on low for 10 minutes. Remove wings from the smoker and toss in the sauce. Place on foil-lined baking trays and finish under the broiler for 2 minutes, or until the skin becomes crispy.

Simple Smoked Chicken Wings
Serves: 8
Cooking Time: 1 Hour 10 Minutes
Ingredients:
- 4 lbs chicken wings
- 1 bottle Italian dressing
- 3 tbsp chicken rub seasoning

Directions:
Add Italian dressing and chicken wings into the zip lock bag and place in refrigerator for overnight. Drain chicken well and rub chicken seasoning over chicken wings. Preheat the smoker to 0 F/148 C using apple wood. Place coated chicken wings in the smoker and smoke for 1 hour. Serve hot and enjoy.

Bacon Wrapped Chicken Lollipops
Serves: 24
Cooking Time: 60 Minutes
Ingredients:
- 4 pounds chicken drumsticks
- 2 pounds sliced bacon
- ½ cup sweet barbecue rub
- Honey as needed

Directions:
Plug in the smoker, fill its tray with hickory woodchips and water pan halfway through, and place dripping pan above the water pan. Then open the top vent, shut with lid and use temperature settings to preheat smoker at 5 degrees F. In the meantime, season chicken with barbecue rub and then wrap with bacon. Place bacon wrapped chicken on smoker rack, drizzle with honey, insert a meat thermometer in it, then shut with lid and set the timer to smoke for 30 to 60 minutes or more until meat thermometer registers an internal temperature of 165 degrees F. Serve straightaway.

Honey Brined Turkey

Serves: 12
Cooking Time: 1 Hour
Ingredients:

- 1 gallon hot water
- 1 lb. kosher salt
- 2 quarts vegetable broth
- 1 lb. honey
- 1 (7-lb.) bag of ice
- 1 (15 to 20-lb.) turkey, with giblets removed
- Vegetable oil, for rubbing turkey

Directions:

Heat up some water until it's warm. Place it in a large cooler. Add in the salt so it dissolves. Stir in the honey and vegetable brother. Add ice to the cooler and stir well. Put the turkey in the brine mixture. You want the breast to be facing upwards. Allow it to brine for twelve hours. After the turkey is done brining, rub it down with vegetable oil. Build a smoke bomb for your grill. Use heavy duty foil to wrap around some hickory wood chips. Set your turkey in the smoker. The turkey should be golden brown on its skin. If not, replace the wood chips. If the skin is golden, be sure to cover it in aluminum foil and allow it to keep cooking. Once done, remove turkey from the smoker and serve.

Turkey In The Electric Smoker

Serves: 10
Cooking Time: 10 Hours
Ingredients:

- 1 (10 pounds) whole turkey
- 4 cloves garlic, crushed
- 2 tablespoons salt, seasoned
- ½ cup butter
- 1 (12 fluid ounce) cola-flavored carbonated beverage
- 1 apple, quartered
- 1 onion, quartered
- 1 tablespoon garlic powder
- 1 tablespoon salt
- 1 tablespoon black pepper

Directions:

Preheat your electric smoker to 225 degrees F and then rinse the turkey well under water, pat dry and then rub it with seasoned salt. Place it inside a roasting pan. Combine cola, butter, apples, garlic powder, salt, and pepper in a bowl . Fill the cavity of turkey with cola, apples, garlic powder, salt, and pepper. Rub butter and crushed garlic outside of the turkey as well. Cover the turkey with foil. Smoke the turkey for 10 hours at 250 degrees F. Once it's done, serve.

Pool Party Wings

Serves: 6
Cooking Time: 3 Hours
Ingredients:

- 24 (6 lbs) chicken wings
- ¾ cup BBQ sauce
- ¼ cup whiskey
- 1 tbsp sugar
- 1/3 cup Dijon mustard
- Salt and freshly ground black pepper, to taste

Directions:

In a small pan, mix together BBQ sauce, whiskey and sugar over medium-high heat and bring to a boil. Remove from the heat and immediately, stir in mustard. Set aside to cool completely. Meanwhile, with a sharp knife, cut each wing through the joints to separate the drumettes from the wings. Sprinkle the wings with salt and black pepper generously. In a sealable bag, place the chicken wings and sauce. Seal the bag and shake to coat well. Refrigerate for overnight. Soak cherry wood chips in water for at least 1 hour. Preheat the smoker to 250 degrees F, using charcoal and cherry wood chips. Remove the wings from bag and discard any excess marinade. Arrange the wings in a large shallow aluminum pan in a single layer. Place the pan into the smoker and cook for about 2 hours. Serve hot.

Thanksgiving Party Turkey

Serves: 12
Cooking Time: 10 Hours
Ingredients:

- 1 (10-15lb) whole turkey, neck and giblets removed
- 1 apple, cored and quartered
- 1 onion, quartered
- ½ cup butter, softened
- Salt and freshly ground black pepper, to taste
- 4 garlic cloves, crushed
- 2 tbsp seasoned salt

Directions:

Preheat the smoker to 225-250 degrees F, using charcoal. For stuffing: in a bowl, add apple, onion, butter, salt and black pepper and mix well. Rub the outer side of turkey with the crushed garlic evenly and sprinkle with seasoned salt. Stuff the cavity of turkey with apple mixture. Arrange the turkey in a disposable roasting pan. With a piece of foil, cover the roasting pan loosely. Place the roasting pan into the smoker. Cook for about 10 hours, basting with pan juices after every 1 hour. Transfer the turkey onto a cutting board and set aside for about 20 minutes before carving. With a sharp knife, cut the turkey in desired sized pieces and serve.

Inspired Turkey Breast
Serves: 10
Cooking Time: 4 Hours
Ingredients:
- 1 (64-ounce) bottle apple cider
- ¾ cup kosher salt
- ½ cup sugar
- ¼ cup apple cider vinegar
- 3 fresh thyme sprigs
- 2 fresh rosemary sprigs
- 10 fresh sage leaves
- 1 garlic bulb, cut in half crosswise
- 4 cups ice cubes
- 1 (5¾-6lb) bone-in turkey breast

Directions:
In a large pan, add all the ingredients except the ice cubes and turkey breast oven over medium-high heat and bring to a boil. Reduce the heat to medium and simmer for about 5 minutes, stirring occasionally. Remove from heat and stir in ice. Set aside to cool completely. In a large food bucket, place the brine and turkey and refrigerate to for about 6-12 hours. Soak pecan wood chips in water for at least 1 hour. Preheat the smoker to 225-250 degrees F, using pecan wood chips. The Remove turkey from brine and with paper towels, pat dry completely. Place the turkey breast into the smoker and cook for about 3½-4 hours or until desired doneness. Transfer the turkey onto a cutting board and set aside for about 15 minutes before slicing. With a sharp knife, cut the turkey breast in desired sized slices and serve.

Fully Smoked Herbal Quail
Serves: 8
Cooking Time: 60 Minutes
Ingredients:
- 4-6 quail
- 2 tablespoon of olive oil
- Salt as needed
- Freshly ground black pepper
- 1 pack of dry Hidden Valley Ranch dressing (or your preferred one)
- ½ a cup of melted butter

Directions:
Pre-heat your smoker to 225 degree Fahrenheit using hickory wood Brush the quail with olive oil and season with salt and pepper Place the in your smoker and smoke for 1 hour Take a small bowl and add ranch dressing mix and melted butter After the first 30 minutes of smoking, brush the quail with the ranch mix Repeat again at the end of the cook time Once the internal temperature of the quail reaches 145 degree Fahrenheit, they are ready!

Sweet And Spicy Chicken Wings
Serves: 8
Cooking Time: 20 Minutes
Ingredients:
- 5 lbs. chicken wings
- 3 tbsps. apple juice
- ½ c. BBQ sauce
- 1 c. honey
- 1 tbsp. garlic powder
- 1 tbsp. chili powder
- 1 tbsp. onion powder
- 2½ tbsps. black pepper
- 1 tbsp. salt

Directions:
Combine together black pepper, seasoned salt, garlic powder, chili powder, and onion powder. Add chicken wings into the ziplock bag then pour dry rub mixture over the chicken and mix well. Place chicken bag into the refrigerator for overnight. Preheat the smoker to 225 F/107 C using apple wood chips. Place chicken wings in smoker and smoke for 20 minutes. After 20 minutes turn chicken and smoke for another 25 minutes or until internal temperature reach 1 F/73 C. Meanwhile, in a small saucepan combine together BBQ sauce, honey, and apple juice and cook over medium heat. Remove chicken wings from smoker and toss with BBQ sauce mixture. Return chicken wings into the smoker and smoke for another 25 minutes. Serve hot and enjoy.

Stuffed Chicken Breast In Masterbuilt Smoker
Serves: 4
Cooking Time: 12 Minutes
Ingredients:
- 1 c. Chopped crawfish
- 1/3 c. chopped red Bell pepper
- ¼ c. chopped Green onion
- 1/3 c. chopped Parsley
- 1 c. shredded Cheese blend
- ½ c. Mayonnaise
- 2 tsps. Cajun Hot Sauce
- 2 tsps. Cajun seasoning
- 4 boneless Chicken breasts
- ½ c. Moppin' Sauce

Directions:
To prepare the Crawfish-stuffed chicken, please ensure that you bring fresh chicken breast just before cooking. It will keep the prepared dish fresh for long. Now, let us prepare the brine. To prepare it, take a large and deep pot. Into the pot, add ½ gallon water, kosher salt (1/cup), and brown sugar (1/3 cup). Add the chicken breast and leave the whole in the refrigerator for a night. Take out the chicken breasts soaked overnight in brine. Take a paper towel and pat it dry. Leave the chicken aside and prepare the stuffing. To prepare the stuffing, take the boiled Crawfish, Green Onion, Red Pepper, Cheese and Parsley in a bowl. Add in the hot sauce and Mayonnaise. Give it a good hand-mix and keep it aside. To prepare the stuffed chicken, you would need to soften the breasts. To do this, wrap the breasts in a plastic film and use a mallet. Beat the chicken breasts slowly, so that all the vacuum is removed from the chicken breasts. Remember, you must gently soften it, not tear it. Now, remove the film from the soften chicken breasts and sprinkle Cajun Seasoning over it. With your hands, nicely rub the seasoning over chicken breasts so that it is nicely seasoned. Now, take the stuffing (approximately 4-5 tbsps), or depending upon the size of the chicken breast and keep it on the top. Roll up the chicken breasts and nicely seal it so that the mixture does not pour out. Meanwhile, prepare the Masterbuilt smoker and add Sassafras woodchips. The temperature of the smoker should be 275 degrees Fahrenheit. Into the heated smoker, place the rolled-up Cajun seasoned chicken breasts. Insert a thermometer probe to check the internal temperature. When the temperature reaches, 160 degrees Fahrenheit, wipe it off with the Moppin' Sauce. The chicken will take about an hour and a half to reach the desired temperature of 160 degrees. Now, cook it for 30 minutes more until the temperature reaches, 165 degrees F. After 30 minutes, remove Chicken Breasts from Masterbuilt Smoker and keep it aside for about 10-15 minutes. Serve it and enjoy!

Cola Glazed Chicken Breasts
Serves: 4
Cooking Time: 45 Minutes-1 Hour
Ingredients:
- 4 bone in, skin on chicken breasts
- ½ gallon hot water
- 4 cups crushed ice
- 1 cup cola
- ½ cup Kosher salt
- ½ cup brown sugar
- 2 Tbsp peppercorns
- 1 cup Cola Barbecue

Directions:
In a large non-reactive bowl, combine water, salt and sugar until salt and sugar are dissolved. Add peppercorns, cola, and crushed ice and stir to combine. Submerge the chicken in the brine and let sit in the fridge for 1 hour. Remove from the brine and dry with a paper towel. Let the chicken sit at room temperature while you preheat the smoker to 250°F. Once the smoker is ready, place each chicken piece directly onto the grate. Smoke the chicken until the internal temperature reaches 155°F. Remove the chicken breasts from the smoker and liberally brush both sides with the Cola Barbecue Sauce. Return the chicken breasts to the smoker and continue cooking until they reach an internal temperature of 165°F. Allow the chicken to rest for 10-15 minutes before serving with additional heated sauce.

Christmas Dinner Duck
Serves: 5
Cooking Time: 4 Hours
Ingredients:
- 1 (5lb) whole duck
- ¾ cup honey
- ¾ cup red wine
- ¾ cup soy sauce
- 1½ tbsp garlic salt
- 2 tbsp freshly ground black pepper

Directions:
Soak pecan wood chips in water for at least hour. Preheat the smoker to 5-250 degrees F, using pecan wood chips. With a fork, poke holes in the skin of duck. In a bowl, add remaining all ingredients and mix until well combined. Rub the duck with the mixture generously, reserving some mixture. Place the duck on the smoker, breast side down and cook for about 4 hours. After 2 hours of cooking, coat the duck with the reserved mixture twice. In the last 30 minutes of the cooking, cover the duck with a piece of foil. Transfer the duck onto a cutting board and set aside for about 10-15 minutes before carving. With a sharp knife, cut the duck in desired sized pieces and serve.

Herb-rubbed Apple Smoked Turkey

Serves:8-10
Cooking Time:6 Hours 40 Minutes
Ingredients:
- 1 whole turkey, prepared(14-lbs, 6.35-kgs)
- Dried thyme – 2 tablespoons
- Powdered sage – 1 tablespoon
- Dried oregano – 2 teaspoons
- Paprika – 2 teaspoons
- Sea salt – 2 teaspoons
- Freshly ground black pepper – 1½ teaspoons
- Dried rosemary -1 teaspoon
- Garlic powder – 1 teaspoon
- Extra-virgin olive oil – ¼ cup
- Freshly squeezed zest of ½ orange
- Preheat your electric smoker to 225°F (110°C)
- Add approximately ½ cup each of apple cider and water to the water pan in the bottom of your smoker, until half filled
- Arrange a drip pan on the shelf above the water pan
- Fill the drawer with apple smoker wood chips

Directions:
In a bowl, combine the thyme, sage, oregano, paprika, sea salt, black pepper, dried rosemary, and garlic powder. Rub the bird's cavity with ⅓ of the seasoning mix. Add the olive oil along with the orange zest to the remaining ⅔ of the seasoning mix and rub all over the turkey's surface. Tuck the turkey's wingtip tightly underneath the bird and place it on the smoker's middle rack. Close the smoker door and set the timer for 6 ½ hours. The bird needs to smoke for 30- minutes for every 1-lbs (0.45-kgs) until its internal temperature on a meat thermometer registers 165°F (74°C). You will, however, need to check every 60 minutes for smoke, add more wood chips if necessary. Check the turkey's internal temperature after 3 hours and every 4minutes thereafter using a meat thermometer. Transfer the turkey to a chopping board and set aside to rest for between 20-120 minutes, before carving.

Seasoned Drumsticks

Serves: 12
Cooking Time: 1 Hour And 30 Minutes
Ingredients:
- 12 chicken drumsticks
- 1 ½ teaspoon minced garlic
- 2 teaspoons onion powder
- 2 teaspoons sea salt
- 2 teaspoons ground black pepper
- 1 teaspoon cayenne pepper
- 2 tablespoons paprika
- 2 teaspoons dried thyme
- 1/2 cup olive oil

Directions:
Plug in the smoker, fill its tray with hickory woodchips and water pan halfway through, and place dripping pan above the water pan. Then open the top vent, shut with lid and use temperature settings to preheat smoker at 0 degrees F. In the meantime, stir together garlic and oil until combined. Place drumsticks on a sheet pan, add garlic-oil mixture and toss until evenly coated. Then stir together remaining spices, sprinkle all over drumsticks until evenly coated and let rest for 10 minutes. Then place chicken on smoker rack, insert meat thermometer, then shut with lid and set the timer to smoke for 1 hour and 30 minutes or more until meat thermometer registers an internal temperature of 1 degrees F. Check vent of smoker every hour and add more woodchips and water to maintain temperature and smoke. Serve straightaway.

Turkey With Chimichurri

Serves: 5
Cooking Time: 4 Hours
Ingredients:
- 5 pounds bone-in, skin on turkey pieces
- Salt and pepper
- 1teaspoon paprika
- ½ teaspoon cayenne
- 2 tablespoons olive oil
- 1 pepper
- 1 onion
- 2 carrots, chopped
- 2 scallions
- 2 tomatoes, chopped
- Homemade Chimichurri Sauce
- ½ cup olive oil
- 1 teaspoon parsley
- 1 teaspoon red pepper flakes
- 2 garlic cloves
- 2 red onions

Directions:
Season the washed and clean turkey with the salt, pepper, paprika and cayenne pepper. Rub it gently all over. Arrange the wood chip inside the smoker and then preheat the smoker to 2 degrees F. Transfer the turkey to the sheet pan and arrange peppers, onions, carrots, scallion, and tomatoes beside it. Drizzle the olive oil on top. Place the pan sheet inside the smoker. Close the electric smoker door and then cook for 4 hours at 250 degrees F. Check the turkey to an internal temperature of 165°F. Now, it is time to make the chimichurri. Blend all the homemade chimichurri ingredients in a blender and puree until combined. Serve the cooked turkey and veggie with the ready to serve the sauce.

Sweet Bbq Wings
Serves: 8
Cooking Time: 1 Hour And 5 Minutes
Ingredients:
- 4 pounds chicken wings
- Honey as needed
- ½ cup BBQ rub
- 12-ounce BBQ sauce

Directions:
Plug in the smoker, fill its tray with apple woodchips and water pan halfway through, and place dripping pan above the water pan. Then open the top vent, shut with lid and use temperature settings to preheat smoker at 5 degrees F. In the meantime, seasoned chicken wings with BBQ rub until evenly coated. Place seasoned chicken wings on smoker rack, 2 pounds per rack, insert a meat thermometer, then shut with lid and set the timer to smoke for minutes. Then transfer chicken wings into a large bowl, add BBQ sauce and toss until evenly coated. Return chicken wings in the smoker, brush with honey and cook for 15 to 20 minutes or until crispy and internal temperature of wings reach to 1 degrees F. Check vent of smoker every hour and add more woodchips and water to maintain temperature and smoke. Serve hot.

Smo-fried Cajun Turkey
Serves: 10-12
Cooking Time: 2 Hours
Ingredients:
- 1 10-12-pound turkey, thawed with giblets removed
- 1 gallon hot water
- 8 cups crushed ice
- 2 cups Cajun Dry
- Turkey Frier
- 2-3 Gallons, Peanut Oil

Directions:
In a large non-reactive bowl, combine water, Cajun Dry Rub, and crushed ice and stir to combine. Submerge the turkey in the brine and let sit in the fridge for at least 1 hour. Remove from the brine and dry with a paper towel. Let the turkey sit at room temperature while you preheat the smoker to 2°F. Once the smoker is ready, place the turkey directly onto the grate, breast side down. Smoke the turkey for 2 hours. Remove the turkey from the smoker and insert directly into a turkey frier, filled according to appliance Directions:, with 325°F peanut oil. Continue to cook the turkey until the internal temperature of the meatiest part of the thigh reads 165°F. Remove the bird from the oil,

drain well, and allow the bird to rest 20-30 minutes before carving.

Grandma's Whole Smoked Chicken
Serves: 4-6
Cooking Time: 3-4 Hours
Ingredients:
- 1 3-4 lb roaster
- 1 gallon hot water
- 8 cups crushed ice
- 1 cup kosher salt
- 1 cup brown sugar
- 1 tsp cayenne pepper
- ¼ cup extra-virgin olive oil
- ¼ cup soy sauce
- 1 Tbsp dried oregano
- 1 Tbsp dried thyme
- 2 tsp onion powder

Directions:
In a large non-reactive bowl, combine water, salt and sugar until salt and sugar are dissolved. Add peppercorns and crushed ice and stir to cool the brine. Submerge the chicken in the brine and let sit in the fridge for 1 hour or as long as overnight. When you are ready to smoke the bird, remove from the brine and dry with a paper towel. Combine the rub ingredients and rub into the skin, under the skin, and inside the cavity of the bird. Let the chicken sit at room temperature while you preheat the smoker to 22F. Place the chicken, breast side down, in the smoker. Smoke the chicken until the thigh meat reaches an internal temperature of 165°F. Remove the chicken from the smoker and allow it to sit, lightly covered, for 15-20 minutes before carving.

Smoked Herbed Chicken Breasts
Serves: 9
Cooking Time: 2 Hours
Ingredients:
- 1 tablespoon fresh herbs (sage, rosemary, and thyme)
- 3 tablespoons olive oil
- Salt and pepper to taste
- 3 pounds chicken breasts

Directions:
Place all Ingredients: in a Ziploc bag. Shake and allow to marinate for hours in the fridge. Preheat the smoker to 2250F. Place apple juice in the water pan and add hickory wood chips into the side tray. Place chicken in the smoker. Cook for 2 hours.

Asparagus Stuffed Smoked Chicken Breasts
Serves: 10
Cooking Time: 1 Hour, 20 Minutes
Ingredients:
* 4-6 boneless, skinless chicken breasts
* Your choice of rub
* 8-12 stalks of asparagus (the thinner stalks are more tender)
* 4-6 slices of bacon (thin sliced seems to crisp up better in the smoker)
* Toothpicks (optional)

Directions:
Apply the rub to the chicken. Allow them to sit in the fridge overnight. Lay the chicken down on a cutting board. Place a piece of asparagus on top, and roll the chicken over the asparagus. Use toothpicks to keep the asparagus in place. Once you've done that, wrap some bacon over the middle of the chicken. Secured it with another toothpick. Sprinkle some rub on top of the "stuffed" chicken with the asparagus and bacon on it. Cover up the chicken and place in the fridge for 4 hours. Overnight if you want that extra flavor. Allow the chicken to cook in the smoker. Allow it to cool for a few minutes before serving.

Smoked Chicken Breasts With Rosemary (masterbuilt Electric Smoker)
Serves: 4
Cooking Time: 2 Hours And 45 Minutes
Ingredients:
* 4 cloves garlic, minced
* 2 Tbsp chopped fresh rosemary, flat-leaf parsley, or another fresh herb
* 1/4 cup fresh lemon juice
* 1/4 cup extra-virgin olive oil; more for drizzling
* Kosher salt and freshly ground black pepper
* 4 chicken breasts boneless and skinless

Directions:
Combine garlic, rosemary, lemon juice, olive oil and salt; generously brush the marinade all over the meat. Cover and refrigerate for 30 minutes. Preheat Masterbuilt Electric Smoker. Allow the smoker temperature to reach 225 degrees Fahrenheit. When it is ready, add some water to the removable pan that is usually on the bottom shelf. Fill the side "drawer" with dry wood chips. Smoke chicken about 2 to 2 1/2 hours when the chicken breast reaches an internal temperature of 1 degrees Fahrenheit. Remove chicken from smoker and let rest for 10 minutes. Transfer on a serving plate and serve.

Well-seasoned Drumsticks
Serves: 4
Cooking Time: 1 Hour 30 Minutes
Ingredients:
* 12 chicken drumsticks
* 1 and ½ teaspoons garlic, minced
* 2 teaspoons onion powder
* 2 teaspoons salt
* 2 teaspoons ground pepper
* 1 teaspoon cayenne pepper
* 2 tablespoons paprika
* 2 teaspoons dried thyme
* ½ cup olive oil

Directions:
Take your drip pan and add water, cover with aluminum foil. Pre-heat your smoker to 220 degrees F Take a large bowl and add breasts, season with salt and pepper, garlic powder Use water fill water pan halfway through and place it over drip pan. Add wood chips to the side tray. Take a bowl and add garlic, oil and mix well Place drumsticks on a sheet pan and add garlic oil mix, toss well Take another bowl and mix remaining spices, sprinkle over drumsticks. Let them sit for 10 minutes Transfer to the smoker and let them smoke for 1 hour and 30 minutes until the internal temperature reaches 165 degrees F Serve and enjoy one done.

Supremely Smoked Alderwood Turkey Breast
Serves: 4
Cooking Time: 3 And A ½ To 4 Hours
Ingredients:
* 4 tablespoon of unsalted butter
* 8 teaspoon of Dijon mustard
* 2 tablespoon of chopped fresh thyme leaves
* 1 teaspoon of freshly ground black pepper
* ½ a teaspoon of kosher salt
* 1 bone-in turkey breast

Directions:
Take a small sized bowl and stir in butter, thyme, mustard, ¼ teaspoon of pepper, salt Rub the turkey breast with the butter mix Cover and allow it to refrigerate overnight Pre-heat your smoker to 250 degree Fahrenheit using Apple wood chips Sprinkle breast with ¾ teaspoon of pepper and transfer to smoker rack Cover and smoke for 3 and a ½ to 4 hours, making sure to keep adding more chips after every minutes Once the internal temperature reaches 165 degree Fahrenheit, remove the turkey and allow it to rest Slice and serve!

Spiced Chicken Thighs
Serves: 6
Cooking Time: 4 Hours
Ingredients:
- 6 skinless, boneless skin-on chicken thighs
- 1 tbsp dried thyme, crushed
- 1 tbsp paprika
- 1 tbsp chili powder
- 1 tbsp cayenne pepper
- 1 tbsp garlic powder
- Salt and freshly ground black pepper, to taste
- 1 cup olive oil

Directions:
Preheat the smoker to 200-220 degrees F, using charcoal. In a bow, add all ingredients except the oil and chicken thighs and mix well. Coat the chicken thighs with the oil evenly and then rub with the spice mixture generously. Place the chicken thighs into the smoker rack and add pecan wood chips at the same time. Cook for about 2 hours. Rotate the chicken thighs and cook for about 1-2 hours. Serve hot.

Romain Chicken Breasts
Serves: 4
Cooking Time: 3 Hours
Ingredients:
- 2 small chicken breasts
- Romaine's hearts
- 1 tomato, diced
- Shavings of parmesan cheese
- Caesar salad dressing
- 1 teaspoon salt
- 1 teaspoon pepper
- ½ teaspoon garlic powder
- 4 large tortillas

Directions:
Take your drip pan and add water, cover with aluminum foil. Pre-heat your smoker to 225 degrees F Take a large bowl and add breasts, season with salt and pepper, garlic powder Use water fill water pan halfway through and place it over drip pan. Add wood chips to the side tray. Transfer chicken to smoker and smoke for 1 and ½ hours until internal temperature reaches 165 degrees F Remove chicken once done, let it rest for 10 minutes, cut into slices Take a large mixing bowl and add romaine hearts, Caesar dressing, parmesan cheese shavings Mix well Warm tortillas on a flat pan on the stove and transfer toasted tortilla to a tray Put a layer of salad, tomatoes, chicken slices and spoonful of dressing on top Fold into rolls and enjoy!

Lemon Pepper Chicken Quarters
Serves: 6
Cooking Time: 1 ½ - 2 Hours
Ingredients:
- 6 Chicken Quarters, dark meat only

- ½ gallon hot water
- 4 cups crushed ice
- ½ cup Kosher salt
- ½ cup brown sugar
- 2 lemons, halved
- 2 Tbsp peppercorns
- ¼ cup Money 2 Tbsp lemon zest
- 1 tsp black pepper

Directions:
In a large non-reactive bowl, combine water, salt and sugar until salt and sugar are dissolved. Add peppercorns and crushed ice and squeeze lemons into the brine. Add squeezed lemons and stir to combine. Submerge the chicken in the brine and let sit in the fridge for 1 hour or as long as overnight. When you are ready to smoke the bird, remove from the brine and dry with a paper towel. Mix black pepper, lemon zest and Money Rub and rub it into the skin, under the skin, and inside the cavity of the bird. Let the chicken sit at room temperature while you preheat the smoker to 22F. Once the smoker is ready, place each chicken piece directly onto the grate. Smoke the chicken until the internal temperature reaches 165°F. Allow the chicken quarters to rest for 10-15 minutes before serving.

Smoked Turkey Breast
Serves: 5
Cook Time: 3 And ½ Hours
Ingredients:
- 1 Bone-in turkey breast of about 7 Pounds
- 1 Cut up, Granny Smith apple
- 2 Cut-up medium onions
- 8 Sprigs of fresh thyme
- 4 Small sprigs of fresh rosemary
- 6 Torn sage leaves
- 2 Teaspoons of seasoning salt
- 1 Teaspoon of paprika

Directions:
Rinse the breast and pat it dry with clean paper towels and loosen the skin over both the sides of the turkey breasts Soak with about to 3 cups of wood chips in hot tap of water Cover with water pan with the aluminum foil; then add the apple, the onion, about 4 sprigs of the thyme, 2 sprigs of rosemary and sprigs of sage leaves. In a small bowl, combine the paprika with the Adobo; then put a generous amount of the mixture between the breast and the skin on the outside of the skin Tuck the remaining herb sprigs under the skin Prepare your smoker by preheating it to a temperature of about 225° F Place the water in the water pan of your Masterbuilt electric smoker and place the body on top of the grill base Place the turkey breast on the top of the grill rack; then cover and smoke at a temperature of about 225°F to 250°F for about 3 and ½ hours Let the eat stand aside covered with foil for about 20 to 30 minutes before slicing and serving it!

Smoked Turkey
Serves: 6
Cook Time: 6 Hours
Ingredients:
- 12-Pound turkey, whole turkey
- 2 Tablespoons of dried thyme
- 1 Tablespoon of powdered sage
- 2 Teaspoons of dried oregano
- 2 Teaspoons of paprika
- 2 Teaspoons of sea salt
- 1 and ½ teaspoons of cracked black pepper
- 1 Teaspoon of dried rosemary
- 1 Teaspoon of garlic powder or onion powder
- The Zest of half orange
- ¼ Cup of extra virgin olive oil
- ½ Cup of apple cider
- ½ Cup of water
- Pecan wood chips or pecan wood

Directions:
Preheat your smoker to a temperature of about 225°F. In a small bowl, combine your dry herbs with the spices Rub the inner cavity of the turkey with about 1/of the dry prepared seasoning Add the oil and the orange zest to the rest of your seasonings and rub the seasonings all over the turkey Put the water and the apple cider in the water pan into the bottom of your electric smoker; filling only half its way Place a drip pan on the shelf above the water pan; then fill the side drawer with the wood chips Tuck the wing tips underneath the turkey; then place the seasoned turkey on top of the middle of the smoker Close the door of the Masterbuilt electric smoker and set its timer for about 6 hours You should start checking the internal temperature of the bird after about 3 hours and every 40 to 45 minutes Remove the turkey from the electric smoker to a cutting board and let rest for about 20 minutes to about 2 hours Serve and enjoy your dish!

Rotisserie Chicken
Serves: 12
Cooking Time: 2 Hours
Ingredients:
- 6 pounds whole chicken
- 1 cup lemon pepper seasoning and more as needed
- Water as needed
- 1-gallon bag

Directions:
Place chicken in the gallon bag, pour in water, and add seasoning. Seal the bag, place in a tray and let soak for 8 hours or overnight in the refrigerator. Then remove chicken from the bag, rinse well, pat dry and season inside-out with lemon pepper seasoning until evenly coated. Plug in the smoker, fill its tray with hickory woodchips and water pan halfway through, and place dripping pan above the water pan. Then open the top vent, shut with lid and use temperature settings to preheat smoker at 2 degrees F. In the meantime, skewer seasoned chicken onto rotisserie grill. Place chicken on smoker rack, insert a meat thermometer into its thickest part, then shut with lid and set the timer to smoke for 2 hours or more until meat thermometer registers an internal temperature of 165 degrees F. Check vent of smoker every hour and add more woodchips and water to maintain temperature and smoke. When done, transfer chicken onto a cutting board, let rest for 15 minutes and then carve to serve.

Get-together Chicken Wings
Serves: 8
Cooking Time: 2 Hours 40 Minutes
Ingredients:
- 6 lbs chicken wings
- 2 tbsp red chili powder
- 2 tbsp smoked paprika
- 1 tsp cayenne pepper
- 1 tsp ground cumin
- 1 tsp garlic powder
- 1 tsp onion powder
- Salt and freshly ground black pepper, to taste
- 2 tbsp olive oil

Directions:
With a sharp knife, cut each wing through the joints to separate the drumettes. In a large bowl, add all the spices and mix well. Coat the chicken wings with the oil Add the chicken wings and coat with the spice mixture generously. Refrigerate for at least 1 hour. Soak apple wood chips in water for at least 1 hour. Preheat the smoker to 225-250 degrees F, using charcoal and apple wood chips. Place the chicken wings over indirect heat and cook for about 2-2½ hours. Now, place the chicken wings directly over coals for about 5 minutes per side. Serve hot.

Red Hot Chicken Wings
Serves: 6-8
Cooking Time: 1-1 ½ Hours
Ingredients:
- 5 lbs chicken wings
- ½ cup your favorite hot sauce (we like sriracha)
- 2 Tbsp black pepper
- 2 tsp chili powder
- 2 tsp red pepper flakes
- 1 tsp onion powder
- 1 tsp garlic powder
- 1 tsp salt

Directions:
In a large zip top bag, combine chicken wings and hot sauce. Let marinate in the fridge for hour. Mix together all rub ingredients in a large zip top bag. Toss the chicken wings into the bag with the rub ingredients and shake the bag vigorously for a few minutes all the pieces are evenly coated. Let the chicken sit at room temperature while you preheat the smoker to 250°F. Smoke the rubbed chicken wing pieces for until they reach an internal temperature of 16F. Meanwhile, heat ½ inch of oil in a large cast iron skillet until the oil reaches 375°F. Fry the smoked wings in batches, in the hot oil for 45 seconds per side. Set the fried wings over a paper towel to drain excess oil.

Smoked Soy Chicken Legs

Serves: 4
Cooking Time: 4 Hours 10 Minutes
Ingredients:
- 3 1/2 lbs chicken legs, rinse and pat dry
- 2 cups apple juice
- 1/4 cup BBQ spice
- 1/2 cup soy sauce
- 1/2 cup Italian salad dressing

Directions:
Add chicken, BBQ spice, soy sauce, and Italian salad dressing in zip lock bag and mix well. Place chicken bag in the refrigerator for overnight. Preheat the smoker to 250 F/121 C using apple wood. Remove chicken from marinade and place in smoker and smoke for hours. After every 30 minutes misting with apple juice. Serve and enjoy.

Smofried Chicken Wings

Serves: 6-8
Cooking Time: 1-1 ½ Hours
Ingredients:
- 5 lbs chicken wings
- ¼ cup Money
- 1 cup Chipotle Lime Mango Barbecue

Directions:
In a large zip top bag, combine chicken wings and rub. Toss vigorously for a few minutes until all the pieces are evenly coated. Let the chicken sit at room temperature while you preheat the smoker to 0°F. Smoke the rubbed chicken wing pieces for until they reach an internal temperature of 165°F. Meanwhile, heat ½ inch of oil in a large cast iron skillet until the oil reaches 375°F. Fry the smoked wings in batches, in the hot oil for 4seconds per side. Set the fried wings over a paper towel to drain excess oil. Toss in warmed sauce for an additional layer of flavor.

Utterly Delicious Duck Breast

Serves: 4-6
Cooking Time: 3 Hours
Ingredients:
- 2 (1lb) boneless duck breasts
- 2 cups apple juice
- 1 tbsp soy sauce
- 1 tbsp white sugar
- ½ tsp paprika
- ½ tsp garlic powder
- ½ tsp dried basil
- Salt and freshly ground black pepper, to taste

Directions:
In a large bowl, add all ingredient except duck breast and mix until sugar is dissolved. In a deep baking dish, place the brine and duck breast. With a plastic wrap, cover the baking dish and refrigerate for about 4 hours. Soak cherry wood chips in water for at least 1 hour. Preheat the smoker to 2 degrees F, using charcoal and cherry wood chips. Place the duck breast onto a smoker rack and cook for about 2½ -3 hours. Transfer the duck breast onto a cutting board and set aside for about 15 minutes before slicing. With a sharp knife, cut the breast in desired sized slices and serve.

German Style Turkey Breast

Serves: 6
Cooking Time: 4 Hours
Ingredients:
- ½ cup honey
- ¼ cup dry sherry
- 1 tbsp butter
- 2 tbsp fresh lemon juice
- Salt, to taste
- 1 (3-3½lb) skinless, boneless turkey breast

Directions:
In a small pan, add the honey, sherry and butter over low heat and cook until the mixture becomes smooth, stirring continuously Remove from heat and stir in lemon juice and salt. Set aside to cool. Transfer the honey mixture and turkey breast in a sealable bag. Seal the bag and shake to coat evenly. Refrigerate for about 10 hours. Preheat the smoker to 225-250 degrees F, using charcoal. Place the turkey breast into the smoker and cook for about 2½-4 hours or until desired doneness. Transfer the turkey onto a cutting board and set aside for about 15 minutes before slicing. With a sharp knife, cut the turkey breast in desired sized slices and serve.

Apple-smoked Duck
Serves: 6
Cooking Time: 4 Hours
Ingredients:
- 6 cups water
- 6 tablespoons kosher salt, plus more to taste
- 1/4 cup packed brown sugar
- 2 bottles (12 ounces each) hard apple cider
- 2 whole ducks (5 to 6 pounds each)
- Freshly ground black pepper, to taste
- 4 apples (cored, quartered)
- 2 sweet onions (peeled, quartered)

Directions:
For the brine, heat water, brown sugar and salt to a boil. Let brine cool to room temperature and stir in hard cider. Remove giblets and neck from ducks as necessary. Rinse ducks with cold water and place in a large glass or plastic container. Pour brine over ducks, cover and refrigerate for at least 8 hours, turning ducks occasionally. Place apple wood chips in the Masterbuilt smoker's wood tray and preheat smoker to 225°F. Remove ducks from brine, pat dry with paper towels and season all over with salt and pepper. Place two apples and one onion inside each duck cavity. Place ducks breast-side up on smoker grate and smoke until the internal temperature of the meat reaches 16F, about 4 hours. Add wood chips to the wood tray as necessary. Remove ducks from smoker and place breast-sides up on a serving platter. Cover ducks loosely with aluminum foil and let rest for about 15 minutes. Remove skin from ducks and carve as desired to serve. Enjoy!

Sweet 'n' Spicy Chicken Wings
Serves: 3-4
Cooking Time:11 Hours 15 Minutes
Ingredients:
- 12 chicken wings
- Chicken rub – 2-3 tablespoons
- Baking powder – 1 tablespoon
- Spicy BBQ sauce, store-bought – ¼ cup
- Runny honey – ½ cup
- Apple juice – 2-4 tablespoons
- Preheat your electric smoker to 225°F (10°C)
- Add the wood chips

Directions:
In a bowl, combine the chicken rub with the baking powder and add to a ziplock bag along with the chicken wings and shake the bag to coat. Place the wings on a tray and put in the fridge, overnight. Add the wings to your smoker and smoke for 1½ hours. Flip the chicken wings over and smoke for an additional 1½ hours. While the wings smoke, prepare the sauce by adding the BBQ sauce to a pan along with the runny honey and apple juice and simmer for 10 minutes, until it begins to thicken. When the second 1 ½ hours have elapsed check the wings internal temperature. If it is not registering 1°F (74°C) smoke for an additional 30 minutes. The total cooking time will be approximately 2 hours 15 minutes. Remove from the smoker and toss in the sauce.

White Wine Turkey Dogs
Serves:10
Cooking Time:2 Hours
Ingredients:
- 10 turkey hot dogs
- Butter – 4 tablespoons
- Mushrooms, chopped – 3 cups
- 1 green pepper, seeded and sliced
- 1 yellow onion, peeled and sliced
- 1 bottle white wine
- 10 hot dog buns
- Preheat the smoker to 225°f (107°c) using peach wood chips

Directions:
Add the butter, mushrooms, green pepper, onion, and white wine to a baking tin. Arrange the baking tin on a lower rack in the smoker and arrange the sausages on the rack above. Smoke for 40 minutes, then add the sausages to the wine mixture. Smoke for another 40 minutes. Arrange the cooked sausages in the buns and top with a little of the cooked mushroom, pepper, and onion. Serve straight away.

Basic Smoked Chicken
Serves: 8
Cooking Time: 3 To 4 Hours
Ingredients:
- 2 whole chickens (4 to 5 pounds each)
- 1 tablespoon salt
- 1 tablespoon freshly ground black pepper
- 1 tablespoon garlic powder
- 1 tablespoon onion powder
- 1 teaspoon dried oregano
- 1 teaspoon dried thyme
- 1/4 cup yellow mustard

Directions:
Pour 2 cups water into the Masterbuilt smoker's water pan. Place apple, cherry, peach or pecan wood chips in the smoker's wood tray and preheat smoker to 225°F. Remove gizzards and necks from chicken cavities if necessary. Rinse chickens inside and out with cold water and pat dry with paper towels. Mix salt, pepper, garlic powder, onion powder, oregano and thyme. Carefully lift skins of chickens and rub some of the spice mixture directly into the meat. Brush mustard over insides and outsides of chickens and rub remaining spice mixture all over the chickens. Place chickens breast-sides down on smoker grate and smoke for one hour. Turn chickens over and smoke until the internal temperature of the meat reaches 165°F, 2 to 3 hours more. Add wood chips to the wood tray as necessary. Remove chickens from smoker, cover loosely with aluminum foil and let rest for about 20 minutes. Carve chickens as desired, serve and enjoy!

Smoked Chicken Thighs In Red Pepper Marinade (masterbuilt Electric Smoker)

Serves: 6
Cooking Time: 2 Hours And 20 Minutes
Ingredients:

- 1/2 cup chicken broth
- 1/2 cup garlic-infused olive oil
- 1 tsp red pepper flakes
- 1 tsp sweet paprika
- 1 tsp Salt and freshly ground black pepper
- 2 lb chicken thighs

Directions:
Place the chicken thighs in a large flat dish so they are in a single layer. In a bowl, combine all remaining Ingredients:. Pour the marinade over chicken thighs. Cover and refrigerate for hours. Remove the chicken tights from marinade and pat dry. Preheat Masterbuilt Electric Smoker. Allow the smoker temperature to reach 225 degrees Fahrenheit. When it is ready, add some water to the removable pan that is usually on the bottom shelf. Fill the side "drawer" with dry wood chips (cherry wood chip). Place marinated chicken thighs on the smoker grate, skin side down. Smoke for 2 hours, rotating throughout cooking. Serve hot.

Spicy Chicken Wings With Dipping Sauce

Serves: 5-6
Cook Time: 2 Hours
Ingredients:

- 4 to 5 Pounds of chicken wings
- ½ Cup of brown sugar, light brown
- ¼ Cup of paprika
- 2 to 2 and ½ teaspoons of sea salt
- ½ Tablespoon of onion powder
- 1 Teaspoon of garlic powder
- ½ Teaspoon of freshly ground black pepper
- 1 Teaspoon of cayenne pepper
- Plain yogurt, 1 Pint
- ¾ Cup of blue cheese, crumbled
- 2 and ½ tablespoons of minced chives
- 1 Pinch of freshly ground black pepper
- 1 Pinch of salt

Directions:
Start by rinsing the chicken wings under running water and pat it dry with clean paper towels Cut off the tips of the wings into half at the joint point Place the portions of the wings in a large bowl In a separate bowl, whisk the sugar with the salt, the paprika, the onion powder, the garlic powder, the pepper, and the cayenne. Add the prepared dry rub to the wings and toss the ingredients with your hands; then set the wings aside while you are preparing your electric smoker Take a rack from your Masterbuilt electric smoker and place on a counter that is lined with clean paper towels Add in the hickory wood chips to the tray of your smoker; then fill the water bowl half the way Open the top of the vent and preheat your electric smoker to a temperature of about 250° F Place the chicken wings in the smoker and smoke it for about 2 hours And while the wings are smoking; when you prepare the dipping sauce; combine the yogurt with the chives, the yogurt, the cheese, the salt and the pepper Check the seasoning and adjust it as needed Serve the chicken wings over a platter with the prepared dipping sauce Enjoy your dish!

Alabama Chicken Sandwiches With White Bbq Sauce

Serves: 8
Cooking Time: 3 To 4 Hours
Ingredients:

- 2 cups mayonnaise
- 1/4 cup white vinegar
- 3 teaspoons freshly ground black pepper (divided)
- 2 teaspoons salt (divided)
- 1 whole chicken (about 4 pounds)
- 2 teaspoons sweet paprika
- 2 teaspoons garlic powder
- 1/2 teaspoon ground cumin
- 1/2 teaspoon ground coriander
- 8 hamburger buns
- Hamburger dill pickle slices (for serving)

Directions:
Pour 2 cups water into the Masterbuilt smoker's water pan. Place oak or pecan wood chips in the smoker's wood tray and preheat smoker to 250°F. For the sauce, mix mayonnaise and vinegar with 1 1/teaspoons pepper and 1 teaspoon salt until thoroughly combined. Place half of the sauce in a covered container and refrigerate until serving. Set remaining sauce aside for basting chicken. Remove gizzards and neck from chicken cavity if necessary. Rinse chicken inside and out with cold water and pat dry with paper towels. Mix paprika, garlic powder, cumin and coriander with remaining 1 1/2 teaspoons pepper and 1 teaspoon salt and rub over inside and outside of chicken.   Place chicken breast-side down on smoker grate and smoke for about 20 minutes. Baste chicken with sauce and continue smoking until the internal temperature of the meat reaches 175°F, 2 to 3 hours, basting with sauce about every 20 minutes and turning chicken over about halfway through cooking time. Add wood chips to the wood tray as necessary. Remove chicken from smoker, cover loosely with aluminum foil and let rest for about 10 minutes. Shred meat with two forks and serve on buns with the pickle slices and remaining sauce. Enjoy!

Supreme Chipotle Wings

Serves: 8
Cooking Time: 1 And A ½ To 2 Hours
Ingredients:
- 2 tablespoon packed light brown sugar
- 1 and a ½ tablespoon of chipotle pepper
- 1 tablespoon of Hungarian smoked paprika
- 1 tablespoon of dry mustard
- 1 tablespoon of ground cumin
- 1 and a ½ teaspoon of salt
- 5 and a ½ pound of chicken wings

Directions:
Take a small sized bowl and add brown sugar, paprika, chipotle, mustard, salt and cumin Transfer the chicken wings to a large re-sealable bag and pour the seasoning mix Seal and shake the chicken Refrigerate for 60 minutes Pre-heat your smoker to 2 degree Fahrenheit with oak woods Transfer the chicken to your smoker rack and smoke for 1 and a ½ to 2 hours Check if the internal temperature is 165 degree Fahrenheit and serve!

Turkey Breast

Serves: 8
Cooking Time: 4 Hours
Ingredients:
- 1 can (12 ounces) beer
- 1/2 cup water
- 1/2 cup chicken stock or broth
- 1 bone-in turkey breast (about 6 pounds)
- 2 tablespoons vegetable oil
- 1 tablespoon kosher salt, plus more to taste
- 1 tablespoon garlic powder
- 1 tablespoon dried rosemary (crushed)
- 1 tablespoon freshly ground black pepper, plus more to taste
- 1 teaspoon dried sage
- 1 teaspoon dried thyme

Directions:
Pour beer, water and chicken stock into the Masterbuilt smoker's water pan. Place hickory or apple wood chips in the smoker's wood tray and preheat smoker to 225°F. Rinse turkey breast with cold water and pat dry with paper towels. Brush oil over turkey breast and set aside. Mix salt, garlic powder, rosemary, pepper, sage and thyme and rub all over turkey breast. Place turkey breast on smoker grate and smoke until the internal temperature of the meat reaches 165°F, about hours. Add wood chips to the wood tray as necessary. Remove turkey breast from smoker, cover loosely with aluminum foil and let rest for about 1minutes. Slice turkey breast as desired and serve. Enjoy!

Bacon-wrapped Chicken Lollipops

Serves: 4
Cooking Time: 60 Minutes
Ingredients:
- 4 pounds chicken drumsticks
- 2 pounds sliced bacon
- ½ cup sweet BBQ rub
- Honey as needed

Directions:
Take your drip pan and add water, cover with aluminum foil. Pre-heat your smoker to 275 degrees F Take a large bowl and add breasts, season with salt and pepper, garlic powder Use water fill water pan halfway through and place it over drip pan. Add wood chips to the side tray. Take a bowl and add chicken, season with BBQ wrap and wrap with bacon Place bacon-wrapped chicken on smoker and drizzle honey on top Smoke for 30- minutes until the internal temperature reaches 165 degrees F Serve and enjoy!

Cajun Style Chicken Breasts

Serves: 6
Cooking Time: 6 Hours
Ingredients:
- 2 lbs skinless, boneless, chicken breasts, trimmed
- 2 tbsp Cajun seasoning
- 1 cup BBQ sauce

Directions:
Soak mesquite wood chips in water for at least hour. Preheat the smoker to 5 degrees F, using charcoal and mesquite wood chips. Rub the chicken breasts with Cajun seasoning generously. Place the chicken breasts into the smoker rack and cook for about 6 hours. During last hour of the cooking, coat the breasts with BBQ sauce twice. Serve hot.

Smoked Chicken Legs

Serves: 3
Cooking Time: 2 Hours
Ingredients:
- 6 chicken legs
- 1 cup olive oil
- 1 tbsp. cayenne pepper
- 1 tbsp. paprika
- 2 tsp. salt
- 1 tbsp. onion powder
- 1 tbsp. dried thyme
- 1 tbsp. garlic powder
- 1 tbsp. pepper

Directions:
Start your smoker up half an hour before you start cooking. In a mixing bowl, stir together all the dry ingredients. Be sure to rub the olive oil all over the chicken legs. Now rub the seasoning over the chicken legs until they're fully coated. Place the chicken legs on the smoking rack. Turn them over so they cook evenly. You may have to add more smoker chips as you do this.

Smoked Chicken Breast In Coffee Marinade (masterbuilt Electric Smoker)

Serves: 4
Cooking Time: 2 Hours And 45 Minutes
Ingredients:

- MARINADE
- 1/4 cup packed dark brown sugar
- 3 cups water
- 3/4 cup strong brewed coffee
- 1 Tbsp mustard seeds
- 1 Tbsp Kosher salt or to taste
- 4 boneless skinless chicken breast halves (6 to 8 oz. each), trimmed and rinsed

Directions:
Combine all Ingredients: for marinade and pour in a large container. Add chicken breasts and toss to combine well. Piercing the chicken with a fork, or cutting it into smaller pieces will help it absorb the marinade. Refrigerate for hours or overnight. Remove the chicken from marinade 30 minutes before smoking. Preheat Masterbuilt Electric Smoker. Allow the smoker temperature to reach 225 degrees Fahrenheit. When it is ready, add some water to the removable pan that is usually on the bottom shelf. Fill the side "drawer" with dry wood chips (such as oak or hickory). Place the chicken breast onto smoker racks; smoke about 2 to 2 1/2 hours when the chicken breast reaches an internal temperature of 160 degrees Fahrenheit.

Old Fashioned Barbecue Chicken

Serves: 4-6
Cooking Time: 3-4 Hours
Ingredients:

- 1 3-4 lb roaster
- 1 gallon hot water
- 8 cups crushed ice
- 1 cup kosher salt
- 1 cup brown sugar
- 2 Tbsp whole peppercorns
- ¼ cup Basic Barbecue ¼ cup of your favorite barbecue sauce (We like the St. Louis Barbecue Sauce.)

Directions:
In a large non-reactive bowl, combine water, salt and sugar until salt and sugar are dissolved. Add peppercorns and crushed ice and stir to cool the brine. Submerge the chicken in the brine and let sit in the fridge for 1 hour or as long as overnight. When you are ready to smoke the bird, remove from the brine and dry with a paper towel. Sprinkle the Basic Barbecue Rub on the skin and inside the cavity of the bird. Let the chicken sit at room temperature while you preheat the smoker to 22F. Place the chicken, breast side down, in the smoker. Smoke the chicken until the thigh meat

reaches an internal temperature of 155°F. Remove the chicken from the smoker and brush liberally with barbecue sauce. Return the chicken to the smoker until it reaches an internal temperature of 165°F. Remove the chicken from the smoker and allow it to sit, lightly covered, for 15-20 minutes before carving.

Chicken With Western Kentucky Mop & Dip

Serves: 4
Cooking Time: 2 1/2 Hours
Ingredients:

- 1 whole chicken (4 to 5 pounds)
- 2 tablespoons kosher salt (divided)
- 2 tablespoons coarsely ground black pepper (divided)
- 3 cups water (divided)
- 1 cup cider vinegar
- 1 cup Worcestershire sauce
- 3 tablespoons lemon juice
- 1/2 cup brown sugar
- 1/2 teaspoon garlic powder
- 1/2 teaspoon onion powder
- 1/4 teaspoon allspice

Directions:
Pour 2 cups water into the Masterbuilt smoker's water pan. Place apple or cherry wood chips in the smoker's wood tray and preheat smoker to 250°F. Remove gizzards and neck from chicken cavity if necessary. Rinse chicken inside and out with cold water and pat dry with paper towels. With a kitchen shears, cut chicken in half lengthwise along the spine and between the breasts. Rub chicken halves all over with 1 tablespoon salt and 1 tablespoon pepper. Place chicken halves skin-sides up on smoker grate and smoke while you prepare the sauce, about minutes. For the sauce, mix 2 cups water with cider vinegar, Worcestershire sauce and lemon juice with remaining 1 tablespoon kosher salt and 1 tablespoon pepper in a medium saucepan over medium-high heat. Heat sauce to a boil, stirring frequently. Pour about half of the sauce into a bowl for basting. For the dip, add brown sugar, garlic powder, onion powder, allspice and remaining 1 cup water to the remaining sauce in the pan, mix until sugar is dissolved and simmer to reduce to desired consistency. Generously brush or "mop" some of the basting sauce over the chicken halves. Continue smoking chicken until the internal temperature of the meat reaches 16F, about 2 hours more, mopping with more sauce about every 30 minutes. Add wood chips to the wood tray as necessary. Remove chicken halves from smoker, cover loosely with aluminum foil and let rest for about 10 minutes. Carve chicken halves as desired and serve with the dip. Enjoy!

Smoked Garlicky Chicken Breast (masterbuilt Electric Smoker)

Serves: 4

Cooking Time: 2 Hours And 45 Minutes

Ingredients:

- 4 chicken breasts boneless and skinless
- 8 cloves garlic minced
- 1/4 cup olive oil
- 1/4 cup honey
- Herbs and spices to a taste
- Salt and freshly ground pepper to taste

Directions:

Heat the oil in small saucepan, and sauté garlic until tender. Remove from heat and stir in honey. Add salt and pepper, and herbs and spices as desired. Place chicken breasts in a baking dish and cover evenly with the garlic and honey mixture. Preheat Masterbuilt Electric Smoker. Allow the smoker temperature to reach 225 degrees Fahrenheit. When it is ready, add some water to the removable pan that is usually on the bottom shelf. Fill the side "drawer" with dry wood chips. Smoke chicken directly on rack for 2 - 2 1/2 hours or until internal temperature reaches 165 degrees (the total cooking time will depend on the cut of the meat). Remove chicken from smoker and let rest for 10 minutes. Serve warm.

Beer Smoked Chicken In Masterbuilt Smoker

Serves: 6

Cooking Time: 13 Minutes

Ingredients:

- 1 Whole chicken
- ¼ c. Dry Rub
- 1 can Beer
- 3 c. Marinade

Directions:

Start by rinsing the chicken cavity and removing giblets. Take the dry rub or seasoning of your choice and properly rub inside and out of the chicken. While rubbing, press the seasoning onto the surface of the chicken and allow it to rest in the refrigerator for an hour. Meanwhile, prepare the Masterbuilt Smoker and empty the beer can in the drip pan. In the can, fill up the marinade and put that can into the cavity of the chicken. Now, keep aside the chicken and prepare the Masterbuilt Electric Smoker. You have to keep it on indirect heat mode and use the woodchips of your liking. For this particular recipe, I would recommend, Applewood; however, if that is unavailable, you can choose one from, Hickory, Mesquite, or Oakwood. Going further, maintain the temperature of the smoker something between 225 degrees F and 275 degrees F. It is time now to place the chicken on Smoker Grill with Beer Can as the base. Cook the chicken for at least 3 hours. If you have used a dripping pan filled with beer and water, that is great; but if you have not done so, then try basting the chicken with the marinade you have. Also, to see the internal temperature of the chicken, poke a thermometer in the thickest part of the meat and wait for the thermometer to read 165 degrees F. If the thermometer reads 165 degrees F, your chicken in beer is ready. Now, once done, remove the chicken from the smoker and let it rest for additional 20 minutes. After 20 minutes, take out your knife and fork and just binge on.

Simple Turkey Breast

Serves: 8

Cooking Time: 15 Minutes

Ingredients:

- 5 lbs. turkey breast
- ½ c. chicken rub seasoning

Directions:

Preheat your smoker to 225 F/7 C using wood chips. Wash turkey and pat dry using a paper towel. Rub chicken seasoning over the turkey and place in smoker. Smoke turkey about 5 hours or until internal temperature reaches 165 F/73 C. Serve and enjoy.

Versatile Chicken Breasts

Serves: 6

Cooking Time: 3 Hours

Ingredients:

- 4 (6-ounce) boneless, skinless chicken breasts
- 2/3 cup Spanish chorizo, chopped
- 2/3 cup cheddar cheese, grated
- 2 tbsp all-purpose spice rub
- 8 bacon slices

Directions:

Soak maple wood chips in water for at least hour. Preheat the smoker to 0 degrees F, using charcoal and maple wood chips. With a sharp knife, gently, create a pocket into each chicken breast. Stuff each chicken pocket with chorizo and cheese evenly. Rub the chicken breasts with the spice rub evenly. Wrap each stuffed chicken breast with 2 bacon slices. Place the chicken breasts into the smoker and cook for about 3 hours. Serve hot.

Tender Sweet Sriracha Bbq Chicken

Serves: 5
Cooking Time: 1 And A ½ To 2 Hours
Ingredients:
- 1 cup of sriracha
- ½ a cup of butter
- ½ a cup of molasses
- ½ a cup of ketchup
- ¼ cup of firmly packed brown sugar
- ¼ cup of prepared yellow mustard
- 1 teaspoon of salt
- 1 teaspoon of freshly ground black pepper
- 1 whole chicken, cut into pieces
- ½ a teaspoon of freshly chopped parsley leaves

Directions:
Pre-heat your smoker to 250 degree Fahrenheit using cherry wood Take a medium saucepan and place it over low heat, stir in butter, sriracha, ketchup, molasses, brown sugar, mustard, pepper and salt and keep stirring until the sugar and salt dissolves Divide the sauce into two portions Brush the chicken half with the sauce and reserve the remaining for serving Make sure to keep the sauce for serving on the side, and keep the other portion for basting Transfer chicken to your smoker rack and smoke for about 1 and a ½ to 2 hours until the internal temperature reaches 1 degree Fahrenheit Sprinkle chicken with parsley and serve with reserved BBQ sauce Enjoy!

Bbq Chicken Legs

Serves: 6
Cooking Time: 4 Hours
Ingredients:
- 3½ lbs chicken legs
- ½ cup soy sauce
- ½ cup Italian salad dressing
- ¼ cup BBQ sauce
- 2 cups apple juice

Directions:
In a bowl, add the soy sauce and salad dressing and ix well. Through a strainer, strain the mixture. Through an injector, inject the chicken legs with the salad dressing mixture. Now, coat the chicken with the BBQ sauce. In sealable bag, place the chicken legs. Seal the bag and refrigerate to

marinate for about 8-10 hours. Soak apple wood chips in water for at least 1 hour. Preheat the smoker to 250 degrees F, using charcoal and apple wood chips. Remove chicken legs from bag. In a spray bottle, place the apple juice and set aside. Place the legs into the smoker over indirect heat and cook for about 4 hours, spraying with apple juice after every 30 minutes. Serve hot.

Easy Smoked Turkey

Serves: 10
Cooking Time: 5 Hours
Ingredients:
- 1 whole turkey, thawed
- 1 packet Cajun seasoning
- 1 bottle Creole marinade

Directions:
Rub the turkey with Cajun seasoning. Place Creole marinade in a syringe tube and inject into the turkey. Allow to marinate in the fridge for 24 hours. Preheat the smoker to 2250F. Place apple juice in the water pan and add hickory wood chips into the side tray. Put the entire turkey in the smoker. Cook for 30 minutes per pound of the bird.

Smoked Turkey Breast With Orange-onion Marinade (masterbuilt Electric Smoker)

Serves: 6
Cooking Time: 4 Hours And 15 Minutes
Ingredients:
- 3 cups orange juice (freshly squeezed)
- 2 Tbsp garlic-infused olive oil
- 1 can (6 oz) Onion soup mix
- 4 lbs turkey breast

Directions:
Whisk orange juice, olive oil, and onion soup mix. Place the marinade and the turkey breast in a big container; cover and refrigerate for hours. Preheat Masterbuilt Electric Smoker. Allow the smoker temperature to reach 225 degrees Fahrenheit. When it is ready, add some water to the removable pan that is usually on the bottom shelf. Fill the side "drawer" with dry wood chips. Smoke turkey, maintaining the temperature inside smoker between 225° and 250°, for 4 hours or until a meat thermometer inserted into the thickest portion is 170°. Let stand 10 minutes before serving.

Authentic Citrus Smoked Chicken
Serves: 12
Cooking Time: 18 Hours 5 Minutes
Ingredients:
- 1 whole chicken
- 4 cups of lemon-lime flavored carbonated beverage
- 1 tablespoon of garlic powder
- 2 cups of soaked wood chips

Directions:
Transfer the whole chicken to a large sized zip bag Sprinkle garlic powder and pour lemon-lime soda mix into the bag   Seal the bag and allow it to marinate overnight   Pre-heat your electric smoker to 225 degree Fahrenheit   Remove the chicken from the bag and transfer to your smoker rack Discard the marinade   Smoker for 10 hours, making sure keep adding more wood chips after every hour   Serve and enjoy!

Weekend Dinner Chicken
Serves: 3
Cooking Time: 1 Hour
Ingredients:
- 1 (3lb) chicken, butterflied, keel bone removed
- 10 cardamom pods
- 5 cinnamon sticks
- 1 tbsp whole cloves
- 2 tbsp canola oil
- 4-6 garlic cloves, chopped
- 1 tbsp fresh ginger, chopped
- 2 tbsp fresh lime juice
- 1 tsp fresh lime zest, grated finely
- Salt and freshly ground black pepper, to taste
- ½ cup water

Directions:
In a bowl of cold water, soak the cardamom, cinnamon sticks and cloves for at least 4 hours.   In a pan, heat the oil over medium heat and sauté the garlic and ginger for about minutes.   Add lime juice, lime zest, salt, pepper and water and bring to a boil. Cook for about 1 minute.   Remove from the heat and set aside to cool slightly.   In a blender, add the onion mixture and pulse until a smooth.   Transfer the paste into a bowl and set aside to cool.   Rub some paste under the skin of chicken and then, coat the entire chicken with the paste evenly. Cover the chicken and refrigerate for about 2 hours. Remove the chicken from the refrigerator 30 minutes before cooking.   Preheat the smoker to 375 degrees F, using charcoal.   After charcoal is covered with a layer of fine gray ash, spread the coals evenly over the bottom of the smoker.   Place the soaked spices over the hot charcoal evenly. Cover the smoker with the lid and heat for about 5 minutes.   Place the chicken over the coals, skin-side down and cook for about 5 minutes.   Flip the chicken and move to indirect heat.   Cook, covered for about 40-50 minutes.   Transfer the chicken onto a cutting board and set aside for about 10 minutes before carving.   With a sharp knife, cut the chicken in desired sized pieces and serve.

Smoked Whole Chicken
Serves: 6
Cook Time: 5 Hours
Ingredients:
- ¼ Cup of packed dark brown sugar
- 2 Tablespoons of chili powder
- 1 Tablespoon of smoked paprika
- 1 Tablespoon of onion powder
- 1 Tablespoon of garlic powder
- 1 Tablespoon of oregano
- 1 Teaspoon of salt
- 1 Whole chicken, of about 4 to 5 pounds

Directions:
Remove the inner parts of the chicken, like the neck and the liver   Run the cold water over the chicken and rinse it very well; then pat it dry   Place the whole chicken over a cutting board and chop the chicken with a meat cleaver down the breast Place the chicken in a pyrex dish   In a bowl, combine the dry ingredients of the rub; then generously rub the chicken with the rub   Wrap the chicken with a plastic wrap over the dish and refrigerate for an overnight.   After the chicken has perfectly marinated, turn on your electric smoker and preheat it to about 225° F   Once perfectly preheated; put the whole chicken on top of the rack breast with the side up and close the smoker Smoke for about 4 to 5 hours; then remove the chicken from the smoker and let sit for about to 10 minutes   Serve and enjoy smoked chicken!

County Fair Turkey Legs
Serves: 8
Cooking Time: 4 To 6 Hours
Ingredients:
- 2 quarts water
- 1/2 cup kosher salt
- 1/2 cup brown sugar
- 8 turkey legs
- 3 tablespoons onion powder
- 2 tablespoons chili powder
- 1 tablespoon garlic powder
- 1 teaspoon freshly ground black pepper
- 1 teaspoon ground cumin
- 2 tablespoons vegetable oil

Directions:
For the brine, heat water, kosher salt and brown sugar to a boil. Remove brine from heat and let cool to room temperature. Place turkey legs in a large glass or plastic container. Pour brine over turkey legs, cover and refrigerate for to 12 hours. Place hickory or pecan wood chips in the Masterbuilt smoker's wood tray and preheat smoker to 5°F.   Mix onion powder, chili powder, garlic powder, pepper and cumin and set aside. Remove turkey legs from brine and pat dry with paper towels. Brush oil over turkey legs and rub with spice mixture.   Place turkey legs on smoker grate and smoke until the internal temperature of the meat reaches 16F, 4 to 6 hours. Add wood chips to the wood tray as necessary.   Remove turkey legs from smoker, cover loosely with aluminum foil and let rest for about 20 minutes. Serve and enjoy!

Smoked Apple Curry Chicken Breast (masterbuilt Electric Smoker)
Serves: 4
Cooking Time: 2 Hours And 45 Minutes
Ingredients:
- 2 cup apple juice (sugar-free)
- 2 cloves garlic, peeled
- 2 tsp curry powder
- 2 Tbsp chopped fresh parsley, optional
- 3 lbs boneless, skinless chicken breast halves

Directions:
Whisk apple juice, garlic, curry powder and parsley in a blender. Pour the marinade in a large container. Place the chicken breast halves and toss to combine well with marinade. Refrigerate for 4 hours or overnight. Remove from marinade 20 minutes before smoking. Preheat Masterbuilt Electric Smoker. Allow the smoker temperature to reach 225 degrees Fahrenheit. When it is ready, add some water to the removable pan that is usually on the bottom shelf. Fill the side "drawer" with dry wood chips. Arrange the chicken halves onto smoker racks, and smoke about 2 to 2 1/2 hours when the chicken breast reaches an internal temperature of 160 degrees Fahrenheit. Serve hot.

Orange Smoked Chicken
Serves: 3
Cooking Time: 10 Minutes
Ingredients:
- 12 oz. chicken breasts
- For rub:
- 2 tbsps. Chicken rub seasoning
- For marinade:
- 1 tbsp. garlic powder
- ½ c. soy sauce
- 2 c. orange juice

Directions:
Add chicken and marinade ingredients into the ziplock bag and mix well. Place chicken bag in the refrigerator for overnight. Preheat the smoker to 250 F/121 C using apple wood chips. Remove chicken from marinade and rub chicken seasoning over the chicken. Place chicken in smoker and smoker for 2 hours or until internal temperature reaches 16F/73 C. Serve and enjoy.

Smoked Turkey Cocktail Bites (masterbuilt Electric Smoker)
Serves: 6
Cooking Time: 2 Hours And 5 Minutes
Ingredients:
- 2 lbs turkey ground meat
- 3 Tbsp mayonnaise
- 2 Tbsp onion grated
- 1 tsp celery salt
- 3 Tbsp walnuts finely chopped

Directions:
In a medium-size bowl, combine ground turkey, mayonnaise, onion, celery salt, parsley. Mix well, cover and chill for 2 hours. Preheat Masterbuilt Electric Smoker. Allow the smoker temperature to reach 5 degrees Fahrenheit. When it is ready, add some water to the removable pan that is usually on the bottom shelf. Fill the side "drawer" with dry wood chips. Place patties in the smoker and smoke 60 to 90 minute or until the internal temperature reaches 1 degrees. Serve hot.

Citrus Goose Breast
Serves: 7
Cooking Time: 6 Hours
Ingredients:
- ½ a cup of orange juice
- 1/3 cup of olive oil
- 1/3 cup of Dijon mustard
- 1/3 cup of brown sugar
- ¼ cup of soy sauce
- ¼ cup of honey
- 1 tablespoon of dried minced onion
- 1 teaspoon of garlic powder
- 8 goose breast halves

Directions:
Take a medium sized bowl and a whisk in orange juice, olive oil, mustard, soy sauce, sugar, honey, onion, garlic powder Mix well and prepare the marinade Transfer the goose breast to the marinade and cover Allow it to refrigerate for 3-6 hours Heat up your smoker to 300 degree Fahrenheit and add some soaked hickory wood chips Transfer the breast to your smoker grate and brush smoke for hours, making sure to keep brushing it with the marinade for the first 30 minutes Keep smoking until the internal temperature reaches 165 degree Fahrenheit Serve and enjoy!

Marinated Chicken Breasts
Serves: 6
Cooking Time: 2 To 2 1/2 Hours
Ingredients:
- 1 red bell pepper (diced)
- 1/4 cup balsamic vinegar
- 1/2 cup extra virgin olive oil
- 2 garlic cloves (minced)
- 2 tablespoons honey
- 1/2 teaspoon kosher salt, plus more to taste
- 1/4 teaspoon freshly ground black pepper, plus more to taste
- 6 boneless skinless breasts

Directions:
For the marinade, puree bell pepper, vinegar, olive oil, garlic, honey, salt and pepper in a food processor or blender until smooth. Rinse chicken breasts, pat dry and place two breasts each on three large sheets of heavy-duty aluminum foil. Drizzle about half of the marinade over the chicken breasts, flip breasts and drizzle with remaining marinade. Fold foil into pouches, seal and refrigerate for at least hours. Place hickory wood chips in the smoker's wood tray and preheat smoker to 250°F. Place foil pouches on smoker grate and pierce with several small slits. Smoke chicken breasts until the internal temperature of the meat reaches 160°F, 2 to 2 1/2 hours. Add wood chips to the wood tray as necessary. Remove pouches from the smoker, open slightly and let rest for about 10 minutes. Slice chicken breasts as desired, season to taste with salt and pepper and serve. Enjoy!

Smoked Chicken Patties (masterbuilt Electric Smoker)
Serves: 6
Cooking Time: 2 Hours And 15 Minutes
Ingredients:
- 2 lbs ground chicken breast
- 4 cloves garlic (finely minced)
- 2 Tbsp fresh parsley, finely chopped
- 1 Tbsp cilantro (chopped)
- 2 Tbsp olive oil
- 3/4 tsp kosher salt

Directions:
Place in a deep bowl all Ingredients: from the list. Using your hands, mix well. Form into 6 patties. Refrigerate until ready to grill (about minutes). Preheat Masterbuilt Electric Smoker. Allow the smoker temperature to reach 275 degrees Fahrenheit. When it is ready, add some water to the removable pan that is usually on the bottom shelf. Fill the side "drawer" with dry wood chips.

Smoke for about 2 hours. Serve hot with your favorite salad and dressing.

Moist Wrapped Chicken Tenders
Serves: 5
Cooking Time: 10 Minutes
Ingredients:
- 1 lb. chicken tenders
- 1 tbsp. chili powder
- 1/3 c. brown sugar
- 1 tsp. garlic powder
- 1 tsp. onion powder
- 1 tsp. paprika
- ½ tsp. Italian seasoning
- 10 bacon slices
- ½ tsp. pepper
- ½ tsp. salt

Directions:
Preheat the smoker to 350 F/6 C. In a bowl, combine together Italian seasoning, garlic powder, onion powder, paprika, pepper, and salt. Add chicken tenders to the bowl and toss well. Wrap each chicken tenders with a bacon slice. Mix together chili powder and brown sugar and sprinkle over the wrapped chicken. Place wrapped the chicken in smoker and smoke for 30 minutes. Serve and enjoy.

Chicken Breast
Serves: 10
Cooking Time: 1 Hour & 15 Minutes
Ingredients:
- 10 individual chicken breasts or a 5 lb. bag of chicken breasts
- 2 tsp. salt
- 2 tsp. paprika
- 2 tsp. garlic powder
- 2 tsp. garlic salt
- 2 tsp. black pepper
- 1/2 tbsp. cayenne pepper
- 1 tbsp. dried thyme
- 1 tbsp. dried oregano
- 4 tsp. brown sugar
- 1 bottle sweet barbecue sauce

Directions:
Be sure to mix all your chicken seasonings together in one large bowl. You'll also want to make sure you have plenty of barbecue sauce to coat each of your chicken breasts. Coat all of your chicken breasts with the seasoning and barbecue sauce. Flip the breast over halfway through smoking. The internal temperature of the meat should reach at least 160 degrees. Allow the breasts to cool down before you serve them.

Orange Crispy Chicken
Serves: 4
Cooking Time: 90 To 120 Minutes
Ingredients:
- For Poultry Spice Rub
- 4 teaspoon of paprika
- 1 tablespoon of chili powder
- 2 teaspoon of ground cumin
- 2 teaspoon of dried thyme
- 2 teaspoon of salt
- 2 teaspoon of garlic powder
- 1 teaspoon of freshly ground black pepper
- For The Marinade
- 4 chicken quarters
- 2 cups of frozen orange-juice concentrate
- ½ a cup of soy sauce
- 1 tablespoon of garlic powder

Directions:
Take a small bowl and add paprika, chili powder, cumin, salt, thyme, garlic powder, pepper and mix well Transfer the chicken quarters to a large dish Take a medium bowl and whisk in orange-juice concentrate, soy sauce, garlic powder, half of the spice-rub mix Pour the marinade over the chicken and cover Refrigerate for 8 hours Pre-heat your smoker to 275 degree Fahrenheit Discard the marinade and rub the surface of the chicken with remaining spice rub Transfer the chicken to smoker and smoker for 1 and a ½ to 2 hours Remove the chicken form the smoker and check using a digital temperature that the internal temperature is 160 degree Fahrenheit Allow it to rest for minutes Enjoy!

Tandoori Chicken
Serves: 6
Cooking Time: 2 Hours
Ingredients:
- 6 chicken leg quarters
- 1 lemon (halved)
- 1 tablespoon kosher salt
- 3 garlic cloves (minced)
- 1 cup plain unsweetened yogurt
- 1 tablespoon garam masala
- 1 teaspoon turmeric
- 1 teaspoon ground coriander
- 1 teaspoon garlic powder
- 1 teaspoon ground ginger
- 1/2 teaspoon cayenne pepper
- Mint sprigs (for garnish)

Directions:
Pierce chicken skin all over with a fork or sharp knife. Rub chicken with lemon halves, garlic and salt. For the marinade, mix yogurt, garam masala, turmeric, coriander, garlic powder, ginger and cayenne pepper. Place chicken in a large plastic zip-top freezer bag, add marinade and turn to coat. Seal bag and refrigerate chicken for 6 to 24 hours. Pour cups water into the Masterbuilt smoker's water pan. Place cherry, pecan or apple wood chips in the smoker's wood tray and preheat smoker to 225°F. Remove chicken from marinade and discard marinade. Place chicken on smoker grate and smoke until the internal temperature of the meat reaches 165°F, about 2 hours. Add wood chips to the wood tray as necessary. Remove chicken from the smoker, cover loosely with aluminum foil and let rest for about 10 minutes. Garnish chicken with the mint sprigs and serve. Enjoy!

Chipotle Turkey Legs
Serves: 4
Cooking Time: 4-5 Hours
Ingredients:
- 4 fresh turkey legs
- ½ gallon hot water
- 4 cups crushed ice
- ½ cup Kosher salt
- ½ cup brown sugar
- 2 Tbsp peppercorns
- 2 cups Chipotle Mango Lime Barbecue

Directions:
In a large non-reactive bowl, combine water, salt and sugar until salt and sugar are dissolved. Add peppercorns and crushed ice and stir to combine. Submerge the turkey legs in the brine and let sit in the fridge for 1 hour. Remove from the brine and dry with a paper towel. Let the turkey sit at room temperature while you preheat the smoker to 250°F. Once the smoker is ready, place each turkey leg directly onto the grate. Smoke the turkey legs until the internal temperature reaches 155°F. Remove the legs from the smoker and brush on all sides with the Chipotle Mango Lime Barbecue Sauce. Return the legs to the smoker and continue cooking until they reach an internal temperature of 165°F. Remove the turkey legs from the smoker and allow the legs to rest for 10-15 minutes before serving with additional barbecue sauce on the side.

Cheesy Turkey Meatballs
Serves: 8
Cooking Time: 1 1/2 Hours
Ingredients:
- 2 pounds ground turkey
- 1/2 cup panko bread crumbs
- 1 egg (beaten)
- 1/2 cup finely grated Parmesan cheese
- 2 teaspoons garlic salt
- 2 teaspoons onion powder
- 2 teaspoons Italian herb mix
- 1/2 teaspoon freshly ground black pepper, plus more to taste
- 4 ounces mozzarella cheese (cut into 48 small cubes)

Directions:
Place apple or cherry wood chips in the Masterbuilt smoker's wood tray and preheat smoker to 225°F. In a large bowl, mix turkey, bread crumbs, egg, Parmesan cheese, garlic salt, onion powder, herbs and pepper until thoroughly combined. Using a 1-tablespoon scoop, divide mixture into about 48 portions. Press a cube of mozzarella cheese into each portion and form into a meatball. Arrange meatballs on a rack, place in smoker and smoke until the internal temperature of the meat reaches 165°F, about 1 1/2 hours. Add wood chips to the wood tray as necessary. Serve meatballs immediately and enjoy!

Smoky Wrap Chicken Breasts
Serves: 6
Cooking Time: 5 Hours 30 Minutes
Ingredients:
- 6 chicken breasts, skinless and boneless
- 18 bacon slices
- 3 tbsp chicken rub
- For brine:
- 1/4 cup brown sugar
- 1/4 cup kosher salt
- 4 cups water

Directions:
Combine together all brine ingredients into the glass dish. Place chicken into the dish and coat well. Soak chicken about 2 hours. Rinse chicken well and coat with chicken rub. Wrap each chicken breast with three bacon slices. Preheat the smoker to 230 F/110 C using soaked wood chips. Place wrapped chicken breasts into the smoker and smoke for about 3 hours or until internal temperature reaches 165 F/ C. Serve and enjoy.

Easiest Bbq Smoked Turkey Wings
Serves: 3-4
Cooking Time:12 Hours 30 Minutes
Ingredients:
- 6 turkey wings, wing tips discarded
- Salt and black pepper
- BBQ sauce of choice
- Preheat the smoker to 225°f (107°c) using cherry wood chips and prepare for indirect cooking

Directions:
Season the turkey wings with salt and pepper and marinade in BBQ sauce overnight. Remove the turkey wings from the marinade and place in the hot smoker. Smoke until the internal temperature registers 165°f (74°c). Baste the wings with more BBQ sauce when they are almost done. Allow to rest for 10 minutes before serving with additional BBQ sauce on the side.

Smoked Chicken Cutlets In Strawberries - Balsamic Marinade (masterbuilt Electric Smoker)
Serves: 6
Cooking Time: 2 Hours And 15 Minutes
Ingredients:
- 3 Tbsp balsamic vinegar
- 20 medium strawberries
- 1/4 cup Extra-virgin olive oil
- 2 Tbsp chopped fresh basil
- Kosher salt and freshly ground black pepper
- 2 lbs boneless, skinless chicken breast cutlets

Directions:
Whisk balsamic vinegar, strawberries, olive oil and fresh basil in your blender. Sprinkle marinade on and rub into the tops, bottoms, and sides of the chicken cutlets. Refrigerate for 2 hours. Preheat Masterbuilt Electric Smoker. Allow the smoker temperature to reach 225 degrees Fahrenheit. When it is ready, add some water to the removable pan that is usually on the bottom shelf. Fill the side "drawer" with dry wood chips. Smoke chicken for about two hours or until the internal temperature reaches 165°F. Serve hot.

Spicy Jamaican Jerk

Serves: 4
Cooking Time: 1 And A ½ Hours
Ingredients:
- 4 chicken leg quarters
- ¼ cup of canola oil
- ¼ cup of cane syrup
- 8 whole cloves
- 6 sliced habanero peppers
- 1 chopped scallions, white and green parts
- 2 tablespoon of whole all spice berries
- 2 tablespoon of salt
- 2 teaspoon of freshly ground black pepper
- 2 teaspoon of ground cinnamon
- 1 teaspoon of cayenne pepper
- 1 teaspoon of dried thyme
- 1 teaspoon of ground cumin

Directions:
Pre-heat your smoker to 275 degree Fahrenheit with mesquite wood Add a handful of whole all spice berries as well Brush the chicken carefully with canola oil Take a blender and add cane syrup, cloves, scallions, habaneros, salt, allspice, pepper, cinnamon, thyme, cayenne, cumin and pulse the whole mixture until you have a smooth and sticky texture Keep 2 tablespoon of the mixture on the side Brush the chicken with remaining mix thoroughly Transfer to smoker rack and smoke for 1 and a ½ hours Remove the chicken from smoker once done and let it rest for 10 minutes Baste with more jerk seasoning and serve!

Smoked Chicken Tenders

Serves: 10
Cooking Time: 2 Hours
Ingredients:
- 4 pounds chicken tenders, rinsed and patted dry
- ½ cup soy sauce
- ½ cup vegetable oil,¼ cup water
- 1 ½ tablespoons sesame seeds
- 2 teaspoons minced garlic
- ¾ grated ginger
- ¼ teaspoon Cajun seasoning

Directions:
In a mixing bowl, combine all Ingredients: and allow to marinate for at least 2 hours in the fridge. Preheat the smoker to 50F. Place water in the water pan and add hickory wood chips into the side tray.Place chicken tenders in the smoker. Cook for 2 hours. Brush every 20 minutes with the marinade.

Smoked White Wings

Serves: 10
Cooking Time: 2 Hours
Ingredients:
- 5 pounds raw chicken wings
- Salt and pepper to taste
- 1 tablespoon garlic powder
- 1 cup apple cider vinegar
- 1 tablespoon white pepper
- ½ tablespoon salt
- ½ tablespoon cayenne pepper
- 1 cup mayonnaise

Directions:
Place all Ingredients: in a Ziploc bag except for the mayonnaise. Marinate for hours in the fridge. Preheat the smoker to 2250F. Place water in the water pan and add mesquite wood chips into the side tray. Place the chicken wings in a tray, Cook for 2 hours. 30 minutes before the cooking time ends, remove the chicken from the smoker and place in a bowl. Stir in the mayonnaise and return the chicken in the smoker.

Smoked Blue Wings

Serves: 10
Cooking Time: 2 Hours
Ingredients:
- 5 pounds raw chicken wings
- Salt and pepper to taste
- 2 tablespoons extra virgin olive oil
- 2 tablespoons garlic, minced
- ½ cup molasses
- 1 cup hot sauce
- 2 cups blue cheese

Directions:
Place all Ingredients: in a heat-proof casserole dish Allow to marinate for hours in the fridge. Preheat the smoker to 2250F. Place water in the water pan and add mesquite wood chips into the side tray. Place the casserole with the chicken in the smoker. Cook for 2 hours.

Smoked Sweet And Spicy Chicken Wings

Serves: 13
Cooking Time: 2 Hours
Ingredients:
- 2 ½ tablespoons black pepper
- 1 tablespoon onion powder
- 1 tablespoon chili powder
- 1 tablespoon garlic powder
- 5 pounds chicken wings
- 1 cup honey
- ½ cup barbecue sauce
- 3 tablespoons apple juice

Directions:
Place all Ingredients: in a Ziploc bag. Shake and allow to marinate for at least 30 minutes in the fridge. Preheat the smoker to 2250F. Place apple juice in the water pan and add apple wood chips into the side tray. Line the rack with aluminum foil. Place chicken in the smoker. Cook for 2 hours. Baste with sauce every 30 minutes.

Smoked Chicken Thighs
Serves: 6
Cooking Time: 4 Hours 10 Minutes
Ingredients:
- 24 oz chicken thighs, skin on
- 2 tbsp black pepper
- 2 tbsp cayenne
- 1 tbsp garlic powder
- 1 tbsp thyme
- 2 tbsp chili powder
- 2 tbsp paprika
- 1 cup olive oil
- 1 tbsp salt

Directions:
Preheat the smoker to 200 F/93 C using wood chips. Combine all dry seasoning ingredients together. Coat chicken with olive oil then sprinkles seasoning over the chicken. Place chicken in smoker and smoke for 2 hours. After 2 hours flip the chicken and smoker for another 2 hours or until internal temperature reaches 16F/73 C. Serve and enjoy.

Smoked Chicken Breast With Dark Sauce (masterbuilt Electric Smoker)
Serves: 5
Cooking Time : 2 Hours And 45 Minutes
Ingredients:
- MARINADE
- 1 cup white wine
- 1/3 cup brown sugar
- 1 Tbsp cider vinegar
- 1 tsp fresh ginger grated
- Salt and ground white pepper
- 2 lbs chicken breasts, boneless, cut into pieces

Directions:
Cut the chicken breast into pieces and rub with salt and white pepper. Combine all Ingredients: for marinade and pour in a shallow container. Add the chicken breast and refrigerate for minutes. Preheat Masterbuilt Electric Smoker. Allow the smoker temperature to reach 225 degrees Fahrenheit. When it is ready, add some water to the removable pan that is usually on the bottom shelf. Fill the side "drawer" with dry wood chips. Smoke about 2 to 2 1/2 hours when the chicken breast reaches an internal temperature of 1 degrees Fahrenheit. Serve hot.

Amazing Mesquite Maple And Bacon Chicken
Serves: 7
Cooking Time: 1 And A ½ To 2 Hours
Ingredients:
- 4 boneless and skinless chicken breast
- Salt as needed
- Freshly ground black pepper
- 12 slices of uncooked bacon
- 1 cup of maple syrup
- ½ a cup of melted butter
- 1 teaspoon of liquid smoke

Directions:
Pre-heat your smoker to 250 degree Fahrenheit Season the chicken with pepper and salt Wrap the breast with bacon slices and cover the entire surface Secure the bacon with tooth picks Take a medium sized bowl and stir in maple syrup, butter, liquid smoker and mix well Reserve 1/3rd of this mixture for later use Submerge the chicken breast into the butter mix and coat them well Place a pan in your smoker and transfer the chicken to your smoker Smoker for 1 to 1 and a ½ hours Brush the chicken with reserved butter and smoke for 30 minutes more until the internal temperature reaches 165 degree Fahrenheit Enjoy!

Apple Brined Smoked Duck Breast
Servings: 4
Cooking Time: 2 hour 40 minutes
Ingredients:
- 2 duck breasts, approximately 2 pounds
- 2 cups apple cider
- 2 cups filtered water
- 1/4 cup course sea salt
- 1 tsp coarsely ground pepper
- 1 clove of garlic, smashed
- 1 bay leaf
- Apple wood chips
- Apple cider and water
- Disposable foil pan

Directions:
In a container large enough to hold the brine and duck breasts, combine the cider, water, salt, pepper, garlic, and bay leaf. Stir well to dissolve all of the salt. Using a sharp knife, score just the fat, not the flesh, of the duck in a 1" diamond pattern. Submerge the breasts in the brine to cover. You can add more cider if needed. Cover and refrigerate for 8 hours or overnight. Remove the duck from the brine and rinse under cold water. Pat the duck dry with plenty of clean paper towels. Take a rack from the smoker and place the duck, fat side up, on the rack. Set the breasts aside to come to room temperature while you prepare your smoker. Discard the brine. Prepare your smoker by filling the side tray with apple wood chips. Fill the water bowl 1/2 way with equal parts plain water and apple cider. Preheat the smoker to between 225°F and 250°F with the top vent open. Place the rack in the middle of the smoker. On an empty rack below place a disposable foil pan to catch any fat drippings. Smoke for 60 minutes and check the internal temperature with a reliable meat thermometer. For medium rare, the temperature should read 145°F. Continue smoking for approximately 60 to 90 minutes longer if the temperature is below that. Remember to check the wood chips and liquid supply every 45 minutes and replenish as necessary. Remove the duck breasts to a cutting board and tent with foil. Allow them to rest for 10 minutes before slicing to ensure they remain moist. Slice and serve the duck with seasonal side dishes. Some recipe ideas are included below.

Brined and Smoked Bone-in Chicken Breasts

Servings: 6
Cooking Time: 2 hour 15 minutes

Ingredients:

- Brine
- 6 bone-in, skin-on, split chicken breasts
- 1 gallon + 2 cups filtered water
- 1 cup coarse sea salt
- 1/2 cup brown sugar
- 1 orange sliced thinly
- 2 tsps whole peppercorns
- 3 bay leaves
- Dry Rub
- 3 TBS paprika
- 1-1/2 TBS garlic powder
- 1-1/2 TBS onion powder
- 2 tsps freshly ground black pepper
- 2 tsps lemon zest
- Water and orange slices for the smoker
- Hickory or mesquite wood chips

Directions:

In a large glass or plastic container, add the water, salt, and sugar. Stir until the salt and sugar are dissolved. Add the orange slices, peppercorns, and bay leaves. Submerge the chicken breasts in the brine. Cover the container with a lid or plastic wrap. Place the container in the refrigerator or inside a cooler with ice. Allow the chicken to brine for 2 to 4 hours.   In a small bowl, whisk together the paprika, onion powder, garlic powder, pepper, and lemon zest. Cover and set aside.   Remove a rack from your Masterbuilt Smoker. Take the chicken out of the brine and carefully rinse it well under cold running water. Pat the chicken dry with paper towels. Rub the chicken breasts all over with the dry spice mixture. Place them on the rack with the skin side facing up. Allow them to come to room temperature for approximately 30 minutes. Prepare the smoker by filling the bowl with water and orange slices. Fill the tray with wood chips. Preheat the smoker with the vent open to 250°F. Place the rack with the seasoned chicken breasts inside the smoker and close the door. Smoke for approximately 1-1/2 to 2 hours. At 1-1/2 hours, check the internal temperature of the meat with a digital meat thermometer. You are looking for between 160 and 165°F. You also want the skin to be browned. Continue cooking until the meat comes to the desired temperature.   Check the wood chips and water every 45 minutes and replenish as needed.   Remove the smoked chicken to a clean cutting board. Cover it loosely with foil and allow the chicken to rest for at least 10 minutes before slicing and serving.   With a sharp knife remove the breast meat from the bone. Slice the breast into 1/4 inch thick portions. Place on a platter and serve with an herbed potato salad. (A recipe follows).

Brined and Smoked Pheasant with a Honey Glaze Recipe

Servings: 6
Cooking Time: 4 hour 30 minutes

Ingredients:

- 2 Whole pheasants with skin on, 2 to 3 pounds each
- 1/2 Cup Kosher salt
- 1/2 Cup brown sugar
- 8 Cups water
- 1 Bay leaf
- 1 tsp dried thyme
- 1/2 tsp dried sage
- 1/2 tsp cracked black pepper
- 1 cup raw amber honey
- Juice of 1/2 lemon

Directions:

In a large pot, place the water and bring to a boil. Stir in the salt and sugar, turn off the heat, and allow the dry ingredients to melt and combine with the water. Set this aside to cool.   Add the herbs and the pheasants to the cooled brine in the pot. Cover and place in the refrigerator overnight (8 to 10 hours). Alternatively, place all ingredients in an ice chest, add some ice, and place the chest in a cool area.   In the morning, rinse the pheasants under cool running water. Pat them dry with paper towels. Place the birds on a wire rack inside a sheet pan. Place the pan inside the refrigerator for 1-1/2 hours to dry the birds. Throw out the brining solution and thoroughly clean the ice chest or pot and your sink of any raw juices.   Remove the pheasants from the refrigerator and leave on your kitchen counter for up to 90 minutes to come to room temperature.   Prepare your smoker by filling the tray with wood chips. Fill the water bowl 1/2 way with equal parts plain water and apple cider. Preheat the smoker to between 200°F and 250°F with the top vent cracked open.   Tie the legs of the birds together and tuck the wings underneath the backs. Place them directly on the bottom or middle racks. (You can smoke sides on the upper racks). Smoke for 1 hour. At 45 minutes, whisk together the honey and lemon juice over a very low heat, just to melt it.   At 1 hour, check the water and wood chips. Replenish every 60 minutes as needed. Baste or coat the birds with some of the honey mixture. Baste again every 30 minutes. Continue to smoke the birds until they reach an internal temperature of 160°F when a thermometer is inserted in the thigh. This will take anywhere from 3 to 5 hours depending on the size of the birds and the temperature of your smoker. Remove the pheasants to a cutting board and tent with foil. Allow them to rest for 20 minutes before carving to ensure they remain moist.   Serve with seasonal side dishes. Some suggestions are below.

Herb Rubbed Smoked Turkey Recipe
Servings: 16
Cooking Time: 6 hour 30 minutes
Ingredients:
- 12 to 14 pound turkey, prepared as directed above.
- 2 TBS dried thyme
- 1 TBS powdered sage
- 2 tsps dried oregano
- 2 tsps paprika
- 2 tsps sea salt
- 1-1/2 tsps cracked black pepper
- 1 tsp dried rosemary
- 1 tsp onion or garlic powder (optional)
- Zest of 1/2 an orange
- 1/4 cup extra virgin olive oil (EVOO)
- 1/2 cup apple cider
- 1/2 cup water
- Apple or pecan wood chips

Directions:
Preheat the smoker to 225°F. In a small bowl, mix together all the dry herbs and spices. Rub the interior cavity of the turkey with 1/3 of the dry seasonings. Add the EVOO and orange zest to the rest of the seasonings and rub all over the outside of the turkey. Place the water and apple cider in the water pan in the bottom of the smoker, filling it only half way. Place a drip pan on the next shelf above the water pan to collect drippings from the turkey. Fill the side drawer with the wood chips. Tuck the wing tips tightly beneath the turkey. Place the seasoned turkey on the middle rack of the smoker, close the door, and set a timer for approximately 6.5 hours. The turkey should smoke for 30 to 40 minutes per pound, until the inside temperature reaches 165°F. Check every hour for smoke. Add wood chips if you don't see any smoke. Start checking the internal temperature of the bird after 3 hours and every 45 minutes with an accurate meat thermometer. Alternatively, use the digital probe thermometer that came with your smoker. Remove the cooked turkey to a cutting board and allow it to rest for a minimum of 20 minutes to 2 hours before carving.

Savory Herb Rubbed and Aromatic Stuffed Smoked Turkey Recipe
Servings: 16
Cooking Time: 7 hour
Ingredients:
- 12 to 14 pound turkey
- 3 TBS extra virgin olive oil (EVOO)
- 3 TBS unsalted butter at room temperature
- 2 cloves fresh garlic minced
- 2 TBS dried thyme
- 1 TBS powdered sage
- 2 tsps dried oregano
- 2 tsps paprika
- 2 tsps sea salt
- 1-1/2 tsps cracked black pepper
- 1 tsp dried rosemary
- 1 apple cut in quarters
- 1 lemon or orange cut in quarters
- 1 medium onion cut in half
- 1/2 cup apple cider (might need more)
- 1/2 cup water (might need more)
- Apple or pecan wood chips

Directions:
Line a drip pan (cookie sheet or similar with a raised edge to hold the drippings) and water bowl with aluminum foil for easier cleanup. Preheat the smoker to 225°F. In a small bowl, cream together the EVOO and softened butter. Mix in the garlic, herbs, and spices. Rub the interior cavity of the turkey with 1/3 of this mixture. Stuff the cavity with the fruits and onion. Rub the outside of the bird with the remaining fat and herb blend. Place the water and apple cider to fill the water pan half way. Place the drip pan on the next rack just above the water pan to collect drippings from the turkey. Fill the side tray with the wood chips. Tuck the tips of the wings tightly beneath the turkey. Place the seasoned turkey directly on the middle rack of the smoker. Insert the digital thermometer into the thigh of the bird, if your smoker has one. Set a timer for approximately 6.5 hours. A turkey generally smokes for 30 to 40 minutes per pound. You want to achieve an inside temperature of 165°F. Check the vent every hour for smoke. Add more wood chips if the smoke has died down. Also, check the water pan and add addition cider and water as needed. Start checking the internal temperature of the bird after 3 or 4 hours and every 45 minutes thereafter with either the digital thermometer or a good meat thermometer. Remove the cooked turkey to a cutting board and allow it to rest for a minimum of 20 minutes before carving. You can tent it with aluminum foil to keep more moisture in.

Seasoned & Smoked Chicken Drumsticks

Servings: 6
Cooking Time: 3 hour 10 minutes
Ingredients:
- 12 chicken drumsticks
- 1/2 cup extra virgin olive oil (EVOO)
- 3 cloves of garlic minced
- 2 TBS paprika
- 2 tsps sea salt
- 2 tsps dried thyme
- 2 tsps onion powder
- 2 tsps cracked black pepper
- 1 tsp cayenne pepper (optional, or adjust to your desired heat level)

Directions:
Mix the EVOO and minced garlic together. Place the drumsticks on a sheet pan and coat all sides with the oil and garlic. Mix together the dried seasonings with a whisk. Using your hands, sprinkle the mixture over the drumsticks, turning to coat all sides evenly. Set the chicken aside while you preheat your smoker. Take a rack or 2 from your smoker for the drumsticks. Add wood chips to the tray of the smoker. Place water in the bowl. Preheat your smoker to a temperature of 220°F. Place the drumsticks on the smoker racks and place the racks inside the smoker. Smoke the chicken legs for 1-1/2 hours and rotate them for even cooking. Add more wood chips and water as needed. Smoke for another 1-1/2 hours and check the internal temperature. You are looking for at least 165°F. Smoke longer if needed to achieve the appropriate temperature. Serve the drumsticks on a platter with lots of napkins and your other favorite party snacks. I think these pair nicely with smoked corn on the cob and a crisp kohlrabi slaw with apples.

Smoked Chicken Breasts with Creamed Spinach Filling

Servings: 4
Cooking Time: 1 hour 30 minutes
Ingredients:
- 1 (10 ounce) package frozen chopped spinach, thawed
- 4 ounces of block cream cheese, at room temperature
- 4 ounces mozzarella cheese, shredded
- 1 garlic clove, minced
- 1/2 tsp sea salt
- 1/2 tsp freshly ground pepper
- 1/8 tsp ground nutmeg
- 4 boneless, skinless chicken breast halves
- 2 TBS extra virgin olive oil
- 2 tsps paprika
- Extra salt and pepper
- Water
- Citrus slices (optional)
- Mild wood chips, such as alder or maple

Directions:
Drain the spinach in a colander and squeeze the excess moisture out with your hands. In a mixing bowl, combine the spinach, cream cheese, mozzarella cheese, garlic, salt, pepper, and nutmeg. If you have a kitchen glove, do this with your hand. Set the filling aside. Remove a rack from your Masterbuilt Smoker. Prepare the smoker by filling the bowl with water and citrus slices, if desired. Fill the tray with wood chips. Preheat the smoker with the vent open to 250°F. Butterfly your chicken on a clean cutting board. Place one hand on top of the breast to hold it in place. With a sharp knife, slice through the center of the breast approximately 3/4 of the way, being sure to leave some chicken intact. You are looking for the breast to open and lay flat like it is a hinged book. Open the chicken and place a piece of plastic wrap on top. Lightly pound each breast with the flat side of a meat mallet just to achieve an even thickness. Don't pound it too thin or tear it. Place equal amounts of the spinach filling on one half of each butterflied breast. Fold the other half over the filling. Tie the chicken breasts with kitchen twine in 3 or 4 spots. Brush each breast all over with olive oil and season with paprika, salt, and pepper. Place the stuffed breasts on the smoker rack. Put the rack inside the smoker and place a sheet pan or disposable pan on the rack below the chicken to catch the drippings. Cook for approximately 1-1/2 hours until the internal temperature reads 165°F when checked with a digital meat thermometer. Continue to cook until the proper temperature is achieved. Remember to check your wood chips and water approximately every 45 minutes. Replenish as needed. Remove the smoked chicken to a clean cutting board. Cover it loosely with foil and allow the chicken to rest for at least 10 minutes before slicing and serving. Using kitchen shears, cut the twine off of the chicken. You can serve the whole breasts or slice them into 3/4 inch thick portions. Serve while still warm.

Smoked Marinated Chicken Skewers
Servings: 6
Cooking Time: 3 hour 30 minutes
Ingredients:
- 3 lbs skinless, boneless chicken breasts
- 1/2 cup soy sauce or tamari
- 1/2 cup raw honey
- 6 TBS toasted sesame oil
- 3 TBS orange juice
- 3 cloves garlic minced
- 1 tsp ground ginger
- 1 tsp cracked black pepper
- 16 oz button mushrooms
- 1 large or 2 medium red or green bell pepper

Directions:
In a large covered dish, whisk together the honey, soy sauce, sesame oil, and orange juice. Stir in the garlic, ginger, and pepper. Set aside 1/3 cup of the marinade in another bowl. Cut the chicken into 1" cubes. Add the chicken to the larger portion of marinade and toss to coat. Cover and place in the refrigerator for approximately 2 hours. After 2 hours remove the chicken from the fridge and set aside to come to room temperature while you proceed to step 3. Soak your skewers in water. Wipe clean the mushrooms. Leave whole the ones that are roughly the same size as the chicken. Large mushrooms can be sliced in half. Slice the pepper in half and remove the seeds, pith, and stem. Cut the pepper into roughly the same size pieces as the chicken. Remove 1 or 2 racks from the smoker to place the skewers on. Prepare your smoker by adding wood chips to the tray and water to the bowl. Preheat the smoker to 250°F. Open the top vent. While the smoker is heating up, assemble the skewers. Start with chicken, then bell pepper, then mushroom and keep going in that order until the skewers are assembled and placed on the rack. Spoon any leftover marinade that the chicken was in over the skewers and discard the rest, except for the portion that was put aside. Place the rack inside the smoker and cook for 30 minutes. Rotate the skewers and cook for another 30 minutes. At 60 minutes check the wood chips and water. Replenish as needed. At 75 minutes brush or mop the skewers with the reserved marinade (not the one that was in contact with raw chicken). Rotate and brush again until all the marinade is used. Smoke the skewers for another 15 to 20 minutes or until the internal temperature of the chicken is at least 165°F to 170°F. Serve the skewers with plenty of napkins or remove the chicken and vegetables to a platter and serve with cooked rice. Also check out Smoked Seasoned Shrimp Skewers and Smoked Sweet and Sour Tofu Skewers recipes.

Sweet and Spicy Smoked Chicken Wings with Yogurt Dipping Sauce
Servings: 4
Cooking Time: 1 hour 50 minutes
Ingredients:
- 5 pounds chicken wings
- 1/2 cup light brown sugar
- 1/4 cup paprika
- 2-1/2 tsps sea salt
- 1 tsp onion powder
- 1 tsp garlic powder
- 1/2 tsp fresh ground black pepper
- 1-1/2 tsps cayenne pepper
- 1 pint plain yogurt
- 3/4 cup crumbled blue cheese
- 3 TBS minced chives
- Salt and freshly ground pepper to taste
- Cucumber and carrot sticks for serving

Directions:
Rinse the chicken wings under cool running water and pat dry with paper towels. If not already trimmed, cut off the wing tips and save these for making soup stock. Cut the wings in half at the joint. You could also leave them whole, if preferred. Place the wing portions in a large bowl or baking dish. In a smaller bowl, whisk together the sugar, paprika, salt, onion powder, garlic powder, pepper, and cayenne. Add the dry rub to the wings and toss with your hands to coat completely. Set the wings aside while you prepare your smoker. Take a rack or 2 from your smoker and place on a counter lined with paper towels. Add mesquite or hickory wood chips to the tray of the smoker. Fill the water bowl 1/2 way. Open the top vent and preheat your smoker to a temperature of 250°F. Place the racks of wings in the smoker. Smoke the wings for 1 hour. Check the temperature with a meat thermometer. You are looking for an internal temperature of 165°F. If needed, smoke for another hour to bring the wings up to temperature. While the wings are cooking, make the dipping sauce: In a medium bowl, mix together the yogurt, cheese, chives, salt and pepper. Check the seasoning and adjust as needed. Serve the wings on a platter with the dipping sauce on the side and plenty of napkins. I like serving carrot and cucumber sticks with the wings.

Games Recipes

Smoked Up Pheasant
Serves: 4
Cooking Time: 5 Hour
Ingredients:
- 2 whole pheasants, skin on, each of 2 pounds
- ½ cup of salt
- ½ teaspoon ground black pepper
- ½ cup brown sugar
- 1 teaspoon dried thyme
- ½ teaspoon dried sage
- 1 bay leaf
- 1 cup honey
- ½ lemon, juiced
- 8 cups of water

Directions:
Take a large pot and place it over medium heat, add water and bring to a boil. Add salt and sugar Remove pot from heat and keep it on the side Add pepper, thyme, sage, bay leaf to the pot and stir well Add pheasants and soak for 8-10 hours Rinse pheasant and pat dry with a paper towel, transfer to fridge and chill for 2 hours more Take your drip pan and add water, cover with aluminum foil. Pre-heat your smoker to 250 degrees F Use water fill water pan halfway through and place it over drip pan. Add wood chips to the side tray. Transfer pheasants to smoker and smoke for 3-5 hours until internal temperature reaches 165 degrees F Take a saucepan and stir in honey, lemon together and cook over low heat Baste the meat with the mixture every hour while smoking Once complete, let them rest in aluminum foil for 10 minutes and slice Serve and enjoy!

Boar Shoulder
Serves: 12
Cooking Time: 4 Hours
Ingredients:
- 6-pound boar shoulder roast
- 3/4 cup salt
- 2 tablespoons ground black pepper
- 1 cup brown sugar
- 1 tablespoon dried rosemary
- 2 whole bay leaves
- 1/4 cup Worcestershire sauce
- 1/2 cup of soy sauce
- 1-gallon water

Directions:
1.   Place a large pot over medium heat, pour in water and bring to boil. Remove pot from heat, add salt and sugar, stir until dissolved and set aside until cooled. Then remaining ingredients except for boar, stir until mixed and pour the mixture into a large bag. Add boar, seal the bag and place in the refrigerator for 8 hours. Plug in the smoker, fill its tray with hickory woodchips and water pan halfway through, and place dripping pan above the water pan. Then open the top vent, shut with lid and use temperature settings to preheat smoker at 275 degrees F. In the meantime, remove boar from the marinade and bring to room temperature. Place boar on smoker rack, insert a meat thermometer, then shut with lid and set the timer to smoke for 4 hours or more until meat thermometer registers an internal temperature of 155 degrees F. Check vent of smoker every hour and add more woodchips and water to maintain temperature and smoke. When done, wrap boar in aluminum foil, let rest for 20 minutes and slice thinly to serve.

Whole Quail
Serves: 6
Cooking Time: 3 Hours
Ingredients:
- 6 whole quail, skin on
- 1 apple, cored and cut into 6 equal pieces
- 1 teaspoon garlic powder
- 2 teaspoons sea salt
- 1 teaspoon ground black pepper
- 1 teaspoon smoky paprika
- 1/2 teaspoon dried thyme
- 1/2 teaspoon dried oregano
- 1/4 of lemon, zested
- 2 1/2 tablespoons olive oil

Directions:
1.   Rinse quail, pat dry and place in a large baking dish. Stir together remaining ingredients and rub the mixture all over the quail until evenly coated. Then cover the dish with a plastic wrap and place in the refrigerator for 4 to 6 hours. Plug in the smoker, fill its tray with hickory woodchips and water pan halfway through, and place dripping pan above the water pan. Then open the top vent, shut with lid and use temperature settings to preheat smoker at 220 degrees F. In the meantime, remove quail from the refrigerator and bring its temperature to room temperature. Place quail on smoker rack, insert a meat thermometer, then shut with lid and set the timer to smoke for 3 hours or more until meat thermometer registers an internal temperature of 145 degrees F. Check vent of smoker every hour and add more woodchips and water to maintain temperature and smoke. When done, wrap quail in aluminum foil, let rest for 15 minutes and serve.

The Great Boar Shoulder
Serves: 4
Cooking Time: 4 Hours
Ingredients:
- 6 pounds boar shoulder, roast
- ¾ cup of salt
- 2 tablespoons ground pepper
- 1 cup brown sugar
- 1 tablespoon dried rosemary
- 2 whole bay leaves
- ¼ cup Worcestershire sauce
- ½ cup of soy sauce
- 1-gallon water

Directions:
Take a large pot and place it over medium heat, add water and bring to a boil Remove pot from heat and stir in salt and sugar Stir until dissolved Add remaining ingredients except for board and mix well, transfer mixture to a zip bag Add board to the bag and seal, let it chill for 8 hours Take your drip pan and add water, cover with aluminum foil. Pre-heat your smoker to 275 degrees F Use water fill water pan halfway through and place it over drip pan. Add wood chips to the side tray. Remove boar from marinade and transfer to the smoker, smoke for 4 hours until internal temperature reaches 155 degrees F Once done, transfer to foil and let it cool for 20 minutes Slice and enjoy it!

Smoked Duck
Serves:4
Cooking Time:6 Hours 45 Minutes
Ingredients:
- 1 whole duck (5-lbs, 2.25-kgs)
- Red wine vinegar – ¾ cup
- Soy sauce – ¾ cup
- Runny honey – ¾ cup
- Garlic salt – 2 tablespoons
- Freshly ground black pepper – 2 tablespoons
- Preheat your electric smoker to 250°F (120°C)
- Add a 50/50 mix of water and apple juice to the water

Directions:
In a bowl, combine the marinade ingredients (red wine vinegar, soy sauce, honey, garlic salt, and freshly ground black pepper). Stir to combine. Set ½ cup of the marinade aside. Add the duck to a suitably sized re-sealable ziplock bag. Pour the remaining ½ cup of marinade over the duck and transfer to the fridge for between 2-4 hours, to marinate. Remove the duck from the marinade and place on the middle rack of your smoker for 60 minutes, basting 5-7 times with the reserved ½ cup of marinade. When the duck is well browned,

cover the bird with aluminum foil and continue smoking for between 2½-4 hours, or until its internal temperature reaches 16F (74°C). Allow to rest and carve.

Bacon Wrapped Dove
Serves: 4
Cooking Time: 1 Hour
Ingredients:
- 4 dove breasts, cleaned
- 4 slices of bacon
- 4 slices of mushrooms, each ¼-inch thick
- 1 teaspoon ground black pepper

Directions:
Plug in the smoker, fill its tray with apple woodchips and water pan halfway through, and place dripping pan above the water pan. Then open the top vent, shut with lid and use temperature settings to preheat smoker at 5 degrees F. In the meantime, season dove with black pepper, then wrap each dove with a slice of bacon and secure with a skewer. Place dove on smoker rack, place meat thermometer, then shut with lid and set the timer to smoke for 1 hour or more until meat thermometer register an internal temperature of 165 degrees F. Serve straightaway.

Delicious Smoked Rabbits
Serves: 4
Cooking Time: 1 Hour 30 Minutes
Ingredients:
- 1 whole rabbit, 3 pounds
- 1 teaspoon garlic, minced
- 1 teaspoon salt
- 2 teaspoons ground pepper
- 1 tablespoon dried thyme
- 2 teaspoons dried oregano
- 1 bay leaf
- 1/3 cup olive oil
- ½ cup dry white wine

Directions:
Rinse your rabbit thoroughly under water and transfer to a large baking dish Stir in remaining ingredients and rub well all over the rabbit Wrap dish well and let it chill for 6 hours in the fridge Take your drip pan and add water, cover with aluminum foil. Pre-heat your smoker to 2 degrees F Use water fill water pan halfway through and place it over drip pan. Add wood chips to the side tray. Transfer rabbit to smoker rack and smoke for 1 hour and 30 minutes until internal temperature reaches 1 degrees F, making sure to keep turning it after every 30 minutes Once done, transfer rabbit to aluminum foil and let it cool, slice and serve Enjoy!

Smoked Wild Goose Breast In Beer Marinade (masterbuilt Electric Smoker)

Serves: 4
Cooking Time: 2 Hours And 30 Minutes
Ingredients:
- 4 goose breasts
- 2 cups strong dark beer
- 1 1/2 tsp Worcestershire sauce
- 1 tsp garlic powder
- 1/2 tsp paprika
- Salt and pepper

Directions:
Place the geese breasts in a ziplock plastic bag. Pour in the beer, Worcestershire sauce, garlic powder, paprika, and salt and pepper. Close the bag and shake to combine all Ingredients: well. Marinate in refrigerated for 2 hours. Remove the goose meat from marinade and par dry on kitchen towel. (reserve the marinade). Preheat Masterbuilt Electric Smoker. Allow the smoker temperature to reach 22degrees Fahrenheit. When it is ready, add some water to the removable pan that is usually on the bottom shelf. Fill the side "drawer" with dry wood chips. Place the goose breasts on the smoker racks. Brush occasionally with the marinade only for the first half an hour. Smoke for about 2 to 2 1/2 hours or the internal temperature reaches 1 degrees F. Let it rest for 10 to 15 minutes before you carve and serve.

Smoked Wild Boar Chops (masterbuilt Electric Smoker)

Serves: 6
Cooking Time: 4 Hours And 15 Minutes
Ingredients:
- 6 wild boar chops
- 2 cups hearty red wine
- 1/2 cup olive oil
- 1/2 cup fresh thyme, chopped
- 3 lemons, freshly squeezed
- 1 tsp Salt and black pepper, fresh ground

Directions:
Season the boar chops with salt and pepper. Place chops in a non-metal container so each chop lays flat. Whisk all Ingredients: remaining Ingredients: for the marinade. Pour marinade over chops. Cover and refrigerate at least (hours, turning every hour or so. Remove the boar chops from the marinade (reserve marinade) and dry at kitchen paper. Preheat Masterbuilt Electric Smoker to a temperature of 250°F–300°F or according to manufacturer's directions. When it is ready, add some water to the removable pan that is usually on the bottom shelf. Fill the side "drawer" with dry wood chips (recommended Mesquite and Pecan wood Smoke the wild boar chops for 3–4 hours or until internal temperature reaches 165°F, basting every 30 minutes with reserved marinade. Remove chops from smoker and let it rest 15 minutes before servings.

Smoked Rabbit With Rosemary Wine Marinade (masterbuilt Electric Smoker)

Serves: 6
Cooking Time: 4 Hours And 15 Minutes
Ingredients:
- 1 rabbit cut into pieces
- For marinade
- 3 cloves of garlic, mashed
- 1 Tbsp fresh rosemary
- 1 1/2 cup of white wine dry
- 1/2 cup olive oil
- 1/2 tsp cumin
- Salt and ground pepper to taste

Directions:
Whisk all Ingredients: for marinade in a shallow container. Place the rabbit meat in marinade and toss to combine well. Cover with plastic wrap and refrigerate for several hours. Remove meat from marinade and pat dry on a kitchen paper towel. Preheat Masterbuilt Electric Smoker. Allow the smoker temperature to reach 22degrees Fahrenheit. When it is ready, add some water to the removable pan that is usually on the bottom shelf. Fill the side "drawer" with dry wood chips. Place the rabbit onto the smoker and smoke for 4 hours or until it reaches an internal temperature of 160 degrees F. Serve hot.

Masterbuilt Electric Smoker Goose Jerky

Serves: 5
Cook Time: 4 Hours
Ingredients:
- 1 Pound of meat
- ½ Cup of soy sauce
- 2 Tablespoon of worcestershire Sauce
- 1 Tablespoon of honey
- 1 Tablespoon of red pepper flakes
- 2 Teaspoons of onion powder
- 2 Teaspoons of garlic powder
- 1 Teaspoon of black pepper

Directions:
Along the grain of the goose meat, cut the eat into thick strips of about 4" of thickness Remove any excess of fat from the goose eat as you slice it Thoroughly combine all your ingredients and let marinate the meat for an overnight into the fridge. Preheat your Masterbuilt electric smoker at a temperature of about 165° F; then fill the water pan with a quantity of water; then add your favorite type of wood chips When the smoker has reached the temperature of 16 F; then add the meat and either skewer it or lay it flat on the racks When you place the meat in the Masterbuilt electric smoker, you can use multiple racks Smoke at a temperature of about 165° F for about 4 to 6 hours Remove the meat from the electric smoker Serve and enjoy or store your delicious jerky!

Masterbuilt Electric Smoker Venison
Serves: 4
Cook Time: 2 Hours
Ingredients:
- 2 Venison tenderloins of about 6 to 8 ounces each
- 1/3 Cup of drinkable dry red wine
- ¼ Cup of extra virgin olive oil
- 1 Tablespoon of tamari or soy sauce
- 1 Teaspoon of Dijon or brown mustard
- 1 Teaspoon of maple syrup or honey
- ½ Diced small onion
- 2 Minced garlic cloves
- 1 Teaspoon of dried rosemary
- 1 Teaspoon of sea salt
- 1 Teaspoon of cracked black pepper

Directions:
Trim the silver skin off of the tenderloins; then prepare your marinade in a large bowl and whisk all together the last ingredients Put the tenderloins in a large sealable baggie Place the bags in a baking dish; then pour the marinade on top of the venison and squeeze any air out Seal the bags very well; then massage to coat the meat very well; then place the dish with the bags into the refrigerator for about 12 hours Remove the venison out of the refrigerator just 20 minutes before you start your smoker. Remove a grill rack from the Masterbuilt electric smoker and place over clean paper towels in order to catch the marinade drippings Prepare your electric smoker by adding wood chips to the baking tray and the water to the bowl. Preheat your electric smoker to a temperature of about 250°F. Open the top vent and when the Masterbuilt smoker is up to the right temperature, remove the venison meat from the marinade and place it on the rack. Discard the extra marinade; then place the rack in the Masterbuilt smoker and cook for about 2 hours Replenish the wood chips and the water every about 45 to 60 minutes. Remove the venison to a cutting board and tent it with a foil; then let rest for about 20 minutes. Serve and enjoy your dish!

Masterbuilt Smoked Rabbit
Serves: 4
Cook Time: 3 Hours
Ingredients:
- 1 Rabbit of about 3 pounds
- ½ Cup of dry white wine
- 1/3 Cup of extra virgin olive oil
- 2 Minced or pressed garlic cloves
- 1 Tablespoons of dried rosemary
- 1 Tablespoons of dried thyme
- 2 Teaspoons of dried oregano
- 2 Teaspoons of cracked black pepper
- 1 Teaspoon of sea salt
- 1 to 2 bay leaves

Directions:
In a large baking dish; combine the ingredients of the marinade; then place the rabbit in the prepared dish and turn the rabbit several times Cover with the plastic wrap and place it in the refrigerator for an overnight and if possible, you can turn the rabbit once or twice Put the rabbit in a large sealable bag; then cut the rabbit into portions Remove the rabbit from the refrigerator minutes before heating your electric smoker Remove the rack from the smoker for the rabbit Add in oak wood chips to the Masterbuilt smoker tray Place water into the bowl of your electric smoker; then add some slices of lemon or white wine to the water; then preheat the smoker to about 240° F Place the whole rabbit over the smoker rack and place the rack in your Masterbuilt smoker; then discard any leftover marinade Smoke the rabbit for about 1 and ½ hours; then turn over for an even cooking. You can add more wood chips if you want and smoke for about 1 and ½ hours Remove the rabbit from the electric smoker to a cutting board and Tent the rabbit with a foil and let rest for about 15 minutes Carve the rabbit into portion to your liking Serve and enjoy with salad and greens!

Sauces, Mobs & Rubs

Sweet Spice Rub
Serves: 125g
Cooking Time: 0 Mins.
Ingredients:
- Brown sugar (¼ cup)
- Salt (1 tbsp.)
- Garlic powder (2 tsp.)
- Chili powder (1 tbsp.)
- Paprika (1 tbsp.)
- Onion powder (2 tsp.)
- Oregano (1 tsp.)

Directions:
Simply place all ingredients into an airtight jar, stir well to combine then close. Use within six months.

Green Salsa
Serves: 125g
Cooking Time: 0 Hours.
Ingredients:
- Small bunch each of parsley, chives and mint
- 1 tsp. capers
- 2-3 anchovies, chopped
- 1 clove garlic, chopped
- Juice of one lemon
- 3 Tbsp. olive oil
- Salt and pepper, to taste

Directions:
Start by chopping the herbs into small pieces and place into a medium bowl. Add the capers, anchovies, garlic, lemon juice, and olive oil, then stir well to combine. Season with salt and pepper to taste then serve and... enjoy!

Paprika Bbq Rub
Serves: 125g
Cooking Time: 0 Hours.
Ingredients:
- Salt (2 tbsp.)
- Black pepper (2 tbsp., ground)
- White sugar (2 tbsp.)
- Paprika (¼ cup)
- Brown sugar (2 tbsp.)
- Cumin (2 tbsp., ground)
- Chili powder (2 tbsp.)

Directions:
Simply place all ingredients into an airtight jar, stir well to combine then close. Use within six months.

Black Bean & Sesame Sauce
Serves: 4
Cooking Time: 5 Minutes
Ingredients:
- ½ can black beans
- 1 tsp. soft dark brown sugar
- 2 tsp. honey
- 1 tsp. Chinese five-spice powder
- ½ tsp. grated ginger
- 1 red chili
- 2 tsps. tahini
- 2 tbsps. cider vinegar
- 2 tsps. soy sauce
- 5 tbsps. water
- Salt
- Pepper

Directions:
Start by opening up your food processor and throwing in all the ingredients. Heat the button, blend until smooth then pour the sauce into a saucepan. Cook over medium heat for 5 minutes until glossy and thick, stirring continuously.

Exotic Rub Mix
Serves: 2
Cooking Time: 2 Hours
Ingredients:
- ½ cup paprika
- ½ teaspoon brown sugar
- 2 tablespoons salt
- 4 tablespoons white pepper
- 4 tablespoons dry mustard powder

Directions:
Set your Smoker to 220 degrees/F Mix the spices together in a bowl Use a cold smoker attachment and fire up the apple chips until the temperature reaches 100 degrees/F Transfer the spice blend to an aluminum pie pan Smoke for 2 hours Store and use!

Texas Style Brisket Rub
Serves: 3
Cooking Time: 5 Minutes
Ingredients:
- 6 tbsps. salt
- 2 tbsps. black pepper
- 4 tbsps. garlic powder
- 10 tbsps. paprika
- 6 tbsps. onion powder
- 2 tsps. mild chili powder
- 1 tsp. ground coriander
- 4 tsps. ground cumin
- 2 tsps. dried oregano
- 1 tsp. garlic powder
- ½ tsp. cayenne pepper

Directions:
Combine the ingredients in a bowl and store in an airtight container. Store in a cool dark place. It can last for 6 months. Use as much as required.

Teriyaki Sauce

Serves: 3
Cooking Time: 5 Minutes
Ingredients:

- 5 tbsps. soy sauce
- 3 tbsps. sake
- 2 tbsps. mirin
- ½ tsp. ginger
- 1 tsp. honey
- 1 sliced spring onion
- Salt
- Pepper

Directions:
Place the honey, ginger, mirin, sake and soy sauce into a bowl and stir well to combine. Transfer this into a small saucepan and place over medium heat. Simmer until thickened, then remove from the heat. Add the spring onion and stir well until combined. Season with salt and pepper to taste, then serve and enjoy.

Easy Mustard Sauce

Serves: 3
Cooking Time: 5 Minutes
Ingredients:

- 1 tbsp. Butter
- 1 chopped Onion
- 1 minced garlic clove
- 1 c. Dijon mustard
- ¾ c. Brown sugar
- ¾ c. White distilled vinegar
- 1 tbsp. hot sauce
- Salt
- Pepper

Directions:
Start by placing the butter into a saucepan and placing over medium heat. When the butter has melted, add the garlic and onions and allow to cook until soft. Add the remaining ingredients, stir well to combine then reduce the heat. Allow it to simmer (uncovered) for around 10 minutes until the sauce starts to thicken. Season to taste, add any extra chili sauce you might like and stir through. Cool to room temperature before serving. Then enjoy!

Cheesy Cowboy Butter

Serves: 1 Cup
Cooking Time: Nil
Ingredients:

- 1 cup unsalted butter, soft
- 4 ounces blue cheese, crumbled
- 1 teaspoon cayenne pepper
- ¼ cup scallions, chopped, white and green parts
- 1 teaspoon garlic powder
- 1 tablespoon brown sugar, firmly packed

Directions:
Cream the butter and cheese together in a food processor Add cayenne pepper, garlic powder, scallions, and brown sugar and blend well Using a sheet of wax paper, roll the mixture into a cylindrical log and wrap it well Chill for 4 hours Use as needed!

Hot Pepper And Vinegar Bbq Sauce

Serves: 3 Cups
Cooking Time: 30 Minutes
Ingredients:

- 2 cups ketchup
- 1 cup firmly packed light brown sugar
- 1 cup hot pepper vinegar sauce
- 2 tablespoons white vinegar
- 2 tablespoons salt
- 1 tablespoon chili powder
- 2 teaspoons freshly ground black pepper
- 1 teaspoon garlic powder
- 1 teaspoon cayenne pepper
- ½ teaspoon ground allspice

Directions:
Place a saucepan over medium heat Add ketchup, brown sugar, vinegar sauce, white vinegar, salt, chili powder, pepper, garlic powder, cayenne, and allspice and bring the mixture to a boil Reduce heat to low and simmer for 25 minutes Use as needed!

Sesame & White Bean Sauce

Serves: 125g
Cooking Time: 0 Hours.
Ingredients:

- ½ can drained and rinsed white beans
- 1 tsp. soft dark brown sugar
- 2 tsp. honey
- 1 tsp. Chinese five-spice powder
- ½ tsp. grated ginger
- 1 red chili
- 2 tsp. tahini (sesame paste)
- 2 Tbsp. cider vinegar
- 2 tsp. soy sauce
- 5 Tbsp. water
- Salt and pepper, to taste

Directions:
Start by opening up your food processor and throwing in all the ingredients. Hit the button, blend until smooth then pour the sauce into a saucepan. Cook over a medium heat for 5 minutes until glossy and thick, stirring continuously.

Memphis Rub
Serves: 4
Cooking Time: 5 Minutes
Ingredients:
- ½ c. paprika
- ¼ c. garlic powder
- ¼ c. mild chili powder
- 3 tbsps. salt
- 3 tbsps. black pepper
- 2 tbsps. onion powder
- 2 tbsps. celery seeds
- 1 tbsps. brown sugar
- 1 tbsp. dried oregano
- 1 tbsp. dried thyme
- 1 tbsp. cumin
- 2 tsps. dry mustard
- 2 tsps. ground coriander
- 2 tsps. ground allspice

Directions:
Simply place all ingredients into an airtight jar, Stir well to combine then close. Use within six months.

The Great Chimichurri Sauce
Serves: 1 Cup
Cooking Time: Nil
Ingredients:
- ½ cup olive oil
- 2 tablespoon fresh oregano leaves
- 2 tablespoons fresh parsley leaves, chopped
- 2 tablespoons garlic, minced
- 2 tablespoons red wine vinegar
- 2 teaspoons red pepper flakes
- Salt
- Freshly ground black pepper

Directions:
Add the listed ingredient (except salt and pepper) to a food processor and pulse until smooth Season the mix with salt and pepper and pulse again Use as needed

Creative Smoked Salt
Serves: 1 Cup
Cooking Time: 1 Hour
Ingredients:
- ½ cup kosher salt

Directions:
Set your Smoker to 220 degrees/F, add wood chips Use a cold smoker attachment and fire up the apple wood chips until the temperature reaches 100 degrees/F Transfer ¼ cup kosher salt to an aluminum pie pan Place in Smoker and smoke for an hour Store in jar and use as needed!

Chili Chipotle Sauce
Serves: 125g
Cooking Time: 0 Hours.
Ingredients:
- 2 Tbsp. vinegar
- Salt and pepper, to taste
- Ginger, 1 Tbsp., sliced
- Garlic, 1 clove, chopped
- Olive oil, 1 Tbsp.
- Cherry peppers, drained, 6 marinated
- Red pepper, ½, chopped
- San Marzano tomatoes, 4 whole, drained
- Chipotle powder, ½ tsp.
- Scallion, 1 large

Directions:
This one is very easy! Simply place all the ingredients into a food processor and blend until smooth. Serve and enjoy!

Montreal Steak Rub
Serves: 3
Cooking Time: 5 Minutes.
Ingredients:
- 2 tbsps. salt
- 2 tbsps. Black pepper
- 2 tbsp. paprika
- 1 tbsp. red pepper flakes
- 1 tbsp. coriander
- 1 tbsp. dill
- 1 tbsp. garlic powder
- 1 tbsp. onion powder

Directions:
Simply place all ingredients into an airtight jar, Stir well to combine then close. Use within six months.

Smoked Red Peppercorns
Serves: 125g
Cooking Time: 1 Hours.
Ingredients:
- Red Peppercorns

Directions:
Start by soaking your woodchips for around an hour and preheat your smoker to 350°F/5°C. Now take a thin sheet pan and sprinkle your peppercorns over the top. Make sure the layer is nice and even. Pop into your smoker for around an hour.

Carolina Barbeque Rub

Serves: 2
Cooking Time: 5 Minutes
Ingredients:
- 2 tbsps. Salt.
- 2 tbsps. Black pepper
- 2 tbsps. White sugar
- ¼ c. Paprika
- 2 tbsps. Brown sugar
- 2 tbsps. Cumin
- 2 tbsps. Chili powder

Directions:
Simply place all ingredients into an airtight jar, Stir well to combine then close. Use within six months.

Lovely Chicken Spice Rub

Serves: 2
Cooking Time: 1-2 Hours
Ingredients:
- 1 teaspoon salt
- 4 teaspoons dried basil
- 4 teaspoons crushed dried rosemary
- 2 teaspoons garlic powder
- 1 teaspoon dry mustard powder
- 1 teaspoon paprika
- ¼ teaspoon ground black pepper
- ¼ teaspoon ground dried thyme
- ½ teaspoon celery seed

- 1 teaspoon dried parsley
- ½ teaspoon ground cumin
- ½ teaspoon cayenne pepper

Directions:
Set your Smoker to 220 degrees/F Mix the spices together in a bowl Use a cold smoker attachment and fire up the apple chips until the temperature reaches 100 degrees/F Transfer the spice blend to an aluminum pie pan Smoke for 1-2 hours Store and use!

Gentle Alabama White Sauce

Serves: 1 Cup
Cooking Time: Nil
Ingredients:
- 1 cup mayonnaise
- ¼ cup apple cider vinegar
- 1 tablespoon hot chili powder
- 1 teaspoon Worcestershire sauce
- ½ teaspoon celery seeds
- ½ teaspoon red pepper flakes
- ¼ teaspoon cayenne pepper
- Salt and pepper to taste

Directions:
In a medium bowl, whisk together mayonnaise, vinegar, chili powder, Worcestershire sauce, celery seed, red pepper flakes, and cayenne Season with salt and pepper Whisk well Use as needed

Cheese & Nuts

Christy's Smoked Pimento Cheese Appetizer
Serves: 6
Cooking Time: 10 Minutes
Ingredients:
- 1 lb. Kielbasa sausage
- Sliced jalapeño peppers
- Saltine crackers
- 12 oz. Pimento Cheese Dip

Directions:
Set smoker to preheat to 225°F. Set your sausages to smoke for 45 minutes - hour then set aside. Arrange your cheese and crackers on a serving platter, slice your sausages and set on top of the cheese while still hot. Lace saltine crackers on a platter, salt-side down. Garnish with Jalapeños and serve!

Splendid Cheeseburger Patty
Serves: 8
Cooking Time: 10 Minutes
Ingredients:
- 1½ lbs. beef, ground
- 1 lb. bacon slices
- 1 tsp. garlic powder
- 1 tsp. salt
- 1 tsp. pepper
- 1 tsp. onion powder
- 4 tbsps. A1 sauce
- ½ c. shredded cheddar cheese
- ½ c. mozzarella cheese
- ¾ c. grated carrots
- 12 hamburger dill sliced pickles

Directions:
Add salt, onion powder, garlic powder and 2 tablespoons of Asauce with the ground beef and blend thoroughly. Put the beef in a Ziploc bag and spread it evenly so that the beef resembles a blanket. Put the beef in the fridge to chill for some time. Make a bacon weave with the bacon strips and set aside. Cut the Ziploc bag and remove the plastic cover from the bef blanket. Layer the remaining A1 sauce, cheese, carrot and pickle over the blanket and fold it tightly to make a roll. Make sure that there are no holes. Now, place the beef roll at the centre of the bacon weave and fold the weave tightly, making sure that there are no holes. Put the fatty inside the smoker and cook for 2 hours at 22degrees. Slice into desired sizes and serve with sauce.

Smoked Brie With Roasted Peppers & Garlic
Serves: 6
Cooking Time: 30 Minutes
Ingredients:
- 1 (15 ounce) wheel double creme brie cheese
- 3 tsp. garlic, minced
- ¾ cup extra virgin olive oil
- 2 green onions, white part only, finely chopped
- 1 (7 ounce) jar roasted red peppers, drained and diced
- 2 tsp. dried thyme or 2 tsp. fresh thyme
- 2 tsp. balsamic vinegar, well-aged
- 1 tbsp. cracked black pepper
- ½ tbsp. coarse kosher salt

Directions:
Take the rind off of the wheel of brie. Set it aside. In a saucepan, heat up the olive oil over a medium high heat. Add in the garlic. Turn the heat down to medium low, and simmer for 15 minutes. Take the saucepan from heat, and transfer the garlic oil to a small bowl to cool down. Add in two tbsp. in another bowl. Add roasted pepper, black pepper, green onions, roasted red pepper, thyme, vinegar, and balsamic. Season it with salt. Be sure to mix it up. Spread the mixture on the top of the brie. Place the cheese in the smoker. Remove and serve with some bread.

Smoked Brie Cheese
Serves: 8
Cooking Time: 5 Minutes
Ingredients:
- 8 oz. blocks Brie cheese

Directions:
Preheat your smoker to a low temperature – make sure it's no higher than 90°F (32°C). Soak the wood chips for an hour. Remove the wood chips from the liquid then pat dry before using. Now add your cheese blocks to the smoker grate and allow to smoke for about 4 hours. Remove from heat and set to cool to room temp. Place into a container, before popping it into the fridge for two weeks. This allows the flavor to really develop. Serve and enjoy.

Smoked Rosemary Cashews
Serves: 3
Cooking Time: 5 Minutes
Ingredients:
- 2 c. cashews
- 1 tsp. packed light brown sugar
- 1 tsp. rosemary
- ¼ tsp. mustard powder
- 2 tsps. olive oil

Directions:
Preheat your smoker to 250°F/0°C and soak the woodchips for an hour. Remove the woodchips from the liquid then pat dry before using. Next, take a medium bowl and add the sugar, rosemary and mustard powder. Stir well to combine, then add the oil. Next throw in the nuts and stir well to combine. Spread in a single layer onto a sheet pan and place into your smoker. Cook for 30 minutes until crispy and dry, or longer if they're not quite done yet. Remove from the smoker, cool in the pan, then serve and enjoy.

Smoked Gouda Cheese
Serves: 4
Cooking Time: 6 Hours
Ingredients:
- 1 lb. Gouda cheese (as much or less as you want)

Directions:
Place Gouda in the smoker. Afterwards place smoked gouda cheese in a plastic bag. Store in the fridge for two weeks.

Smoked Cheese Crisps
Serves: 1
Cooking Time: 90 Minutes
Ingredients:
- 1 block of cheese (can be literally any cheese)

Directions:
Cut the cheese into small cubes. Arrange on a baking sheet placed on an aluminum pan. Arrange the cheeses on the pan. Place cheeses in the smoker. Place the pan on another one that has ice on it. Mix in any spices you desire. Smoke for an additional five minutes, or until the edges turn brown. Allow the cheese to cool before snacking on them.

Garlic And Cayenne Almonds
Serves: 3
Cooking Time: 5 Minutes
Ingredients:
- 1 lb. raw almonds
- 2 tbsps. melted butter
- 1 tbsp. salt
- 1 tsp. garlic powder
- ½ tsp. cayenne pepper

Directions:
Preheat your smoker to 250°F/0°C and soak the wood chips for an hour. Remove the wood chips from the liquid then pat dry before using. Now grab a medium bowl and add the melted butter, salt, garlic and cayenne, then stir well to combine. Add the almonds, and stir well to coat, then transfer to a sheet pan, spreading thinly. Smoke for 2 hours until crispy and dry. Remove the nuts from the smoker, cool completely in the pan, then serve and enjoy.

Smoked Mozzarella
Serves: 6
Cooking Time: 120 Minutes
Ingredients:
- 1 large ball mozzarella (about 1 lb.)
- Vegetable oil, for brushing the cheesecloth
- Salt
- Freshly ground black pepper

Directions:
In an aluminum pan, poke holes in the bottom. Put the cheesecloth on a flat surface. Brush the cloth with the vegetable oil. Season the cloth with the black pepper and salt. After this, put the mozzarella in the center of the cheesecloth and wrap it up. Place the cheese in the aluminum pan. Place the cheese in the smoker. Once the cheese is done remove it from the smoker. Allow it to cool to room temperature.

Hamburger Recipes

Smoked Yummy Chicken Burgers (masterbuilt Electric Smoker)
Serves: 6
Cooking Time: 1 Hour And 45 Minutes
Ingredients:
- 2/3 cup onion, finely diced
- 2 lbs ground chicken breast
- 3 Tbsp fresh parsley, finely chopped
- 2 Tbsp olive oil
- 1/2 tsp ground cumin
- 3/4 tsp kosher salt

Directions:
Clean and chop the onions as finely as you can. Place the onion in a deep bowl and mix all Ingredients: together in a large bowl. Form 4-inch thick patties and place evenly on a cookie sheet. Refrigerate for 30 minutes. Preheat Masterbuilt Electric Smoker. Allow the smoker temperature to reach 225 degrees Fahrenheit. When it is ready, add some water to the removable pan that is usually on the bottom shelf. Fill the side "drawer" with dry wood chips. Place burgers in the smoker and smoke 60 to 90 minute or until the internal temperature reaches 165 degrees Fahrenheit. Serve hot with hamburger buns and your favorite condiments.

Smoked Classic Burgers (masterbuilt Electric Smoker)
Serves: 6
Cooking Time: 1 Hour And 50 Minutes
Ingredients:
- 1 1/4 lbs ground beef
- 1/2 lb ground pork
- 1 onion finely chopped
- 1 Tbsp fresh parsley finely chopped
- 1/4 cup olive oil
- Salt and freshly ground black pepper, to taste

Directions:
Preheat Masterbuilt Electric Smoker. Allow the smoker temperature to reach 225 degrees Fahrenheit. When it is ready, add some water to the removable pan that is usually on the bottom shelf. Fill the side "drawer" with dry wood chips. Mix all Ingredients: together in a large bowl. Form medium patties and place evenly on a cookie sheet. Place burgers in the smoker and smoke to 90 minute or until the internal temperature reaches 150 degrees. Serve hot with mayonnaise, mustard or ketchup.

Smoked Turkey Burgers With Mayo And Mustard (masterbuilt Electric Smoker)
Serves: 6
Cooking Time: 1 Hour And 45 Minutes
Ingredients:
- 1-1/2 lbs ground turkey
- 1/2 cup onion chopped
- 1/2 cup dried breadcrumbs
- 1/4 cup mayonnaise
- 1/4 cup mustard (Dijon, English, or whole grain)
- 1 tsp salt and white freshly ground pepper to taste

Directions:
Combine all Ingredients: in a large bowl. Mix thoroughly and shape into 6 patties. Preheat Masterbuilt Electric Smoker. Allow the smoker temperature to reach 0 degrees Fahrenheit. When it is ready, add some water to the removable pan that is usually on the bottom shelf. Fill the side "drawer" with dry wood chips. Place burgers on smoker racks. Make sure the burgers are not touching. Smoke the burgers until internal temperature reaches 1 degrees. Serve on a burger bun with toppings and condiments of choice.

Smoked "spicy Trio" Burgers (masterbuilt Electric Smoker)
Serves: 6
Cooking Time: 1 Hour And 45 Minutes
Ingredients:
- 1 3/4 lbs combination of lean ground sirloin, lean ground pork, and lean ground veal
- 2 Tbsp ice water
- 1/4 cup ground oats
- 1/4 cup bottled chili sauce
- 1 small onion, minced
- Salt and ground black pepper, to taste

Directions:
Preheat Masterbuilt Electric Smoker. Allow the smoker temperature to reach 225 degrees Fahrenheit. When it is ready, add some water to the removable pan that is usually on the bottom shelf. Fill the side "drawer" with dry wood chips. Combine the meat with the remaining Ingredients: in a bowl. Shape into 6 patties. Place burgers in the smoker and smoke 60 to 90 minute or until the internal temperature reaches 16degrees F. Serve hot with buns and your favorite seasonings.

Smoked Hamburgers With Panko (masterbuilt Electric Smoker)
Serves: 6
Cooking Time: 1 Hour And 45 Minutes
Ingredients:
- 2 lbs. ground beef
- 1 large egg at room temperature
- 2 tsp chili flakes and chili powder
- 1/4 cup panko (Japanese breadcrumbs or common breadcrumbs
- Sea salt to taste
- Lemon juice for serving

Directions:
Mix all Ingredients: from the list in a large bowl. Using your hands knead the ground meat mixture until combined well. Wet your hands under water, and then form the meat into 6 patties. Refrigerate for 30 minutes before grilling. Preheat Masterbuilt Electric Smoker. Allow the smoker temperature to reach 22degrees Fahrenheit. When it is ready, add some water to the removable pan that is usually on the bottom shelf. Fill the side "drawer" with dry wood chips. Arrange your patties in a smoker and smoke 60 to 90 minute or until the internal temperature reaches 150 degrees. Sprinkle with lemon juice and serve immediately.

Other Recipes

Asparagus And Onion Mix
Serves: 4
Cooking Time: 2 Hours
Ingredients:
- 1 and ½ pounds asparagus
- 1 medium white onion, peeled and sliced
- 1 and ½ teaspoon salt
- ¼ teaspoon ground black pepper
- 2 tablespoons lemon juice

Directions:
Take your drip pan and add water, cover with aluminum foil. Pre-heat your smoker to 225 degrees F Use water fill water pan halfway through and place it over drip pan. Add wood chips to the side tray Take a foil pan and spread onion on the bottom, top with asparagus and season with salt and pepper, lemon juice Transfer pan to smoker and smoke for 2 hours Once done, serve and enjoy!

Hearty Jalapeno Peppers
Serves: 4
Cooking Time: 60 Minutes
Ingredients:
- 12 jalapeno peppers
- 8 ounces cream cheese
- 4 ounces cheddar cheese
- 4 ounces mozzarella cheese
- 2 bread heel slices
- 12 bacon slices

Directions:
Take your drip pan and add water, cover with aluminum foil. Pre-heat your smoker to 200 degrees F Use water fill water pan halfway through and place it over drip pan. Add wood chips to the side tray Add all the cheese to your food processor and hit blend button, blend until smooth Cut stems off the pepper and scoop out seeds, fill inside of pepper with cheese mix Tear a small part of the bread from crusts and add into the end of your pepper, this is ensuring that the cheese does not come out oozing Wrap pepper with bacon and secure with a toothpick Transfer to your smoker and smoke for 1 hour
1. Once done, enjoy it!

Rosemary Smoked Cashews
Serves: 16
Cooking Time: 30 Minutes
Ingredients:
- 1 lb raw cashews
- 4 cups water, room temperature
- ¼ cup Kosher salt
- 3 Tbsp melted butter
- 3 tsp dark brown sugar
- 1 tsp table salt

- ½ tsp ground rosemary
- ½ tsp garlic powder

Directions:
In a medium-sized non-reactive bowl, mix water and salt until salt dissolves. Add nuts and allow them to soak for 10 minutes. Arrange the nuts on a sheet tray. Preheat the smoker to 90°F Smoke the nuts for 30 minutes. In a large bowl, combine finishing ingredients. Add smoked nuts and stir to combine. Bake at 375°F for 15-20 minutes, stirring frequently. Allow the nuts to cool completely before serving.

Apple-brined Smoked Turkey
Serves: 15
Cooking Time: 12 Hours
Ingredients:
- 2 quarts apple juice
- 1 cup brown sugar
- 2 tablespoons salt
- 3 oranges, juiced
- 1 thumb-sized ginger, peeled and grated
- 15 cloves
- 6 bay leaves
- 6 cloves of garlic, peeled and crushed
- 1 12-pounds turkey

Directions:
Mix all Ingredients: in a deep stock pan that will fit the turkey. Allow to marinate for at least hours in the fridge. Load the wood tray with apple wood chips. Preheat the smoker to 2250F. Place the seasoned turkey and cook for 8 hours. Cook for 12 hours. Baste the turkey with the sauce every hour.

Sweet And Spicy Smoked Pecans
Serves: 16
Cooking Time: 30 Minutes
Ingredients:
- 1 lb raw pecans
- 4 cups water, room temperature
- ¼ cup Kosher salt
- ¼ cup real maple syrup
- 2 Tbsp butter, melted
- ½ tsp ginger powder
- ¼ tsp cayenne pepper

Directions:
In a medium-sized non-reactive bowl, mix water and salt until salt dissolves. Add nuts and allow them to soak for 10 minutes. Arrange the nuts on a sheet tray. Preheat the smoker to 90°F Smoke the nuts for 30 minutes. Finishing: In a large bowl, combine finishing ingredients. Toss smoked nuts with the finishing ingredients and place on a lightly greased sheet tray. Bake at 375°F for 15-20 minutes, stirring frequently. Allow the nuts to cool completely before serving.

Festival Turkey Legs
Serves: 4
Cooking Time: 8 Hours
Ingredients:
- 4 turkey legs
- 1 bottle lemon-flavored carbonated soda
- 2 tablespoons hot sauce
- 1 tablespoon red pepper flakes
- 1 tablespoon black pepper
- 1 large onion, sliced
- 2 tablespoons honey
- 1 tablespoon steak seasoning

Directions:
Place all Ingredients: in a large mixing bowl. Allow to marinate for at least overnight. Preheat the smoker to 2250F. Place apple juice in the water pan and add apple wood chips into the side tray. Place turkey legs in the smoker. Cook for to 8 hours. Baste the turkey legs with the sauce every hour.

Smoked Cherries
Serves: 1
Cooking Time: 2 Hours
Ingredients:
- 3 cups cherries or 3 cups fruit, of choice
- 12 ounces beer or 12 ounces apple juice

Directions:
Soak the wood chips you're going to use in the beer or apple juice. Arrange the cherries in a single layer over the disposable pan. Only add the fruit to any meat you're cooking two hours before you have to take it out. If not, allow the fruit to smoke for two hours before eating it. Smoke Temp: 160°

The Original Smoked Cauliflower
Serves: 4
Cooking Time: 2 Hours
Ingredients:
- 1 whole cauliflower
- 1 and ¼ teaspoon salt
- ¾ teaspoon pepper
- ½ teaspoon dried oregano
- 2 tablespoons olive oil
- ½ teaspoon dried basil

Directions:
Take your drip pan and add water, cover with aluminum foil. Pre-heat your smoker to 200 degrees F Use water fill water pan halfway through and place it over drip pan. Add wood chips to the side tray Cut cauliflower into florets and transfer to foil pan Add rest of the ingredients and toss well Transfer pan containing cauliflower to Smoker and smoke for 2 hours, making sure to add wood chips after every 30 minutes Serve and enjoy!

Smoked Cabbage Steaks With Dijon Vinaigrette
Serves: 6
Cooking Time: 20 Minutes
Ingredients:
- 1 head of cabbage, cut into 1-inch steaks
- 1 shallot, finely diced
- ¼ cup extra-virgin olive oil
- 2 Tbsp fresh lemon juice
- 1 tsp Dijon mustard
- ½ tsp salt

Directions:
Place vegetables in a shallow roasting pan. Preheat the smoker to 100°F. Smoke vegetables for 20 minutes. Finishing: Brush both sides of the cabbage with vegetable oil and place on a preheated grill. Grill for 2 minutes on each side. In a small bowl, whisk together mustard, shallot, lemon juice, salt and olive oil. Remove the cabbage from the grill and drizzle with the vinaigrette. Serve immediately

Smoked Chorizo With Mustard-caper Sauce (masterbuilt Electric Smoker)
Serves: 8
Cooking Time: 3 Hours And 15 Minutes
Ingredients:
- 2 lbs Chorizo sausages
- For mustard sauce
- 1/3 cup of Dijon mustard
- 1 cup Greek yogurt (plain and unsweetened)
- 3 Tbsp white wine vinegar (good quality)
- 1 Tbsp capers, chopped

Directions:
Prick sausages all over with a fork. Place the water in the pan at the bottom of your smoker. Fill the drawer or tray with wood chips. Preheat your smoker (use a 2-zone or Indirect setup) to about 225°F Set the smoker for 250F and get it smoking with the wood chips/pucks. Place the sausages on smoker racks at least a 1/2 inch apart. Smoke for 3 hours or until the internal temperature is 1F. Transfer the sausages on a platter lined with parchment paper. Stir all Ingredients: for the sauce, and serve in a bowl next to sausages.

Smoked Deer Sausages (masterbuilt Electric Smoker)

Serves: 6
Cooking Time: 6 Hours And 10 Minutes
Ingredients:
- 2 lbs deer sausages (with garlic and basil)
- SAUCE
- 2 cloves garlic minced
- 1/2 cup olive oil
- 3 Tbsp lime juice (freshly squeezed)
- 2 cups fresh mint and parsley mixture, finely chopped

Directions:
Place the water in the pan at the bottom of your smoker. Fill the drawer or tray with wood chips. Preheat your smoker (use a zone or Indirect setup) to about 225°F   Take two skewers (metal or wood). Push the two skewers all the way through the sausages, at a 90-degree angle to each other. The sausages can now easily be turned with a pair of tongs.   Smoke at 1 degrees F for 1 hour, then at 180 degrees F until internal temperature reaches 160 degrees F (insert a meat thermometer in the thickest part of the sausage).   Do not forget to turn every 30 minutes.   Remove sausages from smoker and let cool for 5 - 10 minutes.   Whisk all Ingredients: for sauce in a bowl.   Serve sausages with the sauce.

Mexican Stuffed Cornbread

Serves: 10
Cooking Time: 25 Minutes
Ingredients:
- 1½ cups all-purpose flour
- 1½ cups yellow cornmeal
- ¾ tsp baking soda
- ¾ tsp salt
- 3 eggs
- 1½-2 cups buttermilk
- ¾ cup butter, melted
- 1½ tbsp scallion, minced
- 1½ cups pepper jack cheese, shredded
- 1 lb smoked pulled pork
- 3 grilled habanero peppers, seeded and chopped
- 3 grilled jalapeño peppers, seeded and chopped

Directions:
Soak apple wood chips in water for at least hour. Preheat the smoker to 375 degrees F, using charcoal and soaked apple wood chips.   In a bowl, mix together flour, cornmeal, baking soda and salt. Add eggs, buttermilk, butter and scallion and mix until well combined.   Add ¾ of the cheese and mix well.   In another bowl, mix together the pork and grilled peppers.   Place the mixture into 2 greased loaf pans evenly and tap the pan onto a counter to remove air bubbles.   In the center of each loaf, press the pork mixture downward into the cornbread mixture until the surrounding mixture rise slightly above the stuffing.   Sprinkle the top of both loaves with the remaining cheese.   Place the loaf pans into the smoker and cook for about 25 minutes.   Remove from the smoker and place the loaf pans onto a wire rack for about 5 minutes. Carefully invert the loaves onto wire rack and serve warm.

Smoked Eggs

Serves: 6
Cooking Time: 2 Hours
Ingredients:
- Eggs (as many as you want)

Directions:
Place your eggs on top of the grate.   Allow the eggs to smoke.   Give the eggs a few minutes to cool before eating them.   Smoke Temp: 230

Smoked Vegetables

Serves: 4
Cooking Time: 20 Minutes For A Light Smoke Flavor
Ingredients:
- 1 zucchini, sliced into 1 inch rounds
- 1 lb button mushrooms
- 1 yellow squash, sliced into 1 inch rounds
- 1 red pepper, cut into 1 inch chunks
- 1 onion, cut into 1 inch chunks
- 1 recipe Rosemary Garlic

Directions:
Season the vegetables with the Rosemary Garlic Rub.   Place in a shallow aluminum pan.   Preheat the smoker to 100°F.   Smoke the vegetables for 20 minutes.   Place the vegetables straight into a preheated 400°F oven for 230 minutes.

Smoked Up Peaches

Serves: 4
Cooking Time: 30 Minutes
Ingredients:
- 6 fresh peaches

Directions:
Take your drip pan and add water, cover with aluminum foil. Pre-heat your smoker to 200 degrees F   Use water fill water pan halfway through and place it over drip pan. Add wood chips to the side tray   Transfer peaches directly onto your smoker and smoke for minutes, the first 20 minutes should be skin side down while the final 10 should be skin side up   Remove from smoker and serve, enjoy!

Mixed Veggie Combo
Serves: 6
Cooking Time: 4 Hours
Ingredients:
- 6 small red potatoes, cut into chunks
- 2 zucchinis, cut into ¾-inch-thick disks
- 2 yellow squash, cut into ¾-inch-thick disks
- 1 red bell pepper, seeded and cut into strips
- 1 medium red onion, cut into wedges
- For Vinaigrette:
- 1/3 cup extra-virgin olive oil
- ¼ cup balsamic vinegar
- 2 tsp Dijon mustard
- Salt and freshly ground black pepper, to taste

Directions:
Soak apple wood chips in water for at least hour. Preheat the smoker to 5 degrees F, using charcoal and soaked apple wood chips. For vinaigrette: in a bowl, add all ingredients and net until well combined. In an 8x12-inch casserole dish, place all the veggies and vinaigrette and toss to coat well. Place the dish into the smoker and cook for about 4 hours. Serve hot.

Smoked Cocktail Peanuts
Serves: 16
Cooking Time: 30 Minutes
Ingredients:
- 1 lb raw peanuts
- 4 cups water, room temperature
- ¼ cup Kosher salt
- 2 Tbsp vegetable oil
- 1 tsp granulated garlic
- 1 tsp Cajun ½ tsp table salt

Directions:
In a medium-sized non-reactive bowl, mix water and salt until salt dissolves. Add nuts and allow them to soak for 10 minutes. Arrange the nuts on a sheet tray. Preheat the smoker to 90°F Smoke the nuts for 30 minutes. In a large bowl, combine oil, garlic, Cajun Rub, and salt. Toss in smoked peanuts and stir to combine. Spread the nuts on a sheet tray and bake at 375°F for 15 minutes, stirring frequently. Allow the nuts to cool completely before serving.

Smoked Salmon Cucumbers
Serves: 6
Cooking Time: 25 Minutes
Ingredients:
- 1 large English cucumber
- 1 carton (8 ounces) spreadable chive and onion cream cheese
- 7 to 8 ounces smoked salmon or lox, chopped
- Minced chives

Directions:

Smoke the salmon for the allotted time. Chop the salmon up. Peel your cucumber and cut it into slices that are ¼ inch. Spread some cream cheese on the slices of cucumber. Place a piece of salmon on top of each cucumber slice. Be sure to sprinkle with chives. Serve immediately or store in the fridge for later.

Smoked Almonds
Serves: 16
Cooking Time: 30 Minutes
Ingredients:
- 1 lb raw almonds
- 4 cups water, room temperature
- ¼ cup Kosher salt
- 2 Tbsp extra-virgin olive oil
- 1 Tbsp kosher salt finely ground (coarse salt doesn't stick to the almonds very well)
- 2 tsp chili powder
- 1 tsp fresh ground black pepper
- ½ tsp garlic powder
- ¼ tsp cayenne pepper

Directions:
In a medium-sized non-reactive bowl, mix water and salt until salt dissolves. Add nuts and allow them to soak for 10 minutes. Arrange the nuts on a sheet tray. Preheat the smoker to 90°F Smoke the nuts for 30 minutes. In a large bowl, mix together finishing spices and olive oil. Toss in smoked nuts and stir to thoroughly combine. Bake in a sheet tray at 375°F for 15 minutes, stirring often. Allow the nuts to thoroughly cool before serving.

Smoked Paprika Roasted Potatoes
Serves: 4
Cooking Time: 1 Hour
Ingredients:
- 2 lbs. red potatoes
- 1 1/2 tbsp extra virgin olive oil
- 1 1/4 tsp smoked paprika
- 1 clove fresh garlic, minced very fine
- 3/4 tsp salt
- 1/4 tsp black pepper

Directions:
Be sure to scrub your potatoes clean. Don't peel them. Slice each of the potatoes in wedges. Once the potatoes are cut up, throw them all into a large zipper bag. Add in the olive oil. Be sure to toss the potatoes while they're in the bag. Sprinkle your garlic and other spices into the bag. Shake it again so all the wedges are equally coated. On a disposable foil pan spray it with some cook spray. Arrange your potato wedges on it in one single layer. Allow the potatoes to smoke until they're crisp. Once they're done, allow them to cool for a few minutes before sprinkling some paprika over the top. Enjoy!

Country Smoked Christmas Ham

Serves: 15
Cooking Time: 6 Hours
Ingredients:
- 1 12-lbs ham
- 1 can sliced pineapples, juice reserved
- 1 jar maraschino cherries
- 1 cup brown sugar

Directions:
Load the wood tray with apple wood chips. Preheat the smoker to 50F. Line a large baking pan with aluminum foil. Pat dry the ham and place in the baking pan. Arrange pineapple slices over the ham and put cherries on each hole of the pineapple. Mix together the pineapple juice and brown sugar. Once the sugar has dissolved, pour over the ham. Place the ham in the middle rack of the smoker. Cook for 6 hours. Baste the ham with the sauce every 2 hours.

Tamarind Smoked Turkey Sausages (masterbuilt Electric Smoker)

Serves: 6
Cooking Time: 3 Hours And 25 Minutes
Ingredients:
- 2 lbs mild turkey sausages
- Dressing
- 2 Tbsp tamarind paste
- 2 Tbsp soy sauce
- 1 Tbsp white vinegar
- 1 Tbsp molasses

Directions:
Place the water in the pan at the bottom of your smoker. Fill the drawer or tray with wood chips. Preheat your smoker (use a zone or Indirect setup) to about 225°F Place the sausage on smoker racks at least a 1/2 inch apart. Smoke for 2 - 3 hours or until the internal temperature is 165F. Remove sausages from smoker and let cool for - 10 minutes. In a meanwhile, whisk all Ingredients: for dressing in a bowl. Serve sausages warm with tamarind sauce.

Smoked Maple Butter Soaked Apples

Serves: 4
Cooking Time: 1 ½ Hours
Ingredients:
- Butter

- Brown sugar
- Maple syrup
- 4 apples

Directions:
Be sure to core the apples before placing them on the grill. It's basically a hole in the top of the apple to add in the maple syrup, butter, and brown sugar. Fill each apple up in the middle with the brown sugar, maple syrup, and butter. Place a drip pan beneath the apples. Arrange the apples on the rack together. Once the apples are done smoking give them a few minutes to cool before eating.

Cold Smoked Nuts

Serves: 16
Cooking Time: 30 Minutes
Ingredients:
- 1 lb raw nuts
- 4 cups room temperature water
- ¼ cup Kosher salt

Directions:
In a medium-sized non-reactive bowl, mix water and salt until salt dissolves. Add nuts and allow them to soak for 10 minutes. Arrange the nuts on a sheet tray. Preheat the smoker to 90°F Smoke the nuts for 30 minutes. To finish the nuts, place in a 300°F oven for 15-20 minutes, stirring often.

Thanksgiving Garlic Smoked Turkey

Serves: 15
Cooking Time: 8 Hours
Ingredients:
- 1 12-pound turkey
- 1 cup butter, softened,1 bunch fresh sage
- 1 bunch fresh thyme leaves
- 1 bunch fresh rosemary leaves
- 5 cloves of garlic, minced,2 teaspoons salt
- 1 teaspoon ground black pepper
- 2 lemons, sliced thinly

Directions:
Place turkey in an aluminum pan. Brush the turkey with butter and make sure all surfaces are covered with butter. Rub the sage, thyme, rosemary, garlic, salt, and pepper on the turkey. Arrange lemon slices on top. Load the wood tray with apple wood chips. Preheat the smoker to 2250F. Place the seasoned turkey and cook for 8 hours.

Smoked Chicken Sausages With Fennel Dressing (masterbuilt Electric Smoker)

Serves: 6
Cooking Time: 6 Hours And 15 Minutes
Ingredients:
- 2 lbs chicken sausages
- Dressing
- 1/2 cup olive oil
- 1/2 cup balsamic vinegar
- 1 Tbsp fennel bulb thinly sliced
- 1 garlic clove, minced

Directions:
Place the water in the pan at the bottom of your smoker. Fill the drawer or tray with wood chips. Preheat your smoker to about 5°F. Smoke sausages for 5 to 6 hour or until the outside casing begins to dry, and change to a red color. Remove sausages from smoker and let rest for 5 - 10 minutes. In a meanwhile, whisk together all Ingredients: for dressing in a bowl. Serve hot.

Properly Smoked Mushrooms

Serves: 4
Cooking Time: 1½ Hours
Ingredients:
- 4 (5½-ounce) Portobello mushrooms, stems removed
- 3 tbsp olive oil
- 1 tsp fresh parsley, minced
- 1 garlic clove, minced
- Salt and freshly ground black pepper, to taste

Directions:
Soak hickory wood chips in water for at least hour. Preheat the smoker to 5 degrees F, using charcoal and hickory wood chips. In a bowl, add all ingredients except mushrooms and mix well. Add mushrooms and coat with mixture generously. Place the mushrooms into the smoker and cook for about 1½ hours. Serve warm.

Roasted Broccoli

Serves: 2
Cooking Time: 10 Minutes
Ingredients:
- 6 cups fresh broccoli spears
- 2 tsp. plus 1-1/2 tsp. lemon juice
- 2 tsp. olive oil
- 1/4 tbsp. salt
- 1/4 tbsp. pepper
- 3/4 cup grated Parmesan cheese
- Shaved Parmesan cheese
- purple basil leaves (Optional)

Directions:
In a large bowl put your broccoli in it. Add the pepper, lemon juice, salt, and oil together. Drizzle this mixture over your broccoli. Toss everything if necessary to coat it all. Allow the broccoli to stand for half an hour. Be sure to toss your broccoli one last time before draining out the marinade. Place the cheese in a big Ziploc bag. Place the broccoli inside as well. Shake everything together so the broccoli is evenly coated. Coat the grill rack on the inside of the smoker with oil. Arrange the broccoli on the drill directly over a drip pan. Allow the broccoli to smoke and turn it over halfway through smoking. Serve while still warm. Feel free to garnish with some fresh basil or shaved parmesan.

Cold Smoked Tomato Salsa

Serves: 6
Cooking Time: 20 Minutes
Ingredients:
- 4 large beefsteak tomatoes (or 6 Roma tomatoes)
- 2 cloves garlic, whole
- 1 small onion, quartered
- 1 jalapeno, split lengthwise and seeded
- 2 Tbsp fresh lime juice
- 1 Tbsp chopped cilantro
- ½ tsp salt

Directions:
Place vegetables in a shallow roasting pan. Preheat the smoker to 100°F. Smoke vegetables for 20 minutes. Finishing: Place vegetables in a food processor and pulse until combined. Gently stir in cilantro, lime juice, and salt. Serve with tortilla chips.

Smoked Brussel Sprouts

Serves: 4
Cooking Time: 20 Minutes
Ingredients:
- 1 lb. Brussels sprouts, as uniform in size as possible*
- 2 tsp. olive oil
- 1 tbsp. minced garlic
- 1 tbsp. dry mustard
- 1 tbsp. smoked paprika
- 1 tbsp. kosher salt
- 1/4 tbsp. freshly ground black pepper

Directions:
Be sure to cut the stems off of the Brussel sprouts. Put all the Brussel sprouts in a large bowl and place them in the microwave. Microwave them on high for three minutes. Add salt, olive oil, paprika, garlic, and mustard to the bowl. Mix it all together so they combine well. Let the sprouts cool down for a few minutes before handling them again. Stick to 5 brussel sprouts each on a metal skewer. Place the Brussel sprouts in the smoker. Turn them over halfway through smoking. Put the Brussel sprouts back in the bowl again and toss them with the last of the garlic and oil mixture.

Lemon Rosemary Turkey Breasts

Serves: 17
Cooking Time:12 Hours
Ingredients:

- 1 12-pound whole turkey
- ½ cup lemon juice
- A bundle of rosemary leaves
- Salt and pepper to taste

Directions:
Place turkey in a pan and pour over lemon juice. Sprinkle with rosemary, salt, and pepper. Place an entire rosemary bundle inside the cavity of the turkey. Load the wood tray with hickory wood chips. Preheat the smoker to 22F. Place the seasoned turkey and cook for 8 hours. Cook for 12 hours.

Smoked Cabbage

Serves: 4
Cooking Time: 2 Hours
Ingredients:

- 1 small head green cabbage
- ½ teaspoon salt
- ½ teaspoon pepper
- 1 tablespoon apple cider vinegar
- 2 tablespoons butter
- 2 tablespoons olive oil

Directions:
Take your drip pan and add water, cover with aluminum foil. Pre-heat your smoker to 225 degrees F   Use water fill water pan halfway through and place it over drip pan. Add wood chips to the side tray   Remove the core of your cabbage, fill with vinegar, season with salt, pepper, and rub butter   Season exterior of cabbage with salt and pepper, transfer to foil pan   Place cabbage on the smoker rack and smoke for 30 minutes making sure to add more chips after every 30 minutes   Let it rest and cut into wedges   Serve and enjoy!

Smoked Bananas

Serves: 4
Cooking Time: 30 Minutes
Ingredients:

- 4 bananas unpeeled, cut in half lengthwise
- 4 tsp liquid honey
- 4 tsp lemon juice 5 ml
- 1 tsp ground cinnamon
- 4 tbsp sliced almonds
- Cooking oil

Directions:
Put the bananas on the rack. Afterwards, take the bananas out of the smoker. Remove their skins. Transfer them to a baking sheet that has oil spread on it. Spread a ½ tsp. of lemon juice and honey each on one of each of your banana halves. Also add ½ alam. of almonds and 1/8 tsp. of cinnamon. Start your oven up, and place your bananas in the broiler for about five minutes. Do this until they turn golden brown.

Smoke Roasted Sweet Potatoes

Serves: 4
Cooking Time: 2 Hours
Ingredients:

- 4 large sweet potatoes (6 to 8 oz. each)
- 4 tsp. (½ stick) salted butter, melted
- Coarse salt (kosher or sea) and freshly ground black pepper
- 2 tsp. maple syrup
- 2 tsp. brown sugar, for serving

Directions:
Be sure to clean the sweet potatoes off very well. Pat them dry with paper towels. Put the potatoes in a drip pan. Pour only 2 tbsp. of butter onto your potatoes. Be sure all the sides are coated. Season your potatoes liberally with the salt and pepper. Put the drip pan underneath the grate. Brush the grill of the smoker with some oil before arranging the potatoes on it. Close the smoker and allow the potatoes to smoke. The flesh of your potatoes should be browned, and the flesh tender. Once the sweet potatoes are done, be sure to cut them in half, but lengthwise. Spread the last of the butter and some maple syrup over the potatoes. At this point also sprinkle some brown sugar over the top of the potatoes. Season liberally with salt and pepper for taste. The sweet potatoes can be eaten at this point, even with the skin on.

Amazing Corn

Serves: 4
Cooking Time: 1 Hour
Ingredients:

- 6 ears corn with husk on
- ¼ cup butter, melted
- 1 tbsp light brown sugar
- 1 tsp paprika
- 1 tsp onion powder
- ½ tsp garlic powder
- Salt, to taste
- 3 green onions, sliced thinly

Directions:
Gently pull back husks from corn and remove silks but not husks. In a large roasting pan, soak the corn in water for about 8-1hours. Soak apple wood chips in water for at least 1 hour. Preheat the smoker to 225 degrees F, using charcoal and soaked apple wood chips. Remove corn from water and with paper towels, pat dry them. In small bowl, add remaining ingredients and beat until well combined. Coat corn with butter mixture evenly and sprinkle with green onions. Gently, pull husks back over corn. Place the corn onto smoker and cook for about 1 hour, flipping once half way through. Remove from smoker and keep the corn aside for about minutes. Remove the husks and serve.

Smoked Oysters With Olive Relish

Serves: 1
Cooking Time: 1 Hour, 30 Minutes
Ingredients:

- 1/2 cup chopped pitted kalamata olives
- 1/2 cup chopped seeded peeled plum tomato
- 2 tsp. chopped fresh basil
- 2 tsp. extra-virgin olive oil
- 1 tbsp. capers
- 1 tbsp. fresh lemon juice
- 1/2 tbsp. freshly ground black pepper
- 24 large shucked oysters (on the half shell)
- 12 lemon wedges

Directions:
In a small bowl mix together the olives, black pepper, lemon juice, capers, olive oil, fresh basil, and the plum tomato. On a aluminum foil pan, poke holes in the bottom with a knife or fork. Put another foil pan, but with no holes in it, on an unheated part of the smoker. Pour two cups of water in the pan with no holes in it. Put your oysters in the pan with the holes in it. Once they're done smoking drizzle 1 ½ tsp. of your olive mixture on your oysters. Serve the oysters with your lemon wedges.

Smoked Stuffed Turkey With Vegetables

Serves: 20
Cooking Time: 12 Hours
Ingredients:

- 1 12-pound whole turkey
- 3 tablespoons garlic power
- ¼ cup olive oil
- Salt and pepper to taste
- 1 tablespoon rosemary, divided
- 1 garlic bulb, minced
- 1-pound ground beef
- 1 tablespoon thyme leaves
- 3 large onions, chopped
- ½ cup chopped walnuts

Directions:
Load the wood tray with mesquite wood chips. Preheat the smoker to 50F. Season turkey with garlic powder, olive oil, salt, pepper, and half of the rosemary. Set aside. Prepare the filling by mixing the remaining rosemary, garlic, beef, thyme leaves, onions, and walnuts. Stuff the filling inside the turkey. Place inside the smoker.Cook for 12 hours.

Smoked Corn Recipe

Serves: 4
Cooking Time: 40 Minutes
Ingredients:

- 1/2 cup butter, softened
- 2 tsp. chopped fresh thyme
- 8 ears fresh corn with husks

Directions:
In a small bowl combine the thyme and butter. If not don't already, take the husks off of the corn. Throw away the silk on the corn. Rub your butter mixture over the corn. Pull the husks back over your corn. Place the corn in the smoker. Allow the husks to sit for 10 minutes before serving them.

Go-to-summer Side Dish

Serves: 4
Cooking Time: 1 Hour
Ingredients:

- 2 large zucchinis, slice lengthwise into ½-inch halves
- 2 tsp olive oil
- Salt and freshly ground black pepper, to taste
- 1 tsp balsamic vinegar

Directions:
Soak hickory wood chips in water for at least hour. Preheat the smoker to 5 degrees F, using charcoal and soaked apple wood chips. Coat the zucchini slices with oil and then sprinkle with the salt and black pepper evenly. Place the zucchini slices into the smoker and cook for about 1 hour. Serve warm with the drizzling of vinegar.

Marinated and Smoked Venison Tenderloin

Servings: 4
Cooking Time: 2 hour 15 min
Ingredients:

- 2 venison tenderloins, 6 to 8 ounces each
- 1/3 cup drinkable dry red wine
- 1/4 cup extra virgin olive oil (EVOO)
- 1 TBS soy sauce or tamari
- 1 tsp brown or Dijon mustard
- 1 tsp honey or maple syrup
- 1/2 small onion, diced
- 2 cloves garlic, minced
- 1 tsp dried rosemary
- 1 tsp sea salt
- 1 tsp cracked black pepper

Directions:
Trim any silver skin off of the tenderloins. Prepare the marinade in a bowl, whisking together the 10 last ingredients on the list. Place the tenderloins in a large, sealable baggie or 2. Stand the bags up in a baking dish. Pour the marinade over the venison. Squeeze any air out, seal the bags, and massage lightly to coat the meat. Place the dish with the bag or bags in the refrigerator for up to 12 hours, but not less than 4. Take the venison out of the refrigerator 20 minutes before you start your smoker. Remove a grill rack from your smoker and place on paper towels (to catch marinade drippings). Prepare the smoker by adding wood chips to the tray and water to the bowl. Preheat the smoker to 250°F. Open the top vent. When the smoker is up to temperature, remove the venison from the marinade and place on the rack. Discard extra marinade. Put the rack in the smoker and cook for approximately 2 hours, checking the internal temperature at 60 minutes. You want the meat to be between 140°F and 150°F, depending on how rare or well done you like it. Replenish the wood chips and water every 45 to 60 minutes. Remove the venison to a cutting board and tent with foil. Allow it to rest for approximately 20 minutes. Slice thinly and serve with some autumn sides, such as roasted butternut squash and Brussels sprouts with Bacon.

Provencal Style Marinated and Smoked Rabbit
Servings: 4
Cooking Time: 3 hour 10 minutes
Ingredients:
- 1 whole rabbit, approximately 3 pounds
- 1/2 cup dry white wine
- 1/3 cup extra virgin olive oil (EVOO)
- 2 cloves of garlic, minced or pressed
- 1 TBS dried rosemary
- 1 TBS dried thyme
- 2 tsps dried oregano
- 2 tsps cracked black pepper
- 1 tsp sea salt
- 1 bay leaf

Directions:
In a baking dish large enough to hold the rabbit, mix together the 9 marinade ingredients. Place the rabbit in the dish and turn several times to coat with the mixture. Cover with plastic wrap and place in the refrigerator overnight. If possible, turn the rabbit over once or twice. Better yet, place the rabbit and marinade in a large, sealable plastic bag. Alternatively, you can cut the rabbit into portions so it will fit into a bag. Take the rabbit out of the refrigerator 40 minutes before your smoker is up to temperature. Take a rack from your smoker for the rabbit. Add wood chips to the tray of the smoker. Oak is nice for this recipe. Place water in the bowl. You can add some lemon slices or white wine to the water. Preheat your smoker to a temperature of 240°F. Place the whole rabbit or portions on the smoker rack and place the rack inside the smoker. Discard any leftover marinade. Smoke the rabbit for 1-1/2 hours and turn over for even cooking. Add more wood chips and liquid as needed. Smoke for another 1-1/2 hours and check the internal temperature. You are looking for at least 165°F. Smoke longer if needed to achieve the appropriate temperature. Remove the rabbit from the smoker to a cutting board. Tent with foil and allow it to rest for 15 minutes. Carve the rabbit into portions (legs, thighs, and split saddles) and serve on a large platter with lemon wedges and plenty of Provencal accompaniments, such as, ratatouille, panisses, and a mesclun greens salad with a simple vinaigrette. If you want a sauce, try a white wine and Dijon mustard sauce.

Smoked Classic Deviled Eggs
Servings: 4
Cooking Time: 1 hour
Ingredients:
- 6 large eggs
- 1/4 cup good mayonnaise
- 1-1/2 TBS sweet pickle relish
- 1 tsp Dijon mustard
- 1/4 to 1/2 tsp sea salt
- 1/4 tsp freshly ground pepper
- Paprika for garnish
- Water
- Mild wood chips, such as adler or apple

Directions:
Place the eggs in a soup pot and cover completely + 1 inch with cold water. Put the pot over medium-high heat and bring the water to a boil. Turn off the heat and cover the pot with a well fitting lid. The eggs will continue to cook in the hot water for the next 10 to 12 minutes. Prepare your smoker while the eggs are cooking. Take a rack out of the smoker. Fill the water bowl 1/2 way. Add the wood chips to the side tray. Heat up the smoker to between 200°F and 225°F with the top vent open. Drain the water from the pot and run cold water over the eggs in the pot until they are cool enough to handle. Peel the eggs and return them to the cool water until finished peeling. Drain the eggs completely. Lightly oil the rack and return it to the smoker. Place the eggs in the spaces between the metal grate sections so they don't roll around. Smoke for approximately 25 to 35 minutes until a light bronze color. Cut the hard boiled eggs in half lengthwise. Carefully scoop out the yellow yolks with a spoon, placing them in a mixing bowl. Add the mayonnaise, relish, mustard, salt, and pepper. Stir well to combine until smooth in texture. Fill the cavities of the egg whites with the yolk mixture, achieving some height above the whites. A piping bag can assist with this task. Place the filled egg halves on a platter and chill them in the refrigerator until cool or cold. Sprinkle the tops with paprika just before serving. Serve with cocktail napkins on the side.

Smoked Mac and Cheese with Two Cheeses Recipe

Servings: 6
Cooking Time: 2 hour

Ingredients:
- 1 tsp sea salt
- 1 pound elbow macaroni
- 6 tbsps unsalted butter (3/4 stick)
- 1/2 cup all-purpose flour (AP)
- 4 cups whole milk
- 12 ounces sharp cheddar cheese, grated
- 8 ounces Gruyere cheese, grated
- 1-1/2 tsps sea salt
- 1/2 tsp grated or ground nutmeg
- 1/2 tsp cracked black pepper
- Ingredients for topping:
- 2 tbsps unsalted butter (1/4 stick)
- 1/2 tsp sea salt
- 1-1/2 cups panko bread crumbs

Directions:
Add desired, soaked wood chips to the slide-out drawer of your smoker. Preheat your Masterbuilt Electric Smoker to 225 degrees F. Bring a large pot of water (about a 4 quart pot) to a boil and add 1 teaspoon of the salt. Cook the macaroni in the salted water as directed on the box, approximately 6 to 8 minutes so that it is still a tad al dente. Drain in a colander. While the pasta cooks, grate the cheeses. In the same pot, melt 6 tablespoons of the butter. Gently whisk in the flour a little at a time until it is well blended with the butter. Cook down for 2 minutes until thick. Meanwhile, heat the milk in 2 to 4 cup batches in the microwave until just warm, not boiling. Add the warm milk, 1 cup at a time and whisk it into the roux. Cook for 2 minutes until just creamy and starting to thicken, like a béchamel sauce. Remove the pot from the heat and add the grated cheeses to melt. Stir in the nutmeg, salt, and pepper. Gently stir in the macaroni to coat with the cheese sauce. In a sauté pan, melt 2 tablespoons of butter. Season the melted butter with salt and stir in the breadcrumbs. Pour the macaroni and cheese mixture into a heat-proof or disposable, foil 3 quart baking pan. Cover the top of the dish with the buttery breadcrumbs. Smoke for approximately 1 hour until the cheese is bubbling and the bread crumbs are toasty and browned. Serve while it is piping hot.

Smoked Potato, Ham, and Cheese Casserole Recipe

Servings:
Cooking Time:

Ingredients:
- 2 pounds Yukon gold potatoes, washed well
- 1-1/2 cups chopped yellow onions
- 1 tsp sea salt
- 4 TBS butter
- 1 TBS olive oil
- 5 TBS all-purpose flour
- 2-1/2 cups whole milk
- 2 TBS Worcestershire sauce
- 1/2 tsp whole grain mustard
- 1 tsp sea salt
- 1/2 tsp freshly ground pepper
- 1/4 tsp paprika
- Vegetable or olive oil
- 2 cups shredded mild cheddar cheese
- 2 cups diced cooked ham
- 1/2 cup breadcrumbs
- 3 TBS cold butter, diced
- Water and 2 TBS apple cider vinegar
- Wood chips, such as apple or pecan

Directions:
Wash the potatoes well. Peel them and dice into 1/2 inch cubes. Place the potatoes in a large saucepot and cover with water. Season with 1 teaspoon of salt. Turn the heat to high. As soon as the water boils, reduce the heat to medium-low, add the onions, and cover the pot. Cook until the potatoes are just tender when pierced with a fork, approximately 12 minutes. Drain the potatoes and onions in a colander and set aside while you preheat the smoker and make the sauce. Fill the water bowl of your smoker half way with water and apple cider vinegar. Place the wood chips in the tray. Open the top vent. Preheat your smoker to 350°F. In a medium saucepan over medium heat, melt the butter with the olive oil. Add the flour and whisk until smooth. Continue to cook, whisking constantly, for 2 minutes until slightly thickened. Gradually whisk the milk into the roux. Add the Worcestershire sauce, mustard, salt, pepper, and paprika. Keep cooking and whisking until creamy and thickened but still pourable. Spray or brush a 9 x 13 inch aluminum foil baking pan with vegetable oil. Place half of the cooked potatoes and onions in the pan. Cover the potatoes with half of the cheese. Spread all the ham on top of the cheese. Cover with the remaining potatoes. Pour or ladle the white sauce evenly over the potatoes, ham, and cheese. Add another layer of the remaining cheese over the top. Sprinkle evenly with bread crumbs. Then, dot the top with the diced butter. If freezing a casserole, leave the breadcrumbs and butter off until right before smoking. Place the casserole in the preheated smoker and cook until it is hot and bubbling, approximately 1 hour. Note: If your smoker does not go as high as 350°F, just cook a bit longer. Allow the casserole to sit for 5 minutes before serving. Spoon into bowls or onto plates and enjoy while still warm.

Smoked Sweet and Sour Tofu Skewers Recipe
Servings: 4
Cooking Time: 3 hour
Ingredients:
- 1 block of extra firm tofu, approximately 15.5 ounces
- 16 ounces of fresh pineapple cubes, or cut your own
- 1 bunch fresh, medium to large asparagus spears, washed
- Marinade/Sauce
- 1 cup bottled or canned pineapple juice
- 3/4 cup packed light brown sugar
- 1/3 cup rice vinegar or apple cider vinegar
- 3 TBS ketchup
- 2 TBS soy sauce or tamari
- 1-1/2 TBS cornstarch dissolved in 2 tablespoons water
- 2 scallions sliced thinly
- Vegetable oil spray for the smoker racks
- Toasted sesame seeds for serving

Directions:
Drain the water from the tofu package. Wrap the tofu block in either a clean dish towel or a lot of paper towels. Place this on a plate and press down lightly to release as much moisture as possible without breaking the block. Place the tofu on dry paper towels and allow it to drain some more while you make the sauce. In a sauce pot, place the first 5 marinade ingredients and bring to a simmer over medium high heat, stirring often for about 2 to 3 minutes. Stir or whisk in the cornstarch slurry and scallions. Just heat through until the sauce just starts to thicken, about 1 to 2 minutes. Remove from the heat and set aside to cool. Cut the block of tofu into equal 1" cubes. You should get about 32 to 36 cubes. In a covered container, place 1/2 the marinade. Add the tofu cubes and lightly toss just to coat them without breaking the tofu. Place the covered container in the refrigerator for 30 minutes or up to 4 hours. Cut the pineapple into 1" cubes, if not already prepared for you. Remove the woody ends of the asparagus spears and cut into 1" segments. Set these aside while you prepare the smoker. Remove 1 or 2 racks from the smoker to place the skewers on. Prepare your smoker by adding wood chips to the tray and water to the bowl. Preheat the smoker to 250°F. Open the top vent. Arrange your skewers: Place a pineapple cube toward the end leaving 1 inch of skewer showing, then an asparagus section speared through the middle, followed by a tofu cube and another asparagus piece. Repeat until the skewers are filled, leaving an inch of space at each end. Put the skewers on a plate and brush on 1/2 of the remaining marinade. Spray the smoker racks with vegetable oil to lightly coat. Place the skewers on the racks. Put the racks inside the smoker. Smoke for approximately 45 minutes. Rotate the skewers 180 degrees and brush the rest of the sauce over them. Smoke for another 15 minutes or until the asparagus feels tender *. Sprinkle sesame seeds over the skewers and serve them over white rice or just with napkins to eat casually. Add extra sauce if you have some.

Smoking Hard and Semi-hard Cheeses
Servings: 14
Cooking Time: 3 hour 5 minutes
Ingredients:
- 4 eight ounce blocks of cheese: sharp cheddar, Manchego, gruyere, halloumi, or all four

Directions:
Keep the cheese refrigerated while setting up your smoker. Preheat your smoker to between 75°F and 85°F with the vent open. Place wood chips in the side tray and cold water in the bowl. Place the blocks of cold cheese on a mesh wire rack and place that on a rack inside the smoker. Alternatively, place the cheese directly on the smoker rack. Cold smoke for 2 hours, turning over once or twice. Check for a slight bronze color and taste to see if the cheese has adequate smoke flavor. Continue to smoke for up to 4 hours if desired. Remove the smoked cheese from the smoker and allow it to rest on a rack for approximately 1 hour. If there is a film of oil on the cheese you can blot that off with a paper towel. When the cheese has rested, seal it in plastic wrap or butcher's paper. Place this in the cheese drawer of your refrigerator and leave alone for approximately 7 days for the smoke flavor to mature.

Twice Smoked Cheese and Bacon Potatoes
Servings: 6
Cooking Time: 3 hour 35 minutes
Ingredients:
- 4 large organic Idaho or russet baking potatoes, washed well and patted dry
- 1-1/2 TBS extra virgin olive oil
- 4 strips bacon sliced crosswise into 1/4" pieces
- 6 TBS (3/4 stick) butter, sliced into 8 pieces
- 1/2 cup sour cream
- 1 cup grated cheddar cheese, divided into 1/2 cup measures
- 1/2 cup whole milk
- 1 tsp sea salt
- 1 tsp freshly ground pepper
- 2 scallions, finely sliced
- Mesquite or hickory wood chips

Directions:
Fill the water bowl of your smoker 1/2 to 3/4 full. Place wood chips in the side tray. Preheat smoker to 275°F with the vent open. Coat the potatoes completely with olive oil. Place them on the rack of your smoker. Cook for 2 to 3 hours until soft in the center when pierced with a sharp knife. The internal temperature should be approximately 195°F. Refill the water bowl and wood chip tray as needed. While the potatoes are smoking, place the bacon in a sauté pan on medium-high heat and fry until browned and crispy, approximately 4 to 5 minutes. Drain on paper towels and set aside. Remove the smoked potatoes to a cutting board, leaving the smoker on. Allow them to cool until you can handle them. In a large mixing bowl, place the butter slices, bacon bits, and sour cream. Mix to combine. Using a sharp knife, slice each potato in half lengthwise. Carefully spoon out the insides, leaving a little of the potato in the skins so they retain a bowl-like shape. Place the potato flesh in the bowl with the butter mixture. Smash the potato mixture with a potato masher until all ingredients are well combined. Stir or fold in 1/2 cup of the cheese, milk, salt, pepper, and scallions. Place the skin shells on a foil lined baking sheet. Fill each one with equal portions of the smashed potato mixture. Top each stuffed potato shell with the remaining 1/2 cup of cheese. Place the pan of potatoes in the smoker and cook until warmed though and the cheese has melted, approximately 30 to 45 minutes. Serve the twice smoked and loaded potatoes with grilled, sliced steak and a green salad.

Appendix : Recipes Index

A

A Little Spicy Smoked Lamb Sausage Recipe 73

Alabama Chicken Sandwiches With White Bbq Sauce 107

Alaskan Candied Salmon 88

Ale-brined Catfish With Cilantro Lemon Dipping Sauce 91

Alligator Eggs 24

Amazing Corn 140

Amazing Mesquite Maple And Bacon Chicken 118

Apple Smoked Pork Loin 49

Apple-brined Smoked Turkey 134

Apple-injected Smoked Pork 29

Applesauce 22

Apple-smoked Duck 106

Apple Brined Smoked Duck Breast 118

Asian Honey Pork Chops 43

Asparagus And Onion Mix 134

Asparagus Stuffed Smoked Chicken Breasts 102

Authentic Citrus Smoked Chicken 112

B

Baby Back Ribs With Bbq Sauce 41

Bacon & Endive Salad 25

Bacon Wrapped Chicken Lollipops 96

Bacon Wrapped Dove 124

Bacon Wrapped Smoked Scallops 89

Bacon Wraps 28

Bacon-wrapped Chicken Lollipops 108

Bacon-wrapped Fatty 51

Bacon-wrapped Scallops 88

Bananas Calypso 26

Basic Brisket 45

Basic Smoked Burgers 66

Basic Smoked Chicken 106

Basic Smoked Beef Jerky Recipe 68

Basic Smoked Beef Jerky Recipe 73

Basic Smoked Burgers 69

Bbq Chicken Legs 111

Bbq Lamb Chops 50

Bbq Pulled Pork 48

Beef Jerky 22

Beef Jerky 30

Beef Short Ribs 29

Beefy Jalapeno Fatty 51

Beer Smoked Chicken In Masterbuilt Smoker 110

Best-ever Pork Chops 60

Black Bean & Sesame Sauce 127

Boar Shoulder 123

Brined and Smoked Bone-in Chicken Breasts 119

Brined and Smoked Pheasant with a Honey Glaze Recipe 119

Brown Sugar & Mustard Glazed Ham 32

Burnt End Baked Beans 20

Butterflied Lobster Tails 80

C

Cajun Style Chicken Breasts 108

Cape Cod Lobster Rolls 88

Carolina Barbeque Rub 130

Cheesy Cowboy Butter 128

Cheesy Potatoes 21

Cheesy Turkey Meatballs 116

Cherry Memphis Pork Ribs 40

Chicago Rib Tips 40

Chicken And Guacamole 94

Chicken Breast 114

Chicken With Western Kentucky Mop & Dip 109

Chili Chipotle Sauce 129

Chimichurri Smoked Loin Chops 31

Chinese Style Lamb Shanks 31

Chipotle Turkey Legs 115

Christmas Dinner Duck 99

Christy's Smoked Pimento Cheese Appetizer 131

Cider Brined Pulled Pork 55

Citrus Goose Breast 113

Cola Glazed Chicken Breasts 99

Cold Smoked Nuts 138

Cold Smoked Tomato Salsa 139

Cornbread 23

Country Smoked Christmas Ham 138

Country Style Pork Ribs 57

County Fair Turkey Legs 112

Cowboy Omelet 68

Crazy Smoked Pork Spare Ribs 62

Creamy Shrimp Pasta Salad 89

Creative Smoked Salt 129

Cross-rib Beef Roast 39

Crowd Pleasing Meatloaf 31

Cured Salmon 89

D

Decadent Rump Roast 41

Delicious Lobster Tail 85

Delicious Maple Glazed Smoked Bacon 45

Delicious Portobello Mushrooms 12

Delicious Scallops 86

Delicious Smoked Pork Belly 45

Delicious Smoked Rabbits 124

Deviled Eggs 18

Deviled Ham Crackers 54

Dry Rubbed and Smoked Tri-Tip Roast Recipe 69

Dry Rubbed Pork Chops 60

E

Easiest Bbq Smoked Turkey Wings 116
East Texas Pulled Pork 67
Easy Mustard Sauce 128
Easy Smoked Tuna 83
Easy Smoked Turkey 111
Enticing Salmon 81
Exotic Rub Mix 127

F

Fancy Appetizers 83
Festival Turkey Legs 135
Fiery Pork Loin With Blueberry Chutney 36
Flavorful Beef Brisket 47
Four Cheese Smoked Mac 'n' Cheese 25
Fully Smoked Herbal Quail 98

G

Garlic And Cayenne Almonds 132
Garlic Sauce And Lamb Chops 63
Gentle Alabama White Sauce 130
German Pork Hock 66
German Style Turkey Breast 105
Get-together Chicken Wings 104
Glaze (double for extra sauce) 69
Glazed Meatloaf 47
Glazed Pork Tenderloin 46
Glorious Lamb Shoulder 49
Go-to-summer Side Dish 141
Gourmet Snapper 90
Grandma's Whole Smoked Chicken 101
Green Salsa 127
Groovy Smoked Asparagus 15

H

Halibut With Homemade Tartar Sauce 89
Hamburger Jerky 23
Hasselback Potatoes 27
Hearty Jalapeno Peppers 134
Hearty Ribeye Steaks 57
Herb Rubbed Smoked Rack of Veal 70
Herbed Shrimp 84
Herb-rubbed Apple Smoked Turkey 100
Herby Smoked Cauliflower 11
Hickory Smoked Burgers 64
Homemade Smoked Maple Cured Bacon 74
Honey Brined Turkey 97
Honey Chipotle Salmon With Pineapple Salsa 93
Honey Glazed Cod 87
Honey Mustard Halibut Fillets 91
Honey Smoked Turkey 95
Hot Pepper And Vinegar Bbq Sauce 128
Hot-stuffed Pork Chop 48
Hungarian Pulled Pork Sandwich 35
Herb Rubbed Smoked Turkey Recipe 120

I

Indian Pork Roast 32
Inspired Turkey Breast 98

Irish-style Lamb 42

J

Jalapeno Poppers 20

K

Kansas City Burnt Ends 53
Kimchi Coleslaw 18

L

Lemon Pepper Chicken Quarters 103
Lemon Pepper Tuna 93
Lemon Rosemary Turkey Breasts 140
Let It Cool For 15 Minutes And Serve Standing Smoked Chicken 95
Lip-smackin' Short Ribs 56
Lovely Chicken Spice Rub 130

M

Maple Smoked Salmon Steaks 90
Maple-glazed Nuts 19
Marinated Chicken Breasts 114
Marinated Smoked Beef Short Ribs 70
Marinated Smoked Oysters 81
Marinated Trout 83
Marinated and Smoked Venison Tenderloin 141
Masterbuilt Beef Brisket 61
Masterbuilt Electric Smoker Goose Jerky 125
Masterbuilt Electric Smoker Shrimp Kabobs 80
Masterbuilt Electric Smoker Venison 126
Masterbuilt Smoked Lamb Shank 65
Masterbuilt Smoked Mackerel 79
Masterbuilt Smoked Rabbit 126
Masterbuilt Smoked Seasoned Chuck Roast 63
Masterbuilt Smoked Trout 80
Masterbuilt Smoker Cooker Corned Beef 30
Meats Combo Meatloaf 43
Memphis Bbq Spaghetti 52
Memphis Rub 129
Mexican Stuffed Cornbread 136
Mighty Meaty Beef Tenderloin 29
Mixed Vegetables 18
Mixed Veggie Combo 137
Moist Wrapped Chicken Tenders 114
Molasses Lamb Chops 58
Mole-mole Baby Back Ribs 46
Montreal Steak Rub 129
Moroccan Lamb Ribs 40

N

Naan 21
New York Strip Steak With Bourbon Butter 54

O

Old Fashioned Barbecue Chicken 109
Omega-3 Rich Salmon 83
Orange Crispy Chicken 115
Orange Smoked Chicken 113

P

Paprika Bbq Rub 127
Paprika Herb Rub Garlic & Onion Tenderloin 66
Pastrami 64
Peach-smoked Ahi Tuna Steaks 90
Pecan Tassies 28
Perfect Smoked Beef Burgers 53
Perfectly Cured Salmon 79
Perfectly Smoked Beef Ribs 56
Perfectly Smoked Filet Mignon 65
Perfectly Smoked Pork Butt 37
Perfectly Smoked Pork Spare Ribs 59
Pit Smoked Pork Shoulder 54
Pizza Jalapeño Poppers 24
Pool Party Wings 97
Poor Man's Burnt Ends 52
Pork Belly Burnt Ends 20
Pork Tenderloin Appetizers 27
Properly Smoked Mushrooms 139
Provencal Style Marinated and Smoked Rabbit 142
Pulled Pork Hoagie 68

R

Red Hot Chicken Wings 104
Ribeye Steaks 56
Roasted Broccoli 139
Roasted Pears 20
Romain Chicken Breasts 103
Rosemary Garlic Pork Tenderloins 62
Rosemary Lamb Chops 50
Rosemary Smoked Cashews 134
Rotisserie Chicken 104

S

Saucy Beef Back Ribs 38
Savory And Sweet Pork Ribs 44
Savory and Sweet Smoked Ribs with Classic BBQ Sauce 74
Savory Herb Rubbed and Aromatic Stuffed Smoked Turkey Recipe 120
Scrambled Smoked Fish Bowls 81
Seasoned Chuck Roast 56
Seasoned Drumsticks 100
Sesame & White Bean Sauce 128
Shrimps 85
Simple Beef Roast 60
Simple Brined Trout 84
Simple Pulled Pork 42
Simple Pulled Pork Butt 39
Simple Salt & Pepper Smoked Salmon 84
Simple Smoked Chicken Wings 96
Simple Smoked Salmon 82
Simple Turkey Breast 110
Sirloin Tip Roast 33
Slow Smoked Pork Ribs 37
Smo-fried Cajun Turkey 101
Smofried Chicken Wings 105

Smoke Roasted Apple Crisp 23
Smoke Roasted Sweet Potatoes 140
Smoked "spicy Trio" Burgers (masterbuilt Electric Smoker) 133
Smoked "onion Soup" Pork 33
Smoked Almonds 137
Smoked Apple Curry Chicken Breast (masterbuilt Electric Smoker) 113
Smoked Apple Ribs 49
Smoked Apples with Maple Syrup 15
Smoked Asian Style Pork Tenderloin (masterbuilt Electric Smoker) 35
Smoked Asian Trout 79
Smoked Avocados With Strawberry-mango Salsa 21
Smoked Baked Beans 16
Smoked Banana Foster 25
Smoked Bananas 140
Smoked Bananas for Sundaes and Smoothies 16
Smoked Beef Braciole Finished in Tomato Sauce Recipe 71
Smoked Beef Brisket 61
Smoked Beef Brisket With White Wine Marinade (masterbuilt Electric Smoker) 49
Smoked Beef Tenderloin with Horseradish Sauce Recipe 71
Smoked Blue Wings 117
Smoked Blueberry and Maple Glazed Baby Back Ribs 75
Smoked Bologna 34
Smoked Boston Butt Recipe for Pulled Pork 76
Smoked Brie Cheese 131
Smoked Brie With Roasted Peppers & Garlic 131
Smoked Brisket 72
Smoked Brussel Sprouts 139
Smoked Brussels Sprouts 13
Smoked Brussels Sprouts 16
Smoked Buffalo Chicken Wings 94
Smoked Burgers With Seared Avocado 61
Smoked Cabbage 140
Smoked Cabbage 23
Smoked Cabbage Steaks With Dijon Vinaigrette 135
Smoked Caesar Salad 24
Smoked Catfish 82
Smoked Cheese Crisps 132
Smoked Cheesy Burgers 58
Smoked Cherries 135
Smoked Chicken Breast In Coffee Marinade (masterbuilt Electric Smoker) 109
Smoked Chicken Breast With Dark Sauce (masterbuilt Electric Smoker) 118

Smoked Chicken Breasts With Rosemary (masterbuilt Electric Smoker) 102
Smoked Chicken Cutlets In Strawberries - Balsamic Marinade (masterbuilt Electric Smoker) 116
Smoked Chicken Legs 108
Smoked Chicken Patties (masterbuilt Electric Smoker) 114
Smoked Chicken Sausages With Fennel Dressing (masterbuilt Electric Smoker) 139
Smoked Chicken Tenders 117
Smoked Chicken Thighs 118
Smoked Chicken Thighs In Red Pepper Marinade (masterbuilt Electric Smoker) 107
Smoked Chocolate Bread Pudding 28
Smoked Chorizo Queso 41
Smoked Chorizo With Mustard-caper Sauce (masterbuilt Electric Smoker) 135
Smoked Chuck Roast 59
Smoked Clams 81
Smoked Classic Burgers (masterbuilt Electric Smoker) 133
Smoked Cocktail Peanuts 137
Smoked Coconut Aminos Marinated Flank Steak (masterbuilt Electric Smoker) 57
Smoked Cod 92
Smoked Corn Recipe 141
Smoked Curried Almonds 16
Smoked Deer Sausages (masterbuilt Electric Smoker) 136
Smoked Dry Mustard Beef Round Steak (masterbuilt Electric Smoker) 37
Smoked Dry Rubbed Bottom Round Roast 72
Smoked Duck 124
Smoked Eel 82
Smoked Eggplant 11
Smoked Eggs 136
Smoked Fish Spread 79
Smoked Flank Steak With Curried Pineapple (masterbuilt Electric Smoker) 31
Smoked Flank Steak With Peanut Oil Marinade (masterbuilt Electric Smoker) 34
Smoked French Sour Lamb Cutlets (masterbuilt Electric Smoker) 38
Smoked Garlicky Chicken Breast (masterbuilt Electric Smoker) 110
Smoked Goat Ribs With Garlic (masterbuilt Electric Smoker) 55
Smoked Gouda Cheese 132
Smoked Green Beans With Lemon 13
Smoked Green Beans With Lemon 15
Smoked Halibut Fillets (masterbuilt Electric Smoker) 85
Smoked Ham Hocks Recipe 76
Smoked Ham With Glaze 37

Smoked Ham with Maple & Mustard Glaze Recipe 77
Smoked Hamburger Jerky 63
Smoked Hamburgers 55
Smoked Hamburgers With Panko (masterbuilt Electric Smoker) 133
Smoked Herb Marinated Lamb Skewers 65
Smoked Herbed Chicken Breasts 101
Smoked Hot Pepper Pork Tenderloin (masterbuilt Electric Smoker) 58
Smoked Jumpers 87
Smoked Lamb Breast 59
Smoked Lamb Chops With Fresh Herbs (masterbuilt Electric Smoker) 40
Smoked Lamb Kabobs 36
Smoked Lamb Lollipops 58
Smoked Lamb Shoulder Chops 65
Smoked Leg Of Lamb 44
Smoked Lemony Catfish Fillets (masterbuilt Electric Smoker) 92
Smoked Lemony-garlic Artichokes 14
Smoked Lemony-garlic Artichokes 17
Smoked Lobster 90
Smoked Lobster Tails 91
Smoked Lobster With Herbed Butter (masterbuilt Electric Smoker) 82
Smoked Loin Chops 46
Smoked Loin Chops With Cherry Chutney 64
Smoked Maple Butter Soaked Apples 138
Smoked Meatballs 68
Smoked Molasses Lamb Chops 50
Smoked Molasses Ribeye Beef Steak (masterbuilt Electric Smoker) 50
Smoked Mozzarella 132
Smoked Oysters With Olive Relish 141
Smoked Paprika Roasted Potatoes 137
Smoked Pastrami 32
Smoked Pastrami Burgers 47
Smoked Peaches 26
Smoked Peaches Drowning In Rum With Ice Cream 19
Smoked Pineapple With Honey 21
Smoked Porchetta with Fresh Herbs 77
Smoked Pork Belly 43
Smoked Pork Loin 38
Smoked Pork Loin With Beer-anise Marinade (masterbuilt Electric Smoker) 53
Smoked Pork Loin With Sweet Habanero Rub (masterbuilt Electric Smoker) 34
Smoked Pork Ribs 64
Smoked Pork Ribs With Avocado Oil (masterbuilt Electric Smoker) 67
Smoked Pork Ribs With Fresh Herbs (masterbuilt Electric Smoker) 39
Smoked Pork Ribs With Teriyaki Sauce (masterbuilt Electric Smoker) 36

Smoked Pork Shoulder 33
Smoked Portobello Mushroom 19
Smoked Portobello Mushrooms With Herbs
De Provence 11
Smoked Portobello Mushrooms With Herbs
De Provence 13
Smoked Potato Salad 11
Smoked Potato Salad 12
Smoked Prime Rib 46
Smoked Rabbit With Rosemary Wine
Marinade (masterbuilt Electric Smoker) 125
Smoked Rack Of Lamb 34
Smoked Red Fish Fillets 84
Smoked Red Peppercorns 129
Smoked Ribeye With Herb Rubs (masterbuilt
Electric Smoker) 38
Smoked Rosemary Cashews 132
Smoked Salmon Chowder 87
Smoked Salmon Cucumbers 137
Smoked Salmon With Peppercorn Crust 92
Smoked Salsa 14
Smoked Savory Sardine (masterbuilt Electric
Smoker) 91
Smoked Scallops 86
Smoked Short Ribs 51
Smoked Snow Crab Legs 93
Smoked Sour Baby Ribs (masterbuilt Electric
Smoker) 44
Smoked Soy Chicken Legs 105
Smoked Squash Casserole 12
Smoked Steak Strips 55
Smoked Stuffed Turkey With Vegetables 141
Smoked Summer Vegetables 13
Smoked Summer Vegetables 17
Smoked Sweet And Spicy Chicken Wings 117
Smoked Sweet Onions 19
Smoked Sweet Salmon 85
Smoked Tilapia 92
Smoked Tri-tip Roast 51
Smoked Trout 88
Smoked Trout Potato Skins 27
Smoked Turkey 104
Smoked Turkey Breast 103
Smoked Turkey Breast With Orange-onion
Marinade (masterbuilt Electric Smoker) 111
Smoked Turkey Burgers With Mayo And
Mustard (masterbuilt Electric Smoker) 133
Smoked Turkey Cocktail Bites (masterbuilt
Electric Smoker) 113
Smoked Turkey With Flavors Of Mixed Herbs
94
Smoked Ultimate Flank Steak 45
Smoked Up Peaches 136
Smoked Up Pheasant 123
Smoked Vegetables 136
Smoked Volcanic Potatoes 14

Smoked Volcano Potatoes 14
Smoked Volcano Potatoes 15
Smoked Watermelon 11
Smoked Watermelon Skewers 17
Smoked White Wings 117
Smoked Whole Bologna Roll 78
Smoked Whole Chicken 112
Smoked Wild Boar Chops (masterbuilt
Electric Smoker) 125
Smoked Wild Goose Breast In Beer Marinade
(masterbuilt Electric Smoker) 125
Smoked Yellow Squash 18
Smoked Yummy Chicken Burgers
(masterbuilt Electric Smoker) 133
Smokey Pimento Cheese Appetizer 26
Smoking Hard and Semi-hard Cheeses 144
Smoky Beans Barbecue 27
Smoky Corn On The Cob 12
Smoky Okra 26
Smoky Wrap Chicken Breasts 116
Smoked Chicken Breasts with Creamed
Spinach Filling 121
Smoked Classic Deviled Eggs 142
Smoked Mac and Cheese with Two Cheeses
Recipe 143
Smoked Marinated Chicken Skewers 122
Smoked Potato, Ham, and Cheese Casserole
Recipe 143
Smoked Sweet and Sour Tofu Skewers Recipe
144
South Carolina Pulled Pork 62
Southern Smoked Potato Salad 22
Southwestern Smoked Chili 66
Special Dinner Turkey 95
Spiced Chicken Thighs 103
Spiced Pork Loin 67
Spicy Chicken Wings 96
Spicy Chicken Wings With Dipping Sauce 107
Spicy Cuban Catfish 87
Spicy Honey-apple Bbq Wings 96
Spicy Jamaican Jerk 117
Splendid Cheeseburger Patty 131
Squash Casserole 12
Sticky Smoky Meatloaf 42
Stuffed Cabbage 26
Stuffed Chicken Breast In Masterbuilt Smoker
99
Stuffed Porchetta 29
Stuffed Salmon 86
Stunning Sardine 93
Succulent Tri-tip Roast 35
Succulent Trout 80
Summer Spiced Sausage 59
Supreme Chipotle Wings 108
Supremely Smoked Alderwood Turkey Breast
102

Sweet 'n' Spicy Chicken Wings 106
Sweet And Savory Classical Pork 48
Sweet And Spicy Chicken Wings 98
Sweet And Spicy Smoked Pecans 134
Sweet Bbq Wings 101
Sweet Cola Ribs 30
Sweet Spice Rub 127
Sweet and Spicy Smoked Chicken Wings with Yogurt Dipping Sauce 122
Seasoned & Smoked Chicken Drumsticks 121

T

Tamarind Smoked Turkey Sausages (masterbuilt Electric Smoker) 138
Tandoori Chicken 115
Tangerine Smoked Flans 25
Tender Sweet Sriracha Bbq Chicken 111
Tenderloin Kebabs 42
Teriyaki Sauce 128
Teriyaki Smoked Venison Jerky 24
Tex Mex Pulled Pork Taco Filling 60
Texan Beef Brisket 57
Texas Style Brisket Rub 127
Thanksgiving Garlic Smoked Turkey 138
Thanksgiving Party Turkey 97
The Great Boar Shoulder 124
The Great Chimichurri Sauce 129
The Original Smoked Cauliflower 135

Triple Smoked Burger 54
Tri-tip Roast 36
Tuna Steaks 83
Turkey Breast 108
Turkey In The Electric Smoker 97
Turkey With Chimichurri 100
Twice Pulled Potatoes 13
Twice Smoked Cheese and Bacon Potatoes 145

U

Ultimate Chuck Roast 41
Utterly Delicious Duck Breast 105

V

Versatile Chicken Breasts 110

W

Weekend Dinner Chicken 112
Welcoming Pork Shoulder 52
Well-seasoned Drumsticks 102
White Chocolate Bread Pudding 22
White Wine Turkey Dogs 106
Whole Quail 123
Whole Snapper 86
Wisconsin Beer Brats 33
World's Most Tender "3-2-1 Ribs" 43

Z

Zesty Tuna 82

CPSIA information can be obtained
at www.ICGtesting.com
Printed in the USA
LVHW101101241120
672562LV00007B/67